GROUP PERFORMANCE OF LITERATURE

BEVERLY WHITAKER LONG

University of Texas at Austin

LEE HUDSON

University of Illinois at Urbana

PHILLIS RIENSTRA JEFFREY

University of Texas at Austin

PRENTICE-HALL, INC.   *Englewood Cliffs, New Jersey 07632*

Library of Congress Cataloging in Publication Data

Long, Beverly Whitaker, date
    Group performance of literature.

    Includes bibliographies and index.
      1. Oral interpretation. I. Hudson, Lee,
date— joint author, II. Jeffrey, Phillis
Rienstra, date—   joint author. III. Title.
PH4145.L57   809   77-1655
ISBN   0-13-365346-3

PRENTICE-HALL SPEECH COMMUNICATION SERIES
Larry Barker and Robert J. Kibler, *Editors*

Printed in the United States of America

10 9 8 7 6 5 4 3 2 1

Prentice-Hall International, Inc., *London*
Prentice-Hall of Australia Pty. Limited, *Sydney*
Prentice-Hall of Canada, Ltd., *Toronto*
Prentice-Hall of India Private Limited, *New Delhi*
Prentice-Hall of Japan, Inc., *Tokyo*
Prentice-Hall of Southeast Asia Pte. Ltd., *Singapore*
Whitehall Books Limited, *Wellington, New Zealand*

DEDICATED TO:

Anne Downes
Richard L. Hudson
Annie Klein
Berniece Whitaker

Contents

III   SCRIPTS FOR GROUP PERFORMANCE

Preface

This book is an introduction to a way of studying and presenting literary texts through group performance. We find the activity and the process exciting and informative for performers as well as their audiences. Our study encourages you to *do*—to *perform*—literary texts as an alternative from, or in addition to, your own private, silent perceptions or solo performances. Group performance is yet another way of actively exploring the life of a literary text.

Group Performance of Literature is designed first for students in an oral interpretation class, one usually called Readers Theatre or Chamber Theatre. We hope it will be useful also to students in advanced oral interpretation courses if the instructor is interested in supplementing solo interpretations with group performances.

The book is divided into three parts. The first treats such introductory principles as selection and analysis of literature and techniques of adaptation, rehearsal, and production. This section also includes discussions of features unique to the group performance of poetry, prose, nonfictional literature, and children's literature.

The second part of the book contains a variety of scripts adapted for group performance, each prefaced with an essay by the adaptor/director of the literature. We hope you will read their comments not as directives but as records of probings that led to their decisions about selection, adaptation, and production concept. Many of these decisions were initiated in classroom activities; all were eventually presented for larger audiences.

The scripts represent one director's choices; the essays are his or her descriptions of how they were made as well as discussions of broader concepts that relate to the literature. For example, the essay preceding the adaptation of "Tell Me a Riddle" deals at some length with the elements of lyric fiction; the commentary on "Why I Live at the P.O." includes a consideration of the function of a first-person narrator, and the one prior to *An Evening with Reed Whittemore* treats the relevance of sociobiographical criticism. Each concludes with a bibliography of works consulted in the preparation of the script.

The third section consists of eight additional scripts adapted for group performance, together with an introductory note describing the director's production concept and a bibliography. The directors indicate no elaborate staging directions in the hope that you will enjoy working out your own. Collectively, these scripts as well as those preceded by essays suggest many possibilities for realizing and vitalizing literary texts of various lengths and genres.

In the final analysis, the success of the chapters, essays, and scripts lies in how well they aid you in your own process of selecting, preparing, and presenting literature through group performance in your own classroom, at a festival, or for a campus or community audience.

BWL
LH
PRJ

Acknowledgments

For their contributions to this book, we extend our thanks to the following:

To William Adams, Bill Harbin, Barbara Kaster, and Frances McCurdy for reading the entire manuscript and generously sharing their responses.

To Suzanne Bennett, Frank Galati, Mary Frances HopKins, John Pazeraskis, and Bruce Wagener for substantive suggestions on the manuscript.

To Roddy Austin, Elizabeth Bell, Cheyanne Boyd, Margaret Davidson, Suzanne Skinner and Judith West for clerical work.

To John Skinner for executing the drawings.

To Brian Walker and Natalie Krivanek, of Prentice-Hall, for ideas and support.

To Robert Jeffrey and William Long for assistance and encouragement.

To the Departments of Speech Communication at the University of Texas at Austin and the University of Illinois at Urbana for patience and a host of services.

Credits

TWAIN SKETCHES, page 199

    Reprinted by permission of Harper & Row, Publishers.
    Complete Works of Mark Twain
    Vol. II, *Innocents Abroad*, pp. 169–70, 179, 339–404, 407
    Vol. III, *Puddin' head Wilson*, pp. 44, 50
    Vol. IV, *American Claimant*, pp. 255, 282
    Vol. VI, *Roughing It*, chap. 7, pp. 44–49; chap. 25, pp. 181–182; chap. 12, pp. 98–104
    Vol. V, *Following the Equator*, Chap. 8, p. 98; chap. 27, p. 264; chap. 29, p. 292
    Vol. IX, *Life on the Mississippi*, Chap. 55, p. 407; chap. 4, pp. 43–45
    Vol. II, *What Is Man?*, pp. 139–140, 12–15
    Vol. XIV, *Tom Sawyer Abroad*, pp. 378–383
    Vol. XIII, *Huckleberry Finn*, pp. 113–115
    Vol. XIX, *Sketches Old and New*, pp. 49–55, 280–287
    Vol. XXII, *Literary Essays*, p. 251
    Vol. XXIV, *Speeches*, pp. 145, 256–262, 278, 328, 362. Copyright 1923 by Mark
        Twain Company.

    Mark Twain's Autobiography Copyright 1924 by Clara Gabrilowitsch.
       Vol. I, pp. 94–95, 96–98, 109–113
       Vol. II, pp. 68, 73

    Mark Twain's Letters Arranged by Albert Bigelow Paine. Copyright 1917 by Mark
        Twain Company.
       Vol. I, p. 67
       Vol. II, pp. 675–676, 678, 709

    Mark Twain's Notebook Prepared by Albert Bigelow Paine. Copyright 1935 by
        Mark Twain Company.
       Pp. 236–237, 347

    Eve's Diary, pp. 3, 18, 19, 21, 23–25, 27, 29, 31, 39, 41, 43, 49, 95–105, 109

    Extracts from Adam's Diary, pp. 3–9, 13–17, 23, 11, 39–45, 49, 55–57, 63–65, 71,
       79–83, 87–89

INDIANS SPEAK,   page 291

AN EVENING WITH REED WHITTEMORE, page 93

Lines Composed Upon Reading an Announcement by Civil Defense Authorities
Recommending that I build a Bomb-Shelter in My Backyard

Fifty Poems Fifty, 1970. Reprinted by permission of University of Minnesota Press.
The Fall of the House of Usher
The Girl In the Next Room
The Chair
Reason in the Woods
A Fascinating Poet's Diary

Poems New and Selected, 1967. Reprinted by permission of University of Minne-
sota Press.
Clamming
The Bad Daddy
The Philadelphia Vireo
Dear God
Today
The Departure

I
BASIC PRINCIPLES

chapter 1

Introduction

Impressed by actor Charles Laughton's success as a public reader, Paul Gregory, distinguished film, stage, and television producer, was receptive when Laughton suggested the Hell scenes from George Bernard Shaw's *Man and Superman* as a vehicle for a group reading.[1] This lengthy, rarely produced play, concluding with the Hell sequence, appealed to both Laughton and Gregory because of its clash of ideas and the musicality of Shaw's language. Actors Charles Boyer, Agnes Moorehead, and Sir Cedric Hardwicke joined Laughton and Gregory, to form the First Drama Quartette in 1951. With the Shaw material titled *Don Juan in Hell*, the Quartette played in more than thirty states to enthusiastic audiences and critics. The following year Gregory produced Stephen Vincent Benet's epic poem, *John Brown's Body*, a performance that featured three readers and a fifty-member chorus.

These productions successfully demonstrated for a large public that works not normally dramatized were indeed dramatic, and further, they were, even with minimal

scenery and the presence of manuscripts, theatrically effective.

These "group performance" productions of the early 1950s were innovative in a special sense. They were professionally staged, important theatrical events witnessed by thousands of audience members across the country, and provided additional impetus for an educational activity already present, usually in departments of speech or theatre, in colleges and universities.

During the 1950s and early 1960s, a number of colleges and universities offered courses or sections of courses in "readers theatre," and pioneering essays, notably by Leslie Irene Coger, of Southwest Missouri State University, were published.[2] By the end of the 1960s, most colleges and universities offered readers theatre courses, and

---

[1]Alice Barnhart, ed., "Paul Gregory speaks," *Readers Theatre News* (Winter 1974), p. 3.

[2]Leslie Irene Coger, "Let's Have a Readers' Theatre," *Oral Interpretation* (Cincinnati: The National Thespian Society, 1957), pp. 25–27; "Interpreter's Theatre: Theatre of the Mind," *Quarterly Journal of Speech*, 49, No. 2 (April 1963), 157–64; "Theatre for Oral Interpreters," *The Speech Teacher*, 12, No. 4 (November 1963), 304–7; Leslie Irene Coger and Melvin R. White, eds., *Studies in Readers Theatre* (Brooklyn, N.Y.: S & F Press, 1963).

many high schools and even some junior high and elementary schools incorporated this activity into curricular or extra-curricular programs.

By 1970 another type of group performance, "chamber theatre," was widely taught and practiced throughout the country. Students of interpretation are rightly grateful to its originator, Robert Breen of Northwestern University, for this alternative to the traditional methods of studying and staging narratives. In the late 1940s, Breen had become increasingly concerned because many stories and novels suffered when adapted for film or the stage and because many interpreters tended to adopt a lifeless performance of passages not written in dialogue.[3] Working through these problems at this time, he evolved the concept of "chamber theatre," a method of adaptation and performance that strove for the immediacy of drama in staging novels and short stories while it preserved the narrative voice that characterizes the literary form. In the professional theatre, Paul Sill's *Story Theatre* relied on many of the same techniques Breen devised for chamber theatre.

Today's group performances of literature are indebted to the examples and conventions established in those early productions and published books and essays. In short, the wide array of group performances of literature illustrates that: (1) *the experiential nature of performance is a viable way of studying literature;* and, (2) *audiences desire a public performance of various literary forms.*

Suggested Assignment

In a short essay, synthesize the New York

critics reviews of one of the following professional productions:

1. Sean O'Casey's *Drums Under the Window*, adapted by Paul Shyre.
2. Dylan Thomas's *Under Milk Wood.*
3. *The World of Carl Sandburg*, adapted by Norman Corwin.
4. John Dos Passos's *U.S.A.*
5. *Brecht on Brecht.*
6. George Bernard Shaw and Mrs. Patrick Campbell, *Dear Liar,* adapted by Jerome Kilty.
7. *In White America,* adapted by Martin Duberman.

GROUP PERFORMANCE OF LITERATURE DEFINED

Literary texts are often viewed as scores or symbols for experience. It is also commonly asserted that every text, regardless of its similarities to others, enjoys an existence uniquely its own. If these assumptions are valid, then *each* literary text contains its own notations, directives, or possibilities for performance. These beliefs account for the growing interest in "group performance of literature." Moreover, that phrase is a convenient designation for both the study and the activity. "Group performance" here refers to two or more individuals *doing, realizing, actualizing;* and "of literature" includes that vast storehouse of materials classified as poetry, stories and novels, plays, and nonfictional literature. The phrase is elastic enough for any type of literature and any production style. Its stated focus places the premium on the myriad potentials of the literature rather than on what have sometimes seemed arbitrary sets of conventions.

Conventional productions of plays could no doubt be included in this definition. However, for the purposes of this book, the emphasis is on other literary genres—those less frequently studied through group performance or presented for audiences.

[3]Robert S. Breen, "Chamber Theatre," *Illinois Speech and Theatre Journal*, 26 (Fall 1972), 20–23; public lecture, University of Texas at Austin, April, 1971; "Chamber Theatre," *The Study of Oral Interpretation: Theory and Comment*, Richard Haas and David A. Williams, eds. (Indianapolis: Bobbs-Merrill, Inc., 1975), pp. 207–211.

To reiterate, we hope you will find "group performance of literature" a helpful term in your effort *to restore the oral-aural-physical dimensions of literary texts for which words on a page are symbols and notations for fuller performances.*

SOME VALUES
IN THE GROUP PERFORMANCE
OF LITERATURE

As with all of the arts, determining "value" is extremely difficult. With group performances the problem compounds since we are dealing with two arts—the art of literature and the art of group performance. When the two are successfully fused, the values for both participants and audience will indeed be significant.

Participants

The value of group performance to the participants is potentially immense. As they (director, adaptor, performers, crew) explore the clusters of meanings in the literary text, arrive at a production concept, rehearse and stage their decisions, they become collaborators with the life of the text and with each other. *The process is both active* (actualizing the literature) *and interactive* (responding to other performers, environment, and situations). Directly engaged, the group is in a position to realize those values described by cultural historian Walter Ong, S.J.:

> Acting a role, realizing in a specially intense way one's identity (in a sense) with someone who (in another sense) one is not, remains one of the most human things a man can do.[4]

[4]Walter Ong, quoted from Walker Gibson, *Persona* (New York: Random House, 1969), p. vii.

This kind of "acting" and the liberalizing, humanizing effect it implies is, by extension, available not only to the cast members but to all participants involved in the performance.

Audience

Many performances are eventually presented for an audience—other members of the same class, other classes, assembly programs, campus productions, clubs, festivals, or contests. Such groups of listeners may extend the participating group's experience with the literature as they respond—or fail to respond—to the performance.

The spectrum of possible audience response is almost limitless: ideally, an audience will be informed, interested, persuaded, entertained, moved, or some combination of these and other responses. Most important, if the arts of literature and performance are effectively fused, the audience as well as the performers will enjoy a rich and intense literary experience.

Agnes Moorehead's remembrance of audiences for the original *Don Juan in Hell* strikingly illustrates this kind of meaningful experience:

> Every sentence of Shaw's *Don Juan in Hell* is a challenge to the mind of every person who becomes privately aware of it, either in reading it, or in seeing it performed. Everything that Shaw wrote on sex, marriage, politics, war, a hundred other subjects, is here, in this brief, most brilliant, most penetrating manifestation of his mind and philosophy. There are themes for a dozen plays in it—and the presentation of it offers an opportunity to all of those who care about their minds and souls. *To hear it performed. . .is to come to grips with Shaw's greatness the easy way.*[5]

[5]Agnes Moorehead, "Staging *Don Juan in Hell*," *Western Speech*, 18 (May 1964), 163. (Italics ours.)

chapter 2

The Literature:
Selection and Analysis

SELECTION OF LITERATURE

For hundreds of years dramatic literature has been considered incomplete until it is performed. More and more, we hear a similar claim for other literary genres—poetry, prose fiction, and nonfiction. These too, we believe, may reveal their fullest meaning through performance. While the performance of other literary genres shares many of the same problems and rewards as drama, this book is primarily concerned with literature not written specifically for the stage.

Although libraries are full of material suitable for group performance, some materials are marginally appropriate. The following questions will assist you in the selection process. Negative answers may bring about other choices.

1. Are you, as the director, committed to this literature? Do you believe in its literary value? Are you genuinely excited about spending the time to direct an effective performance?
2. Does the literature seem better suited for a group than a solo performance or a silent reading?

3. Is your adaptation of the script likely to involve so few compromises that the structure, language, or theme of the original text will remain intact?
4. Can you cast this literature? Do the performers have the necessary experience? Is there a sufficient number of interested participants?
5. If a public audience is anticipated, does this literature meet, with reasonable latitude, their expectations in terms of subject, style, and language?
6. If the literature is not in public domain—and particularly if you plan to charge admission—can you secure and afford the rights?

Suggested Assignments

I. Consult one of the anthologies used in literature or interpretation classes on your campus. Choose at least two selections that you believe would be suitable for group performance in light of the preceding questions.
II. List at least five literary texts (mix the genres as much as possible) that you have enjoyed reading and think you

would enjoy adapting and directing for a group performance.

III. Choose two selections from one of the following groups and compare their suitability for group performance:

Poetry:
A. Denise Levertov, "Conversation in Moscow"; Robinson Jeffers, "Roan Stallion"
B. James Dickey, "May Day Sermon"; Allen Ginsberg, "Kaddish"
C. Walt Whitman, *I Sing the Body Electric;* Michael Casey, *Obscenities*

Prose Fiction:
A. Albert Camus, *The Stranger;* Charles Dickens, *David Copperfield*
B. Kurt Vonnegut, "Harrison Bergeron"; Robert Coover, "The Pedestrian Accident"
C. Bernard Malamud, "Angel Levine"; Joyce Carol Oates, "Where Are You Going? Where Have You Been?"

Nonfiction:
A. Lincoln-Douglas Debates; Speeches of William Pitt and Charles James Fox
B. e. e. cummings, *non-lectures;* Oscar Lewis, *Children of Sanchez*
C. Letters of Nathaniel Hawthorne and Herman Melville; Letters of Robert Frost and Louis Untermeyer

ANALYSIS OF THE LITERATURE

After selecting the literature, your next task is a careful study of the text. The significant and exacting nature of this part of the preparation for group performance cannot be overemphasized. The discoveries and decisions articulated in your analysis will affect everything that follows—from production concept to program notes. Simply stated, the objective of this point is to determine *what* the literature means and *how* it means what it does.

Varieties of Analyses of Literature

For centuries, literary critics have evolved theories and methods for exploring literature. The dominant approaches to literary criticism are listed below, together with the key questions associated with the particular approach. The divisions are not mutually exclusive; each does, however, emphasize certain relationships among reality, author, audience, and text.[1]

Mimetic—In what ways does the imaginative work reflect *reality*?

Expressivist—How does the literary work reflect the feelings and ideas of the *author*?

Pragmatic—How does the literature appeal to (e.g., entertain, inform) the *audience*?

Objectivist—How do the parts of the *text* coalesce into a unified whole of internal relationships?

Since analysis is such a significant part of your preparation for group performance, we shall provide an example of it following James Thurber's "The Secret Life of Walter Mitty."

The Secret Life of Walter Mitty
James Thurber

"We're going through!" The Commander's voice was like thin ice breaking. He wore his full-dress uniform, with the heavily braided white cap pulled down rakishly over one cold gray eye. "We can't make it, sir. It's spoiling for a hurricane, if you ask me." "I'm not asking you, Lieutenant Berg," said

[1]M. H. Abrams, *The Mirror and the Lamp* (New York: W. W. Norton & Co., Inc., 1958), p. 6.

the Commander. "Throw on the power lights! Rev her up to 8,500! We're going through!" The pounding of the cylinders increased; ta-pocketa-pocketa-pocketa-*pocketa-pocketa*. The Commander stared at the ice forming on the pilot window. He walked over and twisted a row of complicated dials. "Switch on No. 8 auxiliary!" he shouted. "Switch on No. 8 auxiliary!" repeated Lieutenant Berg. "Full strength in No. 3 turret!" shouted the Commander. "Full strength in No. 3 turret!" The crew, bending to their various tasks in the huge, hurtling eight-engined Navy hydroplane, looked at each other and grinned. "The Old Man'll get us through," they said to one another. "The Old Man ain't afraid of Hell! . . .

"Not so fast! You're driving too fast!" said Mrs. Mitty. "What are you driving so fast for?"

"Hmm?" said Walter Mitty. He looked at his wife, in the seat beside him, with shocked astonishment. She seemed grossly unfamiliar, like a strange woman who had yelled at him in a crowd. "You were up to fifty-five," she said. "You know I don't like to go more than forty. You were up to fifty-five." Walter Mitty drove on toward Waterbury in silence, the roaring of the SN202 through the worst storm in twenty years of Navy flying fading in the remote, intimate airways of his mind. "You're tensed up again," said Mrs. Mitty. "It's one of your days. I wish you'd let Dr. Renshaw look you over."

Walter Mitty stopped the car in front of the building where his wife went to have her hair done. "Remember to get those overshoes while I'm having my hair done," she said. "I don't need overshoes," said Mitty. She put her mirror back into her bag. "We've been all through that," she said, getting out of the car. "You're not a young man any longer." He raced the engine a little. "Why don't you wear your gloves? Have you lost your gloves?" Walter Mitty reached in a pocket and brought out the gloves. He put them on, but after she had turned and gone into the building and he had driven on to a red light, he took them off again. "Pick it up, brother!" snapped a cop as the light changed, and Mitty hastily

pulled on his gloves and lurched ahead. He drove around the streets aimlessly for a time, and then he drove past the hospital on his way to the parking lot.

. . . "It's the millionaire banker, Wellington McMillan," said the pretty nurse. "Yes?" said Walter Mitty, removing his gloves slowly. "Who has the case?" "Dr. Renshaw and Dr. Benbow, but there are two specialists here, Dr. Remington from New York and Mr. Pritchard-Mitford from London. He flew over." A door opened down a long, cool corridor and Dr. Renshaw came out. He looked distraught and haggard. "Hello, Mitty," he said. "We're having the devil's own time with McMillan, the millionaire banker and close personal friend of Roosevelt. Obstreosis of the ductal tract. Tertiary. Wish you'd take a look at him." "Glad to," said Mitty.

In the operating room there were whispered introductions; "Dr. Remington, Dr. Mitty. Mr. Pritchard-Mitford, Dr. Mitty." "I've read your book on streptothricosis," said Pritchard-Mitford, shaking hands. "A brilliant performance, sir." "Thank you," said Walter Mitty. "Didn't know you were in the States, Mitty," grumbled Remington. "Coals to Newcastle, bringing Mitford and me up here for tertiary." "You are very kind," said Mitty. A huge, complicated machine, connected to the operating table, with many tubes and wires, began at this moment to go pocketa-pocketa-pocketa. "The new anaesthetizer is giving away!" shouted an interne. "There is no one in the East who knows how to fix it!" "Quiet, man!" said Mitty, in a low, cool voice. He sprang to the machine, which was now going pocketa-pocketa-queep-pocketa-queep. He began fingering delicately a row of glistening dials. "Give me a fountain pen!" he snapped. Someone handed him a fountain pen. He pulled a faulty piston out of the machine and inserted the pen in its place. "That will hold for ten minutes," he said. "Get on with the operation." A nurse hurried over and whispered to Renshaw, and Mitty saw the man turn pale. "Coreopsis has set in," said Renshaw nervously. "If you would take over, Mitty?" Mitty looked at him and at the craven figure of Benbow, who drank, and at the grave, uncertain faces of the two great specialists. "If you wish," he said. They slipped a white gown on him; he adjusted a mask and drew on thin gloves; nurses handed him shining. . .

"Back it up, Mac! Look out for that Buick!" Walter Mitty jammed on the brakes. "Wrong lane, Mac," said the parking-lot attendant, looking at Mitty closely. "Gee. Yeh," muttered Mitty. He began cautiously to back out of the lane marked "Exit Only." "Leave her sit there," said the attendant. "I'll put her away." Mitty got out of the car. "Hey, better leave the key." "Oh," said Mitty, handing the man the ignition key. The attendant vaulted into the car, backed it up with insolent skill, and put it where it belonged.

They're so damn cocky, thought Walter Mitty, walking along Main Street; they think they know everything. Once he had tried to take his chains off, outside New Milford, and he had got them wound around the axles. A man had had to come out in a wrecking car and unwind them, a young, grinning garage man. Since then Mrs. Mitty always made him drive to a garage to have the chains taken off. The next time, he thought, I'll wear my right arm in a sling; they won't grin at me then. I'll have my right arm in a sling and they'll see I couldn't possibly take the chains off myself. He kicked at the slush on the sidewalk. "Overshoes," he said to himself, and he began looking for a shoe store.

When he came out into the street again, with the overshoes in a box under his arm, Walter Mitty began to wonder what the other thing was his wife had told him to get. She had told him twice, before they set out from their house for Waterbury. In a way he hated these weekly trips to town— he was always getting something wrong. Kleenex, he thought, Squibb's, razor blades? No. Toothpaste, toothbrush, bicarbonate, carborundum, iniative and referendum? He gave it up. But she would remember it. "Where's the what's-its-name?" she would ask. "Don't tell me you forgot the what's-its-name." A newsboy went by shouting something about the Waterbury trial.

. . . ."Perhaps this will refresh your mem-

ory." The District Attorney suddenly thrust a heavy automatic at the quiet figure on the witness stand. "Have you ever seen this before?" Walter Mitty took the gun and examined it expertly. "This is my Webley-Vickers 50.80," he said calmly. An excited buzz ran around the courtroom. The judge rapped for order. "You are a crack shot with any sort of firearms, I believe?" said the District Attorney, insinuatingly. "Objection!" shouted Mitty's attorney. "We have shown that the defendant could not have fired the shot. We have shown that he wore his right arm in a sling on the night of the fourteenth of July." Walter Mitty raised his hand briefly and the bickering attorneys were stilled. "With any known make of gun," he said evenly, "I could have killed Gregory Fitzhurst at three hundred feet *with my left hand*." Pandemonium broke loose in the courtroom. A woman's scream rose above the bedlam and suddenly a lovely, dark-haired girl was in Walter Mitty's arms. The District Attorney struck at her savagely. Without rising from his chair, Mitty let the man have it on the point of the chin. "You miserable cur!" . . .

"Puppy biscuit," said Walter Mitty. He stopped walking and the buildings of Waterbury rose up out of the misty courtroom and surrounded him again. A woman who was passing laughed. "He said 'Puppy biscuit,' " she said to her companion. "That man said 'Puppy biscuit,' to himself." Walter Mitty hurried on. He went into an A. & P., not the first one he came to but a smaller one farther up the street. "I want some biscuit for small, young dogs," he said to the clerk. "Any special brand, sir?" The greatest pistol shot in the world thought a moment. "It says 'Puppies Bark for It' on the box," said Walter Mitty.

His wife would be through at the hairdresser's in fifteen minutes, Mitty saw in looking at his watch, unless they had trouble drying it; sometimes they had trouble drying it. She didn't like to get to the hotel first; she would want him to be there waiting for her as usual. He found a big leather chair in the lobby, facing a window, and he put the overshoes and the puppy biscuit on the floor beside it. He picked up an old copy of *Liberty* and sank down into the chair. "Can Germany Conquer the World through the Air?" Walter Mitty looked at the pictures of bombing planes and of ruined streets.

. . ."The cannonading has got the wind up in young Raleigh, sir," said the sergeant. Captain Mitty looked up at him through tousled hair. "Get him to bed," Mitty said wearily, "with the others. I'll fly alone." "But you can't, sir," said the sergeant anxiously. "It takes two men to handle that bomber and the Archies are pounding hell out of the air. Von Richtman's circus is between here and Saulier." "Somebody's got to get that ammunition dump," said Mitty. "I'm going over. Spot of brandy?" He poured a drink for the sergeant and one for himself. War thundered and whined around the dugout and battered at the door. There was a rending of wood and splinters flew through the room. "A bit of a near thing," said Captain Mitty carelessly. "The box barrage is closing in," said the sergeant. "We only live once, sergeant," said Mitty, with his faint, fleeting smile. "Or do we?" He poured another brandy and tossed it off. "I never seen a man that could hold his brandy like you, sir," said the sergeant. "Begging your pardon, sir." Captain Mitty stood up and strapped on his huge Webley-Vickers automatic. "It's forty kilometers through hell, sir," said the sergeant. Mitty finished one last brandy. "After all," he said softly, "what isn't?" The pounding of the cannon increased; there was the rat-tat-tatting of machine guns, and from somewhere came the menacing pocketa-pocketa-pocketa of the new flame throwers. Walter Mitty walked to the door of the dugout humming *"Auprès de Ma Blonde."* He turned and waved to the sergeant. "Cheerio!" he said. . . .

Something struck his shoulder. "I've been looking all over this hotel for you," said Mrs. Mitty. "Why did you have to hide in this old chair? How did you expect me to find you?" "Things close in," said Walter Mitty vaguely. "What?" Mrs. Mitty said. "Did you get the what's-its-name? The puppy biscuit? What's in that box?" "Overshoes," said Mitty. "Couldn't you have put them on in the store?" "I was thinking," said

Walter Mitty. "Does it ever occur to you that I am sometimes thinking?" She looked at him. "I'm going to take your temperature when I get you home," she said.

They went out through the revolving doors that made a faintly derisive whistling sound when you pushed them. It was two blocks to the parking lot. At the drugstore on the corner she said, "Wait here for me. I forgot something. I won't be a minute." She was more than a minute. Walter Mitty lighted a cigarette. It began to rain, rain with sleet in it. He stood up against the wall of the drugstore, smoking. . . . He put his shoulders back and his heels together. "To hell with the hankerchief," said Walter Mitty scornfully. He took one last drag on his cigarette and snapped it away. Then, with that faint, fleeting smile playing about his lips, he faced the firing squad; erect and motionless, proud and disdainful, Walter Mitty the Undeafeated, inscrutable to the last.[2]

Excerpts from *The Clocks of Columbus: The Literary Career of James Thurber*[3]
Charles S. Holmes

The showpiece of the collection [*My World and Welcome To It*] is "The Secret Life of Walter Mitty." This little story (it is only about four thousand words) is a curious phenomenon: comic in substance, elegant in form and style, it is a work of art in its own right; but it has also become, through one of those mysterious cultural transubstantiations, a part of our modern mythology and folklore. Like Sinclair Lewis' Babbitt, Mitty is a genuine cultural figure, a character whom we immediately recognize; and in his predicament and his absurd daydreams we see a comic image of our own impotence and desperation.

[2]James Thurber, "The Secret Life of Walter Mitty," *My World and Welcome to It* (New York: Harcourt Brace Jovanovich (1942). Copyright © 1942 by James Thurber. © 1970 by Helen Thurber. Originally printed in *The New Yorker*.

[3]From *The Clocks of Columbus, The Literary Career of James Thurber* by Charles S. Holmes. Copyright © 1972 by Charles S. Holmes. Reprinted by permission of Atheneum Publishers.

Mitty's name, like Babbitt's, is now a part of our language ("He's a real Walter Mitty," we say), but it was during World War II that his impact on the American imagination was greatest. The story was reprinted in the *Reader's Digest* in 1943, and the troops immediately made it their own: there was a Mitty International Club in the European Theatre and a Mitty Society in the South Pacific. Bomber pilots in the South Pacific made "Ta-pocketa-pocketa-pocketa" an official password, and painted the Mitty Society emblem—two crossed Webley-Vickers automatics—on the noses of their planes....

...The story of Walter Mitty is not only an archetype of contemporary experience, it is an intensely personal tale as well. Mitty is Thurber's image of himself as romantic daydreamer....

...The central theme of the story is the conflict between the world of fantasy and the world of reality and, as in "The Unicorn in the Garden," this is seen as a part of the conflict between husband and wife. The male is always associated in Thurber's imagination with fantasy, the female with logic and common sense. In reality, Walter Mitty is inadequate to the demands of the real world: his wife bullies him, the parking-lot attendant sneers at his awkward efforts to park the car, he cannot remember the shopping list. But in his secret world of fantasy, derived largely from bad movies, he triumphs over the humiliating forces of the actual.

Mitty's daydreams are the veriest claptrap, made up out of the cliches of popular fiction and movies, and their triteness serves to underline the pathos as well as the comedy of his situation, but at the same time, they are a source of strength, the means by which he makes his life significant. By the standards of the world, Mitty is a pathetic and inadequate figure, but as the closing image of the story suggests, he is in a deeper sense triumphant.

Much of the brilliance of the story is a result of Thurber's mastery of style. Three levels of language interplay throughout. There are the melodramatic cliches of the dream-sequences ("'The new anesthetizer is giving way!' shouted an interne. 'There is no one in the East who knows how to fix it!' 'Quiet, man!' said Mitty in a low, cool voice"); contrasting sharply with these is the flat, colloquial idiom of the scenes of real life ("'Pick it up, brother!' snapped a cop as the light changed"); and holding it all together is Thurber's own narrative style —economical, lightly ironic, and wonderfully expressive ("Walter Mitty drove on toward Waterbury in silence, the roaring of the SN202 through the worst storm in twenty years of Navy flying fading in the remote, intimate airways of his mind"). Examples of Thurber's inventiveness as a comedian of language are everywhere, but the most notable are the mock-technical vocabulary of the hospital sequence ("'Obstreosis of the ductal tract. Tertiary. Wish you'd take a look at him.") and the repetition of the "ta-pocketa-pocketa-pocketa" phrase which runs throughout the tale like a comic leitmotif....

...His passion for perfection extended even to the appearance of his copy: if he made a typing mistake, he redid the entire page. He rewrote "The Secret Life of Walter Mitty" fifteen times, and it took him eight weeks, "working day and night," he told Alistair Cooke....

...In an interview with Maurice Dolbier in the New York *Herald Tribune* (November 3, 1957) there is a totally unexpected story about how Helen's [Thurber's wife] critical judgment improved "The Secret Life of Walter Mitty." In the first version of the story Thurber had a scene in which Mitty got involved in a brawl between Hemingway and an opponent at the Stork Club. Helen objected to the scene on the grounds that there should be nothing topical in the story. "Well, you know how it is when your wife is right," said Thurber to Dolbier; "you grouse around the house for a week, and then you follow her advice."

Notice how Holmes incorporates each of the previously mentioned critical approaches in his own enthusiastic discussion of the story:

Mimetic
In the story, man is cast as a creature caged in dull reality. Such a world under-

standably makes exciting, heroic fantasy essential. The story is "true" to human nature. Also, it is an accurate reflection of a commonly accepted and felt mythology.

Expressivist

Thurber has written of his own need to daydream with a blend of humor and pathos. Some of the success of the story, Thurber said, stemmed from his wife's advice. Also, he sharpened the story with repeated revisions.

Pragmatic

When the story first appeared in the 1940s, its central figure, as well as its language, were sufficiently appealing to start a Thurber-Mitty cult. The story has remained popular because of its power to amuse through comic exaggeration and its latent serious implications about the human dilemma of unrealized dreams.

Objectivist

Thurber blends three levels of language, an interplay held together by the style of the narration. Another unifying feature is the consistently developed tensions between reality and fantasy, the mundane and the imaginative, and husband and wife.

Clearly, some of these approaches yield insights more directly realized in performance than others. Still, each of them contributes to an initial, broad perspective of the literature. They can function as guides for an overall grasp and stimulate and inform plans for a group performance.

Suggested Assignments

I. Carefully read one or more of the selections listed below. Then consult the cited criticism, noting the kinds of questions (stated or implied) that the critic raises, the approach he takes to the text. Which do you find the most convincing? If you discover disagreement about what the story *means,* try to determine whether or not this difference is a matter of divergent premises as to what the literature *should be.*

Do the analyses have a "stretching" effect on your own initial interpretation of the literature—i.e., do they confirm, contradict, or extend your impressions? What do the analyses suggest to you about possible priorities in staging the work for group performance?

A. Katherine Anne Porter, "The Jilting of Granny Weatherall"
   1. Robert G. Cowser, "Porter's 'The Jilting of Granny Wetherall.' " *Explicator,* 21, 34 (1963).
   2. Joseph Wiesenfarth, "Internal Opposition in Porter's 'Granny Weatherall,' " *Critique: Studies in Modern Fiction,* 11, 2 (1969).
   3. Daniel R. Barnes and Madeline T. Barnes, "The Secret Sin of Granny Weatherall," *Renascence,* 21, 3 (Spring 1969).
   4. Peter Wolfe, "The Problems of Granny Weatherall," *College Language Association Journal,* 2 (1967).
   5. John Edward Hardy, "By Self Possessed," *Katherine Anne Porter,* (New York: Frederick Ungar, 1973).
   6. William L. Nance, "The Emerging Pattern," *Katherine Anne Porter and the Art of Rejection,* (Chapel Hill: University of North Caroline Press, 1964).
B. Robert Frost, "Home Burial"
   1. *Frost Centennial Essays* compiled by Committee on Frost Centennial, University of South Mississippi (Jackson: University of Mississippi Press). n.d.
   2. Eben Bass, "Frost's Poetry of Fear," *American Literature,* 43 (January 1972), 603–615.

3. John R. Doyce, Jr., *The Poetry of Robert Frost,* (New York: Hafson, 1962).
4. Langdon Elsbree, "Frost and Isolation of Man," *Claremont Quarterly,* 7 (Summer 1960).
5. Elizabeth Isaacs, *An Introduction to Robert Frost,* (Denver: Alan Swallow, 1962), pp. 142–44.
6. George W. Nitchie, *Human Values in the Poetry of Robert Frost: A Study of a Poet's Convictions* (Durham: Duke University Press, 1960), pp. 83, 93, 99, 123, 129, 166–67.

C. Carl Bernstein and Bob Woodward, *All the President's Men*
1. Anthony Lukas, "All the President's Men," *Commonweal* (August 1974).
2. Robert D. Novak, "The Burglars and Their Pursuers," *National Review* (July 19, 1974).
3. Ward Just, "The Bernstein-Woodward Tapes," *Atlantic Monthly* (July 1974).
4. Joseph A. O'Hare, "Untangling the Web of Watergate," *America,* 30, 3 (June 15, 1974).
5. Doris Kearns, "A Whodunit Without an Ending," *The New York Times Book Review* (June 9, 1974).
6. Richard H. Rovere, ". . . And Nothing but the Truth," *New Yorker* (June 17, 1974).

II. After reading Herman Melville's *Billy Budd,* examine the following analyses:
A. Karl E. Zink, "Herman Melville and the Forms—Irony and Social Criticism in *Billy Budd,*" *Accent: A Quarterly of New Literature* (Summer 1952).
B. William York Tindall, "The Ceremony of Innocence," *Great Moral Dilemmas,* ed. R. M. MacIver. Institute for Religious and Social Studies, 1956.
C. Lee T. Lemon, "*Billy Budd.* The Plot Against the Story," *Studies in Short Fiction,* II (Fall 1964), 32–43.
D. Robert Rogers, "The 'Ineludible Gripe' of Billy Budd," *Literature and Psychology* (Winter, 1964).
E. Richard Chase, "Innocence and Infamy," *Herman Melville: A Critical Study* by Richard Chase. (New York: Macmillan, 1949).
F. H. E. Hudson, IV, "Billy Budd: Adam or Christ?" *Crane Review,* VII (1965).
G. Richard Harter Fogle, "Billy Budd: Acceptance or Irony," *Tulane Studies in English* (1958).
H. Edward H. Rosenberry, "The Problem of *Billy Budd,*" *PMLA* (December 1965).

(NOTE: All of these essays are reprinted in Walter K. Gordon's *Literature in Critical Perspectives* [Englewood Cliffs, N.J.: Prentice-Hall, Inc., 1968].)

III. In one or two sentences, state what each writer asserts the essence of the novel to be. Be prepared to answer the questions raised in Suggested Assignment No. 1.

IV. Study one of the following literary texts and write an informal, multiple-approach analysis similar to Holmes's:
A. William Butler Yeats, "Crazy Jane Meets the Bishop"
B. Richard Howard, "Wildflowers"
C. Jean Stafford, "Bad Characters"
D. Carson McCullers, "A Tree, a Rock, and a Cloud"

Analytic classifications of literature also include the *intrinsic* and *extrinsic*. Are the studies aimed at uncovering extrinsic factors—those that *impinge* on the literature;

or on intrinsic features—those *within* it? One method, dramatic analysis, in its broadest sense, includes both methods and is particularly useful in guiding performance decisions.

Dramatic Analysis

In his *Grammar of Motives,* Kenneth Burke develops the "five key terms of dramatism."

> What is involved when we weigh what people are doing and why they are doing it? . . . We shall use five terms as generating principles of our investigation. They are: Act, Scene, Agent, Agency, Purpose. In a rounded statement about motives, you must have some word that names the *act* (names what took place, in thought or deed), and another that names the scene (the background of the act, the situation in which it occured); also, you must indicate what person or kind of person (*agent*) performed the act, what means or instruments he used (*agency*), and the *purpose.* Men may violently disagree about the purpose behind a given act, or about the character of the person who did it, or how he did it, or in what kind of situation he acted; or they may even insist upon totally different words to name the act itself. But be that as it may, any complete statement about motives will offer *some kind of* answers to these five questions: what was done (act), when and where (scene) it was done, who did it (agent), and how it was done (agency), and why (purpose).[4]

You might, in your extrinsic study of a particular text, ask who (agent) wrote (act) it, when and where (scene), with what means or how (agency), and why (purpose). Answers to these questions are most readily available for works about which scholars have conducted extensive study: e.g., Milton, Donne, Hawthorne, and Dickens, for example. In addition to their usefulness in systematizing observations about the *exter-*

nal nature of the literature, the five key terms can also be applied to the *internal* "drama" of any work.

The following list of questions directs you to several *intrinsic* aspects of the literature, those most frequently translated in interpretation. Derived from the work of Burke, Don Geiger, and others,[5] it raises issues about a text that a group performance can at least partially answer. The interrelationships among answers is apparent; one answer is bound to affect another. Also, in approaching a particular text, some questions assume more importance than others.

   I. THE DRAMATIC SPEAKER
      A. *Who* is uttering the words of the text? (speaker, persona, narrator, character)[6]
         1. Specified *physically?* (species, sex, age, dress, posture, etc.)
         2. Cluster of *attitudes?* (person-

---

[5]Don Geiger, *The Dramatic Impulse in Modern Poetics* (Baton Rogue: Louisiana State University Press, 1967); *The Sound Sense and Performance of Literature* (Glenview: Scott, Foresman and Company, 1963); "A 'Dramatic' Approach to Interpretative Analysis," *Quarterly Journal of Speech* XXXVIII (February 1952), 189–194; Robert Beloof, *The Performing Voice in Literature* (Boston: Little, Brown and Co., 1966). Paul Campbell, *The Speaking and the Speakers of Literature* (Belmont, Calif.: Dickenson Publishing Company. Inc., 1967); Marcia M. Eaton, "Liars, Ranters, and Dramatic Speakers," *Language and Aesthetics,* ed. Benjamin R. Tilghman (Lawrence: The University Press of Kansas, 1973); James L. Kinneavy, *A Theory of Discourse* (Englewood Cliffs, N.J.: Prentice-Hall, Inc., 1971); Joanna H. Maclay and Thomas O. Sloan, *Interpretation: An Approach to the Study of Literature* (New York: Random House, 1972); Alethea Smith Mattingly and Wilma H. Grimes, *Interpretation: Writer, Reader, Audience,* 2nd ed. (San Francisco: Wadsworth Publishing Company, Inc., 1970); Thomas O. Sloan, "Introduction," *The Oral Study of Literature* (New York: Random House, 1966), pp. 3–13; David W. Thompson and Virginia Fredericks, *Oral Interpretation of Fiction: A Dramatistic Approach,* 2nd ed. (Minneapolis: Burgess Publishing Company, 1967).

[6]In this outline, the word speaker encompasses the other three.

---

[4]Kenneth Burke, *A Grammar of Motives* (Cleveland: World Publishing Company, 1962), p. xvii.

ality, bent, disposition, out-
look, tone)

B. From what *perspective,* or point
of view, does the speaker speak?

  1. Within the action? As man-
ipulator of it? As observer?

  2. Objective viewing? Personally involved?

  3. Closer to one character than
others? A reflector of a character? Omniscient to all,
some, one, or none?

  4. Apparently truthful?

  5. Describing an action as it
occurs? As it occurred?

C. *Where* and *when* is the speaker
speaking?

  1. Specified time? (hour, day,
season, year)

  2. Specified scene? (area, locale)

  3. Change of time or scene?

  4. Relation to objects within
the scene?

D. *To whom* is the speaker speaking? (anyone, someone in particular, a generalized group, an absent though specified listener,
him/herself, some combination
of listeners)

II. THE SPEAKER'S DRAMA

A. *What* does the speaker say?
(remember an event? tell a story?
judge a thing or person? observe
an occurrence? give advice?)

B. *How* does the speaker speak?

  1. In what mode? (epic, dramatic, lyric, combination)[7]

  2. With what rhythms? (recur-
rences of silences, sounds,
words, phrases, stanzas, para-
graphs)

  3. With what, if any metrical

patterns? Free verse?

  4. On what level of language?
(jargon, formalities, conversation)

  5. With what language devices? (allusion, metaphor,
hyperbole, etc.)

  6. With what structure? (ram-
bling, associative, topical,
chronological)

  7. With what manipulation of
time? (scene, summary, description)[8]

  8. Is the address direct? Indirect?

C. *Why* does the speaker speak? (to
organize, understand, convince,
relieve, delight in)

  1. Does the presence (or absence) of an audience affect
the speaker's purpose?

  2. Is the speaker's comment on
the human condition different from that of the implied
author?

Let us apply some of these questions to
the following poem:

Elegy
John Ciardi

I. As I hear the family thinking it
This is the body of my good gray practical
  dead
uncle. We are going to bury it today. We
  are
not going to bury it because it is good gray
or practical, but because it is dead. We are
observing, I submit, the proper proprieties.

Were he good gray practical and not dead,
  we
certainly would not bury him. Not today.

---

[7]Joanna Hawkins Maclay, "The Interpreter and
Modern Fiction: Problems of Point of View and
Structural Tensiveness," *Studies in Interpretation,*
ed. Esther M. Doyle and Virginia Hastings Floyd
(Amsterdam: Rodopi NV, 1972), pp. 155–169.

[8]Phyllis Bentley, *Some Observations on the Art
of the Narrative.* Reprinted in Philip Stevick, ed.,
The Theory of the Novel (New York: The Free
Press, 1967), pp. 47–57.

We would let him go on burying himself in
his good gray practical way. It is because
he can no longer bury himself that we

do it for him. We are a family and we
*   observe*
our observances. We have even chosen a
good gray practical day. For, more or less
inevitably, he is dead, and we know how to
put two and two together and get it all

buried. What else is a family for? Do you
*   think*
we would let our uncle bury himself all
these years and not finish the job for him?
Besides, he is unuseably dead. Which, even
as a matter of practicality, changes things:

What good would it do to keep him? He
could only grow more noticeable than
we have ever allowed him to be, or than
would entirely fit his character, or
what we took to be his character, what

the bottle had left of it. He did try us. But
he is dead. This is his body under a good
gray sky with all the practical arrangements
arranged. And the family here, practically
*   mourning.*
But a family. And one that knows what
*   to do.*

II.   As I find myself remembering

But because he bought me my first puppy
*   (a brownsilk*
ears nose and tail all going with a red
*   ribbon*
around its neck) and gave me (on another
*   birthday) my*
first .22 (with which I walked whole
*   continents any*
afternoon) I don't care what rumpot he
*   bloated into*
and floated out of mushy. He is dead. As
*   dead*
as if he had turned into a magnolia and
*   decayed*
open. But by all the sick flowers of this
*   world,*
I remember a gorgeous and a boozy man
*   with*
hairy arms and neat hands and an eye that
*   never*

missed a quail or a pheasant (as I believe
*   my dream).*
And because he was made to hide even his
*   ruin, I kiss*
his stone forehead and leave him my tear
*   openly, for*
myself, perhaps, but openly—who was a
*   dream I had*
young and lived glad in. I did him no good
*   ever*
and I am ashamed to remember how he
*   could laugh once.*[9]

The identity of the poem's speaker (persona) is revealed chiefly through the tensions between a social-familial declaration, which he allows us to overhear, and his own personal remembrance with his statement of grief and shame. The persona is probably male since he admires the hunting skill of his uncle from whom he received a .22 rifle. While he speaks in line 1 and throughout section II, he hears the unfeeling family speaking in the first six stanzas.

The attitude as well as the perspective, action, style, and purpose contrast sharply between sections I and II. In the first, the family members' dominar.t attitude is disgust toward the dead uncle and self-satisfaction for responsibly burying him. They view the body on the day of the funeral, recalling the past only by mentioning the uncle's uselessness and his self-destructive drinking habits.

The family's speeches combine to identify the event, tell of their plans, explain how the uncle had, up until the present, "buried" himself, and point out that his behavior was a source of embarrassment. Throughout this part, the members of the family indicate that they believe they are dutifully behaving like a "family."

Several striking features of the family's language are apparent: the repeated use of the impersonal "we"; the clipped, heavily

[9] John Ciardi, "Elegy," © Rutgers, the State University. Reprinted by permission of the author.

accented lines (e.g., "good gray practical dead/uncle"); the vacuous combinations of words (e.g., "unuseably dead," "proper proprieties," "with all the practical arrangements arranged"). Each device reveals a feigned concern, indifference, and pseudo-grief. The family speaks because they are forced to recognize the death of a relative.

Just as important, they function as a "gray" and empty backdrop for the persona's "elegy" in section II. He, unlike the other members of the family, speaks in a style far less hortatory; his is conversational with freer verse and longer run-on sentences. His use of exaggerations underscores his youthful fondness for and admiration of the uncle: with the gun, he "walked whole continents," and his uncle had "an eye that never missed."

The persona fondly remembers the uncle's association with events of major significance to a young man: birthdays complete with a puppy gift-tied with red ribbon and later his first gun. Although the uncle drank a lot, he was jolly, thoughtful, a crack shot, and a human being who gave far more than he received.

In sincere grief over the loss as well as guilt for his own insensitive adult behavior, the persona leaves the uncle with a kiss, a tear, and a strong sense of gratitude.

Suggested Assignments

I. Prepare an informal dramatic analysis of one of the following poems. Be sure to include comments about the possible presence of more than one *voice* in the poem.
   A. Thomas Hardy, "Ah, Are You Digging on My Grave?"
   B. James Wright, "Mutterings over the Crib of a Deaf Child"
   C. John Frederick Nims, "Love Poem"
   D. Jackson MacLow, "Jail Break"
II. Be prepared to discuss one of the fol-

lowing stories according to a dramatic analysis. Remember that you can use the dramatic analysis framework in looking at *the narrator's action* as well as the *action within the story* he or she tells.
   A. Cynthia Marshall Rich, "My Sister's Marriage"
   B. William Faulkner, "A Rose for Emily"
   C. John Updike, "Pigeon Feathers"
   D. Donald Barthelme, "Shower of Gold"

DIMENSIONS AND LIBERTIES IN ANALYSIS[10]

Clearly, literature does not mean the same thing to all readers. This richness at least partially explains why literature is art. The fact that there are no final or absolute answers can be provocative, even inspiring; it can also be frustrating. The question often arises as to just how far the reading or interpretation of a text legitimately can go. Consider these two claims: *No performance can demonstrate all the interpretations, all levels of meaning in a text; nonetheless there are "wrong" performances that violate the text.*

Asked how far a conductor's liberties extend, one music critic answered: as far as his imagination can take him—so long as he preserves the "known characteristics" of the music. This also applies to the performance of literature. Richly textured literature contains many potentials, and each performance fusion is unique. Still, performing license is not limitless; one's choices are guided by "known characteristics," referred to here as *certainties,* and certainties are to be distinguished sharply from the other in-

[10]Much of this material is drawn from Beverly Whitaker's "Evaluating Performed Literature," *Studies in Interpretation II,* ed. Esther M. Doyle and Virginia Hastings Floyd (Amsterdam: Rodopi NV, 1976).

terpretive dimensions: *probabilities, possibilities,* and *distortions.*

Certainties are the aspects of a text that undoubtedly exist. They are not implied; they *are*. While we may debate their exact meaning and significance, we have no ground for argument about their presence. For example, it is certain that a jealous woman bent on the murder of her rival is the speaker of Robert Browning's "The Laboratory"; it is certain that George Baker's "To My Mother" is written in the sonnet form; and it is certain that Holden Caulfield in J. D. Salinger's *The Catcher in the Rye* tells of his experiences a year after they occur.

Certainties in a literary text inevitably lead to *probabilities,* characteristics implied but not explicitly stated. Supported by evidence inferred from the text, a probability is a weighed likelihood: known facts give rise to provisional conclusions. One of the real joys of literature lies in its unanswered questions. Unanswered questions provoke careful scrutiny and calculated speculations or reasoned deductions. These probabilities may be actualized in performance. Unlike silent readers, performers can only rarely suspend a number of alternative answers; their answers are behaviorally specific.

In addition to certainties and probabilities, performances may demonstrate the literature's *possibilities.* A possible interpretation offers a likelihood, a viable alternate among plausible answers, and the "rightness" of the choice can neither be proved nor disproved absolutely. Based on inferences that range from moderate probabilities to slight chances, this dimension of interpretation, at its best, invites imaginative and creative performances and results in experiences that are illuminating, exciting, and justifiable.

The fewer explicit or strongly implied answers a text contains (or the less highly

defined it is),[11] the more likely the possibilities in performance. Internally consistent and persuasively presented, they may be regarded by listeners as probable or even certain. By their very nature, possible interpretations open the door to marginal—though not necessarily "wrong"—performances. A performance that brings out distant possibilities often competes with or dilutes the certainties or probabilities in the text. The competition or dilution may be so extensive as to produce a performance that violates the text's certainties, thus moving into a fourth dimension of interpretation, *distortion.* While certainties are associated with the stated elements of literature, probabilities with implications, and possibilities with suggestions, distortions present contradictions. Distorted answers make false assertions about the literature; they are marked by the absence of congruence and fidelity to the text. Certainties are so ignored or twisted that the major defining characteristics of the experience the text notates are lost.

This range of dimensions may be illustrated with these statements about "The Secret Life of Walter Mitty." (See chart top of pg. 19.)

Suggested Assignments

I. Prepare a set of certainties, probabilities, possibilities, and distortions for the following poem. Try also to analyze it dramatically by answering the questions: Who is (are) speaking? From what perspective? Where and when? To whom? What does the speaker say? How? Why?

[11]Lee Hudson, "Oral Interpretation as Metaphorical Expression," *Speech Teacher*, 22 (January 1973), 30.

Certainties	Probabilities	Possibilities	Distortions
Mitty enjoys elaborate fantasies in which he is daring, authoritative, and skillful.	Mitty is middle-aged	Mitty is physically smaller than his wife.	Mitty's fantasies show him to be mentally unbalanced.
Mitty, in his everyday life is easily intimidated, prone to forgetfulness, and nagged by his wife.	Mitty's trip to Waterbury takes place in the afternoon.	Mitty, a reckless driver, has had several automobile accidents in the past.	Mitty is tormented by recurring nightmares.

Reason
Josephine Miles

*Said, Pull her up a bit will you, Mac, I want
   to unload there.
Said, Pull her up my rear end, first come
   first serve.
Said, Give her the gun, Bud, he needs a
   taste of his own bumper.
Then the usher came out and got into the
   act:
Said, Pull her up, pull her up a bit, we need
   this space, sir.
Said, For God's sake, is this still a free
   country or what?
You go back and take care of Gary Cooper's
   horse
And leave me handle my own car.
Saw them unloading the lame old lady.
Ducked out under the wheel and gave her
   an elbow,
Said, All you needed to do was jut explain;
Reason, Reason is my middle name.*[12]

II. How might a group performance of the
poem emphasize Miles' observation:
" 'Reason' is a favorite one of my poems
because I like the idea of speech—not
images, not ideas, not music, but people
talking—as the material from which

poetry is made . . . the accents of a limited and maybe slightly misplaced pride we need more of, and oblique accents of it at least sound out the right direction."[13]

THE PRODUCTION CONCEPT

A *production concept* establishes a causal relationship between what you take a piece of literature to *mean* and how it is *actualized*. A production concept embodies what you have *found* (your interpretation through analysis) and what *you intend to do* (adaptation, rehearsal, staging); it is the articulation of your intent. Without a production concept, a performance is left to whim or chance; with one, you, as the director, have an approach from which to work—even though that approach may change. (See Gray's discussion of the major changes in concept that occurred between two productions of "The Nincompoop," pp. 193–95).

Consider the following brief comment about a production concept:

A production concept involves careful exploration of the script for its basic line of action, principal ideas, conflicts, and character relationships in order to define the *es-*

[12]From *Poems 1930–1960* by Josephine Miles, p. 92. Copyright © 1960 by Indiana University Press, Bloomington. Reprinted by permission of the publisher.

[13]From *Poet's Choice*, Paul Engle and Joseph Langland, eds. (New York: The Dial Press, 1962) pp. 107–108.

sence of a script and build a production around that definition. In a recent production of *Romeo and Juliet,* I determined that the play was about young love set in the tarnished world of Verona. In carrying out this concept, we sought to set apart the young lovers as two clear, bright jewels. Romeo wore deep scarlet, while Juliet appeared in lemon yellow. Other members of the rival households carried out the central concept visually by wearing colors of burnished gold, burnt orange, and browns as well as purples and dark reds.[14]

Consider this production concept for Shirley Jackson's novel *We Have Always Lived in the Castle:*

The novel is a paradoxial treatment of the centuries-old theme of innocence and evil. Real innocence ironically marks the character of the emotionally disturbed murderess, Mary Katherine Blackwood, her protector-sister Constance, and her senile uncle Julian. The townspeople personify subtly but forcefully a *real* evil in their social persecution of the Blackwoods and vandalism of their home. One way of emphasizing this thematic tension is to employ throughout the production Mary Katherine's "innocent" point of view: the townspeople actually become gray-faced, over-sized, awkward, snide, strident— or whatever she says they are—standing in sharp contrast to the pleasing warmth and affection in the Blackwood's isolated home-castle.

In addition to clarifying this thematic clash in the novel, I hope to also demonstrate two other facets of the book: (1) the encompassing nature of Mary Katherine's narrative control by casting two performers in that role (one, a youth engaged in a past act; the other, an adult, involved in the present narrative); and (2) the ambiguous time lapse

between the event (the house burning) and the later telling of it, a fictional technique that creates much of the haunting quality and eeriness in the novel.

In this statement the director identifies the basic theme of the novel and the forces through which it is dramatized, the major structural devices to be demonstrated in production, and the dominant response desired from the audience.

In short, the production concept usually treats with varying emphases your answers to four questions: (1) What discoveries or decisions have you made about the literature on literal, thematic, structural and metaphorical[15] levels? (2) What is its essence? (3) Which of the discoveries do you want to translate into your production? (4) What is the effect you desire from your production?

You might find it helpful to select at least three of the essays in the second section of this book. Study the discussions of production concept and consider the kinds of questions each director implicitly or explicitly raises and answers.

Suggested Assignments

I. Be prepared to read and discuss your production concept for one or more of the following: "The Secret Life of Walter Mitty" (pp. 7–10), "Reason" (p. 19), and "Elegy" (p. 16).

II. Search out the New York critic's reviews of one Broadway show of your choice. Try to *infer* from the reviews what the director's production concept may have been.

---

[14]Gresdna Doty, Director of Theatre, Louisiana State University, Baton Rouge, Louisiana.

[15]See Raymond Schneider's "The Visible Metaphor," *Communication Education,* 25 (March, 1976), 121–26.

chapter 3

The Literature Adapted

Just as the framing of a production concept is contingent upon discoveries made as you analyze the literature, so too your rationale for adaptation logically should emerge from the interpretation stated in the production concept.

Adaptation refers to change, alteration, or adjustment. With *any* performance, a degree of adaptation occurs—i.e., the *actualization* of a printed text in a performance (solo or group) necessarily involves a change of medium, an *accommodation* so to speak. Of course, we encourage this kind of change with the tacit assumption that it permits the fuller realization, the "fleshing out" of a text. In this section of the book, however, we are primarily concerned with changes in the language and structure of the text itself.

In adapting literature for group performance, your aim is to enhance the literature for a "sounding" by making necessary modifications without creating *distortions* in the original text. This pivotal point is interestingly illustrated in the program notes for the internationally successful *Emlyn Williams as Charles Dickens*. The notes describe Williams' need to adapt Dickens' work (Dick-

ens himself did so less than a century earlier) because of time and the audience—all in hopes that the performance might lead the audience back to the novels in their entirety.

The Adaptation of *Emlyn Williams* as *Charles Dickens*

In adapting freely but carefully, Mr. Williams has thought it only fair to assume that his audiences know nothing of the books, or have forgotten all they once knew; he felt that if, through his treatment of the text, he could make the performance acceptable to such audiences, there was a chance of coaxing people to lift down from their shelves what they had possibly thought of as a ponderous classic, and to turn its pages as if for the first time, with the feeling that they are about to explore a wonderful new world.[1]

We may deduce from this discussion several challenges and problems in adaptation: (1) literature written for silent reading very

[1]"The Adaptation of *Emlyn Williams as Charles Dickens*," Program notes, Indiana University, 1964.

21

frequently interests performers; (2) much literature is written for longer periods of silent reading than public listening generally provides; (3) some literature, pleasurable for silent reading, can prove dull, confusing, repetitious, or offensive when heard by an audience; and *most important,* (4) performers may choose to limit the literature in order to avoid limiting their own understanding of the text and the listening experiences of an audience.

TECHNIQUES FOR ADAPTATION

The four basic techniques for adaptation include deletion, addition, rearrangement, and extraction. A description of each technique, together with an example, follows.

Deletion

Performers face the constant problem of time requirements. Except in unusually small classes, students rarely have more than ten or fifteen minutes for group performances; and even in workshop or major productions, the maximum time allotted is normally one, or at the most, two hours. With many works, particularly novels, deletion is unavoidable because one must consider the audience's time.

What you delete depends quite naturally upon your production concept. In fact, settling on the production concept makes your adapting tasks infinitely easier: with a clearly stated focus, you "cut in" to preserve that focus, rather than moving through the literary text with an eye to "cutting out." You are in a position to look for the essentials instead of being primed to remove the seeming inessentials.

As with any of the techniques for adaptation, there are no hard, fast, or easy rules. Depending upon your interpretation of the literature, you may decide to delete dialogue tags, episodes, characters, or subplots. The

decision to delete should be carefully weighed against the benefits of inclusion, and it should be relatively easily to justify.

Certain kinds of deletion *deform* the structure of a literary work: e.g., eliminating the lyric passages from Amy Lowell's "The Day that Was the Day" destroys the poetic structure. More insidious is the deletion that reverses the thematic content of the work. One example may suffice. A director who is unsatisfied with the concluding assertion in Archibald MacLeish's *J.B.* might delete the confrontation scene between J.B., Zuess, and Nickles, and thus cut out J.B.'s decision to "go it alone," to rest his determination on being a mere human who wishes to live. Such a deletion, more palatable to some audiences, nevertheless strips away J.B.'s strong insistence that he be his own master, even against overwhelming odds.

Addition

Often deletions necessitate additions to the script. These items, sometimes no longer than a sentence, preserve continuity and set up passages for previous antecedents. Failure to supply this kind of information leads to confusion especially if the audience is unacquainted with the literature. Simple and not necessarily destructive changes can be made. For example, if in the initial introduction of Milo in Reynolds Price's *A Long and Happy Life,* the character of Milo is cut but his name appears later, the director may add an identifying phrase, "Rosocoke's brother." If confusion about time results because of a deletion, the adaptor can simply add such phrases as "the next day," or "two years later."

Rearrangement

Occasionally the director of a group performance will locate material that needs to be reordered for more effective communication. For example, in *Mark Twain's Auto-biography* Charles Neider had to reorganize and unify the original autobiography because it lacked a firm chronology. For slightly different reasons, some of Twain's other works also suggest the need for rearrangement. *The Story of the Good Boy* and *The Story of the Bad Boy* may be combined so that the ironical differences between the boys' behavior and rewards are more humorously emphatic. Combining *Adam's Diary* with *Eve's Diary* results in delightfully contrasting views of the couple's original meeting and subsequent relationship. The use of both diaries provides a stronger narrative thread because Adam and Eve do not always record their impressions about the same periods of time (see p. 218). Another selection by Twain for which rearrangement seems appropriate is "Letter II" from *Letters from the Earth*. In the letter, Satan first writes that man has "imagined a heaven." He then describes man's habits, inclinations, and aversions on earth. Finally, he indicates how these real habits relate to the imaginary heaven. Instead of performing all the habits on earth and then the habits in heaven, the comedy and the irony are sharper if each description of a habit observed on earth is followed by its counterpart in heaven (see p. 217).

Most men do not sing, most men cannot sing, most men will not stay where others are singing if it be continued more than two hours. Note that.

Only about two men in a hundred can play upon a musical instrument, and not four in a hundred have any wish to learn how. Set that down....

...In man's heaven *everybody sings!* The man who did not sing on earth sings there; the man who could not sing on earth is able to do it there. The universal singing is not casual, not occasional, not relieved by intervals of quiet; it goes on, all day long, and every day....

Meantime, every person is playing on a harp—those millions and millions!...Consider the deafening hurricane of sound....[2]

Extraction

Works whose length prohibits them from being read in their entirety often contain episodes or scenes suitable for performance. The most desirable sections are those that require a minimum of explanatory comment and retain their unity when lifted from the complete work. Considerable material of this type is available for performance. A few examples follow:

The Johannesburg sequence in Alan Paton's *Cry, the Beloved Country*

The encounter between Sam Ordway and the Widow Eubanks in William Humphrey's *The Ordways*

Sir Winston Churchill's account of his first speech in *The Early Years*

John Steinbeck's meeting with the Shakespearean actor in *Travels with Charley*

Several of the Chorus' speeches in T. S. Eliot's *Murder in the Cathedral*

Dolly Levi's address to the deceased Mr. Levi in Thornton Wilder's *The Matchmaker*

A section about a specific country in Edna St. Vincent Millay's "I Like Americans"

"The Event" from Robert Penn Warren's *Internal Injuries*

The peroration from Martin Luther King's "I Have a Dream"

Each of these examples can be presented independently of the original text; furthermore, extracting them does not distort the thrust of the complete literary work.

The technique of extraction is used most often in the compilation of scripts, a special form of adaptation discussed below.

[2]Mark Twain, "Letter II," *Letters from the Earth*, ed. Bernard de Voto (New York: Harper & Row, 1962), pp. 15–20.

Compilation as Adaptation

If you wish to study a *class* of works rather than a single work, you assemble material from a variety of sources that, when combined, constitutes a dramatically unified whole. Several constant principles will guide you in the construction of a compiled script: (1) balance, (2) variety, (3) transition, and (4) unity.

A satisfying program balances the length of each selection, the subjects treated, and the tone. The compilation has an overall rhythm independent of that of the individual selections. It should appear progressive and controlled.

Variety in a script refers to a varied, hence more interesting, format design. It is difficult for an audience to remain attentive to one element for more than an hour. Moments of "relief" rechannel audience engagement and energy. This change of pace can be achieved either through arrangement of selections or other changes in sets, music, and lighting.

The transitions between selections are frequently the most challenging design problem. A choppy program, unless specifically intended, appears amateurish and unpolished. To smooth out a program is to connect the selections in some meaningful way. Transitional materials should be carefully integrated into the production concept and design of the entire show. Transitions either break the movement of the production, suspend it, or alter it in some way (e.g., support selection, ironically comment on selection). They are, in short, a powerful structural element. Audiences depend on transitions to provide connectives and reveal the direction of the program. The style of these transitions should be set early in the production. Clean transitions can be achieved (1) by performers who move quickly and purposefully into place for the next selection after setting the last one; (2) by music (preferably live in order to eliminate technical timing problems);

(3) by a narrator whom the audience realizes will direct the production along; (4) by other visual media (e.g., slides announcing selections or providing comment; or (5) by other technical means (e.g., lights, set shifts). Naturally, these transitional devices can be combined in various ways as well.

The program should be unified. This is an aspect of the director's control and sense of a whole in the production concept. All parts should be selected and arranged with this concept in mind and move together in an orchestrated fashion. Some popular concepts in compiled scripts are themes or structures, authors, or literary movements or groups.

Themes or structures. The theme-centered program highlights general statements. Often rhetorical in nature, the theme-centered program can explore social issues ("machines and war," "dehumanization," "ecological awareness"), personal issues ("spiritual searching," "alienation," "ego and identity"), or interpersonal issues ("dimensions of the family," "team spirit," "educational pressures"), to mention just a few.

Other compilations might display a particular structure such as the sonnet or ballad forms. Performers and listeners are often surprised at the wide range of subjects and themes that can be explored within a single structure.

The selection should not be "stretched" unreasonably to fit a certain thematic interest. If the theme is just a small part of the total interest of a given selection, it is unlikely that an audience unfamiliar with it will see its relevance. Also, try to make the theme as specific as possible; for example, a program on "love" probably should deal only with a particular type or aspect of love (e.g., "requited" vs. "unrequited" love). Many of the themes suggested above could be narrowed in a variety of ways to tighten the program. Just how much development you can give a theme will often depend upon time and the selections located.

Authors. Another possible principle for

compilation is the writing of a particular author. Naturally since most authors have written far more than could be presented in a single program, the author-centered script usually has a thematic suborganization such as biographical chronology, range of subject matter or technical virtuosity, social and literary influences, or the tracing of a writer's development.

Literary Movements or Groups. The literary spirit is not easily categorized or "grouped" into movements. A script organized around a literary movement should deal only with general ideas. Most writers, for example, could be placed in any number of groups, and the only reason for categorizing them is to illuminate a particular aspect of their work. This type of compilation also permits including more than one author in the presentation and also, like the author-centered design, has an implicit suborganization. If, for instance, you were planning a program on the black poetry movement, you would probably want to narrow the design to a particular time in the history of black poetry, (e.g., the Harlem Renaissance, the 1960s) and focus on issues, themes, subjects, or styles that characterized the poetry of the time.

Other movements or groups that a compilation could explore include: confessional poetry, folk tales of the Southwest, and avant-garde literature.

Compilation as adaptation is exemplified in the following recently produced scripts:

POEMSNONPOEMS NOW: Pop, Op, and Protest (poetry, slides, and music of the 1960's)

Rain on the Leaves (prose, poetry, and drama by and about the Vietnamese)

Cutlass and Rapier (forms and types of satire)

Prosperity: Around the Corner? (song, prose, and poetry about America's depression years)

Prophets and Peacocks (from short stories, non-fiction, and novels by Flannery O'Conner)

e. e. cummings: Draftsman of Words (poetry, prose, and drama reflecting cummings's romance with language)[3]

Together, these examples reflect the wide range of literary themes that are amenable to compilation. It is a useful and rewarding kind of adaptation if you wish to explore the diversity of a particular writer's work, concentrate on a selected aspect of it, or study the literature of a single genre or country. Many paperback anthologies suggest possible compilations for group performance: *An Irish Treasury, The Medieval Age of Literature, Black Voices, A Whitman Sampler, Anti-Story,* and *Concrete Poetry: A World View.*

If you are interested in showing one writer's artistry, in developing a subject, or underscoring a certain dimension of literature, you will probably devise your own script. In all likelihood, the compilation will involve addition, deletion, rearrangement, and especially extraction.

At its best, the compiled script is a creative synthesis of different but related literature; at its worst, it is unfocused and fragmented. The following questions will help to isolate the challenges and hazards in making a compilation:

1. Does the script possess *unity?* Do the various elements harmonize?
2. Does it contain *contrast*—in tone, length, or style?
3. Is its focus clear?
4. Are transitional materials, if used, *congruent* with the literature and the production concept?
5. Are the materials arranged to form a *whole,* with a beginning, middle, and end? If not, is it deliberately arranged in order to reflect chaos or indecision?
6. Is the compilation *faithful* to each of the individual literary texts?

[3]These scripts were compiled respectively by Beverly Whitaker, Dan Hardy, Lee Hudson, Suanne Bennett, Mary Frances HopKins, and Jean Phillips.

Suggested Assignments

I. In a detailed list, note the changes between the original story and each of the following adaptations in this book:
   A. "Lily Daw and the Three Ladies," p. 299.
   B. "K*A*P*L*A*N on Shakespeare," p. 115.
   C. "Oh Where Oh Where Is There," p. 155.
II. Examine one of the following commercially available scripts for group performance:
   A. Marchette Chute and Laurence Perrine, *The Worlds of Shakespeare*
   B. Martin Duberman, *In White America*
   C. John Barton, *The Hollow Crown*
   After identifying the various techniques of adaptation, answer the questions listed above regarding compilations.

III. Write an essay or prepare an oral report on the technique and probable effects of the changes involved in dramatizing the following literature:
   A. Shirley Jackson, *We Have Always Lived in the Castle,* adapted by Hugh Wheeler, Dramatists Play Service, Inc.
   B. Ken Kesey, *One Flew Over the Cuckoo's Nest,* adapted by Dale Wasserman, Samuel French, Inc.
   C. George Orwell, *Animal Farm,* adapted by Nelson Bond, Samuel French, Inc.
IV. After studying one or more of the following scripts in this book, try to deduce the adaptor's rationale for the transitional material. Then compare your observations with the adaptor's comments in the essay about the script:
   A. *An Hour with Reed Whittemore,* pp. 93.
   B. *Twain Sketches*, pp. 199.

chapter 4

The Literature in Rehearsal and Production

When you select the literature for group performance, analyze it, frame a production concept, and adapt your script, you are functioning chiefly as a literary critic; when you begin rehearsals, you assume another role, that of a director involved with teaching, designing, and administration.

In addition to 'the discussion in this chapter, you will also require additional information from the many excellent sources on the art and craft of performing and directing. As you know, the entire process is far too complex to be reduced to a few pages. Listed below are a few books you will find extremely helpful. You might consider it a "Beginning Bibliography for Directors of Group Performance," and "beginning" is the key word because you will no doubt add many items to it. Collectively, these books touch on every phase of your activity as a director of group performance, although, of course, they do not always share the same approach.

Wallace Bacon. *The Art of Interpretation.* Rev. ed. New York: Holt, Rinehart & Winston, Inc. 1972.

Robert Beneditti. *The Actor at Work.* Englewood Cliffs, N.J.: Prentice-Hall, Inc., 1976.

Richard Boleslavsky. *Acting: The First Six Lessons.* New York: Theatre Arts Books, 1933.

Leslie Irene Coger, and Melvin White. *Readers Theatre Handbook: A Dramatic Approach to Literature.* Rev. ed. Glenview, Ill.: Scott, Foresman, 1973.

Robert Cohen, and John Harrop. *Creative Play Direction.* Englewood Cliffs, N.J.: Prentice-Hall, Inc., 1974.

Williard J. Friederich and John H. Fraser. *Scene Design for the Amateur Stage.* New York: Macmillan, 1962.

Uta Hagen. *Respect for Acting.* New York: Macmillan, 1973.

Richard Haas, *Theatres of Interpretation.* Ann Arbor: Roberts-Burton Publication, 1976.

Francis Hodge. *Play Directing: Analysis, Communication, and Style.* Englewood Cliffs, N.J.: Prentice-Hall, Inc., 1971.

Rudolph von Laban. *The Mastery of Movement.* 3rd ed., revised and enlarged by Lisa Ullmann. Boston: Plays, Inc. 1971.

Joanna Hawkins Maclay. *Readers Theatre: Toward a Grammar of Practice.* New York: Random House, Inc., 1971.

Alethea Mattingly and Wilma Grimes. *Interpretation: Reader, Writer, Audience.* Rev. ed. San Francisco: Wadsworth Publishing Company, Inc., 1971.

Charles McGaw. *Acting Is Believing*, 2nd ed. New York: Holt, Rinehart & Winston, Inc., 1966.

Sonia Moore. *The Stanislavski System in Class Training an Actor.* New York: Viking Press, 1968.

Leland Roloff. *The Perception and Evocation of Literature.* Glenview, Ill.: Scott, Foresman, 1974.

Sam Smiley, *Playwriting: The Structure of Action.* Englewood Cliffs, N.J.: Prentice-Hall, Inc., 1971.

Viola Spolin. *Improvisation for the Theatre: A Handbook of Teaching and Directing Techniques.* Evanston, Ill.: Northwestern University Press, 1963.

Suggested Assignments

I. Prepare a class report on one of the books listed in the preceeding bibliography. If possible, give other members of the class dittoed handouts concerning the book's aim, scope, and any definitions and exercises that you found particularly useful.

II. Select three essays in this book and compare the director's central concerns in rehearsal.

Essentially, rehearsal involves two processes: *exploring* and *setting*. These are intentionally broad categories; the way you handle the objectives unique to each will depend on the nature of your script, the experience and background of individual cast members, and your own personality. The few guidelines offered here should be regarded only as suggestions.

REHEARSALS OF EXPLORATION[1]

During exploratory rehearsals, the direc-

[1]We are indebted for many of these ideas to the comments and practice of Gresdna Doty, James Barton, and Gerald Freedman.

tor provides necessary background for the script, explains the initial analysis, the production concept, and the methods of adaptation. Generally, this information is given at the first rehearsal and is followed by a read-through of the entire script. For some time after this initial explanation, the director is far more likely to raise questions than to answer them; to suggest rather than to tell; to coax and lead rather than demonstrate. This exploring stage involves looking at and delving into the life of the literature from as many angles as possible, those already seen by the director during the study of the script and, just as important, those discovered by the cast as they *perform* the many layered "actions" the script *notates*. The exploring phase of rehearsal is stimulating and significant as you and your cast determine the subtext of individual lines and character relationships.

The Literature's Subtext

The whole matter of subtext—the action or drama beneath what is actually said or done—is the consuming interest in these early rehearsals because the fullest and most credible performances are those in which the subtext is clearly realized and communicated from moment to moment throughout the script. One of the most complete descriptions of subtext and its importance appears in Cohen and Harrop's *Creative Play Direction:*

> Subtext involves all the inner action of a scene or play which is not specifically noted in the text; it is under (*sub*) the text, there to be found by the diligent interpretive study or intuition of the director and actors. It is also there for the study and intuition of critics and audiences, so the director must work carefully if he is to avoid censure.
>
> The subtext of a given moment is the composite of three components which, in the lazy parlance of the theatre, are frequently

mistaken for the whole thing. They are not, and they should be precisely understood:

1. The character's intention (what he wants to do)
2. The character's motivation (why he wants to do it)
3. The character's inner monologue (what he is thinking when he does it)

The subtext of a play [or story, or poem, or nonfiction] therefore is a highly complex network of conscious and unconscious impulses that are as real and theatrical as the external actions. The text is the mere external tip of a giant iceberg of inner action.

As an example of the complexity of this problem, let us look at Othello's single line, "Indeed? Ay, indeed!" [Act III, scene iii, 1.102]. A possible interpretation of the subtext at that moment follows.

Othello's intention: to make light of Iago's hint by mocking Iago's unusual inflection, thereby diverting Iago from continuing.

Othello's motivation: to prevent himself from hearing what he dreads to hear.

Othello's inner monologue: "What the hell is he driving at?"

Iago's intention (while listening to Othello's line): to note how much the hint rattles Othello.

Iago's motivation: to see how fast and hard he should pursue this line of hinting without overstepping his bounds.

Iago's inner monologue: "Yes, he's upset, he's going to pursue this."

The subtext of the moment: Othello, frightened by the possibilities that Iago's hint has opened to examination, tries to avoid further discussion of the subject by the psychological defense mechanism of mocking his subordinate. Iago, a superior psychological analyst, sees through Othello's mechanism, recognizes it for what it is, and discovers that the Moor is open to further suggestion.

Multiply this subtext by every definable moment in the play [script], and every character on stage at every moment, and the magnitude of the subtextual play becomes apparent.[2]

[2]Robert Cohen and John Harrop, *Creative Play Directing* (Englewood Cliffs, N.J.: Prentice-Hall, Inc., 1974.), pp. 126–27.

In addition to working toward as full a grasp as possible of the subtext, the exploratory rehearsals may offer performers a chance, within the group security of the cast, to expand their own resources—vocal, physical, and psychological—for meeting the potentials in the script. Often, directors allocate the first fifteen minutes or so of each rehearsal to physical warm-ups, vocal exercises, and improvisations based on real-life situations but related, on a psychological level, to that portion of the script being rehearsed. If carefully planned and not allowed to go on too long, these sessions can be invaluable in lessening inhibitions and fright, increasing group interaction, and providing a sense of readiness to perform.

Suggested Assignments

I. After rereading Josephine Miles's "Reason" (p. 19), assume that you will be staging the first stanza with four performers. In your preparation, be as specific as possible about the varieties of subtextual interpretation of the four lines. Devise a series of questions that might lead and assist each of the performers.

II. For the same stanza and with the same cast arrangement, plan a series of improvisations, as well as vocal and physical exercises, to help the performers achieve a state of readiness for the performance. (How tense should they be? How loudly do they speak? In what dialect? What is their attitude toward one another? How does their environment of the moment affect their responses?)

Performance Style

Another matter likely to be resolved during exploratory rehearsals is that of performance style. In the long history of performances, two broad distinctions of type are repeatedly recognized: the *presentational,* giving directly to the audience, and *representational,* creating an illusion of reality to which the audience may attend, overhear, as it were. Traditionally, readers theatre productions employ a presentational style and little movement and spectacle. The hypothesis of such productions is that when the playing space is stripped to the barest accouterments, thereby emphasizing the expressive performer's presence and skill, the audience is allowed—or forced—to fill in the details in its imagination, thus enjoying an intense participative experience. Others have argued that no evidence exists to support just how much audiences will or can "image" with minimal stimuli, and further that the rich varieties of literary texts make this kind of precast molding too restrictive in that it ignores the uniqueness of many texts.

Our position is that group performance should be neither restricted nor defined by conventions; instead, each piece of literature invites a close analysis which generates production concepts that include the relationships of performer to performer and performers to audience. *The understood world of the literature then implies manners of performance style.* Choices undoubtedly must be made, but they need not be expedient ones (e.g., "We are using scripts because 'you are supposed to'." Or, worse still, "We are using scripts because we didn't have time to learn the lines."). In short, a given production may reflect a thoughtful preference for either presentational (off stage) or representational (on stage) focus; it may combine both. It may ask an audience both to reflect and be engaged, believe and suspend belief, listen and overhear—all depending finally upon what your study leads you to *show* of the script in performance. Our only firm advice is that you reveal your choice early so that the audience is not left wondering what role to play.

Suggested Assignment

Adapt and be prepared to direct the first paragraph from "The Secret Life of Walter Mitty." In class, try each of the following techniques and be prepared to comment on how well they support your production concept (Suggested Assignment 1, p. 20):

A. Narrator, Mitty, lieutenant, and crew *present* all lines.
B. Narrator speaks to audience while Mitty and crew *represent* the action of the fantasy.
C. Narrator both converses with the audience and watches the action on board; crew remains in the scene while Mitty intermittently both joins it and sees himself far away, even beyond the audience.

Other directorial concerns during the exploratory rehearsals concern movement, or blocking, and design plans. Your original ideas formed during the earlier study of the script are now confirmed or altered as the rehearsals proceed. In order to avoid generalizations, let us consider the tentative decisions reached about half-way through the rehearsals for two different scripts that were performed on the same stage space. We will look at the ground plan (stage map), movement, and elements of stage design.

Antigone, a play by Jean Anouilh

1. *Ground plan:* (See diagram pg. 31.)
2. *Setting*: The set pieces will consist of five reading stands made of light-toned pine to match the wooden panels at the rear of the stage. They will give each performer a "station," blend harmoniously with the permanent features of the playing space, and create a neutral field for the clash in the drama. Furthermore, the use of stands should emphasize both the play's declamatory quality and its conflicts, or debates, between Antigone and the other characters. By minimizing scenic detail, it is hoped that the ideological impasse and the rhetorical-poetic quality of the language and structure will be foremost.

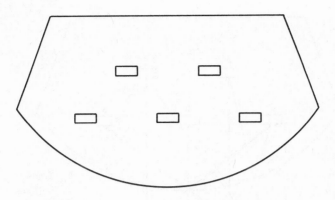

Diagram 1

Scale : 3/4 inch = five feet

☐ Lectern

3. *Movement*: Except for Chorus, who serves as a philosopher-storyteller for the audience and moves freely about, the characters move to and from their designated stations at entrances and exits. Two exceptions occur: for the final scene with the guard, Antigone moves to an up stage position, a movement designed to underscore her loneliness as well as her uncertainty. Also, when Creon's son, Haemon, takes up the debate with Creon, he moves to the center stand, a station occupied earlier only by Antigone. Now, instead of a niece who threatens the stability of the State, Creon must confront his own son and successor to the throne.

Throughout the performance, all characters, except Chorus, will use off-stage focus, the nature of which appears in the following diagram for scenes 10 and 11. The *solid lines* indicate the angle of vision upon Creon's entrance when the guards are presenting their captive, Antigone, who does not look at her uncle-king. The *broken lines* show the focus when the first guard is answering Creon's questions while the other two guards are standing at attention and Antigone is watching for Creon's response. The *dotted lines* show the focus for much of scene 11 when Antigone and Creon confront each other directly and alone. (See diagram 2 top of pg. 32.)

4. *Lighting:* Cross spots for each of the five areas of the stands as well as more general lighting for Chorus will be used. A predominance of blues in the back border lights should work well with the general illumination for the opening tableau and also as background for the localized, low-level light for Antigone and the guard in her final scene.

5. *Costumes*: Antigone will wear a simply styled, long, dark purple dress, an attire that should suggest both royalty and somberness. Creon wears a black suit, white shirt, and dark crimson tie. All of the other characters wear garments of neutral color (black, beige, white) with differences of fabric and line marking their varying standing (e. g., Haemon will wear a stylishly cut off-white suit, and the guards will appear in beige or brown corduroy sports jackets, turtleneck sweaters, and denim trousers.

6. *Make-up*: Except for Creon and Nurse who will need lines and shadows for age, street make-up will be sufficient.

7. *Sound:* Only the gong announcing Antigone's execution will be used.

The Ponder Heart, a novel by Eudora Welty

1. *Ground plan*:
   Act I. The Beulah Hotel lobby and

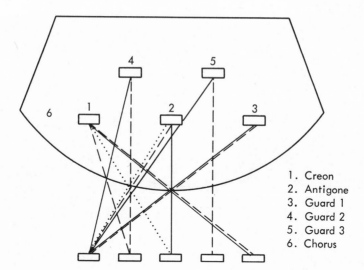

1. Creon
2. Antigone
3. Guard 1
4. Guard 2
5. Guard 3
6. Chorus

Diagram 2

neutral area for street and church. (See diagram no. 3.)

Act II. The courthouse of Clay, Mississippi (with a fragment of the hotel at far stage right). See diagram no. 4 on pg. 33.

2. *Setting*: Although rather worn, the lobby of the hotel should be warm and cozy. Perhaps in light of Edna Earle's interests, it should be a bit overdecorated with flowers, plants, throw pillows, etc. At least a sofa, chair, hassock, table, and

coat rack are necessary for realistic enactment of the novel's action. The dominant set piece is the check-in desk, complete with mail boxes and a sign prominently displaying "Welcome to the Beulah." From this position, Edna Earle, the novel's narrator, controls the story, and much of the time, the town.

Because the opening and closing minutes of Act II are specifically located in the Beulah, a small portion of that set should

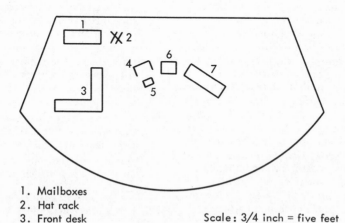

1. Mailboxes
2. Hat rack
3. Front desk
4. Chair
5. Hassock
6. End table
7. Couch

Scale: 3/4 inch = five feet

Diagram 3

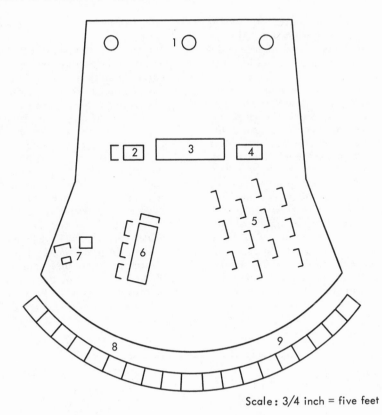

Scale: 3/4 inch = five feet

Diagram 4

1. Flags
2. Baliff
3. Judge
4. Witness stand
5. Jury
6. Prosecution and
   defense
7. Beulah Hotel
8. Peacocks
9. Witnesses

be retained; however, it should not be distracting after the trial begins and the courtroom with its immediate pandemonium comes into view. The judge's bench and the witness stand should be placed in the center of the stage alcove; and, for color as well as specifying locale, three flags—American, Confederate, and Mississippi—could be placed behind the judge.

There is not enough room on stage for the entire Act II cast (35); besides, it might enhance the trial's basic metaphor, a circus, to place the Peacocks (the large rural farm family accusing Edna Earle's uncle, Daniel Ponder, of murdering his wife,

Bonnie Dee Peacock Ponder) on the first row of the audience, along with the trial witnesses. (They can still be seen by the audience since the auditorium is so steeply raked.)

3. *Movement*: Edna Earle's lone listener in the novel will be stretched to include the entire (200) actual audience; she will move about at will in "collaring" them with her story. Even during the trial when her place is somewhat fixed by the judge and the whole riotous event threatens to overshadow her, she can retain control; for unlike the other characters, she operates both *in* the action and *outside* it since she is both participant and recaller. Con-

sequently, she should continue to address the audience directly when she "fills in" with her own observations and various details about the trial proceedings and witnesses.

Although the other characters move about in a realistic, representational style, there are two instances in the script for which *stylized* movement may show the novel's action more clearly. First, when Edna Earle restrains Daniel from telling the *courtroom audience* exactly how Bonnie Dee died and then proceeds to tell that strange story to the *novel's audience* herself, a "freeze" of the rest of the cast could emphasize their ignorance of this part of the story. Second, as Edna Earle moves downstage to tell the audience of Daniel's decision to give all his money away in court, "slow motion" movement by the rest of the cast might heighten that moment when the Ponder "heart of gold"

is demonstrated most clearly—and comically.

Other ways of involving the audience as Edna Earle's listeners lie in the use of entrances and exits. As she explains Daniel and Grandpa Ponder's Friday trips to town when "Daniel spoke to everyone in sight," the two men enter from the center rear door of the auditorium and Daniel can indeed greet the audience. Also, the listeners will perhaps become observers of the trial when the right and left rear doors are used for two entrances at the start of the trial: first, the parade of the Peacocks (all twelve of them) and then, the theatrical sailing in of the county prosecutor, Dorris R. Gladney. The following diagram shows those three entrances in solid lines and the entrances of the remainder of the cast for the trial in broken lines. Hopefully, these actions will envelop a participative audience.

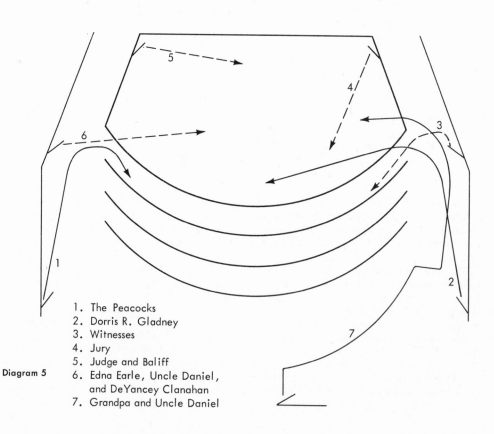

Diagram 5

1. The Peacocks
2. Dorris R. Gladney
3. Witnesses
4. Jury
5. Judge and Baliff
6. Edna Earle, Uncle Daniel, and DeYancey Clanahan
7. Grandpa and Uncle Daniel

4. *Lighting*: Special spotlights will be used when Edna Earle begins and ends her narrative in the Beulah, when Miss Teacake McGee sings in church (red and blue gels to suggest stained-glass windows), and when Edna Earle narrates the actual cause of Bonnie Dee's death. Otherwise, general illumination is used throughout the show.

5. *Costumes*: The novel contains a description of the central costume: Uncle Daniel's white suit, hat, and red bow tie. This dress can be set in contrast to Edna Earle's beige and navy blue, black for the judge and the prosecutor, and pastel cotton for the remainder of the cast. The novel specifies a straw hat entwined with roses for Big John, sunglasses for Narciss, and a "Sunday" dress for Miss Teacake. All of the characters should be in dress of the 1940s period.

6. *Make-up*: Since most of the cast are adults, ordinary street make-up can be used, except for Grandpa Ponder who needs lines and shadows for age, and the coroner, who needs special make-up to denote his blindness.

7. *Sound*: Perhaps distinctively Southern folk music should be played at the beginning and close of each act.

These discussions of specific productions should give you a better idea of the kind of planning that begins during your initial preparation, then jells during the exploratory rehearsals, and is finally executed during the setting rehearsals.

Suggested Assignment

Reread either Anouilh's *Antigone* or Welty's *The Ponder Heart* and be prepared to discuss alternate ways of staging the literature—and there are many. More specifically, what other aspects of these literary texts might be shown in a performance?

REHEARSALS OF SETTING

Setting rehearsals are held to refine, polish, and finish the action of the literature. The director guides the group in locating the rhythm of sequences or units, cleaning up cluttered movement, establishing a sense of precision and authority to the entire effort, and incorporating the use of sound, lighting, properties, costumes, make-up, and so on.

The question will arise as to how much time should be spent doing what during the rehearsal period. While no fixed answers exist, we can suggest a working schedule for a hypothetical thirty-minute performance, a schedule based on the assumption that *at least one hour of rehearsal is needed for each minute of performance*. It does not account for the extra time needed if elaborate technical effects are used. Furthermore, each rehearsal meeting should last (according to this schedule) a minimum of two hours.

Rehearsal	1	General orientation; read through
	2–7	Slow work-throughs (each of the script's five-minute units)
	8	First 15 minutes
	9	Second 15 minutes
	10	Run-through
		(chiefly exploratory)

(chiefly setting)

	11	First 15 minutes
	12	Second 15 minutes
	13	Entire show
	14	Entire show with technical effects
	15	Entire show with technical effects

SOME FINAL CONSIDERATIONS

At this point, the presentation of your adapted script will probably occur in the classroom. However, should you produce it for a larger public, you might want to distribute a program. Carefully designed, the program can give the audience an early clue about the nature of the show. Moreover, if you include program notes you can inform, and perhaps predispose, the audience about some aspect of the literature which they may not know. The cover designs for pro-

ANTIGONE
by Jean Anouilh

Program cover for theatre production of *Antigone*

ductions of *Antigone* and *The Ponder Heart* appear on the opposite page. For *Antigone,* the aim of the design was stark simplicity, and the program notes, taken from a critical essay on the play, were chosen for their cogent discussion of the play's thesis. The program cover for *The Ponder Heart* attempted to alert the audience to the novel's comic tone and its central joyful figure, Uncle Daniel. The notes served to remind the audience of author Welty's place in American letters and the mode of production. The program cover and notes for both follow:

Antigone

Antigone is modeled on the famous tragedy of Sophocles, but Anouilh's play is an interpretation, not merely a restatement. On the surface, the modern heroine rebels for the same reasons as her ancient forebear: out of a sense of injustice over the violation of a sacred law. As in the Greek drama, this conflict opposes the intransigent individual to the tyranny of the state. Yet, in the course of Anouilh's play, the grounds of tension

shift from political to philosophical values; the central issue is the meaning of life itself and the impossibility of maintaining one's purity in a world that demands and imposes compromise. Antigone may not really know why she dies, for Creon convinces her of the futility and senselessness of her resistance, but he overstates his case and only proves that the life Antigone can have is not worth having. Both Antigone and Creon are right; their plea on behalf of contesting principles and values embraces but also goes far beyond the moral and political crisis of the early 1950s.[3]

The Ponder Heart

Published in 1954, Eudora Welty's *The Ponder Heart* won accolades from a reading public already aware of the artistry she demonstrated earlier in both novels and short stories. As one critic remarks, "From her earliest stories, Miss Welty's writing has had a high degree of individuality. Her

[3] Haskell M. Block and Robert G. Shedd, *Masters of Modern Drama* (New York, Random House, 1962) p. 780.

A CHAMBER THEATRE ADAPTATION OF EUDORA WELTY'S

MAY 2, 3, 4   CMA AUD 8 PM

THE

PONDER HEART

Program cover for theatre production of
The Ponder Heart

memory for colloquial speech is unbelievably accurate, and her antic imagination, coupled with her profound compassion and understanding, gives us people much realer than real, stranger, yet more believable than the living."

The Ponder Heart, a comic fantasy of small-town Mississippi life in the 1950s, is Edna Earle's story and she tells it in a rhythmical Southern monologue. Through her eyes we see the sleepy little town of Clay and the value of everyone who counts, most notably her Uncle Daniel.

The style of tonight's show is generally called Chamber Theatre, a variety of Readers Theatre, designed by Robert Breen to dramatize the action in prose fiction while featuring the narrative voice. Chamber Theatre aims to combine the ability of drama to capture the immediacy of action with the ability of the narrator in prose fiction to stall the action in order to examine his characters and their motivation.

A few more comments on directing group performances:

1. As a director, you should be *thoroughly* prepared for rehearsal. Carefully define your objectives for each rehearsal but also be prepared to reset them. Frame them realistically in light of the accomplishments possible during the time period.

2. In rehearsals, be firm about time for starting and stopping, but flexible and open to the performer's ideas about characterization and character relationships.

3. Give the cast as much positive feedback as possible. Let them know how well you think they are demonstrating the literary text.

4. In addition to a close analysis of the literature, the translation of the text into the group performance medium also involves intuition, creativity, and a sense of theatricality.

5. Be prepared to evaluate your efforts in terms of: (a) how the literature was treated—both real and apparent reasons; (b) its effects; and (c) the extent to which the production was a rewarding experience for director, cast, crew, and audience.

chapter 5

Prose Fiction
in Group Performance

"Fiction," "prose," "narrative," "prose fiction," "epic mode" are all ways of referring to the *art of storytelling*. One of the oldest and most practiced of the arts, storytelling even antedates poetry and drama. We are all storytellers and we all "like a good story." A story allows our imagination to participate in events and associations with characters outside our immediate life experience. Stories provide excitement, suspense, romance, travel, adventure, intellectual stimulation, or sentimental escape in a capsulated form, usually the novel or short story. The short story or novel has the same power of all literature—to *make* things happen by simply saying so. Prose writers can create a world, or change the one they are in, by wielding the pen or pounding the typewriter and persuasively involving a reader in an event of imaginative reality. Prose fiction is not dependent upon what has actually happened; it suggests the possible or presents the impossible as a fictive world for the reader to enter.

The traditional structural elements of prose fiction are: (1) point of view, (2) plot,

(3) character, (4) time, and (5) style and theme; all these elements apply directly to group performance.

POINT OF VIEW

Since storytellers relate or narrate the events of their story, *we usually refer to the storytelling voice in the story as a narrator*. There are no limits to the possibilities for this narrator. Often easily identifiable as to age, sex, and personality, a narrator can also assume nonhuman characteristics: for example, the narrator who reflects the thoughts of the speaking bird in Bernard Malamud's story, "The Jewbird," or even more fantastically, the narrator of John Barth's "Night-Sea Journey" whom we gradually discover is a sperm cell. The operation of the narrator within the story is the most basic and often the most significant of all the principles of narrative structure; understanding the narrator and the perspective from which the story is told constitutes the important technique of point of view. *Specifically, the concept of point of view includes: (1) the identity of the narrator; (2) the kinds of information this narrator provides; and (3) the perspective from which this narrator relates or observes the characters and action of the story.*[1] The term "point of view" itself implies an *angle* from which something is seen. For instance, we frequently remind others that circumstances are different when considered from *"our* point of view." Your point of view, however, is conditioned by who you are and your involvement in the action or event. There is no absolutely objective way of reporting an action. Even in the so-called "factual" reporting of a news event, the personal perspective of reporters becomes a part of the news story as they *select* which aspects of the event to include and which to emphasize. Writers of fiction, of course, do not pretend to be objective, although they may construct a narrator who seems to be.

Discovering this narrative voice and the kind of control the narrator holds in the story will direct your development of a production concept for group performance. A helpful way of approaching the narrator's identity and function is to consider the following questions.

Identity of the Narrator

1. What does the story reveal about this narrator? Consider age, social status, sex, education, family, attitudes, values, and interests.
2. Does this narrator seem to be a neutral reporter? An interested observer? An active participant in the story? Is the narrator *both* teller and character?
3. Is this narrator's audience implied or specific? Is he or she aware that he or she is telling a story?

[1] Norman Friedman provides an expanded version of these divisions in "Point of View in Fiction: The Development of a Critical Concept," *PMLA*, 70 (1955), 1160–84.

Kinds of Information This Narrator Provides

1. How informed is this narrator? What does he or she know about the other characters, past events, details of the scene or action?
2. Does the narrator somewhat mystically seem to know everything about everyone —their environment, actions happening simultaneously elsewhere, thoughts, or feelings? (General omniscience.)
3. Does this omniscience, or superhuman access to feelings and thoughts, apply to a single character or selected characters? (Limited omniscience.)
4. How believable is the narrator's information? Is the information or the narrator's observations supported in some way, e.g., by other characters who speak?

Perspective from which This Narrator Relates or Observes the Characters and Action of the Story

1. Does the narrator speak in the third or first person ("he came" or "I came")? Does the use of person shift within the story? When? With what effect?
2. In what ways, other than selecting what is to be told, does the narrator manipulate the characters or the action?
3. Does the narrator at some point seem to turn the story over to another character who tells a story (the story within the story)?
4. Does the narrator appear to "reflect" the thoughts, speech patterns, attitudes, and values of one or more of the characters in the story? Does the narrator "sound like" one of the characters thinking or observing?
5. Is the narrator *engaged* or *detached* from the action and characters in the story? How does this involvement or lack of it affect the way the story is told and the information revealed?
6. Are there major lapses or jumps in time

or place that alter the narrator's perspective and understanding about characters, the action, or him/herself?

When outlined in this fashion, it should be clear just how important the narrator is in the story and in your performance. By answering the questions above, you can frame a short summary of the basic point of view in any story or novel.

The following fictitious remarks about the same event (a campus appearance of Bob Dylan) were constructed to illustrate how point of view controls the reader's perception of the event and reveals something about the narrator. After the narrative statement a summary appears. Naturally an entire story or novel would reveal a far more complex point of view.

1. "Soft folk rock's Pied Piper, Bob Dylan, charmed yet another audience here last night. Through three encores, the winning Dylan demonstrated a magnetism rare for a single performer in today's group-oriented music scene."
   (*Third person, observer; credibility reinforced by mention of encores and knowledge of contemporary music scene.*)

2. "In my twenty years as a university professor of music, I have never been so musically offended as I was at the Dylan concert last night. Voice teachers like myself undoubtedly let out a collective groan as the raspy flat voice (?) of Bob Dylan struck the ear. What more can I say? How can someone so flat be so popular? The youth are now attacking the art of music and are set on destroying the beauty of tonal resonance."
   (*First person, observer; credibility reinforced by music education, experience, and learned jargon ("tonal resonance"); some credibility lost as age of narrator is implied (over 40) and a hostile defensive anti-youth stance adopted. Narrator is conscious of telling a story.*)

3. "College and community fans were ini-

tiated into the live Bob Dylan 'experience' last evening at the auditorium. Displaying warmth and charm, Dylan sang the songs that have made him the most significant folk musician around. I find it difficult to believe, however, that folk music sophisticates could be deceived. Dylan is little more than a warmed-over, discount-house Woodie Guthrie."
(*Shift from third to first person emphasizes distinction between the "popular response" and the "folk sophisticate" response to Dylan. Narrator places self in the sophisticate category. Credibility gained by fairness of presenting both responses, knowledge of the influence of Guthrie on Dylan and his key songs. Credibility is lost by a snobbery and lack of supporting opinion.*)

4. "Last night Bob Dylan *appeared* accompanying his social consciousness with voice, guitar, and harmonica. The audience, over 45,000 in number, thought of a troubled America and the need for change. The young in the audience see a social scene, hassled and screwed up—a heavy number to handle. Dylan reminded them, with his music, what they hope and feel—'the times, they are a changin'.'"
   (*Third person; general omniscience evidenced as narrator claims to know thoughts and feelings of audience. Small glimpse of a reflector as the narrator's diction shifts to youth cliches such as "hassled" and "heavy." Little detail of actual event as focus shifts to audience response. Omniscient narrator lacks "humanness" so credibility difficult to establish. Narrator does not seem to be one of the "young" but knows their response and uses it to make the large point concerning Dylan's message of social change.*)

These four brief examples should illustrate how the point of view *controls* the story. Each paragraph presents a quite different perception of the event and a different voice relating that perception.

To further clarify narrative voice and point of view, these principles will be applied to an entire short short story, Shirley Jackson's "Janice":

Janice
Shirley Jackson

First, to me on the phone, in a half-amused melancholy: "Guess I'm not going back to school . . ."

"Why not, Jan?"

"Oh, my *mother*. She says we can't afford it." How can I reproduce the uncaring inflections of Janice's voice, saying conversationally that what she wanted she could not have? "So I guess I'm not going back."

"I'm so sorry, Jan."

But then, struck by another thought: "Y'know *what?*"

"What?"

"Darn near killed myself this afternoon."

"Jan! How?"

Almost whimsical, indifferent: "Locked myself in the garage and turned on the car motor."

"But why?"

"I dunno. 'Cause I couldn't go back, I suppose."

"What happened?"

"Oh, the fellow that was cutting our lawn heard the motor and came and got me. I was pretty near out."

"But that's terrible, Jan. What ever possessed—"

"Oh, well. Say—" changing again, "—going to Sally's tonight?" . . .

And, later, that night at Sally's where Janice was not the center of the group, but sat talking to me and to Bob: "Nearly killed myself this afternoon, Bob."

"What!"

Lightly: "Nearly killed myself. Locked myself in the garage with the car motor running.

"But why, Jan?"

"I guess because they wouldn't let me go back to school."

"Oh, I'm sorry about that, Jan. But what about this afternoon? What did you do?"

"Man cutting the grass got me out."

Sally coming over: "What's this, Jan?"

"Oh, I'm not going back to school."

Myself cutting in: "How did it feel to be dying, Jan?"

Laughing "Gee, funny. All black." Then, to Sally's incredulous stare: "Nearly killed myself this afternoon, Sally . . ."[2]

Point of View in "Janice"

Identity of the narrator. Although never named or discussed by him/herself or others, we can deduce the following: the narrator is a close friend of Janice's (the narrator seems to be the first person Janice confides in), probably female in her teens, in school (probably college), same social circle as Janice since she too is at Sally's party. The narrator is both narrator and participant in the action of the story. The motivation of the narrator is uncertain; we are not sure *why* she is telling this story—perhaps to gain some of the same attention Janice is seeking. The narrator's diction is less colloquial ("uncaring inflections") than Janice's ("I dunno. 'Cause I couldn't go back, I suppose."), and, as a result, appears more controlled and calculating. She is *aware* that she is telling a story ("How can I reproduce . . .") and assumes some acquaintances in common with her auditor since she does not bother to describe the characters (Janice, Sally, or Bob) in her story.

Kinds of information the narrator provides. The narrator appears, at first reading, to be simply repeating dialogue between Janice, herself, and friends. She inserts, however: (1) very judgmental and controlling modifiers ("half-amused melancholy," "almost whimsical, indifferent"); and (2) an outright pointed remark ("where Janice was not the center of the group"). Three times she recounts the story of Jan-

[2]Shirley Jackson, "Janice," in *Come Along with Me.* Copyright 1938 by Shirley Jackson. Copyright © renewed 1968 by Stanley Edgar Hyman. Reprinted by permission of The Viking Press.

ice's attempted suicide and leaving school while implying that both she and Janice will go on telling it to others. We don't take Janice too seriously because the narrator doesn't and because the way the narrator reports it, Janice too appears unconcerned.

Perspective from which this narrator relates or observes the characters and action. The story is told in the first person by a narrator who is a participant in the action of the story. This participation reduces her credibility since we as readers wonder if she has any vested interests to serve. Also reducing her credibility is her extensive use of extraction as indicated by ellipses. We gradually realize that the narrator is not giving us a whole story but rather adapting it in a very personal way. The narrator gains credibility by extensive use of dialogue or direct discourse; she appears to be letting the characters speak for themselves rather than repeating what they purportedly said. This quoted dialogue adds a sense of "truth" to what was said and seems objective, although we may wonder how the narrator remembers so exactly. The absence of any omniscience is also a credible element in that the narrator does not assume any knowledge that could not be humanly perceived. The focus of the narration is on Janice until it shifts briefly to the narrator as she puts Janice on the spot with her remark "How did it feel to be dying, Jan?" This shift is ironically emphasized by her dialogue tag, "myself *cutting* in."

Point of View in Performance

The group performance of prose fiction clarifies the narrator's role. Through adaptation and staging, a group can illustrate narrative relationships. With this exciting potential in mind, the following practical considerations may help you translate the narrative voice into performance.

1. Perhaps the first major consideration following analysis is to conceptualize the narrator as a *person*. This is not so difficult with a first-person narrator, but visualizing a third-person narrator as a character can be problematic, especially a third-person narrator with omniscience. The tendency to eliminate the narrator entirely or sharply reduce the narrator's role must be very carefully considered since the narrative voice is so central to prose fiction. The adapter has many options. In a story like "Janice" the decision is relatively simple because the first-person narrator is also a character in the story. A single cast member could feasibly step in and out of the action, but a director could decide to cast the character separately from the narrator to emphasize: (a) elapsed time between the events and the telling of them; or (b) the *narrator* (although she went to the party) is not at the party—the *character* is. The narrator is somewhere else later telling of the incident.

2. Take time to formulate an interesting and imaginative handling of the narrator. Too often third-person narrators are routinely seen as properly dressed "authors" or storytellers holding manuscripts or books. While this *can* become a clever part of a production concept (as in "Educating the Young King Arthur" and *The Wind in the Willows*), characterization of the narrator can offer many other possibilities. Consider the various *roles* a particular narrator assumes when characterizing him/herself as confidante, informer, matchmaker, detective, director, news reporter, judge, prophet, and so on. Without ridiculous stretching or distortion, some aspect of the narrator's operation in and manipulation of the story can suggest the narrator's character development in performance.

3. The dialogue tag (a phrase or sentence that describes or comments on a line of dialogue) is the most constant reminder of the narrator's reporting of action and character interaction. The tag can be as incidental as "he said" or as informative as "he said with a scowl; it was the same scowl he *always* displayed when reminded

of her vindictive nature." An adapter should consider the dialogue tags carefully.[3] Below are a few flexible guidelines.

  a. We lose sight of just *who* decided how a given line was to be delivered if the tag is cut. If no tag appears after a line of dialogue in the story, the performer and director decide how to place inflection and emphasis, based on the context and motivation of the character. When a tag does appear after the line of dialogue, the *narrator* determines those matters. Often it is important to know whose perception or direction shapes the delivery. Cutting tags removes this information.

  b. Part of the rhythm of a story can be bound up in the tags, particularly with first-person narrators.

  c. When a tag clearly indicates just who is speaking, it usually is not missed in performance.

  d. When the dialogue tags interfere with a building exchange between characters, for example, the need to capture the tension between the characters may become more important than retaining the tags.

  e. For various purposes and effects, a character may choose to deliver his or her own dialogue tag. The tags are usually more successful if performed *purposively:* to neutralize, reinforce, or contradict the dialogue line itself.

4. Since prose shares many similarities with drama, the usual inclination when staging prose is to rewrite it as a play. Naturally, the practice is common for television, film, and theatre scripts. Shifts in the medium (from print to speech and action) often change the basic structure of the story. If, however, you are interested in retaining and presenting the *prose* structure, you must allow the narrator to function basically as he or she does in the story.

[3]For additional treatment of dialogue tags, see Lilla Heston, "A Note on Prose Fiction: The Performance of Dialogue Tags," *Speech Teacher*, 22 (January 1973), 69–73.

Look again at "Janice." By quickly typing names in the left margin and by cutting or adapting dialogue tags and narration, "Janice" the short story would become "Janice" the play. Much of what is interesting in the story would be unaffected by this decision, such as Janice's compulsive need for attention. Such an adaptation, however, would lose the skillful and subtle *shaping* of the story by the narrator. In a way, the narrator is as intriguing a personality as Janice.

Suggested Assignments

I. Compare the treatments of third-person narrators in the following scripts in Units II and III: "K*A*P*L*A*N on Shakespeare," "Lily Daw and the Three Ladies," "Tell Me a Riddle," and "Oh Where Oh Where Is There."

II. Demonstrate the need of the narrator in "Janice" to have an audience by having her tell the story to one auditor then begin the whole story again with another. There is certainly evidence that the narrator has told the story often enough to get it organized ("First to me . . ."; "And, later, that night . . .").

III. Create a third-person objective narrator for the opening section of the combined "Adam and Eve's Diary" (p. 218) and retell the events from the narrator's perspective. In what ways does this change the effect of the characters? Try the same exercise with a third-person subjective narrator.

IV. For what reasons might two or more narrators be used in staging the following stories?
  A. Flannery O'Connor, "Everything that Rises Must Converge"
  B. Katherine Anne Porter, "Maria Concepcion"
  C. Phillip Roth, "Conversion of the Jews"

PLOT

Plot is the term denoting the structure of events, action, and character development in prose. Far more than a synopsis of the story, plot includes the various ways an author shapes the story; its essence is *change.* Literary critic Norman Friedman points out that change may occur in the protagonist's (1) character, (2) fortune, or (3) thought, or some combination of these.[4] Friedman suggests first examining the protagonist with these potentials for change in mind. The protagonist, or central character, undergoes the greatest change during the story's action; and approaching the plot in this way places the action in its *human* context—the *potential* for change is always present. Friedman identifies three basic kinds of change: character, fortune, and thought.

A character's moral or ethical nature, his or her *character,* intents, purposes, or motives, may change from good to bad, bad to good, meaningful or not, intentional or not, or some slight shift within these extremes. This change, and the sequence of events which precipitate and follow it, can create the structure of the story's action.

A character's *fortune* can change: from wealth to poverty, happiness to unhappiness, and vice versa. Fortune refers to financial, social, educational, or personal pursuits —some meaningful dimension in the character's life. The gain or loss of these elements of fortune may provide the basic organization in the story's structure.

A character's *thought* (attitudes, beliefs, and knowledge) may change as a result of discoveries or realizations made during the story. A character can develop by adapting to situations and surrounding circumstances; or a character can remain static by not perceiving the significance of the action, generally because he or she lacks the self-

[4]Norman Friedman, "Forms of the Plot," *Journal of General Education,* 8 (1955), 241–53.

knowledge necessary for personal growth. A story can reveal the narrowness of a character's thought by showing lack of change, or the fullness of the character's thought by showing development.

Consider the nature of change in the short story "Janice." Since "Janice" is so short, these levels and types of change can be outlined quickly.

1. *Janice* (protagonist)
   a. *Character:* The story contains much evidence of Janice's immaturity: her suicide attempt suggests a retaliation at her parents for not sending her back to school and a cry for attention. It would be difficult to say, based on the little information the narrator provides, whether this is regression from maturity to immaturity. Perhaps Janice always was this infantile. However, her behavior (attempted suicide and pouting, etc.) is brought about by the action revealed in the story. In short, in the story Janice *does* change and act according to her own motives and purposes and to outside events.
   b. *Fortune:* Janice suffers misfortune by having to leave school, but she compensates for this by all the attention she receives for her attempted suicide. Overall, she moves from happiness to apparent unhappiness, and from relative insignificance to the focus of attention.
   c. *Thought:* Undoubtedly thought is the area of potential change least developed in the story. We have no evidence that Janice grows as a result of any action or interaction in the story. When the narrator abruptly strikes a note of realism with "How did it feel to be dying, Jan?" Janice does not come to grips with the implications of the question. She gives a blithe, superficial

response and then reveals her lack of self-perception by continuing to repeat her story.

2. *Narrator*

   a. *Character:* The narrator's motives for telling the story may be simply to inform the listener of a sequence of incidents. This purpose would be understandable; but since we do not know the listener, we do not know just why she is being informed. If the narrator is concerned about Janice ("I'm so sorry, Jan"), then her motivations become nobler. If, however, the narrator is telling the story for similar attention-getting motives, we would say that her character is unchangingly immature. The story is ambiguous; and the narrator's motives remain undefined.

   b. *Fortune:* Regardless of motivation, the narrator undeniably receives someone's attention by telling the story. Therefore fortune changes as others' interests mount.

   c. *Thought:* The narrator does discover several things about her friend Janice. She learns that Janice will not be returning to school; Janice considers her mother responsible; she attempted to kill herself by locking herself in the garage and starting the car; she was rescued by the lawn man; and she tells the story to Bob and then to Sally. More important, the narrator realizes that Janice is enjoying her "drama" ("half-amused melancholy"), is not really concerned about what has happened to herself ("uncaring inflections"), does not know what she really wants, is trying out one story after the other until she receives a satisfactory rise from her listener ("struck by another thought"), needs to be the center of attention,

and is unaware of the significance of what she is saying.

3. *Other Characters: Sally and Bob*

   a. *Character:* These minor characters are not highly defined in the story. It does appear that they are both interested and well-meaning, but there is no evidence that any change in disposition has occurred.

   b. *Fortune:* There is no evidence of change in the story.

   c. *Thought:* Both Sally and Bob learn that Janice is not going back to school and that she has attempted suicide.

Outlines such as this can help you see just where the changes in the story occur, their nature, and who is most affected by them. From this position, you are better able to identify the ways events are related.

Chronological and Associative Plots

The two most basic organizing principles for the changes and events in a story are the chronological and the associative.

Chronological organization is the sequential ordering of events. Proceeding from beginning to end, the chronological arrangement seeks to follow and report the action step by step. Underlying the chronological format is the assumption that one event affects what is to follow; the implication is causal. As a result, the chronology not only traces a sequence but suggests that one situation or event influences another and is influenced by the one before.

If a story is chronologically arranged, it is not only sequential but time-ordered as well. *Time* is in fact the basis of the sequence. A chronology can be charted through years, hours, minutes, or generations. When asked "What happened?" we usually answer in an "and then—and then" developmental way. This is probably the most common organizing principle of story-telling.

"Janice" is extremely well-organized. Clearly chronological, the narrator traces the story of Janice through the story Janice tells. When and to whom Janice tells her story next is the ordering principle. Nearly everything else is omitted from the story. The presence of chronology is unmistakable and is telegraphed in the story by the phrases "First, to me," and "And, later, that night." We, the readers of the story, realize that the sequence and counting of times Janice tells her story is important *to* the story—not only in the organizing of it: the narrator is making sure that the listener is aware of just how often Janice brings up the matter.

Far less systematic, *associative,* or psycho-logical, organization moves from association to association with few or no connectives and captures the drift and flow of random relationships. With the associative format, a writer can represent the illogical "logic" of a dream world or other nonrational processes. This less causal and more frag-mented arrangement can reveal the mind of the narrator as well as probable distor-tions in plot.

Although it contains an underlying chronology, "The Secret Life of Walter Mitty" presents a good example of an asso-ciative organization. Mitty's associations are triggered by some incident, comment, or item in his environment. For instance, his mind jumps from the newsboy's shout about "The Waterbury Trial" headline to his own central role in the following fan-tasy trial scene. Most of the quick shifts in and out of Mitty's mind follow associative logic.

Plot in Performance

Although a given story will stimulate many particular performance ideas for a group, here are some general suggestions for illustrating changes in thought, charac-ter, and fortune and the principles of chron-ological or associative organization.

1. A dramatic and effective way to highlight a discovery, insight, or the acquisition of important information is the *freeze*. The freeze has the same impact on stage as the stop action frame in film; it under-scores and emphasizes a moment by hold-ing it in place. A group can use the *total freeze* (freezing all cast members at a given moment) or the *partial freeze* (freezing certain cast members for a particular reason). You could decide to freeze every-one except the character who is making a discovery, or you could freeze everyone and highlight the effect of the discovery as it is perceived differently by all cast members. When using the freeze, be care-ful to block or place the cast to achieve an interesting group composition, since the freeze has a tableau effect; you should also insure that all performers are en-gaged in a large motion at the time of the freeze or the freeze will appear tenta-tive and not be noticed by the audience.

2. Repetition can also highlight a significant change. Having a character repeat a line of narration or the narrator repeat a line delivered by a character will not only em-phasize the line but will also illustrate through variant inflections the differences in perception between the narrator and the character.

3. If the fortune of a character rises or falls in a story, performers can graphically re-present these changes with symbolic block-ing or by using levels. A given character can actually appear taller as status rises or goals are achieved. If done subtly, the effect is gradual enough to be only un-consciously perceived by the audience.

4. Associative organization of plot structure often involves simultaneity of action. While Walter Mitty is driving or walking he is also fantasizing. This simultaneity can be exciting and effective in group performance. For instance, you could stage one Mitty walking timidly on the sidewalk

in the "real" world and freeze that scene while another performer played the grander, totally confident Mitty taking the witness stand.

5. With both associative and chronological organization, the units of action can be cut and rearranged for convenient adaptation. A chronological organization tends to be in episodes (e.g., "Why I Live at the P.O.") some of which could be eliminated. The absence of connection between the segments of an associative organization makes cutting any given segment possible since it is not logically connected to the preceding section.

6. The visual and sound effects provided by lights, setting, dance, movement, and music should not be overlooked. These effects often underscore significant changes and interesting structural developments in a script.

Suggested Assignments

I. Consider the changes in character, fortune, and thought that do or do not occur in "The Secret Life of Walter Mitty" (p. 7–10) and "The Old Ram" (p. 469). Whose changes shape the plot of the story: participant? listener? How could they be shown in performance?

II. Study one or more of the following stories and outline for each character the kinds of changes that occur. How do changes among the various characters account for the *plot* of the story? How might the changes be shown in group performance?
   A. Melvin Kelley, "Not Exactly Lena Horne"
   B. James Joyce, "Eveline"
   C. Katherine Mansfield, "Miss Brill"
   D. Herman Melville, "Bartleby the Scrivener"
   E. Delmore Schwartz, "In Dreams Begin Responsibilities"

III. Would you classify the plots of the stories listed in II as chronological or associative? How might you translate your decision about this aspect of plot *in* performance?

CHARACTER

Plot is the order of the action in a story; *character* makes that action possible. As the human dimension that propels a story, characters provide often unpredictable directions in their relation to their surroundings, themselves, and their circumstances. Discovering the identity, dimensions, and motivations of the characters in the story is critical to any performance of prose fiction. Like drama, the understanding of individual character and character relationships will enable you to perceive these "human-like" creations.

Levels of Characterization

A helpful and systematic method for delineating character traits is provided by playwright Sam Smiley.[5] Smiley advocates the careful consideration of all characters with the following order of traits in mind. The traits progressively reveal more and more complex *levels of characterization:*

1. Biological	(human or animal, race, male or female)
2. Physical	(physical size, age, voice, health, posture)
3. Social	(class, nationality, education, religion)[6]
4. Dispositional	(personality, temperament, mood)
5. Motivational	(desires, goals, purposes)

[5]Sam Smiley, *Playwriting: The Structure of Action* (Englewood Cliffs, N.J.: Prentice-Hall, Inc., 1971), p. 84.
[6]This "social" level of characterization is suggested by Oscar Brockett, *The Theatre: An Introduction* (Englewood Cliffs, N.J.: Prentice-Hall, Inc., 1974).

6. Deliberative (quantity and quality of character in thought)
7. Decisive   (decision-making)

As you note information about characters, you see their level of development within the story: the more developed, dramatized, or defined the character, the more complex and unpredictable they become. The character thus is more real and less stereotyped. We call multidimensional, highly defined characters "round" and one-dimensional lowly defined characters "flat."[7] A round character has perceivable motives, deliberates, and is capable of decisive action. Such a character appears to have some control over the action and responds and adapts very humanly to changing circumstances.

You gather this varied information about each character by considering: (1) what the character does; (2) what the character says about him or herself; and (3) what the narrator and the other characters say about him or her.

Returning to our troubled heroine, Janice, we see in brief outline just what kinds of information we have about her.

1. Biological: human, female
2. Physical: school age (probably college)
3. Social: American, in school, possibly middle- to upper-middle class, although Janice's mother says they can no longer afford to send her away to school
4. Dispositional: flippant, pouting, self-pitying, whimsical
5. Motivational: need for attention, desire to return to school
6. Deliberative: little thought overall, impulsive, quick shifts of mood

[7]E. M. Forster, "Flat and Round Characters," in *The Theory of the Novel*, ed. Phillip Stevick (New York: The Free Press, 1967), pp. 223–31.

7. Decisive: attempted suicide was Janice's way of combatting her parents' decision

As a result of this brief outline we can quickly see that Janice's psyche is far more important than the more superficial details of her appearance or social circle. Although Janice is an apparently decisive character, the quantity and quality of her thought and deliberation is not very sophisticated. Readers might even question the validity of her one reported decision, her attempted suicide.

Character in Performance

The following suggestions should aid you both in studying characterization and in imaginatively treating character traits.

1. *Improvisation* is one of the most helpful techniques for developing confidence with characterization and arriving at a psychological reality for a character's credibility in performance. Improvising involves identifying with and subjectively exploring the characters and the influences in their development. Performers can expand their identification with a character by placing themselves in contrived situations that demand a sure sense of self-knowledge. These improvisations can construct a past for each character: What was Janice doing two years ago? What conversation with her parents might have ensued when Janice announced the school she wanted to attend and her reasons?

2. To sharpen ensemble relationships between characters, it is helpful to have each character state "I am _____" for each known element of their life and character. This should be followed by a "You are _____" exercise to clarify just how characters see each other.

3. Characters with similar roles or characteristics could feasibly be double cast, i.e. played by the same performer.

4. A director could costume particular char-

acters in similar styles or colors to suggest a visual alliance that represents a larger link of personality.

5. Flat characters could move in a stylized way to emphasize their lack of developed human characteristics.

6. It can be interesting and informative to cast different aspects of the same character. For example, in "Why I Live at the P.O." Sister 1 represents the paranoia of the character while Sister 2 relates the past events. Similar costumes and movements should make it clear to the audience that both performers are actually two distinct parts of the same character.

7. Through staging and blocking it is possible to visually indicate various characters' shared sympathies, traits, dispositions, and motivations.

8. Assigning certain characters' own dialogue tags to them can illustrate their control and consciousness of their attitudes and speech. "Would the characters be capable of saying this about themselves?" is often a good question to ask. There are physical self-descriptions and observations that certain characters simply could never make about themselves even if they were aware of them.

Suggested Assignments

I. Define the levels of characterization in the following scripts in this book; how do the levels differ and how might they be shown in performance?
   A. Lily in "Lily Daw and the Three Ladies"
   B. Kaplan in "K*A*P*L*A*N on Shakespeare"
   C. Badger in *Wind in the Willows*
   D. Vivi in "Tell Me a Riddle"
   E. Wart in "Educating the Young King Arthur"

II. Letting characters talk about themselves is often a fruitful exercise. From their own limited perspective, they may know little. However, let your own understanding of them indicate what they know about themselves and their role in the action of the story. Look at:
   A. Miss Willerton in Flannery O'-Connor's "The Crop"
   B. Hettie in Shirley Jackson's "The Lottery"
   C. Miss Pinkerton in Muriel Spark's "Miss Pinkerton's Apocalypse"

TIME

The dimension of time in fiction usually refers to: (1) when the events of the story happened; (2) when the events are reported by the narrator; and (3) the kinds of time in the story.

The time between the occurrence of the story's action and its being reported can be quite close; not much time may elapse between the event and the telling of it, or on the other hand, a considerable amount of time may separate the incident from the account of it. Both possibilities involve the narrator's temporal relationship to the story and his or her credibility: (a) we could consider that a quick retelling would eliminate the danger of forgetfulness or distortion; or (b), we could wonder whether a quick retelling is premature. The reverse could also be true: a gap between the events and the narration could allow for perspective at the expense of apparently accurate detail.

When the events of the story happened and something of their sequence can be clear from the tense of the verbs or temporal qualifiers ("later," "at once," "finally," "that same evening," for example). As we have discussed earlier, a chronologically organized narrative will reveal its sequence of action through time units. In addition, a narrator can stop the progress of the action, provide background information through flash-backs, then rejoin the story. The narrator's power over the audience's awareness of time is a prime consideration when planning a group performance.

It is more difficult to tell how much time

has elapsed between the action and the narrator's reporting of it. Some narrators appear to have remarkably detailed memories while others do not pretend to precisely reconstruct remembered dialogue in *direct discourse* (She said, "It upsets me to report that I am unable to attend") but instead, tell what the character said in abbreviated *indirect discourse* ("She said unhappily that she couldn't come"). When there is no direct mention of time duration, a significant amount of time may have passed if:

1. The story is highly organized, or the narrator has developed an apparent finesse in the telling of it—economy of detail, carefully constructed suspense or a punch ending.
2. If the narrator has philosophical or otherwise thoughtful reflections on the significance of the action in the story, he or she probably has had some time to consider its importance.
3. Subtle clues in the descriptive passages often imply that time has passed. People are older, scenery is considerably changed, or the technological or environmental developments are more sophisticated from those mentioned in the story.
4. A close study of the characters may reveal aspects of their personalities that have been altered by time such as in a character who has had time to adjust to a significant change in life or who has recovered from a tragedy.

Scene, Summary, Description

Finally, in considering the narrator's ability to create an illusion of a particular time dimension in the story, let us examine author Phyllis Bentley's outline of the various relationships between actual time (AT) and story time (ST).[8] Actual time refers to the time in real life that it takes for an ac-

[8]Phyllis Bentley, *Some Observations on the Art of Narrative* (New York: Macmillan, 1948), pp. 4–26.

tion or statement to occur; story time refers to the time in the story for an action or statement to be related. Bentley indicates that when

AT equals	ST = SCENE
AT less than	ST = DESCRIPTION
AT more than	ST = SUMMARY

The clearest example of *scene* is in dialogue; it takes the same amount of time for a line of speech to be related in the story as it takes to be spoken. When a narrator utilizes *description,* on the other hand, the real action takes less time than it takes for the narrator to relate it. When the narrator *summarizes,* the real action takes considerably longer than the telling of it. Examples of all three can be taken from "Janice":

Scene: "Guess I'm not going back to school..."
"Why not, Jan?"

Description: How can I reproduce the uncaring inflections of Janice's voice, saying conversationally that what she wanted she could not have?

Summary: And, later, that night at Sally's where Janice was not the center of the group, but sat talking to me and to Bob:

In the first instance there is no substantial difference between the actual time it would take to speak the line and the time taken in the story to relate it. In the second instance, description lengthens the event; it takes longer to tell about it than to do it. In the third instance, the summary shortens the amount of time the event actually took.

Manipulations of time allow the narrator to speed up, slow down, or stop the normal procession of time. Writer Eudora Welty sums up the powerful device of time: "While place lies passive, time moves and is a mover. Time is the bringer of action, the instrument of change. . . . Time has the closest possible connection with the novel's meaning, in being the chief conductor of the plot."[9]

Time in Performance

Time is yet another narrative device that fascinates performers and directors alike, and group performance offers possibilities for exploring this dimension not available to the single performer. Consider, discuss, and apply the following suggestions for demonstrating elements of time.

1. Since fictive time propels characters and events at a particular speed, *freeze* or *slow motion* techniques are often necessary to capture the time element. When the narrator stops one segment of action for motivational comment or to recap past incidents before another incident, the freeze will be a graphic display. When an action takes considerably longer to describe than to represent, the characters can move in slow motion to capture the suspended time. In rehearsal, both the freeze and slow motion must be carefully managed and timed if the performance effect is to be smooth and sure.

2. When various segments of action occur simultaneously, the multiple time dimensions can be represented by a group.

3. If a time gap exists between the narrator telling the story and the narrator as a character in the story being told, it is effective to cast both ages of the same person. Typically, a narrator relates an incident that occurred to her or him as a child. By casting both older and younger selves, the effect of time and time's distance on the narrator becomes very clear.

4. If a story regularly flashes back to scenes in the past, a director can create a playing space especially for these flashbacks to clarify the movement of time.

[9]Eudora Welty, "Some Notes on Time in Fiction," *Mississippi Quarterly*, 26 (Fall 1973), 485.

5. The various spectacle effects available to group performances will enhance a sense of the past. Consider the use of a scrim, special lighting, and reverberated sound for creation of a past illusion.

Suggested Assignments

I. With a group, recast "Janice" as if it occurred years later. If the events of her twenties were told by and to someone in her forties, how would the dialogue tags be altered?

II. In discussion and performance try to show the *time* dimensions in the following stories:
A. Edward Lomis, "A Kansas Girl!"
B. J. F. Powers, "The Valiant Woman"
C. James Baldwin, "Going to Meet the Man"

STYLE AND THEME

The complex issue of style involves the *author's* use of *language:* an author's distinctive voice emerges as a result of his or her particular choice of words, punctuation, syntax, and rhythm. Assuming two people desire to make a similar statement, their individual styles would distinguish the ways each would express him / herself. In prose there is usually more than one speaking voice. Usually we hear from the narrator primarily and the other characters who speak. Well-drawn characters, like humans, are discernible by virtue of their particularized speech and usage patterns. The oral performance of prose makes this vocalized level of language usage especially clear. We *do* hear differences between characters' speech because that language is performed.

A careful scrutiny of language, syntax, and speech rhythms is the best beginning for recognizing the style of a character's language. The use of punctuation is also very important because it frequently affects the rhythm of the sentence .There is a different voice in the delivery of a story by Eudora Welty as compared to one by Ernest Hemingway, and some of that difference is reinforced by punctuation.

There are several interesting features in the narrator's use of language in "Janice": (1) when the narrator is in the scene as a character she always refers to Janice as "Jan," while in the narration she always uses the more formal, careful, deliberate, and distant "Janice"; (2) the use of ellipses signals the omission of further conversation that did in fact follow what the narrator has decided to report—the extract focuses very sharply on Janice's school and suicide remarks, a focus that would blur if the entire conversation were presented with many subjects and moods; (3) the excessive use of direct discourse focuses our attention on the characters in the story—if more indirect discourse were used, the focus would shift to the narrator;[10] (4) the narration contains more carefully chosen phrases and words than the dialogue (even when the narrator as character speaks) so that we notice a difference between speeches of the narrator as narrator and the narrator as character. This care with language that the narrator takes suggests her awareness of the reader or listener, whether she is writing or telling the story; we do know that she is *conscious* of telling it.

Theme answers the question "What is this story *about?*" It is a short summary statement about the human condition. Theme is a thread of significance that weaves through the story; it is not the events but what can be made of them or implied by them in a larger sense. Most stories are concerned with one or more central issues; theme statements isolate those issues.

The epigrammatic nature of a thematic statement has the advantage of focusing in on a key meaning, point, or argument in the story but the disadvantage of appearing to grossly oversimplify the impact of the original. The theme of a story is not a one-line paraphrase. The theme or themes can be stated briefly, but refer to the implications of the action, not the action itself. For example, to say " 'Janice' is a story about an adolescent's need for attention" is to sum up thematically the implications of the story's action.

Both style and theme reveal the author's hand at work constructing the story. Although an author turns the story over to a narrator to relate through a particular point of view, traces of the author certainly remain in the story. The stylistic use of language directly reflects the writer's skill at creating characters. The thematic concern in the story reflects the author's value system. Since Wayne C. Booth discussed it in *The Rhetoric of Fiction* the author's implied value system is popularly known as the *implied author*.[11] As in all literature a particular relationship exists between the author and the narrator, speaker, or persona in the story (see "The Poet Writing and the Persona Speaking" in Chapter VI). The "presence" of the implied author is unmistakable in satire, for example, where the reader knows that the narrator's opinions are being ridiculed. The operation of the implied author can also be seen when we are aware of far more than the narrator; we see and understand more because the narrator obviously understands less.

Style and Theme
in Performance

An examination of the style and theme of a story will suggest many possibilities for group performance:

---

[10]See Judith Espinola, "The Nature, Function, and Performance of Indirect Discourse." *Speech Monographs*, 41 (August 1974), 193–204.

[11]Wayne C. Booth, *The Rhetoric of Fiction* (Chicago: University of Chicago Press, 1961).

1. Careful attention to language will sharpen characterization and give the production far more authority.
2. The rhythm of the language and the events in the story directly affects the pacing of the scenes—both within a given scene itself and between scenes.
3. Be careful that your adaptation doesn't distort the style of the selection.
4. Themes may provide metaphors for staging: e.g., the theme of "life is a game" could inspire a game-like set; or "the mechanization of life" theme give to a machine-like set and automatons for characters.

Suggested Assignment

Compare Carson McCullers' "A Tree, a Rock, and a Cloud" with Ernest Hemingway's "A Clean, Well-Lighted Place" in terms of: (a) overall style, (b) the protagonist's style, (c) the narrator's style, and (d) the emergent themes. Frame production concepts for each that would emphasize these aspects of the stories.

Selected Bibliography

BOOTH, WAYNE C. *The Rhetoric of Fiction.* Chicago: University of Chicago Press, 1961.

ESPINOLA, JUDITH C. "The Nature, Function, and Performance of Indirect Discourse." *Speech Monographs,* 41 (August 1974), 193–204.

FRIEDMAN, NORMAN. "Point of View: The Development of a Critical Concept." *PMLA,* 70 (December 1955), 1160–84.

———. "Forms of the Plot." *Journal of General Education,* 8 (1955), 241–53.

HESTON, LILLA. "A Note on Prose Fiction: The Performance of Dialogue Tags." *Speech Teacher,* 22 (January 1973), 69–73.

———. "The Interpreter and the Structure of the Novel." In *Studies in Interpretation,* ed. Esther M. Doyle and Virginia Hastings Floyd. Amsterdam: Rodopi N. V., 1972.

MACLAY, JOANNA. "The Aesthetics of Time in Narrative Fiction." *Speech Teacher,* 18 (September 1969), 194–96.

———. "The Interpreter and Modern Fiction: Problems of Point of View and Structural Tensiveness." In *Studies in Interpretation,* ed. Esther M. Doyle and Virginia Hastings Floyd. Amsterdam: Rodopi N. V., 1972.

WARREN, ROBERT PENN. "Why Do We Read Fiction?" *The Short Story: An Inductive Approach.* New York: Harcourt, Brace, and World, 1967.

chapter 6

Poetry in Group Performance

With an inspired blend of teasing and truth, poet Allen Ginsberg once proclaimed that a "poem" is lines of print that do not make it to the right-hand margin. Beyond the popular tautology that "poems are what poets write," Ginsberg inadvertently summed up the difficulty of defining a literary genre. We can speak of *general characteristics* of a genre (or type of literature), but poetic expression outgrew its convenient, well-behaved definitions centuries ago. Poetry presents us, generally, with a *rhythmic expression of human experience through a tight, well-chosen, intensified language*. One reason that the language becomes intense is that, usually, there is simply not much of it. The poem will hit hard—or miss—its reader. Also, poets are clearly language lovers. They caress the word. With deft blends of imagination and sensitivity, objects and emotions in poems simultaneously appear to us as both special and common.

The oral reader receives a special invitation to the poetic form. With its early origins in song, poetry is a natural form for oral performance. The oral reader is able to *vocally* illustrate the sound structures, or the body of the poem, while also *experiencing* the emotional structures, or the soul of the poem. As a result, if a reader *participates* in the poem—vocally, physically, and emotionally—the poem's internal and external structures tangibly and perceptively converge. The performance revitalizes the poem, first of all, for the reader and—by extension and presentation—for the reader's audience.

Through participation and interaction with others, a group performance of poetic literature involves more than one individual in an experience with poetry. A group is easily able to magnify, by its numbers alone, the interest, excitement, and possibility of performance. While a silent reading or a class discussion of a poem tend to be removed and distant, class *demonstrations* or *performances* activate the literature. Responsiveness and creativity—essential ingredients to the performer—frequently benefit from group vision and participation.

Whether group performance of poetic literature results in readings for a classroom audience or for a larger public audience, careful examination and analysis of the text is clearly the beginning step. *Analysis is the process of extending and sharpening your* initial intuitions and perceptions of the literature. This analytical process can be a silent or oral reading, a written exercise, or an exploratory performance. Through a balance of textual clues and subjective response, concepts for performing the poem will emerge. Performance is a means for developing and generating other performances —i.e., you perform in order to decide what and how to perform a selection. Significantly, *performance itself is a necessary part of analysis and not simply an end result of it.*

The following considerations should aid you in your approach to the group performance of poetry. They apply to both the group working on a particular poem together and a group presenting a larger program of individually performed selected poetry. Many of these points apply as well to a solo performer, but because of the focus of this book, we are primarily concerned with the way a *group* can effectively demonstrate these aspects of poetry. Specifically these considerations are an exploration of (1) dramatic situation; (2) sound structure; (3) visual structure; and (4) programming.

EXPLORATION OF DRAMATIC SITUATION

The "dramatic analysis" (or the systematic examination of the dramatic situation in the poem) emphasizes a constant fact in literature: *someone* is speaking *to someone* through the words of the selection. Unravelling the dramatic situation, the implied or stated particulars of the speaker (*persona*) and environment, is one of the most helpful analytical steps for a performer because performance is a vocal, physical, and emotional *translation* of the dramatic situation from the text into the performance.

Performance as Definition

Performers define through physical and vocal behavior, sets, and costumes the dramatic situation in the literature. In fact all performances, to some degree, define the text. The performance will communicate meanings about the text—just as a definition of a word delimits that word's possibilities for meaning. A performance might be *highly defined*—i.e., displaying a high degree of specificity—or *lowly defined*—i.e., displaying a small degree of specificity. For instance, if the speaker in a poem is sitting on a bench holding an old photograph, a highly defined performance would literalize or strongly suggest these particulars (bench, photograph), while a lowly defined performance would not—i.e., the performer would stand and not hold anything or else conspicuously hold a script. Definition does not refer, however, to just the physical surroundings or environment but also includes other components of the dramatic situation as well. One reader might further define a speaker's anxiety through movement, while another might reduce the definition by depending solely upon a vocal tone to manifest that anxiety. The central concern here is not whether a highly defined performance is "better" than one more lowly defined. *Definition in performance should not exceed the possible bounds of the selection—* i.e., a lowly defined selection should generally not be highly defined in performance and vice versa. When a performance *overdefines* the possible directions in the text, the focus of the performance becomes cluttered, uncertain, dispersed, or misaligned. By contrast, an underdefined performance of a more highly defined selection will appear vague, tentative, indefinite, or confused. The readers' delicate task is to channel their own perceptions and ultimately their audience's perceptions in a similar proportion to the literature.

Although overdefinition or underdefinition can be a problem in any performance, overdefinition is more common when a group works together on poetry. Due to the defining presence of others, a group will naturally present more visual, physical, and vocal information than the individual

reader can. Poetry seems to inspire overde-
fined performances since, in general, poems
are short and often lack dramatic detail.
The conversion into performance should
not force performers to add dramatic elements that do not appear in the text. Placing a speaker conspicuously in a park or a
jail when only a bench is mentioned in the
poem distorts the intentional vagueness of
scene.

In the following poem, "Two Friends"
by David Ignatow, many of these issues
must be dealt with by prospective groups
of performers.

Two Friends
David Ignatow

1 *I have something to tell you.*

I'm listening.

I'm dying.

I'm sorry to hear.

5 *I'm growing old.*

It's terrible.

It is, I thought you should know.

Of course and I'm sorry. Keep in touch.

I will and you too.

10 *And let me know what's new.*

Certainly, though it can't be much.

And stay well.

And you too.

And go slow.

15 *And you too.*[1]

[1]David Ignatow, "Two Friends," reprinted from
Figures of the Human. Copyright © 1963 by David
Ignatow. Reprinted by permission of Wesleyan Uni-
versity.

Poems containing two or more speakers,
such as Ignatow's, may offer a group unique
possibilities in performance to present more
"information." We see the two friends, in
the present tense, in dialogue and action (or
inaction) before us as we hear their speech
(or silence). In staging, two performers can
capitalize on a meaningful physical (spatial)
relationship between the two speakers (prox-
imity, distance, focus, facial expression) as
well as the vocal index of their relationship
(e.g., sympathy, distraction, indifference)
demonstrated by tone, inflection, volume,
and rate. The one-line stanzaic structure of
this poem also typographically reminds
readers that what is not said between the
stanzas is significant—the pauses or units of
silence communicate as well.

Ignatow presents us with a lowly defined
situation. As readers and prospective performers we know very little about these "two
friends" and their dramatic situation. We
do not know *where* they are, *when* they are
speaking, or several facts about them such
as sex and age that would alter the context
of *what* they say. Significantly in this poem
these and other details are omitted. The
spare poem cautions the degree of definition
in performance. Performers who decide to
sacrifice one or more of the dramatic elements in the selection must recognize that
the imposed context into which they have
placed the selection has meaning. For instance, if your group stages "Two Friends"
by having two elderly people (one conspicuously sick) meet in an urban park, the
context would significantly direct the audience's perception of the poem through a
specific situation. All performances will, by
their very nature, define a selection more
than the printed text; we will see and hear
people in *action* instead of imagining them
from the printed words. Perhaps more than
other literary genres poetry frequently both
benefits and suffers in performance because
the traditional poetic techniques of *ambiguity* and *universality* are most quickly lost
in performance, especially of lowly defined

poems. This loss provides exciting alternatives and perspectives on the literature, or
it can result in an unfortunate distortion
depending on the *textual illumination* that
the performance provides.

The irony we find in "Two Friends" depends, to some extent, upon the degree of
ambiguity, or *suspended alternatives* for
interpretation. Several levels of ambiguity
are present in this selection that a group
performance (hopefully more than one)
could illustrate and illuminate.

Consider the following questions as guides
to possible group performance.

1. Are these *really* not "friends" at all but
   insensitive would-be communicators who
   do not listen or respond to one another?
2. Are they such goods friends that they
   understand each other with little said between them?
3. Is the first speaker's concern over health
   a normal recognition of aging or a response to an actual medical condition?
4. Is the tone of the second speaker's voice
   (and the attitude it represents) real concern and sympathy or a set of automatic
   cliches?
5. Are they *trying* to communicate at all?

In these short fifteen lines, Ignatow is
clearly more interested in a *human relationship* than in the particular humans involved. The general *universal* nature of this
human situation is more significant than the
particulars. Because of their lack of detail,
low definitional poems appear to be more
universal.

A highly defined situation in a poem is
clearer to performers if the dramatic detail
becomes a sort of "stage direction" for the
performance. Anne Sexton's poem "Ringing
the Bells" presents a good example.

Ringing the Bells
Anne Sexton

1 And this is the way they ring
   the bells in Bedlam

and this is the bell-lady
who comes each Tuesday morning
to give us a music lesson
and because the attendants make you go
and because we mind by instinct,
like bees caught in the wrong hive,
we are the circle of the crazy ladies
10 who sit in the lounge of the mental house
and smile at the smiling woman
who passes us each a bell,
who points at my hand
that holds my belt, E flat
15 and this is the gray dress next to me
who grumbles as if it were special
to be old, to be old
and this is the small hunched squirrel girl
on the other side of me
20 who picks at the hairs over her lip,
who picks at the hairs over her lip all day,
and this is how the bells really sound,
as untroubled and clean
as a workable kitchen
25 and this is always my bell responding
to my hand that responds to the lady
who points at me, E flat;
and although we are no better for it,
29 they tell you to go. And you do.[2]

Unlike Ignatow's poem, Sexton's provides
details about the speaker and her immediate
situation—the poem is *highly defined*. The
speaker is female, institutionalized in a
mental asylum, engaged in a weekly music
lesson, seated in the lounge in a circle with
others and a "bell lady" in attendance (an
old woman on one side and a young girl on
the other). She is apparently depressed and
pessimistic about the worth of her activity
and her self (high identification with her
bell, E flat). She is aware of more ideal conditions (lines 22–24) but also painfully conscious of the reality of her present situation.
While making automatic physical responses
to directions, she mentally evaluates and
examines her actions—a tension captured by

her paradoxical expression "mind by instinct." She is detached from her self and her activity: she frequently watches herself as if she were someone else and although she appears to understand her responses, she is consciously trapped and resigned to conform. Certainly this skillful and compact poem conveys more "information" than is contained in just the words. The point here is that the information is less ambiguous than the very general situation in "Two Friends."

A group performing "Ringing the Bells" would be able to illustrate several interesting features of this poem in various performances. For instance, a group could: (1) clarify the *physical* surroundings of the poem by using set pieces, props, and costumes; (2) emphasize the flat, rote behavior of these women through mechanical motions; (3) by some means stage the poem's circular structure, which provides an important metaphor for her predicament through rhythmic repetitions and imagery (bells, circle, hive, each Tuesday); (4) explore with two performers the simultaneous *participation* and *detachment* of the speaker during the music session; (5) illustrate symbolically with puppetlike staging that the bell-lady (and the institution she represents—and even conditioned society) controls the actions of the speaker and the other inmates.

Suggested Assignments

I. Read "The Strange Case in Baker Street," "The Bad Daddy," and "Still Life" in "An Evening with Reed Whittemore."

II. For each poem list the specific details that indicate performance behaviors. On the basis of your discoveries which poems would you classify as highly defined, lowly defined, or somewhere in between?

III. What other information would help

you develop specific performance behaviors for Holmes and Watson in "The Strange Case in Baker Street"?

Logical and Symbolic Meaning

The semantic dimension of a poem answers the questions: "What is the poet saying? What is apparently meant?" We assume that if a poet is reasonably successful in the poem, the same meaning will be communicated to a large number of readers. That meaning may be far more than "one dimensional," but if highly ambiguous, that ambiguity should be perceptible as well. Just as Flannery O'Connor says of the short story, a poem defies paraphrase. Most attempts to paraphrase the poem result in trite maxims such as "all men fear death," or "art is an attempt to bring order to the natural world of chaos." We do restate in our minds what we read as we make sense of it but our restatement does not equal the original expression.

Since poetic expression is often short, each word is especially significant. Often this leads readers to expect that poets not only mean far more than they state but that they do not mean what is stated at all. This expectation reflects a general hesitancy to accept the *literal level* in favor of a *symbolic level*. However, readers of poetry should always accept first the literal, stated meaning of the poem before projecting and extending it to the symbolic level. If a poet says that a speaker is standing in the kitchen at the sink washing dishes or is at a gravesite mourning, the reader should believe it. To project "depth" into the situation by deciding that the sink is a baptismal font or the gravesite a sort of judgment arena is to rewrite the poem and deny the poet all possibility of normal expression. If those dimensions are symbolically suggested as the poem progresses, a reader must still remember that the literal had to exist before the symbolic was possible. To see a larger significance in the ordinary is a common poetic manuever, but again, the ordinary must be present to make the extraordinary emerge.

This difference between the direct level of expression and the implied larger level of expression is the difference between the statements in the poem and the more general themes suggested by the poem. In one sense, all language is symbolic—i.e., it refers to something outside itself. In a more colloquial sense, however, the symbolic level of a poem implies a dimension of greater significance than what is stated. Traditionally poetry has exploited the suggestive power of language to reverberate many meanings simultaneously. An awareness of both the stated and the implicit is certainly part of the performer's initial analytical steps.

Suggested Assignments

I. Refer back to pages 15–16 and 19 and examine "Elegy" and "Reason" for their literal and symbolic content.
II. Locate the following poems, all rich on both literal and symbolic levels, and stage them in various ways to demonstrate both levels:
  A. Donald Hall, "In the Old House"
  B. William Stafford, "Father's Voice"
  C. Denise Levertov, "What Were They Like?"
  D. Wole Soyinka, "Telephone Conversation"

The Poet Writing and The Persona Speaking

The distinction between the poet-author and the *persona,* or speaker created *in* the selection, applies to all literature.[3] The lyric

[3]See George T. Wright, "The Faces of the Poet," *The Poet in the Poem* (Berkeley: University of California Press, 1962).

"I" in most poetry, however, raises a typical problem in poetry. The frequent immediacy of the poetic experience and the intensity of the first-person speaker tend to fuse the author with the poem's speaker. The result is that we equate, for instance, Anne Sexton the *person* with the *speaker* of "Ringing the Bells." Yet no matter how closely some details from an author's life parallel incidents in the poetry, *the author is far more than the glimpse attainable in any given poem.* Many performances are considerably distorted by biographical information. Poet Richard Eberhart illustrates this point when he tells of students who, after discovering a member of his family has died from cancer, interpret his poem "The Cancer Cells" as a eulogy. The poem itself would not suggest this to a reader ignorant of the biographical background presenting as it does an imagistic description of what cancer cells look like when viewed under a microscope.

Therefore, while biographical and social-cultural information will often provide relevant insights (see the essay on the Whittemore script), the *extrinsic* material (any information outside the text) involves the partial *real world* of the *author,* while the *intrinsic* material represents the *fictive world* of the *persona.*

EXPLORATION OF SOUND STRUCTURE

Sensitivity to the language of poetry involves hearing the sounds of words as well as understanding them. The poetic medium characteristically explores and exploits sound textures. While written words preserve language, they lack the vocal characteristics of tone, intensity, and inflection.

Sound Texture

"Poetic" language usually means a richer and more imaginative means of expression. A poet who wants to avoid the cliche "crazy as a loon" instead announces "He was crude as a loon on land."[4] Much of this verbal texture—the multi-layered visual and semantic depth—is *sound* textured as well. *Sound texture is the acoustic surface of language.* For example, poet May Swenson surprises and delights with her aural and visual depiction of the lithe carriage of a lion:

> *your loose-skinned belly frilled with fur*
> *you carry easily sinuously pacing on suede*
> *paws*[5]

Swenson auditorily projects the image of the big cat's graceful, smooth step with the continuous rolling sounds in "carry ea*si*ly sinuou*sly*" and the unvoiced softness of "*p*acing on *s*uede *p*aws." Readers need to cultivate their "inner ears" in order to voice these textures in performance.

Individual words can receive a sound-oriented "meaning," or implication, when placed near others. Two of the most common ways that words acquire these sound properties are the *mimetic* and the *onomatopoetic*. When the sound of a word appears to take on the inner characteristics of the object it refers to, it has a mimetic sound quality—i.e., the sound reinforces some internal property of the object or action. For instance, the sound of the word "oil" has a mimetic or imitative quality reminiscent of the substance. The mimetic element makes word sounds curiously reflect and participate in their referents.

When the sound *of* a word appears to represent the sound of the object the word represents, it has an onomatopoetic quality. Aesthetician Monroe Beardsley terms this sound quality the *presentational equivalent* of the word's meaning—the word presents in

sound an equivalent to its meaning.[6] For example, the words "hush," "hiss," or "buzz" when uttered sound like the thing they refer to, unlike "silent," "loud," or "vibrate." Again, as with mimetic sound quality, it is possible to "oversound" words to suggest the things they denote and, for instance, pronounce "shoot" or "thunder" so sonorously as to imply a resemblance to the thing designated. This type of exaggeration does not reveal a sound structure but rather tries to pound it in.

Interesting sound qualities are found most frequently in the poet's use of *rhyme, alliteration, consonance,* and *assonance.* All these language devices depend upon a verbal *group* effect for sound play. Rhymes curiously link certain words that normally would not be thought of together. As a result, for instance, "slow" and "toe" share certain properties when heard together, an identity mysteriously conjured up by the poet who juxtaposes them.

1. *Rhyme.* When words "rhyme," they share the same stressed sounds. Rhyme is usually associated with the last stressed sound in the word, of a line although they can be *visual,* or eye (cough, bough); *slant,* or near (time, nine,); or *internal* in the line and not at the end.

2. *Alliteration.* When *initial* sounds in two or more words are repeated, the effect is called alliteration (*r*ough *R*ichard *r*an). Alliteration can be hidden within words (fil*l*ed a*f*ter aw*f*ul *f*right), but the words must occur in close succession.

3. *Consonance.* When identical *consonants* appear near one another, although the vowels differ, we experience consonance (sweet Sarah sleeps). Consonance occurs also when sounds are the same even though the identical letter does not appear (Phil fell).

[4]Richard Hugo, "The Swimmer at Lake Edward," *What Thou Lovest Well Remains American* (New York: W. W. Norton & Co., Inc., 1975).

[5]May Swenson, "Lion," *To Mix With Time* (New York: Charles Scribner's Sons, 1963).

[6]Monroe C. Beardsley, *Aesthetics: Problems in the Philosophy of Criticism* (New York: Harcourt, Brace, & World, Inc., 1958), p. 235.

4. *Assonance.* When identical *vowel* sounds appear near one another, although the consonants surrounding them differ, we hear assonance (*summer love*).

Suggested Assignments

I. For decades students have enjoyed "feeling" the sounds of poetry by reading them, often in unison. Old favorites are Vachel Lindsay's "The Congo" and Edgar Allen Poe's "The Bells." Experiment with these poems and notice how the repetition of sounds frequently creates or reinforces the meaning of the poems.

II. Poetry written for children is often a delightful way for classes to initiate their study of sound structure. Identify the elements of sound structure described so far in the following poems by Theodore Roethke: "Myrtle," "The Serpent," and "The Sloth."

Sound Symbolism

Poets, performers, critics, and linguists have long argued the issue of "sound symbolism": Do certain sounds or sound patterns have a "meaning"? Assuredly, given sounds do not have any universal meanings or associations, and thus an "s" pattern in a line can be soothing in one instance and harsh in another. Although the context, both sound and semantic, in which the word appears can suggest moods or atmosphere, the individual sounds themselves do not denote anything. Poet John Crowe Ransom describes this as the chameleon-like quality of the phonetic elements in language—their ability to be constantly associated and reassociated. Generally, the descriptive effects of the sound patterns are the most significant. Frequently a poet, craftily weaving auditory effects into the poem, will employ sound clusters far more frequently than these

would occur in ordinary usage. Just as it would be a mistake to assume that those sound clusters always "mean" a certain thing, it would be equally a mistake to assume that they mean nothing at all. An aural sensitivity to the poem will allow the various parts to reflect upon themselves and the whole to which they contribute. In this way sounds can project a particular symbolism in a poem or in the line of a poem, and thus become part of the integrated poetic texture.

Patterned Sound

By placing words with regular features (primarily sound-oriented) into a perceptible pattern, the poet creates a highly rhythmic expression. When something seen or heard in one line returns in a later one, it is simultaneously noticeable both in itself and because of its earlier appearance. This reverberation, or reappearance, creates the rhythmic effect. Thus *rhythm is the recurrence of any language element in the poem at somewhat regular or equal intervals.* This language element could be a word, phrase, syntactical structure, line, pause, couplet, stanza, or even an image.

If the recurring element is a patterned use of stressed and unstressed syllables, the poet's language is termed metrical, or *metered.* Thus, *meter is the patterning of stressed and unstressed syllables.* This patterned syllabic system can consist of: (1) the number of syllables per line (e.g., 4, 5, 5, 4), termed *syllabic meter;* (2) the number of stressed, or accented, syllables per line or stanza (e.g., 3, 4, 3, 4) termed *accentual meter;* (3) or a combination of patterned numbers of unstressed and stressed syllables (e.g., x′, x′, x′) termed *accentual-syllabic,* or *foot meter.* The process of marking stressed (′) and unstressed syllables (x) is termed *scansion.* Although this two-value system (stressed and unstressed) gives an oversimpli-

fied view of the relative stress values within
and between words, it provides a profile of
the working units of stress measurement in
the poem.

Significantly the study of versification, or
prosody (the principles of metrical analysis), is not a "science" but an art. The marking system and terminology of prosody often
suggest "scientific" illusions and convert the
potentially enjoyable study of poetry into a
torturous hide-and-seek scansion search.
Naturally the terminology and the mark-
ings are a convenient form of shorthand,
but scansions are seldom indisputable and
are often ambiguous. The awareness and
sensitivity is essential. Here are a few guidelines:

1. Determine if the poetic structure is metri-
cally *regular*: (a) by visual examination
(does the poem *look* ordered, does it have
boxlike stanzas, the same number of lines
per stanza, capital letters at the beginning
of lines?); (b) by counting the number of
syllables, accents, or feet in successive ver-
tical columns to the right of the poem
so that patterns become more obvious at
a glance; (c) by outlining the rhyme
scheme by placing identical successive
letters of the alphabet at the ends of lines
that rhyme (e.g., an *abab* rhyme scheme
means that the first line rhymes with the
third, and the second with the fourth. An
"x" is used in a rhyme scheme to indicate
a line that does not rhyme with any other
in the poem).

2. If a regular structure is present, distinguish between how the *pattern* controls the
line in the abstract sounding (e.g., iambic,
trochaic) and how the line would be
naturally spoken. James McAuley suggests
scanning the metrical pattern first and
then above it scanning the "speech stress"
pattern.[7] The speech stress scansion indicates how the rhetorical meaning directs
delivery of the line. With both scansions

[7]James McAuley, *Versification: A Short Introduction* (East Lansing: Michigan State University
Press, 1966).

present, the differences between the meter
and the meaning readings of the lines
become clear. While the metrical pattern
is highly controlled, the speech stress pattern will vary with each performer's reading. Take, for example, the following line
from Robert Frost's poem "Provide, Provide":

speech pattern

and nobody will call *you* crone.

metrical pattern

and nobody will call *you* crone.

Rhetorically, Frost italicized the word
"you," indicating a stress on that word,
although his tight iambic pattern (x′)
would dictate an unstressed syllable. This
is an instance of *counterpoint*—when the
meter conflicts with the natural speech
stress, thereby calling even more attention
to the word or phrase.

3. If there is no traditional metrical pattern,
the poem is most likely written in *free
verse*, the rhythm being created by repeated words, phrases, syntactical units,
lines, pauses, or images. When these units
are outlined as illustrated below, numerous internal patterns will emerge. Here
are a few structures from "Ringing the
Bells":

in Bedlam   who comes
in the wrong hive   who sit
in the lounge   who passes
                     who grumbles
                     who picks (twice)
                     who points

Sound Structure in Performance

The sound structures of poetry present
a veritable field day for the performer;
poetry comes alive with single or multiple
voice effects. Since a "sounding" of the poem
characterizes the performance, a performer
must be very aware of the poem's verbal and
rhythmic elements. Some of this awareness

will come from a preparatory analysis and exploratory performances, and from later performances as well.

The group performance of poetry heightens the possibilities for exploring sound texture since the vocal textures of the performers' voices will interact and reveal those in the literature. Group presentations introduce choral possibilities and other multiple voice effects such as vocal overlays, sound effects, echoes. For choral effects, performer's voices are usually integrated much like voices in a chorus.

Many decisions an individual reader faces become complicated when a group performs a selection. Significantly a group performing a given selection (or members of a group performing individually) should generally: (1) be careful to "compromise" between a metrical reading and a sense reading and not discard either totally; (2) avoid any oversounding that removes words from their normal context; (3) respect the delicate balance between suppressing rhymes and pounding them in. Highly rhythmic poems imply highly rhythmic readings. Usually the meter and the sense are well integrated; and if readers restress lines to break a "singsong," they often lose the emphasis of the meaning as well. In addition, readers should regard line endings as "suspended" pauses of relative length. Often a line ends with punctuation of some sort, or the completion of the sense, in which case the line is said to be *end-stopped*. A pause in this case is logical. When the line does not contain end punctuation or a pause in the sense, the line is said to be *enjambed*. Just how long a pause or a final sound should be suspended is an important part of preparing for a performance.

Suggested Assignment

Study the sound structures in one or more of the poems listed below and then answer the questions that follow.

Adrienne Rich, "Meditations of a Savage Child"

Gerard Manley Hopkins, "The Golden Echo and the Leaden Echo"

W. H. Auden, "In Memory of William Butler Yeats"

Felix Pollak, "Speaking: The Hero"

Joyce Carol Oates, "Lines for Those to Whom Tragedy Has Been Denied"

1. Is the poem traditionally metrical or free verse?

2. If the poem is traditionally structured, scan it. If it is free verse, outline the repetitions that create the rhythm.

3. As a class exercise, divide into groups and work out *alternate* performances of the poems: first, demonstrate the rhythm by overemphasizing it; then perform it with attention to the sense of the lines; finally, try to integrate the two in a meaningful way.

EXPLORATION OF VISUAL STRUCTURE

Important clues to a poem's meaning are often visually reinforced or stated in the typography. For instance, the female persona in Marge Piercy's poem, "The Secretary Chant," considering herself engulfed and dehumanized by the impersonal machinelike world in which she lives, types out ironically. "I wonce was a woman."[8] Naturally the visual impact of the "wonce" is underscored by the typographical reproduction of the poem—its visual redundancy in print. The "w" from "woman" is linked with the past "once." In other poems the performer must solve the problem of presenting homonyms, such as in George Baker's sonnet, "To My Mother," where the speaker declares that the mother moves from "mourning to morning." Slides or props could possibly clarify this visual dimension because the

[8]Marge Piercy, "The Secretary Chant," *To Be of Use* (New York: Doubleday & Co., Inc., 1973), p. 5.

oral medium alone does not always define enough in these instances.

A performer is able to signal a line ending through suspended or deliberate pauses. An audience member unfamiliar with the selection, however, could probably not discern which particular pause occurred at the end of a line and which occured somewhere else, unless the line ending was reinforced by a rhyme. Some line endings and stanzaic divisions are very important and are unmistakable in performance when properly observed. Many line endings and stanzaic divisions appear—even under careful analysis—to be arbitrary or constructed with an unclear design. The performer must decide just how functional these formal aspects are in each specific case.

With some highly visual poems, performers can project the poem's shape and design through their physical arrangement in the performing space, or through symbolic movements that underscore the typographical fun in the poem (e.g., the cummings poem "a leaf falls" or "grasshopper"). In addition, the use of slides, transparencies, and graphics can visually supplement the oral performance.

Suggested Assignment

Consider the ways in which a group might *show* the visual designs in May Swenson's *Half Sun Half Sleep* (which contains traditionally stanzaic as well as visual poetry) and in collections of poetry more strictly visual in design, such as Mary Ellen Solt's *Concrete Poetry: A World View* and Emmett William's *Anthology of Concrete Poetry*.

PROGRAMMING

Most group performances of poetry present several poems grouped together in a particular order for a particular purpose. Within a given program, some poems may be performed singly and others by several members of the group. The program format is interesting primarily because of its flexibility of design. Nevertheless, *the program should have a concept that directs the programming design,* a *controlling concept* over and above the individual concepts of each selection. Some popular concepts in programming for a poetry production are: themes, structures, authors, or literary "movements." Here are a few examples:

I. *Themes:* "The Black Poet as Militant"; "Verse and Ecology"; "The American Identity"; "The Jewish Experience in Poetry"; "Individuals Alienated"; "Wars and Weapons"

II. *Structures:* Sonnets, Ballads, Dramatic Monologues

III. *Authors:* "Surrealistic Imagery in the Poetry of Erica Jong"; "Robert Frost's View of Nature"; "The Eulogies of John Ciardi"; "The Assertion of the Individual in the Poetry of Gregory Corso"; "William Carlos Williams: An American Imagist"; "The Engaged Poetry of Denise Levertov"

IV. *Literary Movements or Groups:* Black, Pop, Concrete, Feminist, Protest, Confessional, Black Mountain, Beat, Victorian

Selected Bibliography

BEACHAM, WALTON. *The Meaning of Poetry: A Guide to Explication.* Boston: Allyn and Bacon, Inc., 1974.

BLOOM, EDWARD A., Charles H. Philbrick, and Elmer M. Blistein. *The Order of Poetry: An Introduction.* New York: The Odyssey Press, Inc., 1961.

CIARDI, JOHN. *How Does a Poem Mean?* Boston: Houghton Mifflin Company, 1959.

FUSSELL, PAUL, JR. *Poetic Meter and Poetic Form.* New York: Random House Inc., 1965.

HEMPHILL, GEORGE, ed. *Discussions of Poetry: Rhythm and Sound.* Boston: D.C. Heath and Company, 1961.

MCAULEY, JAMES. *Versification: A Short Introduction.* East Lansing: Michigan State University Press, 1966.

PREMINGER, ALEX, ed. *The Princeton Encyclopedia of Poetry and Poetics.* Princeton: Princeton University Press, 1965.

STAUFFER, DONALD A. *The Nature of Poetry.* New York: W. W. Norton & Co., Inc., 1962.

WRIGHT, GEORGE T. *The Poet in the Poem: The Personae of Eliot, Yeats, and Pound.* Berkeley and Los Angeles: University of California Press, 1960.

chapter 7

Nonfictional Literature
in Group Performance

Literary types that fail to fall neatly into the categories of poetry, dramatic literature, or fictional prose (short stories, novels) are generally called nonfiction and, occasionally, "transitional literary forms."[1] We use here a more inclusive term, *nonfictional literature,* a broad category that includes autobiographies, biographies, diaries, letters, essays, and historical and political documents. Nonfictional literature shares similarities and reveals dissimilarities with the traditional literary genres (fiction, drama, poetry). Often the similarities lead to real difficulties in locating discernible differences between nonfictional literature and strict literary forms. Much factual, historical, and documentary literature, when properly compiled and ordered, shares a peculiar affinity with the dramatic mode. These matters are important to you inasmuch as they affect your decisions to stage nonfictional literature for group performance.

[1]Wallace Bacon, *The Art of Interpretation,* 2nd ed. (New York: Holt, Rinehart & Winston, Inc., 1972), p. 365.

The remainder of this chapter treats: (1) the *challenges* that nonfictional literature present for the director of group performance; (2) *types* of nonfictional literature in group performance; and (3) the *uses* of nonfictional literature and its relationship to group performance.

CHALLENGES OF NONFICTIONAL LITERATURE IN GROUP PERFORMANCE

Some of the challenges of nonfictional literature in group performance include: adaptability, structural simplicity, the nonfictional voice, singularity of voice, and authenticity of voice.

Adaptability

A director would rarely consider "cutting" a poem because of poetry's economy of language, and in many cases, its tight, conventional forms. However, many nonfictional works, because of their emphatic and redundant style, are imminently adaptable or extractable, which makes them desirable as either transitional or focal materials in a group performance.

Structural Simplicity

Fictional prose is an especially attractive genre for group performance. This genre, however, like poetry, is so formally structured that directors must exercise extreme caution in adapting it if they are to retain a sense of the whole work and preserve the integrity of the narrative voice. The complexities of nuance and meaning in much nonfictional prose are usually fewer and less intricately interwoven because: (1) the nonfictional writer's purpose is essentially rhetorical—i.e., to inform, entertain, persuade, or convince; (2) nonfictional writers continually reinforce, reiterate, and retrace for emphasis; and (3) the "point of view" in most nonfictional prose is evident and uncomplicated. Naturally, nonfictional materials are attractive to the director who compiles a theme- or author-centered program or devises a factual drama where both information and perspective are important.

The Nonfictional Voice

Generally, the nonfictional voice is an intensely personal one. Except for biographies and documents, the nonfictional voice is detached from the author by time and space but at the same time clearly bound to him or her. Nonfictional writers do not create a persona or a narrator to speak for them, but carry on a dialogue with the reader in their own person. The nonfictional voice presents two potential problems for the director of group performance: singularity and authenticity of voice.

Singularity of Voice. Some nonfictional literature—specifically letters, diaries, autobiographies, and essays—are so overwhelmingly centered around a single voice and often contain so little dramatic action that they seem hardly amenable to group per-

formance. Clearly, such works can be valuable if they provide one voice among others in a theme- or author-centered compiled script. One interesting alternative, however, is to exploit the variety of personalities present in a single voice by using a different performer for each personality. For example, a careful adaptation of several, or even one, of Anaïs Nin's diaries would reveal a variety of "persons": the child, the "mother confessor," the artist, the sister, the daughter, the lover, the analysand, and the benefactress. These persons represent the more-and-less private voices of Anaïs Nin—the complex facets of her personality. The possibilities for approaching nonfictional literature in this manner are unlimited.

Authenticity of Voice. The nonfictional writer, in a very real sense, *announces* that he or she writes in his or her own voice. The problem arises, then, for the director of group performance to determine how much of the author's real voice should be preserved in performance. The nonfictional author's voice can be authenticated by historical or contemporary records. The nonfictional text will supply clues to the voice but still may not be a sufficient instrument for defining the voice. Consider the questions: "Will an audience wonder if your performance of, say, Nabokov in *Speak, Memory* reveals no trace of the author's Russian heritage?" "Does, or should, audience expectation play a role in your treatment of nonfictional voices?" Each director and group of performers should answer these questions during exploratory rehearsals of nonfictional works. The nature of the individual work coupled with your knowledge of the life and times of the author will direct your decisions.

No "rules" govern the treatment of nonfictional or historical voices in group performance. Extrinsic criticism (an examination of the author's relationship to his environment, to the work of art, and to an audience) will serve a significant function in your approach to nonfictional literature in group performance.

Like group performance, nonfictional writing characteristically features a personality, an event, a theme, a proposition or social or political view, a relationship, a "distorted" portrait, or a "life." Let us consider briefly various *types* of nonfictional literature. We will approach these types on a continuum from the most subjective to the least subjective author involvement, and from the most specific to the least specific audience in the work.

TYPES OF
NONFICTIONAL LITERATURE
IN GROUP PERFORMANCE

Diaries, Letters,
and Autobiographies

These three types of nonfictional literature often exist in the lyric mode. Authors of diaries, letters, and autobiographies create and develop a direct relationship with their audience, though the nature and function of the audience in each of these works vary. A diary, for many writers, serves the function of an alter ego—it operates as a sounding board *for the* self in communion *with* the self. A diarist speaks in the first person and reveals his or her personal perceptions and emotions. The immediate audience in the diary is the writer's "other" self, or alter-ego. A diary emphasizes the subjective profile of the writer. Indeed, Leonard Woolf, writing in the preface to Virginia Woolf's *A Writer's Diary*, explains that his wife's diary

> gives for 27 years a consecutive record of what she did, of the people whom she saw, and *particularly of what she thought about those people, about herself, about life, and about the books she was writing and hoped to write.* . . .
>
> At the best . . . *diaries give a distorted or*

one-sided portrait of the writer, because, as Virginia Woolf herself remarks somewhere in these diaries, one gets into the habit of recording one particular kind of mood—irritation or misery, say—and of not writing one's diary when one is feeling the opposite. *The portrait is therefore from the start unbalanced.* . . .[2]

Diaries, since Samuel Pepys' was deciphered (he wrote it in shorthand) and published in 1825, have held a special fascination for audiences. Pepys' *Diaries*, written between 1660 and 1669, are a spontaneous, lively, and uninhibited record of English life in the 1660s. In them he recreates, among other events, the coronation of Charles II and the Great Fire of London as they directly affected him. On September 3, 1666, the third day of the Great Fire, Pepys records that

> About four o'clock in the morning, my Lady Batten sent me a cart to carry away all my money, and plate, and best things, to Sir W. Rider's at Bednall-Breene. Which I did, riding myself in my nightgown in the cart; and, Lord! to see how the streets and the highways are crowded with people running and riding, and getting of carts at any rate to fetch away things.

Pepys' spontaneity, inhibition, and tone of confidentiality with the listener in the diary (the alter-ego, intimate "friend," "dear" diary) are as appealing as the events he recounts. These qualities are characteristic of diaries since the seventeenth century. Some early diaries and many later ones were not intended for publication, which accounts in large part for the writer's honest, if one-sided, observations.

Letters and autobiographies, like diaries, reveal authors who directly address and establish a peculiar intimacy with their

[2]Virginia Woolf, *A Writer's Diary*, ed. Leonard Woolf (New York: Harcourt Brace Jovanovich, Inc., 1954), pp. vii-viii. (Italics added.)

audience. The letter-writer's audience is necessarily more specific than the autobiographer's. We can easily identify the audience in the letter from the writer's salutation, "Dear _____." The autobiographer addresses a larger, more general audience. The autobiography emphasizes the writer's developing self—confessions of personal crises, aspirations, and disappointments. Letters, on the other hand, have the fundamental purpose, as Lytton Strachey remarked in an essay on Horace Walpole's letters, of "express[ing] the personality of the writer."

Diaries, letters, and autobiographies are unusually personal and often highly intimate. These forms of nonfictional writing can be especially rewarding or embarrassingly inappropriate in group performance. Their tendency to emphasize the intimate details of the writer's private world often offends some audiences, and forces a director and cast to consider the problems of aesthetic distance and "taste."

Essays

Unlike diaries, letters, and autobiographies, essays are addressed to a more generalized audience, though this literary type often reveals a great deal about the author through the style of writing and choice of subject. Montaigne's famous *Essays* of 1580 and 1588 gave the genre its name and characteristically discursive style. In them he declares his views on the nature of man and knowledge. He moves freely from one subject to another, assumes a certain degree of knowledge but avoids technical language, and addresses the general reader rather than the specialist. Later essayists adopted Montaigne's method, and by the middle of the nineteenth century the essay was a well-established and popular genre in England.

Intentionally rhetorical, the essayist expresses a point of view, argues a position, or explains a subject. The essay emphasizes the author's position and admittedly attempts to persuade a reader or audience. Because of their essentially rhetorical nature and often witty style, some formal and many informal—i.e., "familiar," "personal"—essays enjoy a fuller realization in group performance than in silent or solo readings. James Thurber and E. B. White have singly and in collaboration produced many essays highly suitable for group performance. See, for example, "Is Sex Necessary?", a joint effort by Thurber and White. The essays printed by Richard Steele and Joseph Addison in *The Tatler* and *The Spectator* (1709–1712), especially those in *The Spectator,* contain delightful material for group performance. In the tradition of Addison and Steele, modern-day essayists Russell Baker and Art Buchwald write lively (and usually scathing) "editorials" satirizing contemporary figures and mores. Baker's "Doing the Spring Braincleaning" suggests a number of interesting possibilities for group performance (New York *Times,* May 18, 1969, p. 16e).

Suggested Assignments

I. Cast and stage Baker's essay for a classroom performance; include in your production concept what you hope to emphasize, the number of performers, and your production design.

II. What alternative decisions might be necessary if you planned the performance for a group of upper elementary or junior high school students?

Biographies

In the nonfictional forms of literature we have treated so far, the writers have been highly subjective and have written from an idiosyncratic perspective. There is an author-in-the-work directly communicating with a specific or general audience. In the biography, however, some idiosyncrasies remain, but there is a slight shift toward objectivity—"slight" because the biographer, however hard he tries to maintain a distance, always conveys his particular perspective of the subject. In biographies, though, an intervening speaker appears, the "interlocutor" for the person whose life the author examines. The presence of a mediator between the subject and his audience leads some to place biographies in the epic mode, and to advise performers to match the mediator's perspective in the work. The biographer's audience, like that of the autobiographer's and the essayist's, is largely undefined and general, such as the audience for Irving Stone's biographies of Vincent Van Gogh, Rachel Jackson, Clarence Darrow, Mary Todd Lincoln, and Michelangelo. Although many scholars classify Stone's biographies as "fictionalized," others have noted the strict historical accuracy in many of his works.

In a peculiarly sexist comment (not, however for the seventeenth century) John Dryden defined biography as "the history of particular *men's* lives." A biography is a history of a particular person's life. More than a mere chronology of events in the subject's life, these histories usually survey the subject's character, his or her attitudes toward events of the time, and relationships with other people. No two biographies of the same subject will relate exactly the same facts, review the same relationships, or examine the same character traits of the subject. A biography emphasizes both a developing self and the outside influences on that self. Michael Holroyd explains why his two-volume biography of Lytton Strachey reexamines Strachey's works and his relationships with his social and literary associates (the Bloomsbury group):

His life...was very intimately bound up with the Bloomsbury friends, so that I have been obliged also to offer some re-examination of the Bloomsbury world in the light of Lytton's and their own private correspon-

dence. To divide artificially his life from his books, and both of these from the friends who influenced him and with whom he had dealings, would have been to destroy the polychromatic design and meaning of his life. For this reason, the following pages present more than a biography of one man: they unfold a panorama of the social and intellectual environment of an entire generation.[3]

Such biographies offer stimulating and challenging material for directors and students of group performance.

Documents

Few historical novels and even fewer history texts are appropriate in their entirety for group performance, emphasizing as they do cold, statistical data reported by an impassive voice. Many documents—trial proceedings, newspaper accounts, historical letters, journal articles, speeches, legal documents, interviews—in part or in their entirety are, however, rich sources for productions.

In this century we have witnessed the emergence of "reportage" in film and literature and factual, or documentary, drama in the theatre. The procedure of the documentary "dramatist" is similar to that of the director of group performance. The materials are the materials of history, and the aim is, as Martin Duberman explains in the preface to *In White America,* to "combine the evocative power of the spoken word with the confirming power of historical fact." With careful selection (which necessarily involves lengthy research) and arrangement of focal and supporting materials, the documentary dramatist can produce a "play" with a problem, a conflict,

[3]Michael Holroyd, *Lytton Strachey: The Unknown Years, 1880–1910* (New York: Holt, Rinehart & Winston, 1967), p. xvi.

and a resolution (with crises, climax, and denouement). When carefully compiled and ordered, historical documents emphasize character involvements and dramatic situations. In both Peter Weiss' *The Investigation* and Duberman's *In White America* and in the introduction to *The Dramatization of 365 Days* the author-compilers comment extensively on the impetus and sources for their plays. These discussions can be a valuable guide to directors of group performance interested in devising a script from documentary materials.

With devised scripts, the question arises "What is the relationship of the author to the audience?" Playwrights and authors of documentary scripts stand at a distance three times removed from the audience, submerging their voices in those of the characters. The relationships of authors and audiences in diaries, letters, autobiographies, and essays are direct and, occasionally, intimate. However, any author is at best once removed from the audience through the intervention of an implied author, or an author *in the text,* even though he or she speaks in the first person about him- or herself.

All authors, then, begin their communication with the audience at one remove from the audience. The shift from the lyric mode ("I" speakers) to the epic mode involves a shift from first person to third person, from "I" as the subject to "he" or "she" as the subject. This shift establishes a second level of distancing between the author and the audience which is evident, for example, in biographies. In the biography, the writer (author) speaks for the subject—that is, acts as an intermediary, an interlocutor, on behalf of the subject. This author does not directly discuss his or her feelings and attitudes, but those of another person. Although many characters may inhabit the biography, the quality of their personalities, as well as that of the subject, is sifted through the consciousness of the

biographer as he or she interprets their relationships to the subject.

The director of documents for a group performance functions not as a playwright but as a script "deviser." While the document script can be imaginative, it originates in recorded events, conversations, relationships, perceptions. Playwright Tom Stoppard, commenting on his widely acclaimed play *Travesties,* acknowledges his indebtedness to various historical works and admits that the principal characters—Lenin, Joyce, Tzara, and Henry Carr—are not fictional characters. Succinctly clarifying the distinctive roles of the playwright and one who devises a script from documents, Stoppard explains:

> *Travesties* is a work of fiction which makes use, and misuse, of history. Scenes which are self-evidently documentary mingle with others which are just as evidently fantastical. People who were hardly aware of each other's existence are made to collide; real people and imaginary people are brought together without ceremony; and events which took place months, and even years apart are presented as synchronous. For the luxury of such liberties I am indebted to writers who allowed themselves none.[4]

Playwrights create characters who speak and interact; authors of devised scripts create neither events nor characters, but expose both in the materials selected; they develop characters by arranging those materials. In *No Sense of Decency,* for example (see the script in Unit II), the director did not create Joe McCarthy, Roy Cohn, Joseph Welch, and Stuart Symington as characters in a play, but selected documents in which they already existed as principal characters in a past, but very real, human drama. The characters, once exposed through the documents, emerged as fully developed within

---

[4]Tom Stoppard, "Lenin, Joyce, Tzara, and Henry Carr," *Playbill* (December 1975), p. 23.

the context of the event through their sustained presence in the arranged documents.

Many volumes of documents exist that are viable sources for group performances. Trial transcripts, for example, have great potential, such as the obscenity trial of Allen Ginsberg's "Howl." The Watergate scandal has already been dramatized on stage by at least one company, a group of inmates in a Massachusettes federal prison. The William Calley hearings, the Charles Manson murders, the Patricia Hearst case, and the Knapp Commission hearings, on which *Serpico* is based, are other interesting possibilities.

USES OF NONFICTIONAL LITERATURE AND ITS RELATIONSHIP TO GROUP PERFORMANCE

Nonfictional literature is customarily used in two ways in group performance: (1) as transitional material, or (2) as focal material. It is used transitionally in *An Evening with Reed Whittemore, The Nineteenth Great American Laugh,* and *Indians Speak;* it is used both transitionally and focally in *Twain Sketches;* and as the primary source in *No Sense of Decency.* As transitional material, nonfictional literature can provide the connections or links that unify a program. As focal material, nonfictional literature is a promising source for exciting experiments in group performance.

Procedure

In a broad sense, the nonfictional writer and the director of group performance of literature share a number of concerns. First, *nonfictional composition* and *script composition for group performance* are both arts of selectivity and arrangement. However diligently nonfictional writers strive for objectivity and an impersonal, reportorial style, their work, nonetheless, carries their signature. After all, they select certain ma-

terial and arrange it in a manner that reveals a particular point of view. Martin Duberman, author of the documentary drama *In White America,* suggests the relationship between the historian and the literary artist:

> . . . I tried staging the raw material of history itself rather than a fictionalized version of it. The two modes of procedure, of course, are not entirely different. . . . Using historical documents—letters, news reports, diaries, and the like—does not guarantee objectivity; *it would be naive to think that in selecting, abridging, cutting, and juxtaposing the materials of history, I was not also transmuting them.* The past does not speak for itself, and *the ordering intelligence that renders it, necessarily injects some degree of idiosyncrasy.*[5]

While few students of group performance of literature are equally proficient as writers; they share with the nonfictional writer, as Duberman suggests, "a mode of procedure." The director of group performances selects, extracts, adds, deletes, and rearranges the materials for performance. Duberman, a renowned writer of history, functioned in much the same role as the director of group performance. He was concerned, too, with the analogous behaviors of the "professional" historical writer and the literary writer, and the *relationship* between nonfictional composition and script composition.[6]

Among the categories of nonfictional literature in which the writer "necessarily indulges in imaginative combinations of fact and opinion," and where he or she "consciously and extensively" comments upon the material, are biographies, autobiographies, diaries, letters, essays, and documentary drama. Consider, for example, the biographies of Lytton Strachey, the letters

[5]Martin Duberman, *In White America* (New York: The New American Library, 1964), p. 124. (Italics added.)
[6]See Duberman, p. 120.

of G. B. Shaw and Mrs. Patrick Campbell, or the speeches of William Jennings Bryan. However "factual" the data may be in these documents, the author must select and arrange the data as a necessary condition of the art. For example, C. Dwight Dorough, the biographer of *Mr. Sam* (Sam Rayburn, eminent former Speaker of the House of Representatives), *selected* and *arranged* pertinent and voluminous data that confirmed Rayburn's political expertise and his commitment to his constituency. In the same biography, the author chose merely to mention some and to omit other details about his short-lived marriage; he even chose to omit the name of the mysterious Mrs. Rayburn. That such a thorough investigator was ignorant of these facts is unlikely. That he chose to select and arrange *other* details that *in his opinion* exemplified his image of Rayburn is altogether consistent with the biographer's method of composition. In much the same fashion, directors who compile scripts for group performance select materials according to their vision of the subject and arrange them for clarity and impact.

Suggested Assignments

I. Duberman suggests that future performers of *In White America* might use the alternate conclusion instead of the one that appears in the text. As a class project, experiment with both conclusions and write a two-page paper discussing the differences in perspective and probable impact of the two endings.
II. H. Wesley Balk, in his introduction to *The Dramatization of 365 Days* ("An Experiment in Chamber Theatre"), suggests alternative selections from the book that could be used in future productions. One of his suggestions is to dramatize the glossary. Read *The Dramatization of 365 Days* and, following the author's suggestion, incorporate the glossary into the text of the play. How does this inclusion alter the play's perspective? Does this

inclusion produce a different effect on the audience? In what ways?

Perspective

You are probably familiar with Henry James's "House of Fiction," which describes perspective, or vision, for the short story writer and the novelist; this metaphor is also relevant to the nonfictional writer. Describing the windows of his house of fiction, James says:

> ...at each of them stands a figure with a pair of eyes, or at least with a field-glass, which forms, again and again, for observation, a unique instrument, insuring to the person making use of it an impression distinct from every other. He and his neighbours are watching the same show, but one seeing more where the other sees less, one seeing black where the other sees white, one seeing big where the other sees small, one seeing coarse where the other sees fine.[7]

James explains further that

> The spreading field, *the human scene,* is the "*choice of subject*"; *the pierced aperture,* either broad or balconied or slit-like or low browed, is the "literary form"; but they are, singly or together, as nothing without the posted presence of the watcher—without, in other words, the consciousness of the artist. Tell me what the artist is, and I will tell you of what he has *been* conscious.[8]

Nonfictional authors usually intrude on tne subject they have chosen to expose, and the reader is, at times, awkwardly aware of "the posted presence of the watcher." Contrary to Lytton Strachey's insistence, "*Je n'impose rien; je ne propose rien. J'expose*"[9] (I impose

[7]Henry James, "The House of Fiction," in *The Theory of the Novel*, ed. Philip Stevick (New York: The Free Press, 1967), p. 58.
[8]*Ibid.* (italics added).
[9]Lytton Strachey, *Eminent Victorians* (New York: Harbrace Paperbound Library), p. xvi.

nothing; I propose nothing: I expose), he and many other nonfictional writers both impose and propose points of view. Consider Strachey's "unbiased" and "unimposing" description of the correspondence between Voltaire and Madame du Deffand:

> Her letters to Voltaire are enchanting; his replies are no less so; and it is much to be regretted that the whole correspondence has never been collected together in chronological order, and published as a separate book. The slim volume would be, of its kind, quite perfect. There was no love lost between the two old friends; they could not understand each other; Voltaire, alone of his generation, had thrown himself into the very vanguard of thought; to Madame du Deffand progress has no meaning, and thought itself was hardly more than an unpleasant necessity. She distrusted him profoundly, and he returned the compliment. Yet neither could do without the other. . . . In spite of all their differences, they admired each other genuinely, and they were held together by the habit of a long familiarity. The result was a marvelous display of epistolary art. . . . Sometimes one just catches the glimpse of a claw beneath the soft pad, a grimace under the smile of elegance; and one remembers with a shock that, after all, one is reading the correspondence of a monkey and a cat.[10]

Evidence of Strachey's idiosyncratic interaction with his subject and his authorial intrusion abounds in this short excerpt from his biographical essay on Madame du Deffand. It is Strachey's thoughts, feelings, and perceptions, his "generalizations about [the] . . . manners and morals"[11] of Voltaire and Madame du Deffand that grasp and hold a reader's attention. It is unlikely that

Madame du Deffand saw herself as a cat or that Voltaire saw himself as a monkey. It is equally unlikely that the lady would either have seen or described herself as opposed to progress or thought. Voltaire, the great philosopher of the eighteenth century, would doubtless have found it inconceivable that he was incapable, as Strachey asserts, of understanding Madame du Deffand.

We emphasize the problem of perspective in nonfictional writing as a reminder that what the nonfictional writer exposes, as Strachey would have us believe, and what the director of a group performance hopes to expose, is always tempered by the individual vision of either the writer, the director, or both. The moment when the individual talent asserts itself is the exact moment when a particular perspective begins to emerge. The director's signature is immediately apparent in, first, the choice of materials, and second, the overall perspective those materials reflect. If, for example, you choose to compile a group performance script based on the trial of Sacco and Vanzetti, you might include in the script (1) Lila Heston's dramatization of the trial,[12] (2) William Carlos Williams's poem, "Impromptu the Suckers," (3) Vanzetti's letter to Sacco's son written on the eve of his execution proclaiming his and Sacco's innocence, (4) liberal newspaper accounts of the seven-year imprisonment of Sacco and Vanzetti pending their execution, and (5) Biblical and mythological excerpts from stories about the scapegoat (Vanzetti's last words were, "I wish to forgive some people for what they are now doing to me"). Your decision to select and arrange these particular materials reflects a point of view that might be summarized in one or several of the following ways: "I believe that Sacco and Vanzetti were objects of fear and preju-

[10]Lytton Strachey, *Biographical Essays* (New York: Harcourt Brace Jovanovich), pp. 178–79.

[11]The phrase is Norman Friedman's. See Norman Friedman, "Point of View in Fiction: The Development of a Critical Concept," in *The Theory of The Novel*, ed. Philip Stevick (New York: The Free Press, 1967), p. 121.

[12]Lila Heston, ed., "The Trial of Sacco and Vanzetti," in *Man in the Dramatic Mode*, Book 6 (Evanston, Ill.: McDougal, Littell & Co., 1970), pp. 106–123.

dice and that they were not permitted a fair and just hearing in the United States courts of law"; "I oppose oppression in any form"; "I endorse individual freedom"; "I defend the right of every person to voice his or her views" (Sacco and Vanzetti were avowed anarchists); or "I refuse to support any institution that eschews justice." The perspective from which you, as a director, compile or devise a script of nonfictional literature will, of course, be clearly stated in your production concept.

Suggested Assignments

I. Read *Inherit the Wind,* a play by Jerome Lawrence and Robert E. Lee based on the famous Scopes trial of 1925. At the end of the play with whom do your sympathies lie: the defense attorney or the prosecuting attorney? Judging from your reactions to the two characters, write a short paper describing what you believe the playwrights' perspective to be.

II. Read H. L. Mencken's essay "In Memoriam: W. J. B." (William Jennings Bryan) in *Prejudices,* 5th Series (1926) and Vachel Lindsay's poem "Bryan, Bryan, Bryan: The Campaign of 1896, as Viewed at the Time by a 16-Year-Old" (1919). Which of these portraits of Bryan corroborates that of Lawrence and Lee in *Inherit the Wind?* Were you to devise (from documents) your own script based on the Scopes trial, would you use either or both of these descriptions of Bryan? What point of view regarding evolution would your choices betray?

Emphasis

We have so far discussed two characteristics of group performance and nonfictional literature that are in some ways analogous: composition (or procedure) and perspective. A third interrelated characteristic is emphasis. You have seen that for both the nonfictional writer and the director of group performance the procedure of selecting, abridging, and arranging is shaped by a particular perspective. Out of this procedure, and the implied perspective, emerges an emphasis.

Typically, group performance of literature features some aspect of the text and simultaneously preserves the text's integrity. In featuring one or more dimensions of the literature, you are necessarily emphasizing aspects of the text. Indeed, *emphasis* is a special characteristic of the art of group performance.

The production concept that prefaces each script in this text states the emphasis or organizing principle around which the script is adapted and executed. Note that the episodes in "No Sense of Decency," as well as their arrangement in the script, reveal Joe McCarthy as a demagogue and the federal government as a pawn in a cleverly played game. These and not other materials were intentionally selected, condensed, and arranged in order to *feature* the clash of ideologies and the repressive atmosphere that characterized the McCarthy era.

Suggested Assignments

I. Examine *Mystery and Manners* (a collection of lectures and essays by Flannery O'Connor) for a program that would also include some of O'Connor's fiction. Read *Mystery and Manners* before you study her stories and novels.

II. Discuss with another class member who is working on the same project at least five characteristics of O'Connor that you gleaned from the collection of essays. Discuss also your perceptions of her "voice."

III. Read "In Search of Flannery O'Connor" and "What Makes Her 'Different': Flannery O'Connor and Southern Literature" in *The World of Flannery O'Connor* by Josephine Hendin. Do these essays alter your original perceptions? How does this information affect your decisions in selecting and adapting materials from *Mystery and Manners?* Does it alter your perceptions of the way O'Connor *sounds?* Are you aware of her humor? Do you have a fuller understanding of her relationship to her art? What do you hope to feature in your script?

Selected Bibliography

ANGELOU, MAYA. *I Know Why the Caged Bird Sings.* New York: Random House, 1970.

BIANCHI, MARTHA DICKINSON. *The Life and Letters of Emily Dickinson.* New York: Houghton Mifflin, 1924.

BRYAN, W. F. and R. S. CRANE, eds. *The English Familiar Essay,* Boston: Ginn and Co., 1916.

COLLINGWOOD, STUART DODGSON. *The Life and Letters of Lewis Carroll.* Detroit: Gale Research Co., Book Tower, 1967.

CUMMINGS, E. E. *Six Nonlectures.* Cambridge, Mass.: Harvard University Press, 1953.

FRANKFURTER, MARION DENMAN and GARDNER JACKSON, eds. *The Letters of Sacco and Vanzetti.* New York: The Viking Press, 1928.

GARNETT, DAVID, ed. *Carrington: Selected Letters and Extracts from Her Diaries.* New York: Ballantine Books, 1970.

LEWIS, OSCAR. *The Children of Sanchez: The Autobiography of a Mexican Family.* New York: Random House, 1961.

GOLDMAN, ERIC F. *The Crucial Decade and After.* New York: Alfred A. Knopf, Inc., 1956.

MAILER, NORMAN. *The Armies of the Night.* New York: The New American Library, Inc., 1968.

NABOKOV, VLADIMIR. *Speak, Memory: An Autobiography Revisited.* New York: Capricorn Books, 1970.

NIN, ANAIS. *The Diaries of Anaïs Nin,* ed. Stuhlmann. Vols. I–V. New York: Harcourt Brace Jovanovich, 1966, 67, 69, 71, 75.

O'CONNOR, FLANNERY. *Mystery and Manners.* New York: Farrar, Straus & Giroux, 1970.

ST. JOHN, CHRISTOPHER, ed. *Ellen Terry and Bernard Shaw: A Correspondence.* New York: G. P. Putnam's Sons, 1919.

WOOLF, LEONARD, ed. *A Writer's Diary: Being Extracts from the Diary of Virginia Woolf.* New York: Harcourt Brace Jovanovich, Inc., 1954.

chapter 8

Children's Literature
in Group Performance

The box office receipts of Metro-Goldwyn-Mayer and Twentieth-Century Fox attest to the popularity of such children's classics as *The Wizard of Oz, Snow White and the Seven Dwarfs,* and *Bambi.* The film industry's successes point to the conclusion that children's literature in performance provides a delightful and enriching experience for children. While adults derive a special pleasure from staged performances of children's literature, we are specifically concerned with the values this medium provides the child audience—the reasons and the ways a group performance of literature increases the child's personal enjoyment, stimulates vicarious experience, and broadens perceptions.

Literature written for the young satisfies certain well-established and fundamental needs of children. Child psychologists and educators note that children express certain needs in greater or lesser degrees as they approach various stages of maturation. Recognizing and satisfying these needs plays an important role in the child's intellectual and emotional growth: children require peer acceptance, parental and filial love,

physical sustenance, and intellectual stimulation. They also seek and embrace aesthetic fulfillment. While educators have long recognized the importance of literature and dramatic productions (and art, cinema, music, dance) in serving adult aesthetic needs, they have sometimes ignored this significant dimension of child development. Pleasurable literary experiences can stimulate children's artistic appreciation.

LITERATURE AS EXPERIENCE
FOR CHILDREN

Not accidentally, books written for children are dominated by personified playing-cards, talking rabbits, professorial spiders, live jacks-in-the-box, market-going pigs, and extra-terrestial beings. The authors who have provided milestones in children's literature—*Aesop's Fables, Robinson Crusoe, Songs of Innocence, A Visit from St. Nicholas, A Wonder-Book for Girls and Boys, Alice's Adventures in Wonderland, Treasure Island, Nights with Uncle Remus, The Tale of Peter Rabbit* and *A Child's Garden of Verses*—did so by recalling the child in themselves and by inventing bizarre but believable worlds that appealed to children's imaginations. Agnes Repplier, in her Introduction to *An Anthology of Modern Verse,* describes literature's special appeal to children:

> In the matter of poetry, a child's imagination outstrips his understanding; his emotions carry him far beyond the narrow reach of his intelligence. He has but one lesson to learn—the lesson of enjoyment.[1]

Repplier implies that the three primary links between children and literature are: (1) the child's imagination, (2) an emotional instead of a predominately intellectual response, and (3) a response of pleasure, or enjoyment. As was pointed out, writers of children's literature write from the child's point of view—they recall the child in themselves. Literature that (1) piques the child's imagination, (2) elicits an empathic response, (3) produces pleasure, and (4) evokes youthful identification will probably actively engage children with the world of the text.

Many gifted writers address both child and adult audiences, e.g., Emily Dickinson, T.S. Eliot, Robert Frost, Randall Jarrell, Theodore Roethke, May Swenson. The essential components of a poem, play, short story, or novel remain the same whether written for adults or children: a limerick usually contains five lines of which the first, second, and fifth are trimeter and the third and fourth dimeter, with an *aabba* rhyming pattern, as in "The Music Master":

> *"My Sons," said a Glurk slurping soup.*
> *"We would make a fine musical group.*
> *Put your spoon to your lip*

> *And slurp when you sip,*
> *But don't spill. Like this, children—oop!"*[2]

Ciardi's limerick recreates a world readily identifiable to young children: who but a child really appreciates a "Glurk," and knows the full pleasure of the sound and feel of his own slurp? Who enjoys more than the child the unexpected opportunity to witness playful, childish behavior in an adult? Regardless of how skillfully crafted a piece of literature is, if it reflects either the adult's point of view or the point of view of the child filtered through that of the adult (e.g., Phyllis McGinley's "Thirteen" or William Stafford's "Fifteen"), then the literature is probably not written *for* children.

Just as writers recognize and address the needs, expectations, interests, and pleasures of children, directors of children's literature in group performance must explore the text's certainties, probabilities, and possibilities (review Chapter 2 for a full discussion of these concepts) that will, when actualized, further heighten the selection's value to children. Ciardi, for example, asks his audience to envision a "Glurk" demonstrating to a group of children the art of slurping soup. The scene, essentially ordinary, can become a delightful "happening" for youngsters. Consider staging the poem with a fully costumed (obviously absurd) "Glurk," a quartet (or sextet or octet) of children—the "Sons"—and a number of spoons. How much more pleasurable for the young audience to literally see and hear—and probably join—this demonstration than to merely read it silently. The sounds and rhythms, the Glurk's absurd appearance and gestures, and the sudden identification with the children in the poem are almost certain to appeal to the child audience.

[1]Agnes Repplier, "Introduction," in *An Anthology of Modern Verse*, A. Methuen, ed. (Toronto: Methuen Publishers, 1921), p. xiii.

[2]John Ciardi, "The Music Master," *Someone Could Win a Polar Bear* (Philadelphia: J. B. Lippincott, Co.), 1970.

Suggested Assignments

I. Randall Jarrell's *The Bat Poet* addresses a child audience. After examining the book, note the ways it (a) appeals to the child's imagination, (b) elicits an empathic response, and (c) provides pleasurable experience.

II. Examine the ways in which Jarrell writes from the child's point of view?

A child's introduction and developing relationship with literature is a rewarding experience. A necessary and initial step in making literature rewarding is, of course, the instructor's concern for the needs and expectations of children and a familiarity with the literature they like. Let us examine a segment of Randall Jarrell's "A Sick Child," a poem written for children, to explore some of the ways it might engage or involve children in the world of the poem. First, realizing that children are essentially self-centered and innocently covetous, we may say that the youthful impulse expressed in the poem is to insist:

I want . . . I want a ship from some near star
To land in the yard, and beings to come out
And think to me: "So this is where you are!

Come!" . . .

These lines illustrate particularly appealing elements of literature written for children:

1. a dramatic speaker embodying characteristics common to many children.
2. a world in which the known and unknown, ordinary and extraordinary, fantastic and mundane converge.
3. an event or action containing a beginning, a middle, and an end and revealing a chorus of "voices."
4. a sense of immediacy and intimacy produced by dialogue.
5. unexpected and pleasurable action.
6. sensory dimensions combined in patterned, repeated phrases, images, and sounds.

The Dramatic Speaker

The poem's dramatic speaker is a young boy who is either feigning illness or actually ill. He entertains himself by imagining a terse, well-ordered little drama in which he is the central character. We can easily establish the centrality of his character by noting the frequency of his self-references: "I," "me," and "you" (he is also the "you" addressed in these lines). The frequent self-references and the repeated statement of his desire ("I want . . . I want") illustrate the typical egocentricity of young children. The object of his wishes, a spaceship, is typical of children's desires.

Imaginative Qualities

Elements of the *unknown* (the ship is from a star), the *mysterious* ("beings" address him), and the *fantastic* (the beings "think" to him) alter and extend the child's concept of self. His ordinary, secure world merges with the *extraordinary* environment of his imagination. The familiarity of the young speaker's yard takes on new dimensions of excitement when the (space) ship lands there bringing with it the wonder of life in outer space. The mystery attached to the "beings" is transferred to and, hence, transforms the speaker as they establish *him* as the object of *their* search. He changes from an ordinary child to a very special one whose uniqueness derives from knowing the unknown, from being desired by the most desirable ("So this is where you are!/ Come!"). That these beings think rather than speak to him contributes further to their specialness. The dialogue is also unusual since it is transmitted through telepathy. The speaker, in this portion of the poem, articulates a vision many children identify with and respond to: a vision that transforms the impossible world into the possible with the speaker in the center (see "Oh Where Oh Where Is There" and "Alice in Wonderland").

Formal and Sensory Qualities

Unity, cohesion, and sound repetitions are additional dimensions of this poem and other literary works that provide special pleasures for children. For example, the repetition of "want" in the first line of the segment, of "come" in the second and fourth lines, and the near and full rhyme of "yard/are/star," and "some/come" appeal to the auditory sense of children. Unity and cohesion characterize the stanza cited from "A Sick Child": a single thought appears (the statement of the child's desire signaled by "I want . . . I want); the thought develops; and the wish is fulfilled when the beings beckon the speaker to "Come!" Like most short stories, novels, plays, and scenes within plays, this short segment of the poem contains a beginning, middle, and end in which all parts are logically related to convey a single episode. The child seeks and responds to this kind of order.

Certain kinds of imagery, too, provide a special enjoyment because they invite children to indulge their senses: to taste and see, to hear, to touch, and to smell. The sensory dimension of literature largely accounts for its magnetic attraction to children when presented in group performance. A fuller treatment of this performative dimension of literature appears later in the chapter.

Suggested Assignment

Now that you've observed various dimensions of one segment of Jarrell's "A Sick Child," examine the entire poem. After studying the poem, consider the following elements of the dramatic situation and the speaker's drama:

1. the nature of the speaker (physical and attitudinal features that identify him).
2. his act (what activity he performs or thought he conveys).
3. his manner of expression (how he uses language to convey his thoughts).
4. where the action takes place (his mind, a specific physical locale, a designated time).
5. why he performs this particular act (his purpose).
6. who hears him (only himself or others; if others, are they identified and do they help shape the drama?).

A Sick Child
Randall Jarrell

The postman comes when I am still in bed.
"Postman, what do you have for me today?"
I say to him. (But really I'm in bed.)
Then he says—what shall I have him say?

"This letter says that you are president
Of—this word here; it's a republic."
Tell them I can't answer right away,
"It's your duty." No, I'd rather just be sick.

Then he tells me there are letters saying
*   everything*
That I can think of that I want for them
*   to say.*
I say, "Well, thank you very much. Goodbye."
He is ashamed, and turns and walks away.

If I can think of it, it isn't what I want.
I want . . . I want a ship from some near star
To land in the yard, and beings to come out
And think to me: "So this is where you are!

Come." Except that they won't do,
I thought of them . . . And yet somewhere
*   there must be*
Something that's different from everything.
All that I've never thought of—think of me![3]

While it is imperative to recognize literary works that appeal to children, it is equally important to present them in ways that engage the child's interest. In the following discussion we will suggest possibilities for the group performance of children's literature, noting particularly the special demands of a child audience.

CHILDREN'S LITERATURE IN GROUP PERFORMANCE

Many children's literature textbooks recommend choral reading, story-telling, reading aloud and dramatizations of literary selections as methods for teaching literature in the elementary and middle grades. Some of these textbooks offer instructions on "How to Read Poetry Aloud," and refer to very young children as "the read-aloud audience." We agree with these authors and suggest further that the children can perhaps enjoy an even fuller participation in literature through group performance, a medium that actualizes the oral, aural, visual, and kinesthetic dimensions of the literary experience.

You may recall the analogy between music and literature we made in our introductory chapter. Just as bars and notes constitute the symbols for the ultimate actualization of a musical composition, the poem, novel, or short story also often serves as the written construct for the actualized literary text. Of course, musical scores usually do not require dialogue or staging, but they are intended for translation through a medium more expressive than the inner ear, or the silent voice. Likewise, much literature, especially that written for children, should be both seen and heard. The vital and differentiating element in children's literature is the "to whom" dimension—the audience. *What* writers choose as subject matter and theme, as well as *how* they choose to present them, are necessarily affected by the audience *for whom* they write. Similarly, directors of group performances of children's literature will be concerned with the special demands of the child audience.

The Child Audience

The Child as Child.   From Aesop to William J. Smith (see his *Typewriter Town,* a collection of illustrated poems), writers of literature for children have responded first to the child as child and not to the child as miniature adult. Their literature contains elements that appeal to children's interests, pique their imagination, and encourage identification. Children become absorbed in productions designed and executed to heighten interests, imaginations, and identification through the following staging principles: (1) *Credibility*—the director should design and render all aspects of the production credible *within the context* of the story (children are quick to detect deception). (2) *Action*—"Show it, don't tell it."[4] (3) *Characters*—emphasize the qualities of one-dimensional, stereotyped, or caricatured (flat) characters. (4) *Rhythm*—emphasize patterns of rhythm which alternately "seize and relax" attention. Any repeated element (a color, phrase, prop, or sound) becomes a rhythmic quality of the production. (5) *Conflict*—emphasize conflict, contrast, and surprise whether in character, plot, scene. (6) *Exaggeration*—exaggerate voice quality, facial expressions, and physical gestures. (7) *Spectacle*—use lighting, costumes, make-up, and music to highlight important characters, scenes, movements, and progressions that "connect" the beginning, middle, and end of the story.

Staging Principles for a Child Audience

Credibility.   Children are inveterate believers—their belief begins with themselves,

[4]See Charlotte Chorpenning's discussion of staging principles for children's literature in her *Twenty-One Years with Children's Theatre* (Anchorage, Ky.: The Children's Theatre Press, 1954).

extends to their observed world, and includes all that is convincingly demonstrated to them. Literature written and performed for children must demonstrate real or imagined experiences. The author who is both sufficiently inventive and masterfully convincing writes from a perspective described by James E. Higgins in *Beyond Words: Mystical Fancy in Children's Literature:*

> Inventiveness, remember, is not to be judged by how *far out* the imagination of the writer may take his readers, but rather by the degree to which he can make the readers believe in the world he has created.[5]

Children's willingness to believe accounts in part for their eager acceptance of and participation in group performance of literature. This belief factor in the psychology of children is rooted, Piaget tells us, in their perceptions of reality:

> ... childish assumptions deal with a reality which is far more fluctuating than ours, one which is perpetually shifting its level from the plane of observation to that of play, and vice versa. In this respect, reality is for the child both more arbitrary and better regulated than for us. It is more arbitrary, because nothing is impossible, and nothing obeys causal laws. But whatever may happen, it can always be accounted for, for behind the most fantastic events which he believes in, the child will always discover motives which are sufficient to justify them. . .[6]

To the child, it is perfectly agreeable for Rose's *Chair* to narrate the young girl's adventures en route to the mountain (see "Oh Where Oh Where Is There") because, for the child, nothing is necessarily impos-

sible. If, however, the director of the production decided midway through the story to make the chair an inanimate prop, instead of the initially established personified storyteller, the story would probably lose its credibility for the child audience. Also believable to the child is that the Mole, Badger, and Rat (*The Wind in The Willows*) function in a seemingly human society and behave like human beings; it is also quite credible for Alice to consort with a rabbit, a caterpillar, and a mouse. These characters invite children to shift "from the plane of observation to that of play," and they readily comply.

The plane of play, to which children naturally gravitate according to Piaget, is vividly and imaginatively realized in group performance of literature. Consider, for example, the various imaginative functions the circle of balloons serves in the staging of "Oh Where Oh Where Is There": (1) they represent first the circular design of the world; (2) they create the illusion of a clump of bushes; (3) they appear as clusters of bushes around the mountain; and (4) they define, graphically, the world below Rose as she perches atop her chair on the mountain. Consider, too, the playful and joyous effect the director of *Alice* produced with her stylized use of animated playing cards. The element of children's credulity challenges the director's ability to arouse the child's imagination.

Action. Some of the characteristics of literature that appeal to the child's imagination are adventure, exaggeration, fantasy, and absurdity. These are elements that adapt well to showing rather than telling the events in children's literature. The timeless appeal of *Alice's Adventures in Wonderland,* for example, rests in part on Lewis Carroll's deft presentation of one bold, absurd, fantastic encounter after another. An imaginative production of this story would attempt to match Carroll's presentation in

[5] James E. Higgins, *Beyond Words: Magical Fancy in Children's Literature* (New York: Teachers College Press, Columbia University, 1970), p. 28.

[6] Jean Piaget, *The Language and Thought of the Child,* trans. Marjorie Gabain (New York: World Publishing Co., 1973), p. 216.

performance (see *Alice in Wonderland,* Unit III), showing the characters and adventures as they unfold. Each adventure in the book is further marked by surprise and absurdity. No one is more amazed than Alice at her alternate Brobdingnagian and Lilliputian stature. Nothing is more absurd and enticing to either Alice or her readers than a talking rabbit who wears a waistcoat and ponders the time of day. Carroll's narrator reports that:

(When she thought it over afterwards it occurred to her that she ought to have wondered at this, but at the time it all seemed quite natural.) But, when the Rabbit actually *took a watch out of its waistcoat pocket,* and looked at it, and then hurried on, Alice started to her feet, for it flashed across her mind that she had never before seen a rabbit with either a waistcoat pocket or a watch to take out of it, and, burning with curiosity she ran across the field after it. . . .

In performance, children see the physical activities of Alice and the rabbit, as well as Alice's astonishment and burning curiosity. Note the number of action phrases in this short passage that, when translated into movement, gesture, or expression, command the child's attention: language connoting *movement*—"took a watch out," "hurried on," "started to her feet," "ran across the field"; language connoting *gesture*—"look at it" (the watch); and language connoting *expression*—"flashed across her mind," "burning with curiosity."

The adventure and absurdity in *Alice in Wonderland* suggest great latitude for performance. At one point Alice grows to nine feet in height, sheds "gallons" of tears, and encounters a mushroom as large as she (after she has dwindled considerably). Alice's story is a fantasy, a magical tale of her imaginative world ("the hot day made her feel very sleepy and stupid"). Children delight

in seeing this magical tale enacted on stage: the giant mushroom, the pipe-smoking caterpillar, the personified playing-cards, and the eccentric rabbit dashing to and fro.

Characters. A distinctive characteristic of the child audience is its ready acceptance of stereotyped, caricatured, or otherwise "flat" characters. Flat characters are wholly and comfortably predictable (Cinderella, Hansel and Gretel, Heidi, the Wicked Witch of the West, all of the Dwarfs, the Tooth Fairy, and Santa Claus). While some of these characters are not necessarily good, they are easily recognizable and memorable —the dimensions of characterization accessible to children. Additionally, they embody an inherent but ill-defined source of humor in many cases. Indeed, E. M. Forster reminds us that "Flat characters were called 'humorous' in the seventeenth century. . . .,"[7] and further explains that

They are constructed round a single idea or quality. . . . The really flat character can be expressed in one sentence. . . .

One great advantage of flat characters is that they are easily recognized whenever they come in—recognized by the reader's emotional eye, not by the visual eye, which merely notes the recurrence of a proper name. . . .

A second advantage is that they are easily remembered by the reader afterwards. They remain in his mind as unalterable for the reason that they were not changed by circumstances; they moved through circumstances. . . .[8]

In the same essay Forster suggests that we may not remember the actions of flat characters or the greater dilemmas they face; what we are likely to remember is the "figure" and the "formula that surrounds"

[7] E. M. Forster, "Flat and Round Characters," *The Theory of the Novel,* ed. Philip Stevick (New York: The Free Press, 1967), p. 224.
[8] *Ibid.,* pp. 224–26.

them.[9] Thus, Cinderella, the sooty-faced urchin turned princess, and her demeaning stepmother are both figures that indelibly imprint themselves on our memory and so do the formulae that direct their behaviors: children *know* that beneath all that soot lie the qualities of a princess (beauty, integrity, honesty, cleanliness, charity), that Cinderella will encounter obstacles (their exact nature is insignificant) en route to her throne, and that she will ultimately acquire her throne. The pattern is well established, and children expect to see it fulfilled. Similarly, Rose ("Oh Where Oh Where Is There"), the adolescent in search of her identity, is a flat character who (1) can be summed up in a single phrase, (2) is recognizable and memorable, (3) is predictable, and (4) adheres to a familiar formula—she embarks on and completes a journey.

Flat characters are not necessarily shallow nor do they lack human dignity or depth of insight; rather, they are singularly directed and tenaciously pursue the singular direction of their vision. Children, while unable to digest the complexities inherent in "round" characters, accept and embrace fully drawn flat characters.

Rhythm. Children derive a particular kind of pleasure from the flow or movement of a piece of literature—its rhythm. Traditionally, rhythm has been equated with meter or the regular recurrence of stresses in a line of poetry, as in the nonsense verse, "Hickory, dickory, dock/The mouse ran up the clock." Many contemporary scholars and literary critics define rhythm more broadly as "variations upon a pattern of expectation."[10] This definition of rhythm would include any recognizable movement precipitated by the *regular interruption* of a *pattern of properties* in literature. Therefore,

any element that both appears systematically and is systematically interrupted can be described as a "rhythmic" quality. Whether or not a poem's rhythm arises from its meter or from the various other identifiable and regular patterns, we are concerned here primarily with its effect on a child audience. Although Paul Fussell equates meter with rhythm in the following description, his account clarifies some of the physical effects:

> The impulse toward metrical organization seems to be a part of the larger human impulses toward order: meter is what results when the rhythmical movements of colloquial speech are heightened, organized, and regulated so that pattern emerges from the relatively phonetic haphazard of ordinary utterance.... Most theorists agree that poetic meter, even when most primitive, produces a pleasant effect.... The pleasure universally resulting from foot-tapping and musical time-beating seems to suggest that the pleasures of meter are definitely physical and that they are as intimately connected with the rhythmic quality of man's total experience as are the similar alternating and recurring phenomena of breathing, walking, and love-making.... Children and the unsophisticated receive from meter primarily physical pleasure which manifests itself in foot- or finger-tapping, head-nodding, and the like....[11]

Charlotte S. Huck and Doris Young Kuhn agree that young children seem to have an innate appreciation for rhythm:

> The young child is naturally rhythmical. He beats on the tray of his high-chair, kicks his foot against the table, and chants his vocabulary of one or two words in a sing-song fashion. He delights in the rhythm of "Pat-a-cake, pat-a-cake, baker's man," or "Ride a

[9]*Ibid.*, p. 226.

[10]Harvey Gross, *Sound and Form in Modern Poetry* (Ann Arbor: University of Michigan Press, 1968), p. 14.

[11]Paul Fussell, "Meter," *Princeton Encyclopedia of Poetry and Poetics*, ed. Alex Preminger, enlarged ed. (Princeton, N.J.: Princeton University Press, 1974), p. 497.

cock-horse to Banbury Cross" before he understands the meaning of the words. . . .[12]

The child audience responds most enthusiastically and spontaneously when a group performance magnifies multiple rhythmic patterns through a chorus of voices, producing a "dance" of movement. Indeed, Charlotte Chorpenning, long-time director of the Chicago Goodman Theatre for Children, insists that "patterns of rhythm unify the play and the [child] audience."[13]

Lewis Carroll's young friend Secunda begged for "nonsense" in his story of Alice's adventures underground. Pure musical nonsense is what Carroll gave her in the form of "The Lobster Quadrille," "Father William," "How Doth the Little Crocodile" and, of course, the famous "Jabberwocky," to which Alice responded with little understanding but with great pleasure. Nonsense verse provides rhythmic "experience"—visual, auditory, and kinesthetic—for the child audience. Furthermore, the recurrence of these verses, spaced as they are throughout the story, serves as one source of rhythm that unifies both the story and the audience. The beat and rhyme of

"You are old, Father William" the young man said,
and your hair has become very white:
And yet you incessantly stand on your head—
Do you think, at your age, it is right?

appeals to children because they are measured, regular, and steady, evoking the rhythms of their daily lives. Though this verse is rhymed, the metrical composition

alone (four beats in the first and third lines and three beats in the second and fourth lines) would compel the child to move with the poem. It is the "repeat of a beat, somewhere/ an inner chime that makes you want to/ tap your feet or swerve in a curse;/ a lilt, a leap, a lightning-split"[14] that creates a joyful emotional response in children; and the orchestration of rhythms in a group performance magnifies the response.

Conflict and Contrast. Literature to which children respond joyously tries to elicit their participation to establish a communion between child and literature. A child audience, engaged by a literary selection in group performance, becomes the selection's fulfillment. Children who enjoy a group performance of Alice's story are not merely observers of her exploits, but rather her companions. They, too, *grow* and *diminish* in size, suffer recriminations when Alice alludes to the cat in front of the mice, and *fear* with her the Queen's wrathful sword. They, like Alice, do not question the White Rabbit's destination (his whereabouts are never explained) nor stop to wonder why the Red Queen runs incessantly "to keep in the same place" or the Cheshire Cat *vanishes* but his grin remains behind, for they are actively involved in the situational conflicts and contrasting personalities.

No two characters (except the card *deck*), are exactly alike in mode of dress or manner of speech and behavior. Children, curious and imaginative, are intolerant of too much sameness and applaud and appreciate variety and contrast. It seems that children, particularly, respond intuitively to the metaphorical nature of all things. How unlike a "normal" twelve-year-old girl Alice appears because she consorts with animals and playing cards; yet, how similar to a "nor-

[12]Charlotte S. Huck and Doris Young Kuhn, *Children's Literature in the Elementary School,* 2nd ed. (New York: Holt, Rinehart, & Winston, Inc., 1968), pp. 389–90.

[13]Chorpenning, *op. cit.,* p. 37.

[14]Eve Merriam, "Inside a Poem," *There Is No Rhyme for Silver,* illustrated by Joseph Schindelman (New York: Atheneum, 1962).

mal" twelve-year-old girl she seems just because she is contrasted with these creatures.

Alice spends most of her time alternately offending and trying to placate the fantasy world inhabitants. She seems never to be out of trouble and exists in a perpetual state of conflict, constantly anticipating the next complication. A performance promises to catch the audience's attention when at the outset they are confronted with Alice's energy in conflict with her boredom and the White Rabbit's distress at being late.

Exaggeration. Enlarging, magnifying, or amplifying voice quality, cadences, facial expressions and movement are essential to the group performance of children's literature, according to Charlotte Chorpenning.[15] Without distorting a text through performance, which exaggeration implies, a vocal, verbal or physical translation of a text does amplify it. The human body is, after all, a more sophisticated "magnifying" instrument than a sheet of paper. Lewis Carroll, aware of the power of performance to engage children, first performed the original version of *Alice in Wonderland* for three young friends of his on a summer outing in 1862. As he tired of telling his story to them, insisting "The rest next time," they persistently demanded "It is next time!" Two years later Carroll presented them with the first manuscript version of Alice's adventures as a Christmas gift. Carroll, perhaps fearing that the story might lose some of its vitality in print, supplied illustrations to accompany the text. That *Alice in Wonderland* was first spoken and subsequently illustrated may account for a large part of its success when it is enacted. Carroll's three young friends—Prima, Secunda, and Tertia—might well have begged for encores of Alice's story because he supplied the subtleties of inflection, pause, and tonal change as he related her adventures. Remember Alice's boredom with her sister's book be-

cause "it had no pictures or conversations in it," and her insistent question, "what is the use of a book without pictures or conversations?" Group performance can recapture the vitality of images and dialogue that the printed words only partially represent—by exaggerating verbal and vocal qualities and cadences, facial expressions, and movement.

Spectacle. The element of spectacle is among the most effective dramatic elements in the group performance of children's literature for a child audience. Lighting effects, sound effects, costumes, make-up, interesting scenic designs—anything that contributes to the "high drama" of the occasion—receive enthusiastic approval from children. Recall the child's anticipation of the annual county fair or the "Shrine" circus featuring clowns, trapeze artists, performing animals, dare-devil events of every description, spook houses, grotesque fat ladies and deformed Siamese twins, elaborate magic acts, and the general panorama of deafening sounds and garish costumes. Garish and unpalatable to us, perhaps, but to children, a virtual wonderland of intrigue, excitement and imaginative identification. The element of spectacle heightens and extends a child's playful participation as it illuminates, reinforces, and promotes the production's continuity and unity.

Suggested Assignment

For a major class project read, write out a production concept, and adapt T. H. White's *Mistress Masham's Repose;* pay particular attention to the elements of conflict and action in the story; note the stock qualities of the governess, the vicar, and the little girl; and observe closely the text's exaggerations.

As you work on character development and staging that will appeal to a child audience, consider the following questions: (a) How will you indicate the difference in size of the orphaned girl and the colony of

---

[15]Chorpenning, *op. cit.*, p. 6.

Known Characteristics		Inferred Characteristics
Certainties:	Probabilities:	Possibilities:
1. the speaker is a child.	1. the speaker is a male child.	1. the speaker is between 7 and 10 years of age.
2. the scene exists in his imagination.	2. he addresses himself.	2. he is actually in bed and addresses another as well as himself.
3. he contrives the conversation; it does not literally occur between the speaker and the postman or the child and the beings.	3. he is not actually ill, but uses illness as an excuse for daydreaming.	3. he is actually ill, and this provides impetus for daydreaming.
4. he is self-involved, self-examining.	4. he is seeking an identity or self-concepts.	4. he discovers something about the inexplicable nature of the individual.

Lilliputians? (b) What physical and vocal characteristics will emphasize the vicar's unscrupulous nature? (c) How much spectacle is necessary for a convincing setting? (d) Will the protagonist (the little girl) begin to subtly assume some of the governess's qualities when she tries to control the Lilliputians? (e) What particular gestures, vocal tones, and speech rhythms are necessary to indicate the governess's callousness?

Invite a group of sixth and seventh graders from a local public school to your performance of *Mistress Masham's Repose.*

Analysis of "A Sick Child" for Group Performance

We have emphasized the importance of analysis as the initial step in developing a production concept and arriving at a text's certainties, probabilities, and possibilities. Reconsider the production possibilities of Jarrell's "A Sick Child" in light of some of its known and inferred characteristics. First, let us assume that we've decided to compile a script on "Children and Dreams," in which "A Sick Child" will be included. The script could also include such works as "My Conversation with The Sky":

> *Once I walked up to the Sky and said, "Hi, Sky. What are you doing?"*

> *"Oh, just hanging around. It is rather boring," said the Sky.*
> *"One thing, Sky. I thought you couldn't fly. Is it still true?"*
> *"Definitely. Why do you ask such stupid questions?"*
> *"Well, I hate to ask this next question, but if that is true, how do you stay up there?"*
> *The Sky didn't answer, because he was falling down to earth!*[16]

We would devote to each poem the kind of attention given earlier to "A Sick Child." In addition, we would examine the known and inferred characteristics of each poem following the schema above for "A Sick Child."

While these observations about the poem are cursory and incomplete, they supply a foundation for approaching production possibilities for the child audience. Many decisions for staging the poem will emerge from the tensions between the text's known and inferred characteristics. For example, this scene can be more or less literally or fully staged. However, since we are considering performance possibilities for the child audience, the poem will have to be

[16]Lisa Jill Braun, "My Conversation with the Sky," in *Wishes, Lies and Dreams: Teaching Children to Write Poetry* by Kenneth Koch (New York: Chelsea House Publishers, 1970), p. 129.

staged in ways that will engage *the child* and maintain the poem's integrity. There are at least three possibilities (and any combination thereof) for staging this poem that tap the child's imagination, and they arise from a combination of the poem's certainties, probabilities, and possibilities:

1. The entire poem is spoken by the child speaker as he observes the fantasy being "acted out" elsewhere on stage.
2. The poem is told from the child speaker's point of view, while a realistic or animated film depicts the encounters and conversations he relates.
3. The entire drama is literalized with the child speaker performing as narrator and the other "characters" taking over their lines as dictated by the text.

In each instance some or all of the following dimensions of the poem can be behaviorally translated in performance:

1. Ambiguities exist between the actual and "make-believe" world: twice, the speaker says that he is in bed, yet his conversation with the postman and the "beings" suggests other physical locations as well.
2. The speaker, *in some fashion,* hears and sees both the postman and the beings.
3. The speaker envisions himself as central to the world of the poem: "This letter says that you are president . . . ," and ". . . there are letters saying everything/ That I can think of that I want for them to say."
4. There is an *implied* "other" listener in addition to the postman and the beings: parentheticals, "(But really I'm in bed)"; dialogue tags, "I say to him"; and imperatives, "think of me," suggest the presence of another listener.

Clearly, the literal degree to which this poem (and many others) is performed depends upon the director's production concept.

Suggested Assignment

Return to "My Conversation with the Sky" and chart the poem's certainties, probabilities, and possibilities. As you arrive at these decisions, also note possible distortions of the poem.

In this poem, the "sky" is a character with a distinctive voice and personality. How will you, as a director, distinguish this character from the child speaker? Is it necessary to indicate—and if so, how?—that the sky "was falling down to earth"? Who else does the speaker address besides the sky? Himself? Another, more general, audience? These are questions you must answer before you can stage the poem.

The delight children take in their own fantasies is heightened by the validity literature gives them. Because, as Carl R. Rogers reminds us, "the young human being is intrinsically motivated to a high degree,"[17] literature frequently evokes and sustains curiosities that might otherwise rest in the interest of more practical concerns. Rogers insists that the young person

. . . is curious, eager to discover, eager to know, eager to solve problems. A sad part of most education is that by the time the child has spent a number of years in school this intrinsic motivation is pretty well dampened. Yet it is there and it is our task as facilitators of learning to tap that motivation, to discover what challenges are real for the young person, and to provide the opportunity for him to meet those challenges.[18]

The group performance of children's literature challenges and extends the child's imagination.

---

[17]Carl R. Rogers, *Freedom to Learn* (Columbus, Ohio: Charles E. Merrill Publishing Co., 1969), p. 131.

[18]*Ibid.*, p. 131.

Selected Bibliography

ALMY, MILLIE. *Ways of Studying Children.* New York: Teachers College, Columbia University Press, 1969.

ARBUTHNOT, MAY HILL and SHELTON L. ROOT, JR. *Time for Poetry,* 3rd ed., illustrated by Rainey Bennett and others. Glenview, Ill.: Scott, Foresman, 1971.

BREWTON, JOHN E. and SARA W., comps. *Index to Children's Poetry.* New York: H. W. Wilson, Co., 1942, 1954, 1965.

BROWN, HELEN A. and HARRY J. HELTMAN, eds. *Choral Readings for Fun and Recreation.* Philadelphia: Westminster, 1956.

CAMERON, ELEANOR. *The Green and Burning Tree: On the Writing and Enjoyment of Children's Books.* Boston: Little, Brown & Co., 1969.

CONRAD, EDNA and MARY VAN DYKE. *History on the Stage; Children Make Plays from Historical Novels.* New York: Van Nostrand Reinhold, Co., 1971.

COOK, ELIZABETH. *The Ordinary and the Fabulous: An Introduction to Myths, Legends, and Fairy Tales for Teachers and Storytellers.* New York: Cambridge University Press, 1969.

DUNNING, STEPHEN. *Teaching Literature to Adolescents: Poetry.* Glenview, Ill.: Scott, Foresman, 1966.

EASTMAN, MAX. *The Enjoyment of Poetry.* New York: Charles Scribner's Sons, 1951.

Library Association. *Chosen for Children: An Account of the Books Which Have Been Awarded the Library Association Carnegie Medal, 1936–1965,* rev. ed. London: The Library Assoc., 1967.

II

ESSAYS AND SCRIPTS
FOR
GROUP PERFORMANCE

An Evening with Reed Whittemore[1]

Compiled and Directed by Mary Francis HopKins

Louisiana State University

The relationship between poets and their poems has long fascinated theoretical critics, other literary scholars, and the general reader. Can we expect the poet in real life to be like the persona in the poem? What if the poet uses a mask, creates a character? Is it irrelevant, even misguided, to expect the poem to provide the key to the poet's personality? Whatever our stance on this issue, one conclusion is obvious: a study of the full works of a poet gives us a sense of the writer behind the poems. Authors simply cannot erase all traces of authorial intrusion. Whether they speak directly or through a character, we know something about them if only because of the information or experiences they choose to share and the voices they choose to create. When poets speak primarily in their own voices, however varied in mood and tone, we get a strong sense indeed of the poet behind the poems.

Reed Whittemore emerges as witty, urbane, charming, self-effacing—qualities that make him highly presentable to an audience. Furthermore, though his work is repeatedly and understandably characterized as humorous, "almost nobody accuses him of writing light verse."[2] This paradox is particularly interesting for the performer. Though Whittemore's poems are clever and fun, and, many of them at least, readily understandable to an audience on first reading, they betray an underlying seriousness worth attending to and a craftmanship worth our studied appreciation.

Whittemore poems are fun. Whether he is mocking himself or poking fun at figures from history and literature, his tone is light and ingratiating, his wit sharp and perceptive. Even the nonmocking poems such as "Still Life" and "On a Summer Sunday," make us smile with pleasure. His humor is always acceptable to us and, on the surface at least, not discomforting, aimed as it is at himself or long dead or fictional figures.

Our delight often lies in dramatic irony:

[1]The original title was "A Visit with Reed Whittemore," but Mr. Whittemore thought "visit" misleading, hence the more ambiguous "evening." For all three performances at L.S.U., "afternoon" would have been used.

[2]Michael Benedict, "Listening and Not Listening," *Poetry*, 112 (1968), 194.

Darwin will remain an underachiever. Though a degree of snobbery is doubtless present in this kind of pleasure (we are proud to be in on the joke), it is mitigated by the wit and warmth of the tone. Erudite references also account in part for Whittemore's firm reputation as a sophisticate. He draws from a seemingly boundless store of information about history, philosophy, current events, and literature. Sometimes his sources are obvious, but an imperceptive reader may miss the subtlety of an echo like the final line of "The Party."

It is not only the wealth of historical and literary allusion that marks Whittemore's sophistication. His stance toward himself, toward the ennervating ease of modern life, and the thoughtlessness of technology, is always slightly mocking, as if he is amused at the subject and amused at his own preoccupation with it.

We must not allow our delight in the sophisticated wit and charm of the poems to obscure their underlying seriousness. Especially in the later poems the poet's concern for the plight of modern man borders on pessimism. He cares about the human condition. The voice of fury is no less authentic because it is more suave than crude, modulated, not ranting.

Some of Whittemore's most satisfying poems deal with the process of writing. Still modest, still self-disclaiming even when speaking of his forte, he nevertheless raises interesting questions about the role and duty of artists and their role in society. One would be hard pressed to find a stronger affirmation of the poet's powers than the concluding lines of "Three Poems to Jackson." Poets do not create illusions, do not "play" at rebuilding the world; instead they reconstitute reality.

The few complaints one reads about Whittemore's poems are statements more of disappointment than censure. Delighted with his achievement, some reviewers want him to take greater risks, explore a wider range of emotions. Perhaps he should. Perhaps he will. As performers we need not be overly concerned with the challenges critics habitually urge upon the strong. Instead, we can rejoice at what he has done, is doing, and share our appreciation with an audience.

PRODUCTION CONCEPT

The aims in compiling the script were threefold: (1) to provide poems representative of Whittemore's entire works, (2) to give the audience a sense of Whittemore's personality—at least his "public," "accessible" personality—through the poems and his own prose comments, and (3) to illuminate the variety and structure of the poems through the use of multiple readers. Prose comments found in print and brief explanatory materials were juxtaposed with the poems.

PRODUCTION PLAN

Sources of the Script

The poems, obviously, came from the poet's published works. Fortunately for the compiler in search of prose comments, Whittemore conducted a series of lectures at Beloit College that were later published with some other essays as *From Zero to the Absolute,* a collection used in compiling this script.[3] Other prose comments came from three sources: a volume published by the NCTE for the 1966 convention, *Poems for Young Readers; Poet's Choice;* and *The Boy from Iowa.* For publication in the present volume, the poet rewrote some of the excerpts to bring them up to date.

I used the prose comments to create a dialogue with a commentator-host and to introduce groups of poems. Poems were

[3]For full information on this and other sources, see bibliography.

grouped thematically, and each section was introduced by the student performing as Whittemore or the host or both. The commentary merits explanation. Its banality contrasts almost painfully with the poet's style. Ideally the entire show would be the words of the poet, but sometimes appropriate comments were not to be found in his printed works, and the sections needed to be separated. As William Stafford once remarked, almost apologizing for his commentary between poems in performance, "I like to put a little insulation between the poems." The nonliterary narration may be justifiable only on that basis: its use as "insulation" helps to create the structure of the show.

Methods of Devising the Script

Arrangement and rearrangement, as suggested above, provided the method for devising almost the entire script. The poems could be grouped topically as follows:

I. Ridicule of historical and literary figures: "Paul Revere's Ride," "The Fall of the House of Usher," "The Strange Case in Baker Street," "Charles Darwin"

II. Family relationships: "The Girl in the Next Room," "The Chair," "Clamming," "The Bad Daddy"

III. The home: "The Farmhouse," "Still Life"

IV. Nature: "The Philadelphia Vireo," "Reason in the Woods," "Three Poems to Jackson"

V. Being a poet: "Today," "A Fascinating Poet's Diary," "The Departure," "Dear God"

VI. Final statement: "Lines Composed upon Reading an Announcement by Civil Defense Authorities Recommending that I Build a Bomb-shelter in My Backyard"

Although each segment contains some variety in tone and structure, the program as a whole moves from lighter to more serious matters. The opening poems are short, almost purely humorous, and designed for immediate response. The comparatively heavy "Poems to Jackson" and "Dear God" come late when the audience has already become engaged with the program and involved in the poetry.

The poet's comments were extracted, usually whole, from longer stretches of prose. Occasionally some deletion within segments was necessary, but most of the pieces were already short, tailored to fit. Finding appropriate prose passages and deciding where to use them was by far the most time-consuming step in the preparation.

Deletions occurred, as mentioned, in only a few of the prose extracts. "Dear God," long enough to unbalance a thirty-minute show, had to be cut, in the places indicated. But the omissions are similar in tone and thought to what stands, and what is left makes the point. More important, what is left gives a fair sense of the poem as a whole. All the other poems are intact.

ORIGINAL PRODUCTION

Casting and Rehearsals

I did not decide on the number of performers until the end of tryouts. The only certainties were the host-commentator, a Reed Whittemore (male), and three or more readers, preferably both men and women. It was only incidental that the six readers chosen to do the poems were three men and three women.

The commentator and Reed Whittemore were designated at the first meeting, but assignment of the poems came only after four or five rehearsals. Partly for the ensemble effect and partly to insure full comprehension of each poem, as a group we first studied each poem, and the cast alternated reading them. "The Bad Daddy" demanded a male reader. "Sherlock Holmes" invited a British accent, and "Dear God" called for the most experienced performer. Other considerations were merely a comparatively even distribution of poems among performers and avoidance of a patterned order.

No distinctive activities marked the rehearsals, but they were never dull. Each rehearsal period consisted of the usual activities: exercises, practice, discussion.

Stage Composition

The minimal staging used for this performance was dictated by the restrictions of the performing area and the demands of the script itself. In most of the poems the speaker's action is just to talk, usually to the world at large, and the dramatic situation is simple. The speakers are not highly characterized or emotional, and they do not seem particularly private or introspective. Both the commentator and Whittemore are likewise open and somewhat impersonal. Because neither the speakers nor their situations are highly defined, and

because the language and thought were of major importance, minimal staging seemed appropriate.

Fortunately the literature did not demand elaborate staging. The setting was wholly informal—a large room with no raised area, no lighting facilities, no curtains or screens to define a stage. Mainly to be seen, the six performers who read the poems sat on stools. To emphasize the fact that they were offering the work of the poet, and to conform with the largely unstructured dramatic situations in the poems, the performers used scripts, which rested on stands in front of the stools. The stools were grouped irregularly in a sort of curve. We avoided a pattern in order to establish informality. To set them off from the readers of the poems, Whittemore and the commentator sat in chairs that rested on small platforms for visibility. All the performers were seated when the audience came in, and they did not move during the performance.

Selected Bibliography

BENEDICT, MICHAEL. "Listening and Not Listening." *Poetry,* 112 (1968), 194–98.

JACOBSON, JOSEPHINE. "Political Poet." *The New Republic,* 171 (October 12, 1974), 26–27.

LIEBERMAN, LAURENCE. "The Expansional Poet: A Return to Personality." *Yale Review,* 57 (December 1967), 258–71.

MURPHY, ROSALIE. "Whittemore, (Edward) Reed." *Contemporary Poets of the English Language,* ed. Rosalie Murphy. New York: St. Martin's Press, 1970.

Poems for Young Readers. 56th Annual NCTE Convention, November 24–26, 1966.

Poet's Choice. Eds. Paul Engle and Joseph Langland. New York: Dell Publishing Co., Inc., 1966.

TURCO, LEWIS. "Of Laureates and Lovers." *Saturday Review,* 50 (October 14, 1967), 31–33, 99.

WHITTEMORE, REED. *An American Takes a Walk and Other Poems.* Minneapolis: University of Minnesota Press, 1956.

———. *The Boy from Iowa: Poems and Essays.* New York: Macmillan, 1962.

———. *Fifty Poems Fifty.* Minneapolis: University of Minnesota Press, 1970.

———. *From Zero to the Absolute.* New York: Crown Publishers, Inc., 1967.

————. *The Mother's Breast and the Father's House.* Boston: Houghton Mifflin Company, 1974.

————. *Poems New and Selected.* Minneapolis: University of Minnesota Press, 1967.

YOUNG, VERNON. "October Thoughts." *Hudson Review,* 23 (Winter 1970–71), 733–46.

AN EVENING WITH REED WHITTEMORE

Cast of Characters

W: Reed Whittemore
H: Host-Commentator
R1-R6: Six Readers

H: Good evening, everyone, and welcome to "An Evening with Reed Whittemore." Some of you may have met him already. His first book of poems came out in 1947, and as long ago as 1956, when his second book hit the market, James Dickey said of him, "He is as wittily cultural as they come, he has read more than any young man anybody knows, has been all kinds of places, yet shuffles along in an old pair of tennis shoes and khaki pants, with his hands in his pockets. . . ." This informality, this unwillingness to take himself too seriously, comes through to us more in his poems than in his wardrobe, and he is someone we enjoy being with. He teaches English at the University of Maryland.

W: I am an imposter (I have no graduate degree, none . . .)[1]

H: And is now the editor of the magazine, *The Carleton Miscellany*.

W: No, not any more. I was its editor for four years and before that I was the editor of another little magazine, called *Furioso*; but I'm clean now, having written a pamphlet about little magazines and at one time or another met half the little magazine editors in the country.[2]

[1]*From Zero to Absolute* by Reed Whittemore, © 1967 by Reed Whittemore. Used by permission of Crown Publishers, Inc. New York, p. 174.
[2]Written by the poet for this script. Hereafter designated *Poet*.

H: *Furioso* was published in his college days at Yale as a quarterly . . .[3]

W: In the first issue we announced that *Furioso* would be published every two weeks. In the second issue, which appeared nine months later, we announced that *Furioso* would be published every two or three months. In the next issue, which appeared four months later, we omitted mention of our frequency and merely stated that the next issue would be "printed somewhere in Europe, possibly in Italy." We were wrong about that too; the next issue was printed in the United States a year and a half later. Then the war came and disrupted our schedule.[4]

H: In 1964 he served as poetry consultant at the Library of Congress.

W: . . . there was the problem of what I was supposed to do. I had been told that I was to be consulted about the acquisition of books and manuscripts for the Library, but for weeks I couldn't even find the books and manuscripts the Library already had—thirteen million of them. And nobody brought me any books and manuscripts to be wise about. I was left dealing with a number of newspaper reporters, all of whom asked me right away what the Poetry Consultant *did*. My predecessor's reply to that—which became mine—was that the Poetry Consultant's job was to explain what the Poetry Consultant's job was.[5]

H: Some of his flippant attitude toward himself seems to extend to the literature he teaches as well as to historical figures.

R1: "Paul Revere's Ride".

> Is it one if by land, two if by sea?
> Or two if by land? Or what?
> What farms, what villages are those to be
> Roused from their midnight rut?
>
> Worry, worry, worry. There! A light?
> Of course not. But for an empty head
> I'd quit this profitless, cold post to plot
> The Revolution home in bed.
>
> Yet if the British from the Tower hunts me down.
> Then I mount swiftly; then I fiercely ride,
> Bearing fresh news of the infamous Crown
> To agitate the countryside.
>
> But if the British do,
> I wonder, is it one if by land, or two?

R2: "The Fall of the House of Usher"

> It was a big boxy wreck of a house
> Owned by a classmate of mine named Rod Usher,
> Who lived in the thing with his twin sister.
> He was a louse and she was a souse.

[3]*Poet.*
[4]*The Boy from Iowa,* p. 92.
[5]*Zero,* p. 153.

While I was visiting them one wet summer, she died.
We buried her,
Or rather we stuck her in a back room for a bit, meaning to bury her
When the graveyard dried.

But the weather got wetter.
One night we were both waked by a twister,
Plus a screeching and howling outside that turned out to be sister
Up and dying again, making it hard for Rod to forget her.

He didn't. He and she died in a heap, and I left quick,
Which was lucky since the house fell in right after
                Like a ton of brick.

R3: "The Strange Case in Baker Street"

My dear Watson, all
That a man may know and knowing clutch
Is thrust upon the turmoil of his will
By sight, smell, hearing, taste and touch.

The footprints in the garden, the plucked and trampled rose
Sooner than the law the outlaw find.
Murder will incessantly disclose
No body to the naked mind.

Yes, good is something inside going bad
Unless the senses take it out to catch
The butcher in the plaid
Suspenders, the butler with the poisoned match.

But bad is something outside making good
Until the senses do what senses should.

R5: *(Holmes puts on heavy spectacles, grasps firmly his magnifying glass, and crawls about the room rapidly on his hands and knees examining the fabric of the carpet.)*

R3: Elementary, Watson. Yet the case
Crowning all, the last great deception,
Now lies disclosed. And though I place
All conviction in my ravening perception,

This that I have found, this culprit for this act
I least envisaged. Even the Boston Murders,
The Anarchist at Greenwich, and the Tortured Fact
Pass now as felonies or drab disorders.

For the perfect crime is solved; the hidden logic
In every clever microscopic clue
Has led me as by miracle or magic
To the master criminal of all, dear Watson, you.

You'll facilitate formalities decidedly

By coming quietly.

R5: "Charles Darwin"

R6: You care for nothing but shooting, dogs, and rat-catching, and you will be a
disgrace to yourself and all your family.

> —Robert Waring Darwin, to his son Charles

R5: At Darwin's birth Goethe and Hegel,
Coleridge, Wordsworth and, for the rhyme, Schlegel
Were brightening Europe with synthesis, mystery,
Love and immaterial history.

In eighteen nine. Eighty years later,
With Darwin dead, and his apes turned pater,
New men rose as the age's guide—
Shaw, Huxley, Jekyll, Hyde.

Had rat-catcher Charles done it all? Had he shifted
The course of his culture with something he lifted
Sedulously from the orphaned fauna
Of some little islands off someone's Guiana?

Possibly.

If so, we thank Robert Darwin for it,
Who drove his son to survive, fit.

H: This last poem is from a group called "Fathers and Sons." Parenthood is
something the poet knows firsthand because he has four children. The group of
poems to follow express various modern parental attitudes.

R3: "The Girl in the Next Room"

Baby girl, you have insomnia.
I know. I am forty-nine times your age. I have insomnia.
It brings us together.

In there, what are you thinking?
Softly you woof woof, like the neighbor's dog.
Gently your feet pound the crib, like the moon's hammers.
And now you are humming.
But what are you thinking?

In here, I, forty-niner, your comrade,
Am thinking darkly of moons and worlds and flesh,
As old sleepless ones do, softly.
Do you have dark thoughts?

I wish I could ask you, hear your reply,
In there,
The two of us close and soft, far from the day.

But if I went in you would tease,
and not say.

R6: "The Chair"

So the baby chair overturned on the soft carpet,
And the baby herself, who had felled it, said it Fall Down,
Yes, yes, said I, Fall Down; and Boom, said she,
Happily, giving our love a bone.

I sat reading the paper.
She tiptoed off to the kitchen to implement Boom.
When she returned she was hitched.
There was the story,
And picture too: baby and groom.

I put down the paper
I righted the chair.
Dearest baby, wrote I in the wax weave of the carpet,
Why did you give your dada the air?

R4: "Clamming"

I go digging for clams once every two or three years
Just to keep my hand in (I usually cut it),
And I'm sure that whenever I do so I tell the same story
Of how at the age of four, I was trapped by the tide
As I clammed a sandbar. It's no story at all,
But I tell it and tell it. It serves my small lust
To be thought of as someone who's lived.
I've a war too to fall back on, and some years of flying,
As well as a high quota of drunken parties,
A wife and children; but somehow the clamming thing
Gives me an image of me that soothes my psyche
Like none of the louder events: me helpless,
Alone with my sandpail,
As fate in the form of soupy Long Island Sound
Comes stalking me.

I've a son now at that age.
He's spoiled. He's been sickly.
He's handsome and bright, affectionate and demanding.
I think of the tides when I look at him.
I'd have him alone and sea-girt, poor little boy.

The self, what a brute it is. It wants, wants.
It will not let go of its even most fictional grandeur,
But must grope, grope down in the muck of its past
For some little squirting life and bring it up tenderly
To the lo and behold of death, that it may weep
And pass on the weeping, keep the thing going.

Son, when you clam,
Watch out for the tides and take care of yourself,
Yet no great care,
Lest you care too much and brag of the caring
And bore your best friends and inhibit your children and sicken
At last into opera on somebody's sandbar. Son, when you clam,
Clam.

H: Sometimes, a husband and father runs out of patience—with his family, with himself.

R6: "The Bad Daddy"

The bad daddy who has been angry with the whole family, one by one,
Now retires to his study to be sullen and think of death.
He has aches in his neck and stomach that he is afraid to see the doctor about.
He has a sense of his mind's slopping off into fuzz.
He feels that he is becoming allergic to cigarettes,
That he can't digest steak, that he needs glasses, that he is impotent.
He knows he is bored by his friends, bored by novels, Shakespeare, youth.
He thinks that if it rains one more day he will kill himself.
He lies on the cot in his study covered by a child's security blanket too short to
    sleep under,
And he improvises idly, a few two-minute commercials for a different life, thus:

Dear Son: In the war between the Earthmen and the Martians,
Keep your feet dry, your messkit clean, your weapons oiled.
Get plenty of sleep, drink not nor fornicate, speak
When spoken to, write home once a week, get to know your chaplain.
If upon your return I should be wandering amid the shades of the departed,
Call the president of the bank who will deliver to you
A sealed manila envelope containing three french hens, two turtle doves
And your further instructions. Vale. Your sire.

Dear Mathilda: Though we have not spoken a word to each other for thirteen years,
We are sympatico, you and I. We commune across the miles; we yearn; we dote.
I watch you drive away in your furs in the Rolls to the shoe shop.
I hear you banging pots and pans in the bunker,
And my heart, woman, twitches and the salt tears come,
Tum-te-tum. Your Daddy-o.

Dearest Daughter: It was good, awfully good to have that nice little note from you.
Jimmy danced up and down, Mama had tears in her eyes.
We pulled out the scrapbook
And found that the last time you wrote was your fifteenth birthday,
When you were pregnant. Remember?
And now you write that you've won the Insurgents' Prize,
And at Berkeley! Of course we're terribly proud.
But as old-fashioned moralists we doubt the wisdom of compliments,
And anyhway you should know that your mother and I
Really think you're a frightful bitch. Love. Dad.

So now the bad Daddy feels much more like himself.
His typewriter pants pleasantly in its shed; the beast is fed.
Down the long waste of his years he sees, suddenly, violets.
He picks them and crushes them gently, and is at peace.
Gettem all, bad daddy, and sleep now.

H: Home for Reed Whittemore for twenty years was Northfield, Minnesota. Some of his best poems are simple ones about his homelife there.

W: Northfield is a town with not one but two presidents as well as a mayor. Each of our two presidents is surrounded by a large brain trust with long views. A member of the trusts can look out through the clear air for miles and see nothing but brains. In the center of the whole complex are a pool hall, a liquor store, and a movie house; on the fringes is corn, soon snow.[6]

R5: "The Farmhouse"*

Our house is an old farmhouse, whose properties
The town had gradually purchased, leaving it
Only a city lot and a few trees
Of all that wood and busheldom and breeze
It once served. It is high and square,
And its lines, such as they are, have been muddled by several
Conflicting remodelers, whose care
In widening, lengthening, adding on, letting in the air
Has left it with four kinds of windows, three porches
And a door that leads to a closet that is not there.

The city houses around us have borrowed from verse
And the Old Dominion; their cosmopolitan
Muddle is elegant next to ours.
We think of moving, and say we'll add no more dollars
To those already spent making a box
Of what was, is and will be, forever, a box,
When there's land, empty and unboxed, down a few blocks
Waiting.
We say this as we pull down, pull up, push out,
And generally persevere with our renovating—
That is, making new again—knowing
That houses like our house are not made new again
Any more than a man is. All that growing
Up and away from the land, that bowing
To impersonal social forces that transform
Wheatfields into rows of two-bedroom ramblers
Must be acknowledged; but the warm
Part of our country boy will not conform.
It remains, behind new windows, doors and porches,
Hugging its childhood, staying down on the farm.

[6]Zero, pp. 165–66, abridged (deletions within excerpt).

*Reprinted with permission of Macmillan Publishing Co., Inc. from *The Self-Made Man* by Reed Whittemore. © 1959 by Reed Whittemore.

R1: "Still Life"

> I must explain why it is that at night, in my own house,
> Even when no one's asleep, I feel I must whisper.
> Thoreau and Wordsworth would call it an act of devotion,
> I think; others would call it fright. It is probably
> Something of both. In my living room there are matters I'd rather not meddle with
> Late at night.

> I prefer to sit very still on the couch, watching
> All the inanimate things of my daytime life—
> The furniture and the curtains, the pictures and books—
> Come alive,
> Not as in some childish fantasy, the chairs dancing,
> But with dignity,
> The big rocker presiding over a silent
> And solemn assembly of all my craftsmen,
> From Picasso and other dignities gracing my walls
> To the local carpenter benched at my slippered feet.
> I find these proceedings
> Remarkable for their clarity and intelligence, and I wish I might somehow
> Bring into daylight the eloquence, say, of a doorknob.
> But always the gathering breaks up. Everyone there
> Shrinks from the tossing turbulence
> Of a cough, a creaking stair.

W: I'm a city poet, and I've only rarely felt that trees and hills were profitable objects for me to conduct my poetic transactions with. Mostly, as I say in one poem, I feel like a fool out there with the birds. I commune with the famous line by Wordsworth, "Little we see in Nature that is ours," but for the wrong reasons.[7]

R2: "The Philadelphia Vireo"

R1: . . . Anyone unable to tell a Vireo from a Warbler is hardly ready to recognize this species.—*A Field Guide to the Birds* by Roger Tory Peterson

R2: One can't do much in these woods without a bird book.
> Right on my porch sits a light-breasted thing I named phoebe, building a nest;
> And the pines by the house are held by a reddish-brown thrush and his
> > reddish-brown mate,
> Along with the smallest bird on the place, some warbler or finch,
> Who struts down below on the needles on match-stick legs.
> Far out and high I hear what I think is a mocking bird; then there are crows,
> Robins, jays, a few pheasants, what-all. I march up and down with my bird book,
> > scholarly.
> Interested in the variety of sounds and shapes,
> Amused by my own insufficiencies as stalker of wild life,
> But otherwise little disposed to be moved: to commune, to identify.

> Back at the house I page through an angry Tolstoi berating the Greeks

[7]*Zero*, p. 52.

For beguiling the artless Christians with pre-Christian nudes.
I close Tolstoi. He should have sniped at the birds too while he was at it,
Little pagans, for putting so many poets in bushes with bird books.
It's a bad day and I feel like a fool out here wtih these chirpers,
And now I'm writing these lines, dissonant things, and thinking bird things,
Because I'm a professional bird and am programmed to sing.
So I sing: chrrk, chrrk.

But why should I run down the birds? They have energy, they are strange.
There is wonder in energy, strangeness. Art needs that, man needs that,
And I seem to be in these woods for that, though writing a man-book.
So I say to my phoebe, the one on the porch, the builder,
Who is flying in sticks to her nest like a drunken west wind: bird,
Man thinks, though he thinks too much for all he knows of thee, well of thee.

R4: "Reason in the Woods"

"The tree is lazy. It wastes time.
I am lazy. I waste time.
So I must be
A tree," said the rock.

R5: "No, you rock," said the bird,
"Try again."
R4: "The tree is lazy. I'm a rock.
I must not be
Lazy," said the rock.
R5: "That's better," said the bird.
R: "I may be lazy,"
Said the tree,
"But I'm no tree.
I'm a birch."
R2: "They talk so stupidly,"
Said the man,
And rammed into the lazy rock birch bird tree.

W: My affection for birds and brooks is great, but I have never assumed that I could contribute much as a poet to their presence. Accordingly I have tended to work a bit differently on the edges of nature—somewhere near the town line.[8]

R6: "Three Poems to Jackson"*

I

Darkness comes early, stays late
In my winter country; the frost
Goes four feet down; trees are like sticks;
A light snow lingers

[8]*Zero,* pp. 52–53.
*Reprinted with permission of Macmillan Publishing Co., Inc. from *The Boy from Iowa* by Reed Whittemore. © 1959 by Reed Whittemore.

For a month or two, getting dirty. I write every day
But throw much away.

My third book will appear in the spring, a small book,
A slight book,
Containing no plays or long narrative poems,
Borrowing hardly at all from the Middle Ages,
Making few affirmations, avoiding inversions,
Using iambics distrustfully, favoring lines
Of odd lengths and irony.
                   I am forty.
I seem to know the dimensions of what I can do
And the season to do it in.
Give me a few more winters like this one, and spring—
Will cease to be a disturbance, and I'll be
Solid,
Jackson.

II

Steam on a winter stream. Cold air
Meeting warm water
Condenses? I suppose so.
But why should the water not freeze
Like me? I don't know.
I am mufflered, mittened, booted and earflapped
Like a child. I am taking the air.
The air is bitter.
The water is dark, incredibly dark; I look down
And see nothing and see that Narcissus
Was a summer child, a child who knew green
Scum and tadpoles, not
Black water.

Nature would rather we rest our psyches in winter.
She gives us no looking glass; she withdraws
From our poems, leaving us
Only our own thoughts, words and inflections
To find solace in. When we look out
We see nothing like us; we live
In a land of the dead with our mittens on; if we
Walk all day in the rutted road by the stream,
We find not even a stranger to befriend us.

But I am forty.
I look down from the stone bridge to the water,
And I see, yes, my face. It sends me,
Jackson.

III

And the lawyers said, and the wisemen said,
"It is better to come to terms " With what?

108

With all that ice, stickery, black water?
Of course not. Given a choice we choose
To walk in the meadows, pick clover, commune with
What there is to commune with. It is moral.
How then come to terms?
What the lawyers meant, and the wisemen, was that we
Trundle out to the stone bridge and play at terms.
Then the snow sparkles,
The stream converts to a prize-winning shot from a Kodak,
And we think of spring.

I have a book of lyrics coming out
In the spring.
I am twenty.
The spirit is strong within me; I have not
Come to terms with winter but bludgeoned winter
To my terms.
        Is the air warm?
I take off my coat.
          Is the grass soft?
Off, shoes.
And so on.
One does these things as a poet. I am a poet,
Jackson.

H: As a poet Mr. Whittemore has participated in the usual activities of a professional
poet. He reads his poems for audiences—

W: I have never dared to improvise a poem on the spot on the stage—or perhaps I
should say that I've never had enough presence of mind to do so—but I've
conducted enough poetry readings to know you have to go into it feeling
irresponsible but eloquent, which is to say that you have to have a few drinks first.
Our occupational hazard. And you have to draw the audience in on the happening
by hook or crook. (Katherine Ann Porter is reported to drop her gloves; I tend to
stutter appealingly and look helpless.)[9] It's best for a professing poet like me to
make small jokes about institutions. If he doesn't, someone will say he has sold
out—and maybe they will anyway.[10]

R3: "Today"

Today is one of those days when I wish I knew everything, like the critics.
I need a bit of self-confidence, like the critics.
I wish I knew about Coptic, for example, and Shakti-Yoga.
The criticis I read know them, and they say so. I wish I could say so.
I want to climb up some big publishing mountain and wear a little skullcap and say
    so: I know.

Confidence, that's what I need—to know—
And would have if I came from California or New York. Or France.
If I came from France I could say such things as, "Art opened its eyes on itself at

[9]*Zero*, p. 73, abridged.
[10]*Zero*, p. 7.

the time of the Renaissance."
If I came from California I could say, "Christianity was shortcircuited by
   Constantine."
If I came from New York I could say anything.

I come from Minnesota.
I must get a great big book with all the critics in it
And eat it. One gets so hungry and stupid in Minnesota.

W: Ambitious statements are expected of poetry consultants. On one of my very first
days in Washington a reporter asked me if I thought the world was getting better or
worse. I said I didn't know, which was disappointing to her. One must learn not to
disappoint the press, and the press, like the rest of the world, seems to expect of
its poets and poetry consultants information not available elsewhere. This is
perhaps one of the basic misunderstandings about poetry, and one the poets
themselves have cultivated; I was very flattered to be asked whether the world was
getting better or worse.[11]

R2: "A Fascinating Poet's Diary"

I am keeping this diary because I am fascinating.
My impacted wisdom teeth are fascinating.
My diet, my sex life, my career, these also are fascinating.
As are my newspaper clippings. Fascinating.
And all in my little book.
Up to now I have stuck to fascinating facts in my book,
Starting at six a.m. when I rise, shave, and write in my book,
And ending at ten-thirty when I retire with Agatha Christie and my book:
But starting today I propose to include fascinating dreams in my book
In fact I have just had a smasher
In which I find myself wearing a fascinatingly old-fashioned six-button book.

Oh, little book, oh sweetie, how you adorn me!

H: Most of Mr. Whittemore's writing expresses concern for the self in the modern
world—the place of the self in the space age, the conflicts between the self and
the pressures of the world.

W: I wrote this next poem at the MacDowell Colony just before I left for Washington,
D.C. I was struck by the difference between my "job" in the woods—which was to
write poems—and the worldly job ahead of me; so I wrestled with the problems of
what the world would expect of me (and presumably not get) and what the world
would do to my writing (I thought it might stop it).[12]

R5: "The Departure"

The artist must leave these woods now.
He must put his books and files back in the car,
And stuff his bags with shirts and shorts and sweaters,

[11]*Zero*, p. 130.
[12]*Poems for Young Readers*, National Council of Teachers of English, 1966, p. 4, abridged.
Reprinted by permission of Reed Whittemore.

And clean his room and take a load to the dump, wherever the dump is,
And go the rounds and say goodbye to the artists—goodbye—
And the trees—goodbye—
And cash a check and fill up with gas and set out
For the world again, the world, to talk up art.

The world likes that.
It likes to get news of the spirit fresh from the woods,
What birds are saying, and frogs. It sits in its cities,
Thirsty. The artist will fix that.
He will bring in a carload of essences quick on the thruway,
Mists for everyone's parlor, and sunsets, done up nice.
Cities want their essences done up nice.

So the artist must leave these woods now. For that.
He takes a last walk in the woods: what is the news, woods?
And the woods reply in their woodsy way that the news
Is woods, woods,
And he hears the news, notes it down and walks back
To his shirts and sweaters, while out of the sky
Art in its arty way keeps saying: goodbye.

W: The scene for this next poem is also the artists' colony in New Hampshire, where the self gets a real workout. The self gets pushed away in a little studio, all alone in the woods, with nothing but a blank wall and a few birds and trees to look at. The poem is in the form of a letter, and the letter is to God, and it is very long—several minutes even. So we'll read only parts of it.[13]

R5: "Dear God"

Though I don't believe in you, I've decided to write you,
Do with my words what you will—do you have a file?—
But don't imagine me sitting down here pining away for an answer.
It's not that kind of letter,
But a common poetic trick you would know about, if you kept up,
For talking at large to one's self without feeling ill.
A number of other poets have tried such things, whose names I won't mention,
And not one of them have been happy with your reply.
Nor I. So don't worry, I'll do the worrying, about you, and art, and man,
Especially man. You fly your atoms. . . .

One can't make an easy living exploring the self—that's for sure—
Which may be the reason such explorations enchant us so much,
Too much. We take a big healthy hunk of artist
Who likes to talk, drink, make love, play tennis
And so on, and what do we tell him? We make him a patient.
We say: you need to be alone, desperately, you need privacy.
Take a month, take two, three, get away someplace—
New Hampshire's nice—

[13]*Zero,* p. 168, abridged.

Get away and get to it: write, paint, sculpt, create, create.
And of course he does get to it, like mad. Who wouldn't? The woods are lovely,
Dark, deep, just dandy in every respect except that the life in them
Becomes a kind of irrelevance or aside.
The patient is well, perhaps even happy, but just barely breathing.
He's art, all art, and his art is all art, and shows it.
Sometimes, fed up, he thinks he'd be better off, though he wouldn't be,
If he set up shop in the middle of some city sidewalk. . . .

And as for that breezy, happy, pastoral alternative, peace,
Imagine a bright blue day,
A justice day, a rights day, a day when a bruised peach would go to court,
And the patrons of art are out on the streets commissioning
Portraits of upstairs halls, plays for long Riviera yacht trips,
While Shakespeare fans out alarmingly from Central Park,
And General Motors buys a controlling interest in the Association of Literary
    Magazines of America—
Imagine that blue, blue day, and the self, with its wall
Staring all day at the blankness, then tearing up paper,
Blackening canvasses, fiendishly chopping up granite
In sheer impotence—
Imagine it grinding home in your loveliest sunset
To kick the dog in the yard and blow down the pretty home, whoof,
With the children inside at TV and the wife in the kitchen
Pow, and have a quick six drinks and rage off to a bad movie
To return again, again to clamber all lonely,
Shh, into its bed where it falls asleep reading a road map. . . .

Enough. I'll write a book later. It's too muggy now.
All the bits and pieces of nature that in a better world than this one would be yours
Are indefinite at the edges. I can see no artists at all, but I know they're out there,
Struggling against the heat and the walls to retain their integrity
Which some of them know and some of them don't know that they can't possibly
keep.
But going hard at it anyway, as I am
I don't know what else to tell you. I look all around me, and inside,
And am shamed mostly,
Not by country or freedom, not by Congressmen
(Them I'll put in the book),
But by the spectacle of the self, the pompous self,
The minuscule godlet strutting behind the wall,
Surviving, thriving, bragging, beating his chest, despite all.
Dear God, could you bless him?

W: I like this next one partly out of malice toward the editors of *The New Yorker*, who
rejected it six or seven years ago on the grounds that while they liked it it was no
longer timely. There may have been other reasons—rejection slips are seldom
honest—but I prefer not to think of them. It still seems o.k. to me, and three lines in
the last stanza are among the best I've written (that makes them really hot, of
course):[14]

[14]*Poet's Choice*, edited by Paul Engle and Joseph Langland, Dell Publishing Co., New York, 1966, p. 178. Reprinted by permission of Reed Whittemore.

R6: "Lines

R2: Composed upon Reading an Announcement by Civil Defense Authorities Recommending that I build a Bomb-shelter in My Backyard"

R6: I remember a dugout we dug in the backyard as children
And closed on top with an old door covered with dirt
And sat in, hour by hour, thoroughly squashed,
But safe, with our chins on our knees, from the world's hurt.
There, as the earth trickled down on us as in an hourglass,
Our mothers called us, called us to come and be fed,
But we would not, could not hear them, possessed as we were
By our self's damp stronghold among the selfless dead.

Now, they say, willy nilly I must go back,
And under the new and terrible rules of romance
Dig yet another hole in which like a child
My adult soul may trifle with circumstance.
But I'll not, no, not do it, not go back
And lie there in that dark under the weight
Of all that earth on that old door for my state.
I know too much to think now that if I creep
From the grown-up's house to the child's house I'll keep.

W: I'll probably never follow those instructions in an emergency, but I like to think I would; so the poem gives me a pleasant image of me as I would like to be—what more could a poet want from his own lines?[15]

H: Reading Reed Whittemore's poems and identifying with his wit, his perception, his humility, allows us images of ourselves as we would like to be. What more could we ask from his lines? What more could we ask from An Evening with Reed Whittemore?

---

[15]*Ibid.*

"Mr. K*A*P*L*A*N and Shakespeare"*

by Leonard Q. Ross

Adapted and Directed by Lee Hudson
University of Illinois at Urbana

In *The Education of H*Y*M*A*N K*A*P*L*A*N*, Leo Rosten's[1] delightful assault on language itself, Mr. Parkhill, an adult education teacher, parries punctuation and pronunciation with hero Hyman Kaplan in his beginners' grade of the American Night Preparatory School for Adults ("English—Americanization—Civics—Preparation for Naturalization"). Just whose education is actually in progress is never entirely clear—while Mr. Kaplan and the other students are "educated," Mr. Parkhill learns about education. We the readers enjoy the entire process.

In a mixed bag of tricks, Rosten can simultaneously capture and caricature humans in an anxious, precarious situation—the adult education class. Humor is what he produces best. We do not find the bite of satire, the mockery of parody, nor the ridicule of travesty—just the frolic of the enjoyably humorous, the tickling truth of the comic eye, and in Kaplan's case, the ear as well.

Rosten's triumph in the book is his characterizations of the various individuals that people those evening classes. Beyond the distinguishable physical and behavioral characteristics, Rosten preserves the dialect (or some incredible graphic substitute) of the characters. This *dialect humor* and its counterpoints provide the root of Kaplan's captivating charm. Through malapropism after mispronunciation, Mr. Parkhill grinds his teeth through "Recitation and Speech" class with frayed nerves and an unbelievable dispensation of strained patience. He limps his linguistic way through class after class correcting Kaplan's highly original delivery of the English language: the superlative of

[1]Leo Rosten (Leonard Q. Ross), *The Education of H*Y*M*A*N K*A*P*L*A*N* (New York: Harcourt, Brace & World, Inc., 1937).

good becomes "high-class"; Abraham Lincoln—Ab*ram* Linc*ohen;* and King George III—Kink Jawdge Number Tree, dat tarrible autocrap who—. Kaplan informs us that "for eatink smashed potatoes I am usink a knife an' fog!" and, as if nothing is sacred, Mr. Parkhill's name is irreverently voiced as "Mr. Pockheel." Kaplan's tongue is certainly well matched with his imagination.

The use of dialect in literature is common. We find it in poetry from Tennyson to Frost; in fiction from Twain to Welty; and in drama from Aristophanes to Williams. Portraying peculiarities of dialect is a creative, not a transcriptional, art. Rosten has written elsewhere that an author's recording of dialect is a process of transformation—"that which he hears into that which you could not."[2] Writers who translate into a native idiom clearly represent regional characteristics through the use of regional speech—we know Miss Caravello's Italy through Miss Caravello's Italian.

Language's ability to reflect an individual's world-perception enables us to meet these students and see their situation somewhat as they see it. Although very little background information exists about the various characters, we feel that we do know them to a predictable level of familiarity. Their humanness, in short, comes to us through their idiosyncratic language. One striking example is in the chapter "Mr. K*A*P*L*A*N and the Magi." This episode portrays the class's dramatic, sentimental selection and presentation of a Christmas gift for Mr. Parkhill—a black and gold smoking jacket with a green-tongued dragon on the pocket. Kaplan makes the ceremonial "spitch" and then, at its conclusion, mutters to Mr. Parkhill that perhaps he was too formal in his address but that "avery void I said—it came fromm *below mine heart!*"[3]

2*The Return of H*Y*M*A*N K*A*P*L*A*N* (New York, Harper & Brothers, 1959), p. 14.

3*The Education of H*Y*M*A*N K*A*P*L*A*N,* p. 79.

Since we become so fond of the characters' innocence and naivety in this educational process, we value *their* perceptions and realize that these would be lost if "standardized." There is a not-so-subtle hope that Kaplan and the class will successfully resist the fiercest of Mr. Parkhill's efforts. We realize that for them to retain their individual visions, they must retain their means of expressing them.

Local speech in Rosten's classroom constitutes a linguistic potpourri. This melting pot of language usage ultimately creates a masterful phonetic *tour de force.* Rosten's eager characters fight the barriers of an illogical, standardized English and emerge from this verbal war as battered, but still battling victims.

"Mr. K*A*P*L*A*N and Shakespeare" is one of the sixteen chapters in Rosten's book. Mr. Parkhill listens to colleague Miss Higby ("who had once begun a master's thesis on Coventry Patmore") and decides to try using Shakespeare to improve the English and the poetic sensibilities of his variegated international class. What follows is not only undeniably impossible to paraphrase—Rosten's skillful tongue-twisting makes it equally impossible to translate. Mr. Kaplan manages in a few short Yiddish pages to recast, rewrite, replot, and reconceive the immortal Bard. He defeats the pedagogical finesse of Miss Higby and Mr. Parkhill, and the heritage of Shakespeare himself.

PRODUCTION CONCEPT

The production concept for "K*A*P*L*A*N and Shakespeare" was to capture the humor of the situation in the classroom and the humor of the interaction between the characters as it emerges through their use and misuse of language. Dialect humor is a humor of the ear that emphasizes the importance of "voice" in performance.

PRODUCTION PLAN

"K*A*P*L*A*N and Shakespeare" was directly extracted (almost verbatim) from the chapter of the same title in Leo Rosten's collection of previously printed stories, *The Education of H*Y*M*A*N K*A*P*L*A*N.* In addition, Rosten's *Spoken Arts* recording was utilized in the script composition.[4] This recording varies considerably from the the printed version of the text in the Harbrace edition. Two phrases, present on the record, were added to the script: Kaplan's admonition to Mr. Bloom "Batter tink a minute!" and his explanation of the candle extinguishing "Go ot! Go ot! Short candle! and he's the kink so it goes ot."

Besides extraction and addition, I also rearranged a few elements and deleted some others. For clarification, the title of Mr. Parkhill's class was drawn from the first chapter ("English—Americanization—Civics —Preparation for Naturalization"); and because of cast composition Mrs. Yampolsky became a Mr. The deletions included: (1) the short summary question period (to focus on the "Recitation and Speech" part of the class), and (2) two nonspeaking characters, Scymzak and Schneiderman, (for casting reasons).

I carefully preserved the narrator's comments since the narrator provides such a necessary and humorous commentary on the characters' thought and action, both past and present. Rosten's narrator zeroes in on motivations and fears and describes with vivid skill the setting and situation of the story. I was also interested in the narrative structure of the work and in the operations of that most articulate narrator whose directional pointer often leads us right to the source of the humor.

[4] *The Education...and Return of H*Y*M*A*N K*A*P*L*A*N* (New York: Spoken Arts, Inc.).

ORIGINAL PRODUCTION

The impetus for this production was the Saddleback Interpretation Festival. The theme for the festival was "Shakespeare." Since I was not ready to shoulder the Bard and shuffle some scene into the necessary format, a parody seemed the only solution. Colleague Alethea Mattingly alerted me to the wisdom that was K*A*P*L*A*N.

Working with primarily graduate students from the University of Arizona I was able to achieve several purposes; they were currently both teachers and students and, for the most part, were older. Naturally this age added a credibility to the adult education class setting.

Conveniently the set for the show was a classroom, and with a few props a normal "space" became a "set." Costumes aided the performers in their characterizations; and after reading all of Rosten's book and its sequel, *The Return of H*Y*M*A*N K*A*P*L*A*N,*[5] they were better prepared to move into their *alter egos*. This was especially true of the minor characters who have so few lines but *must* have a constant sense of self and some stage business to fill out their character.

Blocking was very straightforward; the placement and movement of the narrator was the only creative problem. The narrator "froze" the action to provide motivation and shifted it to slow motion when it was necessary to slow stage time to "fit" narrative time. The performers did not use scripts since the scene was so literally depicted.

The entire production was a delight. Rosten's humor wears extremely well.

[5] *The Return of H*Y*M*A*N K*A*P*L*A*N* (New York: Harper & Brothers, 1959).

Selected Bibliography

Rosten, Leo (Leonard Q. Ross), *The Education of H*Y*M*A*N K*A*P*L*A*N*. New York: Harcourt, Brace & World, Inc., 1937.

————. *The Joys of Yiddish*. New York: McGraw-Hill, 1968.

————. *The Return of H*Y*M*A*N K*A*P*L*A*N*. New York: Harper & Brothers, 1959.

————. *The Education . . . and Return of H*Y*M*A*N K*A*P*L*A*N*. New York: Spoken Arts, Inc.

MR. K*A*P*L*A*N ON SHAKESPEARE

Cast of Characters

N: Narrator   **C:** Miss Caravello
H: Miss Higby   **Y:** Mr. Yampolsky
P: Mr. Parkhill   **K:** Mr. Kaplan
B: Mr. Bloom

(Miss Higby and Mr. Parkhill enter stage left, Miss Higby is miming conversation. Narrator is in room and follows them as they cross to stage right).

N: It was Miss Higby's idea in the first place. She had suggested to Mr. Parkhill that the students came to her class unaware of the *finer* side of English, of its beauty and, as she put it,

H: "the glorious heritage of our literature." She suggested that perhaps poetry might be worked into the exercises of Mr. Parkhill's class—the beginners' grade of the American Night Preparatory School for Adults ("English—Americanization—Civics—Preparation for Naturalization"). The beginner's grade had, after all, been subjected to almost a year of English and might be presumed to have achieved some linguistic sophistication. Poetry would make the students conscious of precise enunciation; it would make them read with greater care and an ear for sounds.

N: Miss Higby, who had once begun a master's thesis on Coventry Patmore, *loved* poetry. And, it should be said in all justice, she argued her cause with considerable logic.

P: Poetry would be excellent for the enunciation of the students, thought Mr. Parkhill.

N: *(Short break here for time lapse. Students enter randomly, greet each other, low class noise).* So it was that when he faced the class the following Tuesday night, Mr. Parkhill had a volume of Shakespeare on his desk, and an eager, almost an expectant, look in his eye. The love that Miss Higby bore for poetry in general was as nothing compared to the love that Mr. Parkhill bore for Shakespeare in particular. To Mr. Parkhill, poetry meant Shakespeare. Many years ago he had played Polonius in his senior class play.

P: *(Mr. Parkhill strikes desk with pointer to get their attention).* Tonight, class, I am going to try an experiment.

N: The class looked up dutifully. They had come to regard Mr. Parkhill's pedagogical innovations as part of the natural order.

P: I am going to introduce you to poetry—great poetry. You see—

N: *(Mr. Parkhill mimes his "lecture" using same words as narration to follow).* Mr. Parkhill delivered a modest lecture on the beauty of poetry, its expression of the loftier thoughts of men, its economy of statement. He hoped it would be a relief from spelling and composition exercises to use poetry as the subject matter of the regular Recitation and Speech period.

P: I have written a passage on the board and will read it for you. Then, for Recitation and Speech, you will give short addresses, using the passage as the general topic, telling us what it has brought to your minds, what thoughts and ideas.

N: The class seemed quite pleased by the announcement. However Mr. Norman Bloom sighed with a businesslike air: you could tell that for him

B: poetry was merely another assignment, like a speech on "What I Like to Eat Best" or a composition on "A Day at a Picnic"

N: Miss Caravello

C: to whom any public performance was unpleasant

N: tried to look enthusiastic, without much success. And Mr. Hyman Kaplan, the heroic smile on his face as indelibly as ever, looked at Mr. Parkhill with admiration and whispered to himself:

K: Poyetry! Now is poyetry! My! Mus' be progriss ve makink awreddy!

P: The passage is from Shakespeare

N: Mr. Parkhill announced, opening the volume. An excited buzz ran through the class as the magic of that name fell upon them.

K: Imachine!

N: murmured Mr. Kaplan.

K: Jakesbeer!

P: *Shakes*peare, Mr. Kaplan!

N: Mr. Parkhill had taken a piece of chalk and, with care and evident love, had written the following passage on the board in large, clear letters:

P: *(Parkhill reads somewhat woodenly with exaggerated emphasis on rhythm—body and pointer used)*

Tomorrow, and tomorrow, and tomorrow
Creeps in this petty pace from day to day,
To the last syllable of recorded time;
And all our mysteries have lighted fools
The way to dusty death. Out, out, brief candle!

Life's but a walking shadow, a poor player
That struts and frets his hour upon the stage,
And then is heard no more; it is a tale
Told by an idiot, full of sound and fury,
Signifying nothing.

N: A reverent hush filled the classroom, as eyes gazed with wonder on this passage from the Bard. Mr. Parkhill was pleased at this.

P: I shall read the passage again, Listen carefully this time to my enunciation—and—er—let Shakespeare's thoughts sink into your minds.

N: Mr. Parkhill read:

P: *(Parkhill now reads with overdone emotion that builds).* Tomorrow, and tomorrow, and tomorrow . . .

N: Mr. Parkhill read very well and this night, as if some special fire burned in him, he read with rare eloquence.

P: Out, out, brief candle!

N: In Miss Caravello's eyes there was inspiration and wonder.

P: Life's but a walking shadow . . .

N: Mr. Bloom sat with a heavy heart, indicating cerebration.

P: It is a tale told by an idiot . . .

N: Mr. Kaplan's smile had taken on something luminous; but his eyes were closed: it was not clear whether Mr. Kaplan had surrendered to the spell of the Immortal Bard or to that of Morpheus.

P: Well, I shall allow a few minutes for you all to—er—think over the meaning of the passage. Then we shall begin Recitation and Speech.

N: Mr. Kaplan promptly closed his eyes again, his smile beatific. The students sank into that revery miscalled thought, searching their souls for the symbols evoked by Shakespeare's immortal words.

P: Miss Caravello, will you begin?

N: *(Mr. Parkhill and Miss Caravello exchange places in slow motion movement timed to fit the narration. All class is reacting in slow motion).* asked Mr. Parkhill at last. He took Miss Caravello's seat. He always took the seat of the student reciting during Recitation and Speech period. It seemed to establish a comradely rapport in the class; besides it was easier to hear and watch the student speaking.

C: Da poem isa gooda, Itsa have—

P: It *has.*

C: It hasa beautiful wordsa. Itsa lak Dante, Italian poet—

K: HA!

N: cried Mr. Kaplan scornfully.

K: Shakesbeer you metchink met Tante? *Shakesbeer*? Mein Gott!

N: It was obvious that Mr. Kaplan had identified himself with Shakespeare and would tolerate no disparagement of his *alter ego.*

P: Miss Caravello is merely expressing her own ideas,

N: said Mr. Parkhill pacifically

P: Actually, he felt completely sympathetic to Mr. Kaplan's point of view.

K: Hau Kay,

N: agreed Mr. Kaplan, with a generous wave of the hand.

K: But to me is no comparink a high-cles men like Shakesbeer mit a Tante dat's all.

N: Miss Caravello, her poise shattered, said a few more words and sat down. *(Miss Caravello takes seat. Mr. Yampolsky goes to front of class. Parkhill takes Yampolsky's seat).*

Y: This is full deep meanings. Is hard for a person not so good in English to unnistant. But I like.

K: *Like!*

N: cried Mr. Kaplan with a fine impatience.

K: LIKE? Better *love*, Yampolsky. Mit Shakesbeer mus' be *love*!

N: Mr. Parkhill had to suggest that Mr. Kaplan control his aesthetic passions. Mr. Yampolsky staggered through several more nervous comments and retired.

N: *(Mr. Yampolsky sits, Parkhill gestures to Mr. Bloom and takes his seat as Bloom goes to front of class).* Mr. Bloom was next. He gave a long declamation, ending:

B: So is passimistic ideas in the poem, and I am optimist. Life should be happy—so we should remember this is only a poem. Maybe is Shakespeare too passimistic.

K: You wronk, Bloom! Batter tink a minute!

N: cried Mr. Kaplan with prompt indignation.

K: Shakesbeer is passimist because is de *life* passimist also!

N: Mr. Parkhill, impressed by this philosophical stroke, realized that Mr. Kaplan, afire with the glory of the Swan of Avon, could not be suppressed. Mr. Kaplan was the kind of man who brooked no criticism of his gods. The only solution was to call on Mr. Kaplan for his recitation at once.

P: Mr. Parkhill was indeed curious about what fresh thoughts Mr. Kaplan would utter after his passionate defenses of the Bard. Mr. Kaplan, will *you* speak next?

N: Mr. Kaplan's face broke into a glow; his smile was like a rainbow.

K: Soitinly

N: *(Kaplan goes to front. Parkhill takes his seat).* he said, walking to the front of the room. Never had he seemed so dignified, so eager, so conscious of a great destiny.

P: Er—Mr. Kaplan,

N: added Mr. Parkhill, suddenly aware of the possibilities which the situation

P: (Kaplan on Shakespeare)

N: involved:

P: Speak *carefully*.

K: *Spacially* carefull villl be, Ladies an' gantleman, you hoid all kinds minninks abot dis piece poyetry, an'—

P: *Poetry*.

K: —abot dis piece *poetry*. But to me is a difference minnink altogadder. Ve mus' tink abot Julius Scissor an' how *he* falt!

N: Mr. Parkhill moved nervously, puzzled.

K: In dese exact voids is Julius Scissor sayink—

P: Er—Mr. Kaplan, said Mr. Parkhill once he grasped the full import of Mr. Kaplan's error. The passage is from "Macbeth."

N: Mr. Kaplan looked at Mr. Parkhill with injured surprise.

K: *Not* from Julius Scissor?

N: There was pain in his voice.

P: No. And it's—er—Julius *Cae*sar.

N: Mr. Kaplan waited until the last echo of the name had permeated his soul.

K: Podden me, Mr. Pockheel. Isn't *seez*or vat you cottink somting op mit?

P: That, said Mr. Parkhill quickly, is scissor. You have used "Caesar" for "scissor" and "scissor" for "Caesar."

N: Mr. Kaplan nodded, marvelling at his own virtuosity.

P: But go on with your speech, please. Mr. Parkhill, to tell the truth, felt a little guilty that he had not announced at the very beginning that the passage was from Macbeth. "Tell us *why* you thought the lines were from "Julius Caesar."

K: Vell.

N: said Mr. Kaplan to the class, his smile assuming its normal serenity.

K: I vas positif, becawss I can *see* de whole ting.

N: He paused, debating how to explain this cryptic remark. Then his eyes filled with a strange enchantment.

K: I see de whole scinn. It's in a tant, on de night before dey makink Julius de Kink fromm Rome. So he is excited an' ken't slip. He is layink in bad, tinking: "Tomorrow an' tomorrow an' tomorrow. How slow dey movink! Almost cripps! Soch a pity de pace!

N: Before Mr. Parkhill could explain that "petty pace" did not mean "Soch a pity de pace!" Mr. Kaplan had soared on.

K: De days go slow, fromm day to day, like leetle tsyallables on phonograph racords fromm time. An' vat abot yestidday? tinks Julius Scissor. Ha! All our yestiddays are only makink a good light for fools to die in the dost!

P: Dusty death doesn't mean—

K: An' Julius Scissor is so tired, an' he vants to fallink aslip. So he hollers, mit fillink, Go ot! Go ot! Short candle! So it goes ot. *(Voice drops to a whisper).* But he ken't slip. Now is bodderink him de idea fromm life. 'Vat is de life altogadder?' tinks Julius Scissor. An' he gives ensswer, de pot I like de bast. 'Life is like a bum actor, strottink an' hollerink aroud de stage for only vun hour bafore he's kicked ot. Life is a tale told by idjots, dat's all, full of fonny sonds an' phooey!

P: Mr. Parkhill could be silent no longer. "Full of sound and fury!" he cried desperately.

K: Life is monkey business! It don' minn a ting. It signifies nottink!' An' den Julius Scissor closes his ice fest—

N: Mr. Kaplan demonstrated the Consul's exact ocular process in closing his "ice"—

K: —an falls dad!

N: The class was hushed as Mr. Kaplan stopped. In the silence, a tribute of the fertility of Mr. Kaplan's imagination and the power of his oratory. *(Mr. Kaplan slowly moves to his seat. Mr. Parkhill goes to front).* Mr. Kaplan went to his seat. But just before he sat down, as if adding a postscript, he sighed:

K: Dat vas mine idea. But ufcawss is all wronk, becawss Mr. Pockheel said de voids ain't abot Julius Scissor altogadder. It's all abot an Irishman by de name Macbat.

N: Then Mr. Kaplan sat down. It was some time before Mr. Parkhill could bring himself to criticize Mr. Kaplan's pronunciation, enunciation, diction, grammar, idiom, and sentence structure. Mr. Parkhill discovered that he could not easily return to the world of reality. He was still trying to tear himself away from that tent outside Rome, where "Julius Scissor" cursed with insomnia, had thought of time and life—and philosophized himself to a strange and sudden death.

Mr. Parkhill was distinctly annoyed with Miss Higby.

No Sense of Decency:
The Army-McCarthy Hearings

Compiled and Directed by Phillis Rienstra Jeffrey

The University of Texas at Austin

A televised episode lasting thirty-six days, an almost 3,000-page government document, and a period in American history labeled "The McCarthy Era" constitute a saga of drama and tyranny—the now famous Army-McCarthy Hearings.[1] In 1950, when a gripping fear of Communism pervaded America, the junior senator from Wisconsin, Joe McCarthy, needed a campaign issue that would secure his seat in the United States Senate. He made the cold war into a hot issue by using every available means as chairman of the Committee on Government Operations to expose real and imagined Communists. He labeled this activity his "fight for America." The list of people and institutions that fell prey to his tactics and accusations is long; it includes President Eisenhower, President Truman, the Protestant clergy, General George C. Marshall, the Catholic *Commonweal*, the president of Harvard University, the C.I.A., the Departments of State and Justice, and finally, the Department of Defense.

In the summer of 1953, the young, wealthy, and draftable G. David Schine, one of McCarthy's staff members, was notified that his draft status was about to change, and that he was eligible to be drafted by the armed forces. His invitation from the United States Army displeased Senator McCarthy and his chief counsel Roy Cohn, Schine's friend and colleague. The McCarthy forces set in motion a campaign to high pressure the Army to refrain from drafting Schine. When they learned that the Army would not cooperate in obtaining either a deferment or a direct commission for Schine, the McCarthy committee publicized widespread espionage at Fort Monmouth. Department of Defense officials retaliated with a letter to certain senators warning that if McCarthy did not halt the destructive publicity, they would issue charges against the senator for seeking preferential treatment for Private Schine. Continued abuse from the McCarthy staff forced the Army to file the threatened charge. McCarthy's countercharge of blackmail and

[1]A fuller discussion of this script can be found in Phillis Rienstra, "No Sense of Decency: A Readers Theatre Production of the Army-McCarthy Hearings," Unpublished Masters Thesis, The University of Texas at Austin, 1970.

treason by the Army was filed several days later. The furor over the dispute became so disruptive that the Congress was compelled to investigate the charges and counter-charges. That investigation emerged as the Army-McCarthy Hearings, the primary source of the documentary drama, "No Sense of Decency."

"No Sense of Decency" is representative of documentary drama, or the Theatre of Fact, that originated with Erwin Piscator's Political Theatre established in 1919. The terms "epic" and "proletarian," as well as "political," characterize Piscator's concept of drama that defied conventional, realistic theatre and commanded an audience to assume the role of critical viewer. Piscator's intent was to impose his leftist ideology upon the viewer[2]

Bertolt Brecht, following the path cleared by Piscator, used the stage as a vehicle for political agitation, creating scripts based on historical incidents that implored critical inquiry. The playwright demanded "productive" audience participation in the drama; he achieved this partially through the use of alienation, the process of "making strange" through songs, narration, films, and other theatrical devices, the events on stage to objectify the audience's role and move it to action.

Similar to the political, historical, and epic drama in aim, the documentary drama, unlike its predecessors, derives its script from documented fact. However, the selection, arrangement, condensation, and execution of those facts are clearly and admittedly propagandistic and biased. Drama of this nature is factual, historically contemporary, and reformative in intent. So too is "No Sense of Decency."

PRODUCTION CONCEPT

The compilation of a script of the Army-

[2]Stanley Hart, Judith Bierman, and James Hart, *The Play and the Reader* (Englewood Cliffs, N.J.: Prentice-Hall, Inc., 1966), p. 383.

McCarthy Hearings seemed especially exciting and appropriate in the 1970s because (1) "Documentary Drama," the current interest in reported facts as drama, underscored the potential of nonfictional material for group performance, and (2) the effects of McCarthyism are still noticeably present today. In this script, selected aspects of the original hearings are structurally and rhythmically organized to feature the clash of ideologies that characterized the McCarthy era, and to reveal Joe McCarthy as a demogogue.

PRODUCTION PLAN

Sources of the Script

The United States Senate transcript of the Army-McCarthy Hearings was the primary source of the script. Other sources included biographies and autobiographies of McCarthy's contemporaries, press coverage during the period, and "Point of Order," a documentary film of the hearings.

Just as integral to the script as the dialogue between the characters are the *Voice* and the *Narrator*, observers who explain the event and interpret the action on stage. Most of their lines were not taken from the government document but from secondary sources cited in footnotes to the script. Their purpose was to encourage audience participation and critical evaluation.

I employed three of the commonly accepted techniques of adaptation: addition, deletion, and rearrangement.

Addition. While the documents of the hearings contained "dramatic" elements (e.g., immediacy, discordant moods, and intensity), additional materials were needed to clarify and reinforce the theme. Added materials, spoken chiefly by the Voice and the Narrator, clarified the following points: (1) the historical period, (2) the character of Joseph McCarthy, (3) the events leading up to the hearings, (4) the charges and countercharges submitted by the Army and the McCarthy coalition, and (5) the other characters.

An objective reporter (the Voice) announcing period epithets (e.g. "The Age of Suspicion," "The Age of Blacklisting") provided the background to the era and introduced McCarthy through a series of quotations and descriptions of him from the time he entered public life (1941) to the time of the hearings (1954). The Narrator, the other added "Voice," recounted the events preceding the hearings, reviewed the charges and countercharges in the dispute, and called upon the characters to introduce their own roles objectively and directly to the audience in order to establish a distance between them, an "alienation" concept often used in documentary drama.

Intermittent comments by the Voice, freezing the action on stage, further characterized McCarthy and intensified the play's focus on the danger of his tactics. All commentary by the Narrator, except his final lines, served as explanatory transitions from one episode to another.

Deletion. The technique of deletion was necessary in devising "No Sense of Decency." Of the approximately 3,000 pages in the document, 780 pages were adapted for this one-hour production. Within the sequences used, phrases were deleted and reconstructed to provide a more fluent text. For example, in General Miles Reber's explanation below, the lines in parentheses were deleted in the script.

Mr. Cohn informed me that Mr. Schine had been a junior ship's officer in the Army Transport Service (and had served in that capacity for approximately one year beginning in the fall of 1946) and that Mr. Schine had at that time the assimilated rank of first lieutenant. It was emphasized to me in (looking into the possibility of) obtaining this commission, because the status of Mr. Schine under the Selective Service Act was about to change. (The next morning I inquired as to whether or not an individual

who had Mr. Schine's purported qualifications could be given a direct commission in the Officers' Reserve Corps. The response to my inquiry was in the affirmative.) I later learned that Mr. Schine had not been a junior ship's officer in the Army Transport Service, so the commission was impossible to obtain.

Rearrangement. The sequence of events in the adapted script did not follow as it appeared in the hearings. Episodes were arranged to allow McCarthy's "indecency" to grow on the audience, as his behavior in successive sequences became increasingly despicable. During the hearings, for example, the incident involving Fred Fisher, attorney Joseph Welch's young law partner, preceded the volatile scene between Symington and McCarthy. In the script the order is reversed because the calm indictment by Welch is more devasting to McCarthy than Symington's furious denunciation.

Selection of Characters

McCarthy Faction	Army Faction
Joe McCarthy (Republican Senator)	Robert T. Stevens (Secretary of the Army)
Roy Cohn (McCarthy's assistant)	Joseph Welch (Counselor for the Army)
	Miles Reber (Testifying for the Army)

Investigations Committee:
Stuart Symington
(Senator, Democratic Party)

Karl Mundt
(Chairman, Investigating Committee)

Others:
Voice (Objective Reporter)
Narrator

Summary of Script Organization

Similar to reportage or documentary productions, "No Sense of Decency" is episodic in structure (i.e., it is composed of single units that contain a beginning, a middle, and an end). The Prologue introduces the forthcoming clash and is followed by six episodes arranged to reveal progressively harmful characteristics of McCarthy. The script can be outlined as follows:

I. *Prologue*—A foreshadowing of the clash.
  A. Introduction of the Age and the senator with period epithets by the Voice.
  B. Review of the incidents precipitating the hearings by the narrator.
  C. Self-descriptive character introduction in the third person.
  D. Review of the charges and countercharges in the dispute by Senator Symington.
II. *Episode I*—McCarthy's use of insinuation and innuendo with General Miles Reber.
III. *Episode II*—McCarthy's use of intimidation with Secretary of Defense, Robert T. Stevens.
IV. *Episode III*—McCarthy's use of "The Multiple Untruth" with Secretary Stevens, Senator Symington, and Counselor Joseph Welch.
V. *Episode IV*—McCarthy's accusation of treason by every branch of the federal government: the climax.
VI. *Episode V*—McCarthy's unconscious confession of his role in the spy-and-informer system in the federal government.
VII. *Episode VI*—Welch's denunciation of McCarthy.[3]

ORIGINAL PRODUCTION

In keeping with the spirit of a documentary production, the objective was not to

[3]Reprinted from Phillis Rienstra, "Resurrecting the Past: Historical Documents as Materials for Readers Theatre," *The Speech Teacher*, 21, No. 4 (November 1972), 312.

create an illusion, but rather to repeat selected parts of an event. In keeping with the production concept, the arrangement and staging of "No Sense of Decency" was based on two considerations: first, to provide (for the director, performers, and audience) a broader understanding of the particular historical period, and a perspective vivifying it as literature; and second, to elicit a critical response from the audience.

Rehearsals

Since the script was devised primarily to serve a social function, I spent several days explaining the McCarthy Era and the manifestations of McCarthyism in the present decade to the cast and crew. Of equal importance was the cast's understanding of the script's structure. The language of "No Sense of Decency" contains little poetic imagery or elevated expression, except in the case of Counselor Joseph Welch. The language is of ordinary men responding spontaneously to each other with much irony, exaggerated and lengthy oratory, colloquialisms, and allusions to their present situation.

As the performers developed a clear understanding of the drama and the composition of their roles, subsequent rehearsals involved sessions whenever necessary. Daily rehearsals began one month before production.

Stage Composition

Setting. The factors considered in developing a set for "No Sense of Decency" were simplicity, clarity, and consistency with the text. To suggest the original caucus room, a selected group of set pieces was used. Two 6' x 2½' conference tables, separated by a platform slightly raised and constructed of crates, were placed parallel to each other on the stage. Attached to the conference table edges and extending to the stage floor were two 6' long and 29" high corrugated cardboard constructions covered with walnut contact paper. The outer rectangular ends were similarly covered. A slightly taller (36″) construction of the corrugated cardboard was attached to each inner, downstage leg of the conference tables, and seamed to the larger constructions, masking the front of the witness stand. The added height of the center covering focused attention on a character as he assumed his position in the witness chair, which was placed on the raised platform.

Microphones appeared on the conference tables in front of the characters, but were equipped only for recording the performance and not for projecting sound. Additional props on the conference tables were glasses of water and name plates. On each side of the stage were two 10′ x 10′ screens on which 2″ x 2″ slides were rear-projected. Senator Karl Mundt, the Voice and the Narrator (all of whom sat in the auditorium) used microphones equipped for sound projection.

Visuals. Because there were two large permanent screens on either side of the stage, the visuals for the production appeared in groups of four. The forty different groups projected during the hour presentation served two purposes: (1) to support or extend the Voice's commentary; and (2) to clarify the dialogue on stage.

Blocking. All characters, except the Narrator and the Voice, entered the playing area from the house wings. After each principal introduced his role in the third person, he moved to a position either on stage or on the first row in the audience.

Senator McCarthy and his Chief Counsel Roy Cohn were seated at the conference table stage left, parallel to the table where their questioners sat. Senator Symington and Counselor Welch assumed the same position at the table on stage right.

Senator Symington, Joseph Welch, Senator McCarthy, and Roy Cohn were at all times present on stage. Senator Karl Mundt, acting moderator, sat in the first row of house seats behind a conference table. Seated on either side of him were the two witnesses in the hearings, Major General Miles Reber, and Secretary of the Army Robert Stevens, who when called upon to testify, approached the stage steps and assumed their position in the witness chair, returning to their initial positions after testifying. Placement of these characters below and in front of the stage area illuminated the roles they played in the hearings without detracting from those on stage. This composition was similar to the setting of the hearings, where the principals were surrounded by spectators and separated from the inquisitors and witnesses. Hopefully, the placement of both the Voice and the Narrator in the house reminded the audience that the event being viewed was not divorced from reality.

Minimal movement occurred on stage. The performers maintained initial positions almost constantly throughout the drama. Witnesses moved from their positions to the witness chair when called upon to testify. The only other movement occurred during particularly heated arguments between the characters, when Joseph Welch delivered the Fred Fisher story, and when performers froze. A freeze became part of the stage movement in two instances: (1) when the Voice interrupted the drama to underscore what the performers were saying; and (2) during the Narrator's last commentary. The problems of physically manipulating scripts during fiery exchanges made them impossible to use. It was also reasoned that the use of scripts would have impaired the spontaneity of the dialogue.

Selected Bibliography

"Agnew on the Warpath." *Life Magazine,* 69 (October 16, 1960), 26.

BERGER, JOHN and ANNA BOSTOCK, trans. *Brecht: Poems on the Theatre.* Loestoft, Eng.: Scorpion Press, 1961.

DE ANTONIO, EMILE. "McCarthy." Printed insert accompanying Broadside Records Album No. BR450, 1968.

"The Country Below the Surface," *Time Magazine,* 63 (March 8, 1966), 83.

KENDRICK, ALEXANDER. *Prime Time: The Life of Edward R. Murrow.* Boston: Little, Brown and Company, 1969.

LATHAM, EARL. *The Communist Controversy in Washington: From the New Deal to McCarthy.* Cambridge: Harvard University Press, 1966.

MANNES, MARYA. "Did or Did Not...," *The Reporter,* 10 (June 8, 1954), 40–41.

MARCONI, GERALD. "The Theatre of Fact: Contemporary Documentary Drama." Unpublished Master's thesis, Catholic University of America, Washington, D.C., 1969.

MATUSOW, HARVEY. *False Witness.* New York: Cameron and Kahn, 1955.

Point of Order (Motion Picture). Point Films. Released by Point Films, 1964.

ROVERE, RICHARD H. *Senator Joe McCarthy.* New York: Harcourt Brace Jovanovich, 1957.

————. "The Most Gifted and Successful Demogogue This Country Has Ever Known," *New York Times Magazine* (April 1967), 23–24, 115–18, 20.

RORTY, JAMES, and MOSHE DECTER. *McCarthy and the Communists.* Boston: Beacon Press, 1954.

STRAIGHT, MICHAEL. *Trial by Television.* Boston: Beacon Press, 1954.

United States Congress, Senate, Special Investigation on charges and counter-charges involving: Secretary of the Army Robert T. Stevens, John G. Adams, H. Struve Hensel and Senator Joseph McCarthy, Roy M. Cohn, and Francis P. Carr. *Hearings, Special Subcommittee on Investigations,* 83d Congress, 2nd Session, on S. Res. 189, April 22–June 17, 1954. Washington D.C.: Government Printing Office, 1954.

THE ARMY — McCARTHY HEARINGS
THE ARMY McCARTHY HEARI
THE ARMY McCARTHY HEAR
THE ARMY McCARTHY HEA
THE ARMY McCARTHY H

NO SENSE OF DECENCY

Program cover for theatre production of *No Sense of Decency*

NO SENSE OF DECENCY: THE ARMY-McCARTHY HEARINGS

Cast of Characters and Key to Abbreviations

CT1: Conference Table 1
CT2: Conference Table 2
GF: Group Freeze
H: House
JM: Joseph McCarthy
JW: Joseph Welch
KM: Karl Mundt
MR: Miles Reber
N: Narrator
NH: Newspaper Headlines
PIC: Picture

RC: Roy Cohn
RS: Robert Stevens
S1: Screen 1
S2: Screen 2
S3: Screen 3
S4: Screen 4
SCR: Senate Caucus Room
SS: Stuart Symington
VG: Visual Group
V: Voice

Prologue

The Narrator and the Voice are seated in the audience. Karl Mundt, Roy Cohn, Robert Stevens, and Joe McCarthy enter down left, and Miles Reber, Stuart Symington, and Joseph Welch enter down right as all four screens (VG 1)* display scenes of the empty Senate caucus room.

V: The 1950s. The age of suspicion *(VG 2: Screen 1, NH–"Red Party is Red Threat"; Screen 2, NH–"Should Reds Teach?"; Screen 3, NH–"Loyalty Oaths Issued"; Screen 4, NH–"The University Doesn't Make Communists Out of Any of us"). The*

---

*All visuals remain displayed until otherwise indicated.

age of blacklisting *(VG 3: Screen 1, PIC–June 23, 1950, issue of* COUNTERATTACK*; Screen 2, PIC–*RED CHANNELS *entry on Leonard Bernstein; Screen 3, PIC–*RED CHANNELS *entry on José Ferrer; Screen 4, Mock Headlines–"Accuses," "Demands," "Denies").* The age of Congressional hearings *(VG 4: Screen 1, NH–"Witnesses Bare Red Plot to Infiltrate Boy Scouts" and "Boy Scouts Infiltrated by Reds? They Say Not"; Screen 2, NH–"Communist Threat Creates Problem for United States"; Screen 3, NH–"University of Texas Books Nest in Rest Search"; Screen 4, NH–"Ex-Spy Vows Red Bosses Ordered Copper Strike").* The age of McCarthyism *(VG 5: Screen 1, NH–" 'McCarthy to Austin Move' Argued in House' "; Screen 2, NH–"Ex-Red Involves Joe's Staff"; Screen 3, NH–"Ex-Commie Matusow Turns to Authorship"; Screen 4, NH–"McCarthy Calls for List of Communists in News Field").* Nineteen forty-one—Wisconsin circuit judge Joe McCarthy destroys document substantiating legal action taken by Wisconsin Department of Agriculture against local dairy[1] *(VG 6: Screen 1, NH–"Secret FBI Man Reveals: 35,000 Students Recruited Here for Red Fifth-Column"; Screen 2, NH–"History Little Help in 'Censure Joe' Case"; Screen 3, NH–"Coincidence May Keep Joe Away"; Screen 4, NH–"McCarthy Censure Debate Ends in Near Empty Senate").* Nineteen forty-four—Judge McCarthy neglects to report over $40,000 in stock market speculation to the Internal Revenue Service[2] *(VG 7: Screens 1, 3, 4–blank: Screen 2, PIC–Joseph McCarthy).* Nineteen forty-six—Disregarding the constitution and laws of Wisconsin, Judge McCarthy campaigns for U. S. Senator even though his term as circuit judge does not expire until 1951[3] *(VG 8: Screen 1, Blank; Screen 2, PIC–McCarthy and Campaign Poster; Screen 3, PIC–Campaign Poster "Republication Joseph McCarthy for U. S. Senate"; Screen 4, PIC–"Tailgunner Joe").* Nineteen forty-seven—Judge McCarthy elected as U. S. Senator from Wisconsin on his "Tail Gunner Joe" war record.[4] Nineteen forty-eight—Senator McCarthy was not a tail gunner in the Second World War, and was never wounded in the war. He never appeared on the war front. Nineteen fifty—Ambassador-at-Large Philip Jessup . . . has shown "an unusual affinity for Communist causes," the Senator reports[5] *(VG 9: Screens 1, 2, 4–blank: Screen 3, New York Times front page PIC of Philip Jessup testifying).* Nineteen fifty-one—Senator McCarthy reported of President Truman, after the President's dismissal of General Douglas MacArthur, that the President was a "son-of-a-bitch" and the firing must have come from a night of "bourbon and benedictine"[6] *(VG 10: Screens 1, 2, 4–blank: Screen 3, PIC–Harry Truman).* Nineteen fifty-two—Father Leon Sullivan, Catholic missionary imprisoned by Chinese Communists, reported: "I would rather return to my Chinese Communist prison cell than avail myself of Senator McCarthy's 'protection.' His is as great, if not a greater threat to American freedom than the military might of the Kremlin, and, believe me, I do not underestimate either the Kremlin's might or its

---

[1]James Rorty and Moshe Decter, *McCarthy and the Communists* (Boston: Beacon Press, 1954), p. 82.

[2]*Ibid.*, p. 83.

[3]*Ibid.*

[4]Emile de Antonio, "McCarthy" (printed insert accompanying Broadside Record Album No. BR450, 1968), p. 1.

[5]Earl Latham, *The Communist Controversy in Washington: From the New Deal to McCarthy* (Cambridge: Harvard University Press, 1966), p. 275.

[6]Eric Goldman, *The Crucial Decade and After* (New York: Random House, 1960), p. 203.

cleverness"[7] *(VG 11: All screens blank).* Nineteen fifty-three—Senator McCarthy's opinion of the very revered General George C. Marshall is: "He is a man steeped in falsehood," and that the general would, "Sell out his own grandmother"[8] *(VG 12: Screens 1, 2, 4, blank; Screen 2, PIC–General George C. Marshall with Eleanor Roosevelt).* Nineteen fifty-four—Senator McCarthy charges: The Army is blackmailing me and using one of my staff members, G. David Schine, as a hostage to halt my investigation of Communist infiltration in their Department (VG 13: Screens 1 and 4, blank: Screen 2, PIC–David Schine; Screen 3, NH–"Veil of Lies Hides Key in Army Probe").*

N: In the summer of 1953, the young, wealthy, and draftable G. David Schine, one of McCarthy's staff members, was notified that his draft status was about to change, and he was eligible to be conscripted into the armed forces. His invitation from the United States Army displeased Senator McCarthy and his Chief Counsel Roy Cohn, Schine's friend and colleague. The McCarthy forces set in motion a campaign to high pressure the Army to refrain from drafting Schine. When they learned that the Army would not cooperate in obtaining either a deferment or a direct commission for Schine, the McCarthy committee publicized widespread espionage at Fort Monmouth. Department of Defense officials retaliated with a letter to certain senators warning that if McCarthy did not halt the destructive publicity, they would issue charges against the senator for seeking preferential treatment for Private Schine. Continued abuse from the McCarthy staff forced the Army to file the threatened charge. McCarthy's countercharge of blackmail and treason on the part of the Army was filed several days later. The furor over the dispute became so disruptive that the Congress was compelled to investigate the charges and countercharges. *(VG 14: Screen 1, SCR with caption "June 22, 1954"; Screens 2, 3, 4 SCR without caption).* That investigation was the now famous Army-McCarthy Hearings, a documentary drama whose principle characters are:

KM: Senator Karl Mundt, temporary chairman of the Senate Subcommittee on Investigations. His role is to keep the hearings at the proper level of the dignity of the Senate *(VG 15: Screens 1 and 4, SCR; Screens 2 and 3, PIC–Senator Karl E. Mundt).*

SS: Senator Stuart Symington, Democratic member of the committee. He stands in direct opposition to McCarthy's tactics *(VG 16: Screens 1 and 4, SCR; Screens 2 and 3, PIC–Senator Stuart Symington)*

JW: Counselor Joseph Welch, seasoned courtroom lawyer, who is appearing on the Army's behalf. He is to prove that the McCarthy committee did exert pressure for preferential treatment for Private Schine *(VG 17: Screens 1 and 4, SCR; Screens 2 and 3, PIC–Joseph N. Welch, Special Counsel for the Army).*

MR: Major General Miles Reber, an Army witness subpoenaed to relate his role in trying to obtain a commission for Private Schine *(VG 18: Screens 1 and 4, SCR; Screens 2 and 3, PIC–Major General Miles Reber).*

RS: Republican Secretary of the Army, Robert Tenbrooke Stevens, called to defend the Army's charges against McCarthy and characterized as "a goldfish among

---

[7]Rorty and Decter, *op cit.,* p. 86.

[8]Alexander Kendrick, *Prime Time: The Life of Edward R. Murrow* (Boston: Little, Brown and Company, 1969), p. 41; Richard Rovere, "The Most Gifted and Successful Demagogue This Country Has Ever Known," *New York Times Magazine* (April 1967), p. 115.

barracudas"[9] *(VG 19: Screens 1 and 4, SCR; Screens 2 and 3, PIC–Robert T. Stevens, Secretary of the Army).*

RC: Roy Cohn, Chief Counsel for the McCarthy committee, and longtime friend and ally of the Senator *(VG 20: Screens 1 and 4, SCR; Screens 2 and 3, PIC–Roy M. Cohn, Chief Counsel for McCarthy).*

JM: Senator Joseph Raymond McCarthy, Junior Senator from Wisconsin. His immense power derives from his reputation as "Mr. Anti-Communist." He is called by his friends simply "Tail Gunner Joe" *(VG 21: Screens 1 and 4, SCR; Screens 2 and 3, PIC–Senator Joseph McCarthy).*

Episode I[10]

(Karl Mundt crosses down center of house; Robert Stevens crosses down left of house; Roy Cohn crosses down left; Joe McCarthy crosses up left; Miles Reber crosses down right of house; Stuart Symington crosses down right; Joseph Welch crosses up right.)

SS: In the excitement over these hearings I think the charges and countercharges made have been forgotten. The charge is: did Senator McCarthy and two members of the staff use improper pressures for Mr. David Schine with the Army. The countercharge is that there was blackmail on the part of the Army and the use of Mr. Schine as a hostage. Now those are the charges that have been made, and they are so diametrically in conflict that, as I see it, they cannot possibly be reconciled *(VG 22: Screens 1 and 4, SCR; Screens 2 and 3, blank).*

KM: Thank you very much, Senator Symington. I will now call the first witness.

JM: A point of order, Mr. Chairman. May I raise a point of order? The specifications filed here by Mr. Stevens and Mr. Adams are entitled, "Filed by the Department of the Army," and if I understand, the committee unanimously voted that Mr. Stevens, Mr. Hensel, and Mr. Adams were parties to this dispute, but the Department of the Army has never been made a party to this dispute. I have heard, Mr. Chairman, from people in the military all the way from generals, with most upstanding combat records, down to privates recently inducted, and they indicate they are very resentful of the fact that a few Pentagon politicians, attempting to disrupt our investigations, are naming themselves the Department of the Army. I would suggest that the Chair direct Mr. Hensel, Mr. Stevens, and Mr. Adams to list themselves as individuals who are here to prove that a private in the Army got special consideration.

KM: The Chair will say that the statement of Mr. Stevens is not before it at the present time. You may raise your point of order when Mr. Stevens is the witness, if you so desire at that time.

JM: Mr. Chairman, I maintain it is a disgrace and reflection upon every one of the million outstanding men in the Army to let a few civilians who are trying to hold up an investigation of Communists, label themselves as the Department of the Army. I do not think . . .

KM: The Chair will hold that the point of order would not be raised at this time.

JM: May I finish?

[9]*Time Magazine* (March 8, 1954), p. 23

[10]Army-McCarthy Hearings. Unless otherwise noted, the script is taken from segments of the Hearings, pp. 1–780.

KM: I will call the first witness.

JM: I object to the attempt to make this a contest between me and the Army. I do not have any respect for the civilians in the Pentagon who have been working night and day to attempt to shift an investigation of Communism, Communist infiltration, into an investigation of one private in the Army.

KM: You will be overruled at this time because it is not appropriate.

JM: I would like to make it very clear that there is no contest between Senator McCarthy and the Department of the Army. All that Senator McCarthy has been trying to do is expose the Communists who have infiltrated the Department of the Army, a very small percent.

KM: I will call the first witness. The Chair suggested that perhaps you reread the official presentation which is before this committee and which makes it very clear the participants involved. Major General Miles Reber, please take the stand. *(Miles Reber crosses up center.)* State your name and rank, please.

MR: Major General Miles Reber of the United States Army.

KM: State what you were doing in July of 1953.

MR: In July of 1953 I was Legislative Liason of the Army.

KM: What were your duties in that capacity?

MR: I was to insure the maintenance of proper relations between the Congress and the Army.

N: In July, the McCarthy committee made their first request of General Reber for preferential treatment for Private Schine. The general was to obtain a commission for the private.

KM: What, exactly did the McCarthy committee request of you with reference to G. David Schine?

MR: They demanded that I obtain a direct commission for Private Schine.

KM: Will you state what qualifications Mr. Cohn claimed to have been possessed by Mr. Schine,at that time?

MR: Mr. Cohn informed me that Mr. Schine had been a junior ship's officer in the Army Transport Service, and had served in that capacity for approximately one year beginning in the fall of 1946, and that Mr. Schine had at that time the assimilated rank of first lieutenant. It was emphasized to me that there was a very definite necessity for speed in looking into the possibility of obtaining this commission because the status of Mr. Schine under the Selective Service Act was apparently about to change. I later learned that Mr. Schine had not been a junior ship's officer in the Army Transport Service, so the commission was impossible to obtain.

KM: Did anyone from the McCarthy committee contact you at any other time during the month of July on behalf of G. David Schine?

MR: Yes, Sir, on numerous occasions.

KM: Were telephone calls from Senators unusual?

MR: No, Sir, telephone calls from Senators were not unusual.

KM: And that has been common practice, I would say, since the time which your memory runneth not to the contrary, is it not? You know of the tremendously important work in which Senator McCarthy was then engaged, did you not?

MR: I certainly did, Sir.

KM: And that was the investigation of Communists and of the infiltration of Communists in industry, in every branch of the government, as well as in the Army?

MR: That was my understanding.

KM: Does any endeavor on the part of any individual or group of individuals occur to you as being more important and especially at this particular time, than that of the tracking down and ferreting out of Communists, whether they be in the Army or anywhere else in this country?

MR: Certainly not to my knowledge, Sir.

KM: And that was the work that Senator McCarthy and G. David Schine were doing, was it not?

MR: That is correct, Sir.

KM: And you were told by both Senator McCarthy and Mr. Cohn that Schine was an expert, trained investigator, with a background of experience, possessing a peculiar knowledge of what constituted a Communist and the means and best methods of detecting a Communist. They told you that, did they not?

MR: That is correct, Sir. *(Group freeze. VG 23: Screens 1 and 4, SCR; Screen 2: PIC–Telegram to Owen Lattimore informing him of McCarthy's espionage charge; Screen 3, PIC–Telegram from Owner Lattimore denying charge of Communist espionage).*

V: "Owen Lattimore (eminent professor at Johns Hopkins University) is the chief Soviet espionage agent in the United States," the Senator reports.[11] But it was the conclusion of the Tydings Committee that, "We find no evidence to support the charge that Owen Lattimore is the 'top Russian spy' or, for that matter, any other sort of spy."[12] McCarthy still says: "There is no academic freedom where a Communist is concerned." *(VG 24: Screens 1 and 4, SCR; Screens 2 and 3, blank.)*

KM: Now, General, you have spoken of numerous calls from Senator McCarthy and numerous others from Mr. Cohn. Taking into consideration the vital work in which they told you Schine was engaged, I believe you say that you did not regard the efforts of Senator McCarthy as being improper in any respect in his efforts to get some, shall we say, preferential treatment for Schine so that he could assist in carrying on this investigative work of the Senate; is that right?

MR: I do not believe, Mr. Mundt, I said anything about the propriety of those calls.

KM: What about Mr. Cohn?

MR: I felt that Mr. Cohn was persistently after me, Sir.

KM: Did you know that at that time—that is, July 1953—and perhaps before that time, the McCarthy Investigating Committee was laying the groundwork for an investigation of Communist infiltration at Fort Monmouth?

MR: I did not, in July of 1953, know that.

KM: Do you know that G. David Schine participated in the investigation of Fort Monmouth?

MR: It is my understanding that he did.

KM: Fort Monmouth is the very site upon which the defenses against both the atomic and the hydrogen bomb are planned and laid, is that correct?

MR: It is the Signal Corps Research and Development Activity, Sir.

KM: So it was vital to the interests and the safety and the security of the nation that there of all places be no employee or no member of the Army at Fort Monmouth

[11]Owen Lattimore, *Ordeal by Slander* (Boston: Little, Brown and Company, 1950), p. 1.

[12]Latham, p. 279.

who was a doubtful security risk. That is correct, is it not? And that is the character of work that was carried on by the senator, the members of the staff, including Schine, with the result that thirty-three questionable civilian employees were discharged or suspended. *(Group freeze. VG 25: Screens 1 and 4, SCR; Screen 2, NH–"Hearing Confused in Monmouth Case;" Screen 3, blank).*

V: McCarthy charges that Ruth Levine was discharged from Fort Monmouth as a security risk. But Ruth Levine was not employed at Fort Monmouth.[13] *(VG 26: Screens 1 and 4, SCR; Screens 2 and 3, blank.)*

MR: It is a matter of general knowledge that various people were suspended at Fort Monmouth, and I don't believe it is a matter of general knowledge as to reasons why those individuals were suspended.

JM: General, when you called to our office and when you had this great success in helping promote Schine to the extent that he is a private, don't you think that you should have at least told me about the fact that you were the brother of the man who has all this difficulty with Mr. Cohn and Mr. Schine, if I can use the word?

MR: Senator McCarthy, if I had had the slightest idea then or now that any difficulty that Mr. Cohn and Mr. Schine had had with my brother would have affected my actions in this case, I certainly would have told you. I have not had that idea until the present moment.

JM: Would it in any way affect your testimony, do you think?

MR: It certain would not affect my testimony.

JM: General, you were before this committee a number of times, is that right, when I was chairman?

MR: I actually only testified once—on the eighth of September, 1953. I did, in my capacity of chief of Legislative Liaison, furnish your committee a great deal of information from time to time.

JM: At that time we asked—as I recall, I repeated the question a number of times—asked you whether or not you felt that the committee should be entitled to the names of individuals at the Pentagon who had protected and covered up Communists. At that time I had difficulty getting an answer from you on that. I am firmly convinced the reason we are spending our time on the question of whether or not Private Schine received special consideration is because we are getting close to the nerve center in the Pentagon of the civilian politicans over the past ten or twenty years who have covered up.

KM: The Senator's time has expired.

SS: Mr. Chairman, I have one question. Did Mr. Cohn complain to you at any time during this period of any bias, alleged bias, that you might have against him by reason of your brother?

MR: No, none whatsoever. The first conversation that I have heard from either Senator McCarthy or Mr. Cohn about my brother occurred in this hearing today. I can tell the committee absolutely unequivocally that I acted without any bias of any kind in this case.

SS: General Reber, was there anything that you would have done within your power that was left undone to get the commission for Mr. Schine?

MR: No, Sir.

JM: Are you aware of the fact that your brother was allowed to resign when charges

[13]Rorty and Decter, p. 58.

that he was a bad security risk were made against him as a result of the investigations of this committee?

KM: Mr. Chairman, I must object to that on the grounds that it is wholly irrelevant.

JM: If his brother was forced to resign from a high position in the State Department as a result of activities on the part of this committee, resigned because he was a bad security risk, even by no reflection upon the General, I do think that it is important to have that in the record insofar as the possible motive of his testimony is concerned.

SS: There has been no testimony that the statements that the senator makes as facts are true, and until they are established in this record as facts, then the question is incompetent. Let us have a ruling on this, because we may be trying members of everybody's family involved before we get through.

JM: Did your brother retire or resign from the State Department as a result of his being investigated by the McCarthy committee?

MR: Until you brought this question up I had never heard that my brother retired as a result of any action of this committee. The answer is "Positively No" to that question.

JM: Let me ask this question: Do you know now or do you have any reason to believe that your brother resigned because charges involving security were brought against him?

MR: As I understand this procedure, a very serious charge has been made against my brother in this room. I would like to answer that charge publicly right now, to the most honest extent of my knowledge. My brother retired from the Department of State—*(Group freeze.)*

V: The slander amalgam—Senator McCarthy refers to the New York *Post* as the "Uptown Edition" of the *Daily Worker* . . . The Washington *Post* as the "local edition" . . . and the Milwaukee *Journal* as the "Milwaukee edition."[14] The slander amalgam—Vice President Agnew refers to Democrat Senator Albert Gore as the "Southern regional chairman of the Eastern Liberal Establishment" . . . and Democratic Senator Frank Moss as the "Western regional chairman of the Eastern Liberal Establishment."[15]

JM: A point of order. I just want to make the record clear that if General Reber is going to go into the grounds upon which his brother was separated, if that is considered pertinent, then I feel that I have a right to cross-examine him upon that subject.

SS: Mr. Counsel, may I say that the statement has been made in this room and is apparent to millions of Americans that General Reber's brother was dismissed as a security risk. I want to state in the record that the statement cannot be stricken from all the newspapers tonight, or from the television audience, and radio audience, and I think in fairness he should be given the opportunity to answer the statement limited to that charge that his brother was dismissed as a security risk.

JM: I am not concerned with General Reber's brother. I asked the question on the basis of motive. but if the general now denies that his brother was allowed or forced to resign because of security reasons, if the committee thinks that is pertinent, then I feel that I must demand the right—whether the demand is granted or not—I must demand the right to cross-examine the general on that subject and also produce witnesses from the State Department on this subject.

[14]*Ibid.,* p. 74.

[15]"Agnew on the Warpath," *Life Magazine* (October 16, 1970), p. 26.

SS: Mr. Chairman, these extraneous accusations that are being made against people who are not parties to this proceeding, do carry over the air and on television and in the press. It has been stated here that the general's brother was dismissed as a security risk. I contend that he has a right on the same forum at this time to either confirm or deny, and that should end it, because it is not important to these proceedings whether he is dismissed as a security risk or as a chicken thief or as a gentleman.

JM: Mr. Chairman, my position is that if the general is going to give us a statement about the reason for his brother's dismissal, gratuitously, then I should have the right to cross-examine him, period. *(Group freeze.)*

V: The demagogue is "a man of loose tongue, intemperate, trusting in tumult, leading the populace to mischief with empty words."[16] *(Miles Reber crosses down right of house; Robert Stevens crosses up center.)*

Episode II

N: The McCarthy Investigating Committee charges that Secretary of the Army, Stevens and Mr. Adams made constant attempts to trade off preferential treatment for Private Schine as an inducement to the subcommittee to halt its exposition of Communist infiltration in the military, especially at the radar installation of Fort Monmouth. Senator McCarthy demands that the secretary admit to his eagerness in halting the investigation.

JM: Now Bob, this is a very simple question, can you tell us today, whether or not you wanted the hearings at Fort Monmouth suspended?

RS: I wanted to stop the hammering of the Army over the head and head lines of the press which were creating the impression that there was widespread espionage at Fort Monmouth when such was not the case.

JM: How did you finally succeed in getting the hearings suspended?

RS: How did I finally succeed?

JM: Yes. They are suspended as of today. We both agree to that, I believe. How did you finally succeed?

RS: They aren't suspended, as far as I know.

JM: You know that the hearings were suspended the day you or someone filed your charges against Mr. Cohn, Mr. Carr, and myself. You know that, don't you? Let's not be coy.

RS: I am not being coy at all. I don't think that has anything to do with it, Senator McCarthy.

JM: Was not that the way you got them suspended?

RS: If you are talking about Fort Monmouth, I think those hearings were suspended quite a long time ago.

JM: Then we will talk about all the hearings into Communist infiltration in the Army, so there is no question about their having been suspended a long time ago. The day before you filed your charges against my chief counsel, my chief of staff, and me, Bob, we asked for information on those who were responsible for the promotion, the honorable discharge, and the favorable stateside duty for the Fifth Amendment Communist. You know that was done, Mr. Secretary, the day before you filed those charges, so don't come here and tell us they were suspended a

---

[16]Rovere, p. 115, citing Euripides, *Orestes*.

long time ago. Mr. Stevens, do you want to tell us today under oath that you feel that the filing of your charges had nothing to do with the suspension of our hearings?

RS: I don't think that the Army's allegations against you could stop the work of the Congress of the United States. I certainly hope it can't.

JM: Answer my question, will you? Will you answer the question?

RS: May I have the question read?

JM: If you don't remember it, you certainly may.

KM: "Mr. Stevens, do you want to tell us today under oath that you feel that the filing of your charges had nothing to do with the suspension of our hearings?"

RS: I will stand on the answer I made.

JM: I will ask the Chair to order you to answer the question, Bob. I think you owe us that answer.

RS: May we have the answer that I gave read?

JM: Will you take time out, Mr. Chairman? *(Robert Stevens crosses down left of house.)*

N: The letter of the law applies to whomever the senator wishes but not to the senator himself. *(Joseph McCarthy crosses up center.)* As we hear Counselor Welch wring a confession from McCarthy of the organized spy-and-informer ring in the federal government, we find the senator "taking the Fifth." Welch insists on knowing where McCarthy obtained a classified letter from J. Edgar Hoover to the Army, warning that Department of Communist infiltration at Fort Monmouth.

JW: Senator McCarthy, when you took the stand you knew, of course, that you were going to be asked about the letter, did you not?

JM: I assumed that would be the subject.

JW: And you, of course, understood that you were going to be asked the source from which you got it?

JM: I won't answer that.

JW: Could I have the oath that you read to us wholly by the reporter?

KM: Mr. Welch, that doesn't seem to be an appropriate question. It's the same oath you took.

JW: The oath included a promise, a solemn promise by you to tell the truth and nothing but the truth. Is that correct, Sir?

JM: Mr. Welch, you are not the first individual that tried to get me to betray the confidence and give out the names of my informants. You will be no more successful than those who have tried it in the past.

JW: I am only asking you, Sir, did you realize when you took the oath that you were making a solemn promise to tell the truth to this committee?

JM: I understand the oath, Mr. Welch.

JW: And when you took it, did you have some mental reservation, some Fifth or Sixth Amendment notion, that you could measure what you would tell?

JM: I don't take the Fifth Amendment.

JW: Have you some private reservation when you take the oath that lets you be the judge of what you testify to?

JM: The answer is that there is no reservation about telling the whole truth.

JW: Thank you, Sir. Then tell us who delivered the documents to you?

JM: The answer is No. You will not get the information.

JW: You wish then to put your own interpretation on your oath and tell us less than the whole truth?

JM: You can go right ahead and try until doomsday. You will not get the names of any informants who rely upon me to protect them.

JW: Will you tell us where you were when you got it?

JM: No.

JW: Were you in Washington?

JM: The answer was I would not tell you.

JW: How soon after you got it did you show it to anyone?

JM: I don't remember.

JW: To whom did you first show it?

JM: I don't remember.

JW: To whom did you first show it?

JM: I don't recall.

JW: Can you think of anyone to whom you showed it?

JM: Oh, I assume that it was passed down to my staff most likely.

JW: Name the ones on your staff who had it.

JM: I wouldn't know.

JW: You wouldn't know?

JM: No. (Group freeze.)

V: "Senator Flanders from Vermont disapproves of Senator McCarthy's tactics." But, Senator McCarthy relates that the Vermont Senator is "senile." And he thinks "They should get a net and take him to a good quiet place." *(Joseph McCarthy crosses up left.)*

Episode III

N: Chief Counsel for the McCarthy Committee, Roy Cohn, testified that Secretary Stevens requested *(VG 27: Screens 1 and 4, SCR; Screen 2, McCarthy's cropped pic of Schine and Stevens; Screen 3, blank.)* to have his photograph taken alone with G. David Schine at McGuire Air Force Base. Cohn's testimony clearly implied that the Army cooperated in giving Schine preferential treatment, that the secretary of the Army flew from his Washington, D. C., office to McGuire Base and made special arrangements to be photographed smiling at Schine. On the following day Mr. Welch, counsel for *(VG 28: Screens 1 and 4, SCR; Screen 2, McCarthy's cropped pic of Schine and Stevens; Screen 3, Pic of Francis P. Carr, Col. Bradley, Schine and Stevens showing Army's crop and McCarthy's crop.)* the Army, submitted as evidence the actual photograph, a photograph in which four people appear—Secretary Stevens and Colonel Bradley from the Army, Private Schine and Francis P. Carr from the McCarthy Committee. The McCarthy staff cropped the photograph to show only Private Schine and Secretary Stevens, who were standing next to each other. Their purpose in altering the photograph to show just Private Schine and Secretary Stevens was to substantiate their claim that Stevens had ingratiated himself to Schine in order to stop McCarthy's investigation of Communist infiltration in the Army. *(VG 29: Screen 1 and 4, SCR; Screen 2, Pic of Bradley, Schine and Stevens from movie*

"Point of Order"; Screen 3, Pic of Bradley, Schine and Stevens from movie "Point of Order.")

JW: And produced as if it were honest. Mr. Chairman, I have a point of order. Here is the photograph that was offered yesterday in evidence, and in respect to which Mr. Stevens was not only examined but cross-examined. I show you now a photograph which, I charge was an altered, shamefully cut-down picture, so that somebody could say to Stevens, "Were you not photographed alone with David Schine," when the truth is he was photographed in a group. I would like to offer the picture that I have in my right hand as the original, undoctored, unaltered piece of evidence.

JM: I think we should have the third man identified, and we should have Mr. Welch sworn and have him tell how the picture has been doctored, if it has been doctored. I am curious to know how. I think the fact that there is a third man in here, if this is an accurate picture—and I assume it is—the third man should be identified. Again, Mr. Chairman, I suggest that Mr. Welch, if he is going to make charges such as he has, should be put under oath and tell how this was doctored, and who doctored it. Mr. Chairman, may I have that picture? Mr. Chairman, Mr. Welch has made the statement under the guise of being a point of order that this picture was doctored, and I look at it now and I don't have the other picture before me. May I have it?

JW: This is the doctored picture.

JM: I think, Mr. Chairman, when counsel for Mr. Adams and Mr. Stevens and Mr. Hensel—

KM: Senator McCarthy, may the Chair say—

JM: Mr. Chairman, couldn't we have an understanding here that when I start to make a point of order that I may finish without interruption?

KM: Make a point of order and then speak to it.

JM: The point of order is this: That Mr. Welch, under the guise of making a point of order, has testified that a picture is doctored. I now have before me, and I may say this: Yesterday was the first time I saw either of these pictures, and he makes the completely false statement that this is a group picture, and it is not.

KM: Senator McCarthy, may I say—

JM: May I finish my point of order?

KM: The Chair advises the senator that he is engaging in a statement of cross-examination rather than a point of order.

JM: I am getting rather sick of being interrupted in the middle of a sentence.

SS: I would like to say if this is not a point of order, it is out of order. The Chair says it is not a point of order.

JM: Oh, be quiet.

SS: I haven't the slightest intention of being quiet. The Chair is running this committee and you are not running it.

JM: Mr. Chairman, may I suggest that when I want to say something, I not be interrupted in the middle of a sentence and that Mr. Symington and no one else have the right to interrupt unless he addresses the Chair, and unless the Chair recognizes him. I am getting awfully sick of sitting down here at the end of the table and having whoever wants to interrupt in the middle of a sentence. Now, Mr. Welch made a statement and I raised a point of order that it was not a proper point of order that he raised, and that he said this picture was doctored, and may I suggest to the Chair as a point of order in fairness to whoever produced the picture that Mr. Welch point out wherein the picture was doctored. I can see no doctoring, except that a Colonel Bradley, who will be a witness here, his picture was not included. When Mr. Welch under the guise of a point of order said this was a group picture, I suggest that the Chair make the record clear that Mr. Welch was not speaking the truth, and that the only change—

SS: Mr. Chairman, Mr. Chairman—

JM: Mr. Chairman—

KM: Do you have a point of order?

JM: Call it a point of order or call it what you may, when counsel for Mr. Stevens, and Mr. Hensel, and Mr. Adams makes a statement and he is allowed to do it without interruption, and if that statement is false, do I have a right to correct it, or do we find halfway through my statement that Mr. Welch should not have made his statement and therefore I cannot point out that he was lying?

SS: I would like to make a point of order, myself. The Chair has stated twice, and I heard it, that what was being said was not a point of order, and I believe that if we are going to keep these hearings at the proper level, of the dignity of the Senate, we have to follow the rulings of the Chair. Now, Mr. Cohn, don't you think it was important yesterday when Mr. Stevens testified under oath that he had no recollection about having a picture taken "alone" with David Schine, and Mr. Mundt asked and it became very material to this question whether this picture was taken alone or with someone else. Don't you think you should have called attention to the fact that this picture might not be complete?

RC: I did not catch the word "alone," and I did not attach any significance to it then, and I don't recall even hearing it. I recall questioning about a picture of Secretary Stevens and Private Schine. If I had known that there were other persons in the picture, I would have been glad to supply that. I might say I think it is completely unimportant, whether or not Colonel Bradley is standing to the side while this picture is taken or not.

SS: But don't you think that Mr. Mundt very rightfully asked the question of Mr. Stevens: "Did you have a picture taken alone with Private Schine," and just let me finish my question, because the picture that had been handed to Mr. Mundt showed the two of them together?

JM: A point of order, Mr. Chairman. May I suggest that the question asked by Mr. Mundt be read into the record. In all fairness to the witness, the question should be read. The question as asked does not contain the word "alone". Later on the word was asked, starting on page 433 of the record.

SS: Since when did I ever suggest to other members of this committee or witnesses what questions they ought to ask?

JW: Mr. Cohn, I assume you would like it understood that I am not your counsel?

RC: There is not a statement that has been made at this hearing which I am in more complete agreement, Mr. Welch, although I say I am sure you are a lawyer of great ability and maybe I would be fortunate if I had you as my counsel. I have no counsel here. Roy Cohn is here speaking for Roy Cohn, to give the facts. I have no counsel, and I feel the need for none, Sir.

JW: In all modesty; Sir, I am content that it should appear from my end that I am not your counsel. Would someone hold up what I call the big picture so that this witness can see it? Mr. Cohn, you have spoken of that picture as representing Mr. Stevens smiling at Schine. Will you look at it now with me?

RC: Let's have it closer. Mr. Welch, may I confess to a slight case of nearsightedness here, and I hope that is not nearsightedness, in connection with my duties, but it is when it comes to these things. I would like to have that right up here.

JW: I think you have betrayed some nearsightedness. Have it as close as you like.

RC: Mr. Welch, I might say here again, I will be very glad to answer your questions here. I don't think I am quite as clever as you are, and I am afraid I am not going to be able to answer your questions.

JW: Oh, Mr. Cohn, my question now is this: You have referred to that picture as showing Mr. Secretary Stevens smiling at David Schine. Are you now close enough to the picture so that you would like to qualify that statement?

RC: Sir, I will accept your characterization of the picture.

JW: It is a grim smile on Stevens' face.

RC: I accept it. If you want to call Mr. Stevens' smile a grim smile, Sir, I fully accept what you say. To me it is a picture of Secretary Stevens. If it is a grim smile, so be it. It is a picture of Private Schine. They are standing next to each other. They are facing each other. Their eyes are meeting. They are looking at each other. If the smile is grim or if it isn't grim, I know not, Sir.

JW: Not too fast, Mr. Cohn; not too fast. Mr. Stevens is looking to his right, isn't he?

RC: Well, Sir—

JW: Isn't he? You can answer that one easily.

RC: Mr. Welch, do you want to imply that I am not answering it? You asked me a question, and then you say with the implication as though I can't answer it.

JW: Well, answer it. Mr. Stevens is looking to his right, isn't he?

RC: Sir, if you will give me the chance, I will try to answer it.

JW: By all means, Sir.

RC: Thank you. The picture, to me, looks as though Mr. Stevens and Private Schine are looking at each other.

JW: My question was a simple one. Mr. Stevens is looking to his right, is he not?

RC: Yes, I would say he probably is looking to his right, and Private Schine is standing to his right.

JW: On Mr. Stevens' right are two figures, is that correct?

RC: Yes, that is correct. To Mr. Stevens' right there are two figures.

JW: One is Private Schine?

RC: Yes, Sir.

JW: And further to Mr. Stevens' right is Colonel Bradley?

RC: Standing sideways.

JW: It would take someone with clairvoyance to know to whom Secretary Stevens is looking, would it not?

RC: No, Sir. I don't think so. It would take someone with common sense who can look at a picture and see what is in it.

JW: I think I observe on Colonel Bradley's face a faint little look of pleasure. Do you, sir?

RC: I would say I know that Colonel Bradley had a good steak dinner shortly afterward. Maybe he was anticipating it. I do know that Colonel Bradley looks to me as though he, too, is looking at Private Schine.

JW: If Bradley is feeling good about a steak dinner, Schine must be considering a whole haunch of beef.

RC: Yes, sir, and Mr. Stevens, possibly you may be right, the grimness on his face might have come after Senator McCarthy told him that hearings showing what was going on in Communist infiltration in the Army would begin the next Tuesday. *(Group freeze. VG 30: Screen 1, Mock newspaper heads "Accuses," "Demands," "Denies"; Screen 2, "Accuses," "Demands," "Denies"; Screen 3, "Accuses," "Demands," "Denies"; Screen 4, "Accuses," "Demands," "Denies.")*

Episode IV[17]

V: 1952, Senator McCarthy says: "The issue between Republicans and Democrats is clearly drawn; it has been deliberately drawn by those that have been in charge of twenty years of treason. Now, the hard fact is . . . that those who wear the label 'Democrat' wear it with a stain of historic betrayal." And . . . "The Democratic Party has time after time and irrevocably, labeled itself as the party which stands for government of, by, and for Communist crooks and cronies. Which means that if they return to power, you get another . . . twenty years of the same."[18]

SS: The charge by the junior senator from Wisconsin that we've had another year of treason under *(VG 31: Screen 1, "Accuses," "Demands," "Denies"; Screen 2, Herblock cartoon depicting burglars gathering evidence for McCarthy; Screen 3, Herblock cartoon depicting McCarthy burning doctored photo and faked letter; Screen 4, "Accuses," "Demands," "Denies.")* President Eisenhower, the charge that the C.I.A. is infiltrated and infested with Communists, the charge that the Department of Defense is full of Communists, the charge that the Department of Justice, that the Attorney General of the Department of Justice—there's something phony about him, and the charge that the hydrogen bomb plants and the atomic bomb plants are full of Communists—well, where do we go from here as the American people? It would appear some of us want to end up in this country with just plain anarchy.

JM: Will he, Symington, be willing to go under oath, the same as the rest of us are going under oath, the same as I have gone under oath and will go under oath, the same as the Republicans have gone under oath and tell us the truth of what part he had to play with these hearings? If he will merely consent to go on the stand and tell us why and how it happened that, number one, he got the political adviser of the Democratic Party to guide under cover the Republican Secretary of the Army and, number two, while our very sanctimonious Stu was a—

SS: Senator McCarthy, I resent that reference to my first name—you better go to a psychiatrist. I need no psychological bribe from you—nobody in the Senate knows more about how to avoid testifying than the junior senator from Wisconsin and everybody in the United States knows that fact is true. At different times when they wanted to put you under oath, you didn't want to go.

JM: Mr. Symington has said that no one knows better than the senator from Wisconsin how to avoid testifying. I have now at this time made the offer to go on the stand and let him question me about everything. I don't care how irrelevant it is.

SS: Mr. Chairman, I have decided to testify under oath before this committee. I believe

[17]*Point of Order* (Motion Picture) Point Films. Released by Point Films, 1964.

[18]de Antonio, p. 1.

that I will have performed a public service of overwhelming importance if any action of mine can induce you to answer under oath the allegations formally preferred against you by the Senate Subcommittee and to which you have heretofore persistently refused to respond except to denounce the subcommittee. Accordingly, I propose that we agree on the following points: (1) You will agree to an investigation by a committee of the Senate—I will agree to take the stand in the present proceedings and to testify as to the events preceding the institution of these hearings. I trust that you will confirm your agreement with this program. If you are in accord, please sign as indicated below. Senator, here is the letter and if you will sign it, then we can get this matter settled.

JM: Mr. Symington, I think, I'm glad we're on television, I think the millions of people can see how low an alleged man can sink. He's been asked here to come before the committee and give the information which he has in regard to this investigation. He retorts by saying that he wants all of the old smears investigated. Now, may I say this, Mr. Chairman, if that is necessary in order to get Symington on the stand—that will be done. If the Vice President—

SS: Just sign the letter—

JM: I will not sign the letter with false statements in it—

SS: Sign the letter. I's very simple. It's in the record. All you have to do is sign it and then we'll be all—

JM: Don't pull that phony thing on me.

SS: Sign the letter. Here it is, Senator, it's got my signature on it. Sign it.

JM: You have a document with false statements in it. I will not sign and agree that's true. I don't—you're not fooling anyone. You're not fooling anyone, Mr. Symington. I have offered to go before any committee, do anything you ask, if I can just get you to come down here and take the oath so we can get the answers to some questions. Now, you're not, you're not fooling anyone at all.

SS: Senator, Senator, let me tell you something. The American people have had a look at you for six weeks. You're not fooling anyone either. In all the years that I have been in the government, based on the testimony that's been given before this committee under oath, I think the files of what you call my staff, my director, my chief of staff have been the sloppiest and most dangerously handled lies that I have ever known of since I've been in the government. *(Roy Cohn crosses up center.)*

Episode V

N: David Schine flew to New York upon instructions from the McCarthy Committee to retrieve the photograph of Secretary Stevens and himself. Several McCarthy Committee members conferred about the treatment *(VG 32: Screen 1, "Accuses," "Demands," "Denies"; Screen 2, Pic of Francis P. Carr, Col. Bradley, Schine, and Stevens showing Army's crop and McCarthy's crop; Screen 3, Pic of Francis P. Carr, Col Bradley, Schine, and Stevens showing Army's crop and McCarthy's crop; Screen 4, "Accuses," "Demands," "Denies.")* of the picture. Mr. Welch questions Roy Cohn, McCarthy staff member, about his role in reproducing the "cropped" photograph.

JW: Mr. Cohn, you just told us that you were under continuous instructions, for a period of a week or more, to furnish a picture of Stevens and Schine, is that right. Sir?

RC: No, Mr. Welch, it was over a period of two or three days.

JW: Two or three days?

RC: Yes, sir.

JW: And like a good hired man, in the end you produced, didn't you?

RC: Yes, sir.

JW: Mr. Cohn, isn't the simple truth that no blow-up of the original Schine picture was needed in the first instance?

RC: I don't follow the question.

JW: Let me put it to you this way: We have been able to get alone all right in the courtroom with the very thing that was brought down from New York, haven't we? Do you see it?

RC: Well, I think I just assume that the only reason it was blown up was so that it would be exhibited easier.

JW: Well, then, the only thing to do was to bring in the photostat of the original picture, with three people in the case, isn't that right?

RC: I wasn't asked for it and I didn't deliver that.

JW: I think that is right. You were asked for something different from the thing that hung on Schine's wall.

RC: I never knew what hung on Schine's wall.

JW: Did you think this came from a pixie? Where did you think this picture that I hold in my hand came from?

RC: I had no idea.

JM: Will counsel for my benefit define—I think he might be an expert on that—what a pixie is?

JW: Yes, I should say, Mr. Senator, that a pixie is a close relative of a fairy. Shall I proceed sir? Have I enlightened you? Mr. Cohn, when we come right down to this caucus room, we can do very well with exhibit three which I hold in my hand, can't we?

RC: I think it would suffice, but I also think that even your blown-up picture is much larger and would be much nicer to handle and would be better for the television cameras and for the audience.

JW: Mr. Cohn, you just told Senator Mundt that you had no malicious intent when you handed in what I shall call now the smaller picture; is that right?

RC: That is correct, sir.

JW: Are you intensely sorry that you did it?

RC: Due to the fact that—

JW: I don't care due to what fact.

RC: Due to the fact that it has wasted so much time, I am sorry.

JW: Only that, sir?

RC: Yes, sir.

JW: Your conscience, then, doesn't bother you to this moment, is that right?

RC: I did nothing wrong, in my conscience, and it does not bother me.

JW: Don't you think a terrifically unfortunate situation was created when Mr. Stevens sat in this chair and was confronted with your doctored picture?

RC: I respect the secretary of the Army as I do any other cabinet member of this country, and I wouldn't want to do anything to harm him.

JW: Did you hear the question asked him as to whether or not his picture was taken alone with Schine?

RC: I cannot testify that I was in the room at that time. I may have been.

JW: Did you fail to catch the word "alone?"

RC: I did fail to catch the word "alone."

JW: Now I turn to Mr. Cohn's testimony, and I observe that you testified: "And as a matter of fact, I did not even catch the word "alone" put there by Mr. Mundt." It is unfortunate that the two men who had the key to this small fraud, as I claim it was, failed to hear that word "alone."

RC: Do you claim I was involved in a fraud, Mr. Welch?

JW: I claim that there was at least a small fraud or else a terrible, unfortunate mistake. *(Group freeze.)*

V: April, 1954, Senator McCarthy *(VG 33: Screen 1, "Accuses," "Demands," "Denies"; Screen 2, PIC—Edward R. Murrow; Screen 3, PIC—Edward R. Murrow; Screen 4, "Accuses," "Demands," "Denies.")* named Edward R. Murrow the "symbol, the leader, and the cleverest of the jackal pack which is always found at the throat of anyone who dares to expose individual Communists and traitors."[19]

RC: *(VG 34: Screens 1 and 4, "Accuses," "Demands," "Denies"; Screens 2 and 3, blank.)* I resent the implication, and I have testified that I took the responsibility.

JW: Now as to the hearing of the word "alone," have you observed that Mr. Cohn is slightly hard of hearing as he is slightly nearsighted? Is your hearing good?

RC: Excellent.

JW: Had you heard that word "alone" in Mr. Mundt's questions would you have sprung to the defense of Secretary Stevens?

RC: You are asking me a hypothetical question.

JW: Yes, I am, indeed.

RC: I may have, yes, sir, if I had heard it.

JW: You would have been quick to spring to his defense?

RC: Possibly.

JW: From which it follows you know an injustice was done him, don't you?

RC: No, I would not say that.

JW: Were you going to spring to his defense in a case where no injustice had been done him?

RC: I didn't get that, Mr. Welch.

JW: My question is in two parts: First, if you had heard the word "alone," in Mr. Mundt's question, you have, I think, said you would have been quick to spring to Secretary Stevens' defense, is that right?

RC: I did not say that, sir. I said I may have.

JW: You would have liked to, wouldn't you, in fairness?

RC: I may have.

JW: And if you were going to spring to his defense, it would have been because you thought a very unfortunate situation was created by what you did to that picture?

RC: Possibly so.

---

[19]Rorty and Decter, p. 75.

N: *(Roy Cohn crosses down left.)* "Eight days before the hearings ended, on June 9, the Army counsel led Roy Cohn through a mocking, destructive cross-examination, and McCarthy sat fuming."[20] Now Welch is pressing Cohn as to why, if subversion was so serious at Fort Monmouth, he had not come crying alarm to Secretary Stevens.

JW: Mr. Cohn, what is the exact number of Communists, or subversives, that are loose today in these defense plants?

RC: The exact number that is loose, sir?

JW: Yes, sir.

RC: I don't know.

JW: How, roughly, how many?

RC: I can only tell you, sir, what we know about.

JW: Well, that's one hundred thirty, is that right?

RC: Yes, sir, I'm gonna try to particularize for you if I can.

JW: I'm in a hurry; I don't want the sun to go down while they're still in there if we can get 'em out.

RC: I'm afriad we won't be able to work that fast.

JW: Well, I've got a suggestion about it, sir. How many are there?

RC: I believe the figure is approximately a hundred and thirty.

JW: Approximately one-three-o.

RC: Yes, those are people, Mr. Welch—

JW: I don't care, you told us who they are. In how many plants are they?

RC: Just one minute, sir. I'd say sixteen, offhand.

JW: Sixteen plants. Are you alarmed at that situation, Mr. Cohn?

RC: Yes, sir, I am.

JW: Nothing could be more alarming, could it?

RC: It's certainly a very alarming thing.

JW: Will you not, before the sun goes down, give those names to the F.B.I. and at least have those men put under surveillance?

RC: Sir, if there is need for surveillance in the case of espionage or anything like that, I can well assure you that Mr. John Edgar Hoover and his men know a lot better than I, and I might respectuflly suggest, who should be put under surveillance. I do not propose to tell the F.B.I. how to run its shop. It does very well.

JW: And they do it, and they do it, don't they, Mr. Cohn?

RC: When the need arises, of course.

JW: Then they've got the whole hundred and thirty, have they, Mr. Cohn?

RC: I am sure of it, sir, and a lot more.

JW: Well, then what's all the excitement about, if J. Edgar Hoover is on the job, chasing these hundred and thirty Communists?

RC: Mr. Welch; all the excitement—

JW: Well, then as a second line of defense, let's send the hundred and thirty names to the Department of Defense tonight, would you mind doing that?

[20]Eric Goldman, *The Crucial Decade and After* (New York: Random House, 1960), p. 275.

RC: Whatever the committee directs on that, sir, I'll—

JW: I wish the committee would direct that all the names be sent both to the F.B.I. and to the Department of Defense with extreme suddenness.

JM: In view of Mr. Welch's request that the information be given once we know of anyone who might be performing any work for the Communist Party, I think we should tell him that he has in his law firm, a young man named Fisher whom he recommended, incidentally, to do work on this committee, who has been for a number of years, a member of an organization which is named, oh, years and years ago, as the legal bulwark of the Communist Party. I certainly assumed that Mr. Welch did not know of this, uh, young man the time he recommended him as the assistant counsel for this committee, but he has such terror, and such a great desire to know where anyone is located, who may be serving the Communist cause, Mr. Welch, and I thought we should just call your attention to the fact that your Mr. Fisher, who is still in your law firm today, whom you asked to have down here, looking over the secret and classified material, is a member of an organization, not named by me, but named by various committees, named by the attorney general, as I recall, and I think I quote this verbatim as the "legal bulwark of the Communist Party." I have been, uh, rather bored with your phony request to Mr. Cohn, here, that he, personally, get every Communist out of government before sundown. Therefore, we will give you the information about the young man in your own organization. Whether you know that he was a member of that Communist organization or not, I don't know. I assume you did not, Mr. Welch, because I get the impression that while you are quite an actor, you play for a laugh, I don't think you have any conception of the danger of the Communists. *(Group freeze.)*

V: One month before the Army-McCarthy Hearings, CBS commentator *(VG 35: Screens 1 and 4, "Accuses," "Demands," "Denies"; Screen 2, blank; Screen 3, Caption "See It Now," Murrow's TV Show)* Edward R. Murrow exposed McCarthyism on his "See It Now" show. At the program's conclusion he warned, "There is no time for men who oppose Senator McCarthy's methods to keep silent. We can deny our heritage and our history, but we cannot escape responsibility for the result."[21] *(VG 36: Screens 1 and 4, "Accuses," "Demands," "Denies"; Screen 2, PIC—Don Hollenbeck; Screen 3, Caption—"See It Now.")* CBS colleague, Don Hollenbeck endorsed, "I want to associate myself with every word just spoken by Ed Murrow."[22] Three months *(VG 37: Screen 1 and 4, "Accuses," "Demands," "Denies"; Screen 2 and 3, NH—"Don Hollenbeck in Suicide by Gas" with pic.)* later Hollenbeck committed suicide. Reason: continued attacks on him as one of Murrow's "pinkos."[23]

JW: *(VG 38: Screens 1 and 4, "Accuses," "Demands," "Denies"; Screens 2 and 3, blank.)* Mr. Chairman, under these circumstances, I must myself have *(Joseph Welch crosses up right.)* something approaching a personal privilege. Senator McCarthy, I did not know senator, senator, sometimes you say, "May I have your attention." May I have your attention?

JM: You have one ear.

JW: Now, this time, sir, I want you to listen with both. Senator McCarthy, I think until this moment—

[21]Kendrick, p. 53.
[22]*Ibid.*
[23]*Ibid.*

JM: Just, just a minute. Let me ask—Jim, Jim will you get the news story to the effect that this, this man belongs to the, this Communist front organization—

JW: I will tell you that he belonged to it.

JM: Will, will you get, the citations, order the citations showing that this was the legal arm of the Communist Party, and the length of time that he belonged, and the fact that he was recommended by Mr. Welch. I think that should be in the record.

JW: Senator, you won't need anything in the record when I finish telling you this. Until this moment, senator, I think I never really gauged your cruelty or your recklessness. Fred Fisher is a young man who went to the Harvard Law School and came into my firm and is starting what looks to be a brilliant career *(Joseph Welch crosses up right)* with us. When I decided to work for this committee, I asked Jim St. Clair to be my first assistant. I said to Jim, "Pick somebody in the firm to work under you that you would like." He chose Fred Fisher, and they came down on an afternoon plane. That night when we had taken a little stab at trying to see what the case was about, Fred Fisher and Jim St. Clair and I went to dinner together. I then said to these two young men, "Boys, I don't know anything about you except that I've always liked you. But if there is anything funny in the life of either one of you that would hurt anybody in this case you speak up quick." And Fred Fisher said, "Mr Welch, when I was in the law school, and for a period of months after, I belonged to the Lawyer's Guild," as you have suggested, senator. He went on to say, "I am secretary of the Young Republicans League in Newton, with the son of Massachusetts' governor. And I have the respect and admiration of my community, and I am sure that I have the respect of the twenty-five lawyers or so in Hale and Door." And I said, "Fred, I just don't think I'm going to ask you to work on the case. If I do one of these days that will come out, and go over national television, and it will just hurt like the Dickens." And so, senator, I asked him to go back to Boston. Little did I dream that you would be so reckless and so cruel as to do an injury to that lad. It is true he is still with Hale and Door, it is true that he will continue to be with Hale and Door. It is, I regret to say, equally true that he shall always bear a scar needlessly inflicted by you. If it were within my power to forgive you for your reckless cruelty, I would do so. But your forgiveness will have to come from someone other than me. If there is a god in heaven, it will do neither you nor your cause any good. *(Group freeze.)*

V: September, 1970, former Supreme Court Justice Abe Fortas warns that there may be ". . . an imminent collision with 'a wave of reactionary oppression' worse than the repression of the McCarthy era."

JM: Mr. Chairman, Mr. Chairman. May I say that Mr. Welch talks about this being cruel and reckless, he was just baiting, he has been baiting Mr. Cohn here for hours. Now, I just give this man's record, and I want to say, Mr. Welch, that it has been labeled long before he became a member. As early as 1944—

JW: Senator, may we not drop this. We know he belonged to the Lawyer's Guild, and Mr. Cohn nods his head at me—I did you, I think, no personal injury, Mr. Cohn.

RC: No, Sir.

JW: I meant to do you no personal injury. And if I did, I beg your pardon. Let us not assassinate this lad further, senator. You have done enough. Have you no sense of decency, sir? At long last, have you left no sense of decency? *(Group freeze.)*

N: "For a long few seconds the hush in the room continued. One of the few rules Chairman Mundt had tried hard to enforce was the one against demonstrations, and six policemen were present to assist him. But suddenly the room shook with applause. For the first time in the memory of Washington observers, press photographers laid aside their cameras to join in the ovation for Welch."[24] *(VG 39: Screens 1 and 4, "Accuses," "Demands," "Denies"; Screens 2 and 3, PIC—SCR with spectators.)* "Here were all the dread familiar methods of a totalitarian: The relentless, interminable breaking down of the witness; the deliberate evasion of the basic issues; the constant diversionary moves to obscure them. Here were the totalitarian cliches, the inversions of Communist labels: 'Pentagon Politicians,' 'Fifth Amendment Communists,' 'Leftist Press.' Here was the radical attempt to wreck the Executive Branch of the United States Government. Here, most appalling of all, was the open admission and condonement of a spy-and-informer system within our government—The Loyal American Underground."[25] *(VG 40: Screens 1, 2, 3, and 4, PIC—Empty Senate Caucus Room. Karl Mundt exit house right. Miles Reber exit house right. Robert Stevens exit house left. Roy Cohn exit down left. Stuart Symington exit down right. Joseph Welch exit down right. Joseph McCarthy exit down left.)*

[24]Goldman, pp. 278–79.

[25]Marya Mannes, "Did or Did Not . . ." *The Reporter* (June 8, 1954), pp. 40–41.

Oh Where Oh Where is There*

by Gertrude Stein

From The World Is Round
Adapted and Directed by Sue Pratschner
University of North Dakota

I first saw *The World Is Round,* Gertrude Stein's novel for children, performed as a solo reading in an oral interpretation class. The audience, including myself, was delighted by the reading. I felt that an adaptation for group performance would be successful since: (1) the piece lent itself to group performance with more than one "voice" in the novel; (2) the lyrical qualities of Stein's poetic prose would be most fully appreciated when read aloud; and (3) many possibilities for staging this imaginative selection existed to make it appealing, especially to children.

Gertrude Stein's verbal innovations and creative freshness demanded special consideration from director and performers alike —sound dominates sense and "meaningful contexts" of traditional prose sentences have been exuberantly discarded. This rhythmic verbal hypnosis was certain to captivate and charm the ears of both adult and child audiences. A group performance with analo-

*Script is adapted from *The World Is Round* © 1939, renewed © 1967, by Gertrude Stein, a Young Scott Book, by permission of Addison-Wesley Publishing Co., Inc.

gous supportive visual design promised to extend that experience even more.

The World Is Round demonstrates most of Stein's better-known word structure games: (1) excessive use of repetition; (2) recontextualized or uncontextualized word meanings with unconventional sentence constructions; and (3) high energy, movement, and motion in the lines. Simultaneously, Stein convinces her reader or listener that there is method in her madness *and* imaginative madness in her method. She repeats words to keep them *present* in the mind thereby fighting the transient quality of language—i.e., that it passes out of the mind when it disappears from eye or ear. She will repeat repeat repeat to *insist* the word and create a "continuous presentness" for that word. "Roundness" of sound and meaning is a direct result of her repetition, for just as the word is leaving it returns again. In *The World Is Round,* Stein goes even further with this device by creating a circular narrative. In addition, Stein removes words from their normal context or interjects seemingly incongruous words into an otherwise conventional sentence. Since

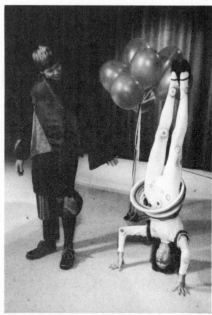

Scenes from O Where O Where is There. (University of North Dakota)
(a) Rose and the chair spin around and around the world.
(b) The chair looks upon Rose, who is always thinking.
(c) Rose climbs the mountain with the help of the blue garden chair.
(d) Rose and the chair pause, for it is hard to go on.

a word's meaning is largely determined by the context in which it appears, she will strip away its old meaning by removing its old context. In short, she exposes the word to the imagination by recontextualizing it. Finally, movement or motion in Stein's prose results from her repetition of words, phrases, and sentences and her profuse use of verbs. In her essay "How Writing Is Written" Stein explains that her use of verbs energizes her writing: "The other thing which I accomplished was getting rid of nouns. In the twentieth century you feel like movement. . . . You know that in your lives movement is the thing that occupies you most—you feel like movement all the time."[1]

While these devices are "interesting" to the overly analytic adult, children more easily delight in the rhythms, rhymes, and frequent imaginative "nonsense" in Stein's prose; these devices enhance the appeal of *The World Is Round* to children.

PRODUCTION CONCEPT

The production concept for "Oh Where Oh Where Is There" was to illustrate and embody some special characteristics of Gertrude Stein's vibrant use of language, particularly her use of excessive repetition, the motif of "roundness," and the continual energy and flow of motion in the prose. This concept directed all steps in the production, from script adaptation through set selection, costume construction, blocking, and special effects.

PRODUCTION PLAN

Methods of Devising the Script

The World Is Round is the story of a girl named Rose and her journey up a moun-

[1]Gertrude Stein, "How Writing Is Written," in *How Writing Is Written: Volume II of the Previously Uncollected Writings of Gertrude Stein,* Robert Haas ed. (Los Angeles: Black Sparrow Press, 1971), p. 153.

tain where she searches for answers to her questions about her identity. Other characters include her cousin Willie (who secretly follows Rose on her journey and ultimately marries her) and a lion named Billie, a gift from Willie to Rose.

Parts of the book were extracted in their entirety to establish the central story line and to adhere to the twenty-minute time limit of a festival presentation. Characters included in the extracted parts were Rose and a narrator. Since the novel focuses on Rose's quest, I concluded this script with Rose's reaching the mountain summit and omitted the last chapter.

The technique of deletion was used with discretion to preserve the rhythm of Stein's poetic prose. Therefore the only internal deletions consisted of specific mentions of the other minor characters not necessary to the central story line.

Selection of Characters

The perspective of the novel includes two viewpoints: (1) Rose's perspective of herself and (2) the broader perspective of the world and its effect on Rose as indicated by the omniscient narrator. Consequently, two performers were used to convey these perspectives simultaneously—Rose and a narrator who also functioned as Rose's blue garden chair. Lines reflecting a more universal perspective were assigned to the narrator. In addition, the narrator-as-chair was given other lines to establish his support and encouragement of Rose. To add vocal interest and variety, listing sequences in the narrative lines were alternated between Rose and the narrator.

ORIGINAL PRODUCTION

Casting

In the original production the size of the readers visually reinforced their roles. Rose was played by a petite female who suggested a nine-year-old girl; the narrator was played by a male who was larger than Rose and who could represent her chair. Both performers could move with agility and sing. In addition, their diversified experience in theatre and interpretation productions permitted a more intricate style of presentation.

Rehearsals

Rehearsals began three weeks before performance and ranged from one to three hours. The first three days were spent in oral reading of the script to sensitize the readers to the rhythm and assonance of Stein's language. Then the basic stylistic concepts of roundness and of children's games were communicated to the performers. The illusion of roundness became an important aspect of the production concept. For example, the set consisted of round balloons; the costumes were constructed with circles, cones, cylinders, and balls; and the blocking incorporated spins, turns, and movements around the balloons. The second stylistic extension of the production concept was the use of children's games. The intent was to involve the child audience and create a continual flow of motion to harmonize with Stein's language. Working within this general framework, the performers and I had a brainstorming session to experiment with specific movements. Those found workable were then incorporated into the script in appropriate places. For example, two games that were suggested for the one mountain-two mountain sequence were hopscotch and one-potato, two-potato. The one-potato, two-potato counting device was selected since the action was more economical and fit the rhythm of the language. Due to the nature of this movement, blocking could not be finalized until the script was memorized two weeks later. The last week was spent in polishing and included three rehearsals for the performers to adjust to their stiff, unusually

shaped costumes. The production was conceived and rehearsed in a group with contributions from director, performers, and a faculty supervisor.[2]

Stage Composition

Setting. Considerations important to the set design were: creation of a metaphorical world for Rose; extension of the "roundness" motif; encouragement of desirable movement; appeal for a child audience; and mobility for touring. The set consisted of five groups of big, round, red helium-filled balloons (red, the traditional color of roses) anchored to blue weights. The five groups of balloons were arranged like the five dots on a die in a 20' x 30' area; six balloons were grouped in the center cluster, four and five balloons in the other clusters. They were tied with bright yellow strings five feet long except the center group, which was tied with multicolored strings suggesting the rainbow. Each string was looped at its midpoint and near the lip of the balloons. As Rose made her journey up the mountain, she pulled the balloons down at intervals and looped the string through hooks on each weight, lowering the entire group of balloons. This device visually reinforced the concept of ascent. All the balloons were at floor level when Rose reached the top of the mountain.

Blocking. The children's games used as a basis for the blocking enhanced two motifs suggested by the script: the concept of roundness and the supportive relationship between Rose and the chair. These formal and informal children's games included: spins (Rose by herself, or with her arms linked back-to-back with the narrator, or

[2]The faculty supervisor for this production was Professor Suzanne Bennett, Department of Theatre Arts, University of North Dakota. The original performers were: Mary Jane Crook as Rose, and Joel Vig as narrator—both students at the University of North Dakota.

with the two of them square dance style), one-potato, two-potato, headstands, singing, mimicked movement, leapfrog, and patty-cake. The narrator-garden chair supported Rose on her journey by verbal and physical "assists" including a duck walk, wheelbarrow movement, elephant walk, and Rose sitting on his shoulders when she reaches the top of the mountain. (The major movements are indicated, where used, in the script.)

Sound. We adapted familiar children's song melodies to Stein's lyrics such as: "Little Tommy Tucker" for "I am a little girl," "I am Rose," and "Oh where oh where is there"; "White Coral Bells" for "Mountains are high"; an ascending scale of major thirds for "Dear mountain tall mountain"; and the round "Three Blind Mice" for "Here I am."

Costumes. The costume design[3] was based on a modified Bauhaus[4] concept—a design that uses form and color innovatively to disguise the human shape—which facilitated the transformation of the narrator into an inanimate chair.

Both costumes were constructed of stiff foam materials covered with shiny sibone fabric. The chair was covered appropriately in blue accented with green, while Rose's skirt of tubular foam was in gradated rainbow colors. Circular designs on Rose's yellow leotards and tights were sprayed on.

[3]Costumes were designed by Karen Thornberg, graduate student, Department of Theatre Arts, University of North Dakota.

[4]The Bauhaus Institute was founded in Germany in 1919 for the study of art, design, and functional architecture.

Selected Bibliography

GOLDBERG, MOSES. *Children's Theatre: A Philosophy and a Method.* Englewood Cliffs, N.J.: Prentice-Hall, Inc., 1974.

GROPIUS, WALTER, ed. *The Theatre of the Bauhaus.* Middletown, Conn.: Wesleyan University Press, 1961.

HAAS, ROBERT, ed. *A Primer for the Understanding of Gertrude Stein.* Los Angeles: Black Sparrow Press, 1971.

————. *How Writing Is Written: Volume II of the Previously Uncollected Writings of Gertrude Stein.* Los Angeles: Black Sparrow Press, 1974.

ORFF, CARL, and GUNILD KEETMAN. *Music for Children.* A set of records manufactured in the United States, recorded in Europe by Angel Records, n.d.

STEIN, GERTRUDE. *Lectures In America.* New York: Vintage Books, 1935.

————. *The Autobiography of Alice B. Toklas.* New York: Random House, Inc., 1933.

————. *The World Is Round.* New York: Avon Books, 1939. Copyright renewed 1967.

————. *What Are Masterpieces?* New York: Pitman Publishing Corp., 1940.

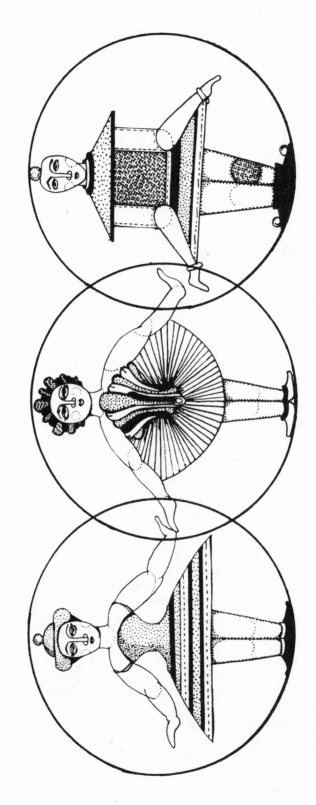

"oh where, oh where is there" from
gertrude stein's the world is round

Program cover for theatre production of "Oh where, Oh where is there"

OH WHERE OH WHERE IS THERE

Cast of Characters

N: Narrator
R: Rose

The Narrator and Rose are standing next to the two front balloon groups respectively. They walk to center, join hands, and spin.

N: Once upon a time the world was round and you could go on it around and around. Everywhere there was somewhere and everywhere there they were men

R: women

N: children

R: dogs

N: cows

R: wild pigs

N: little rabbits

R: cats

N: lizards

R: and animals

N: That is the way it was. And everybody dogs

R: cats

N: sheep

R: rabbits

N: and lizards

Both: and children

N: all wanted to tell everybody all about it and they wanted to tell all about themselves.

R: *(Breaking out of spin goes to stage left.)* And then there was Rose.

N: Rose was her name and would she have been Rose if her name had not been Rose. She used to think and then she used to think again. Would she have been Rose if her name had not been Rose and would she have been Rose if she had been a twin.

R: Rose was her name all the same and her father's name was Bob and her mother's name was Kate and her uncle's name was William and her aunt's name was Gloria and her grandmother's name was Lucy. They all had names and her name was Rose,

N: but would she have been she used to cry about it would she have been Rose if her name had not been Rose.
(Narrator and Rose holding hands, spin.) I tell you at this time the world was all round and you could go on it around and around. *(Rose breaks out of spin to stage left.)* Rose sang songs and these were the songs she sang.

R: I am a little girl and my name is Rose
Rose is my name
Why am I a little girl
And why is my name Rose
And when am I a little girl
And when is my name Rose
And where am I a little girl
And where is my name Rose
And which little girl am I
Am I the little girl named Rose
Which little girl named Rose.

N: And she sang this song and she sang and sang.

R: Why am I a little girl
Where am I a little girl
When am I a little girl
Which little girl am I

N: And singing that made her so sad she began to cry. *(Rose cries on narrator's shoulder.)* Rose cried and cried and cried until she stopped and at last her eyes were dried. *(Rose and Narrator repeat spin.)*

N: And all this time the world just continued to be round. *(Rose and Narrator standing back to back, link arms.) (Narrator faces front.)* When mountains are really true they are blue.

R: *(facing front)* Rose knows they were blue and blue was her favorite color. She knew they were blue and they were far away or near just as the rain came or went away.

N: *(facing front)* The rain came or the rain went away any day. And so Rose would look and see and deary me the mountains would be blue. And then one day she saw a mountain near and then it was all clear. *(Rose breaks away, pointing to imaginary mountains offstage.)* This was the way Rose knew what to say. Listen.

R: Mountains are high

Up there is a sky
Rain is near
Mountains are clear
Mountains are blue
That is true
(Rose and narrator play one-potato, two-potato.) And one mountain two
mountains three mountains or four
When there are mountains there always are more
Even from the door

N: So Rose would say when every day she came that way.

R: Rose was at school there.

Both: *(Narrator cradles Rose in his arms.)* There the mountains were and they were
blue, oh dear blue blue just blue, dear sweet blue yes blue.

N: And then Rose began to think. It was funny about Rose, she always could just
begin to think. Rose was always thinking.

R: *(Standing on her head.)* It is easy to think when your name is Rose.

N: Nobody's name was ever Blue, nobody's, why not. Rose never thought about
that. Rose thought she thought a lot but she never did think about that.

R: *(Coming down from head stand)* But mountains yes Rose did think about
mountains and about blue when it was on the mountains and feathers when
clouds like feathers were on the mountains and birds when one little bird and
two little birds and three and four and six and seven and ten and seventeen and
thirty and forty little birds all came flying and a big bird came flying and the little
birds came flying and they flew higher than the big bird and they came down
and one and then two and then five and then fifty of them came picking down on
the head of the big bird and slowly the big bird came falling down between the
mountain and the little birds all went home again. Little birds do go home again
after they have scared off the big bird.

N: How Rose thought when she was thinking. Rose would get all round thinking her
eyes her head her mouth her hands, she would get all round while she was
thinking and then to relieve her hearing her thinking she would sing.
She sang song of the mountain
She sang

R: *(Rose and Narrator play stacking hands.)* Dear mountain tall mountain real
mountain blue mountain yes mountain high mountain all mountain my mountain,
I will with my chair come climbing and once there mountain once there I will be
thinking, mountain so high, who cares for the sky yes mountain no mountain yes
I will be there.

N: Tears come to her eyes.

R: Yes mountain yes I will be there.

N: *(Pointing to mountains off stage)* And then as she looked she saw that one
mountain had a top and the top was a meadow and the meadow came up to a
point and on the point oh dear yes on the point yes Rose would put a chair and
she would sit there and

R: *(Duplicates pointing)* yes she did care yes there she would put a chair there
there and everywhere she would see everywhere and she would sit on that
chair,

Both: yes there.
(Rose and Narrator spin square-dance style.)

N: And she did and this was how she did it. All alone she did it. She and the chair there there, and it was not blue there, no dear no it was green there, grass and trees and rocks are green not blue there no blue was there

R: *(Breaking down spin to stage right)* but blue was her favorite color all through. She had decided about the chair it was a blue chair a blue garden chair otherwise scratches and rain and dew and being carried all through would do a chair harm but not a blue garden chair,
(Rose and Narrator wheelbarrow around balloons.)

N: So Rose left early so no one saw her and her chair she held before her and

Both: the mountain was high and so was the sky and the world was round and was all ground and she began to go,

R: even so it was very long way to go even if a mountain does not grow even so, climb a mountain and you will know even if there is no snow. Well shall I go

N: Rose said as she was going, nobody does like to go nobody does say no and so Rose did go, even so she did go. As she began to go it was early morning you know.

R: *(Pulling down balloon group)* The birds began to stir. And then she heard some birds making funny screams as they flew.

N: Did the blue garden chair have arms or was it without arms, I am wondering.
(Narrator does a tap dance.)

A hill is a mountain, a cow is a cat,
A fever is heating and where is she at.

R: *(Both resume wheelbarrowing)* She is climbing the mountain a chair in her arms, and always around her she is full of alarms.

N: Why not, a chair is something but not to talk to when it is too cold to be a lot too white to be blue, too red to be wed. *(Rose pulls balloon group down.)*

R: *(Rose and Narrator play leapfrog.)* there was a simple noise

N: just a noise

R: and with a noise there were eyes and with the eyes there was a tail

N: and then from Rose there was a wail

R: I wish I was not dead said Rose but if I am I will have torn my clothes, blackberries are black and blueberries are blue strawberries are red and so are you

N: said Rose to Rose and it was all true. *(Rose and Narrator duckwalk diagonally back and forth.)* She could not sit down on her chair because if she did sit down on her chair she would think she was already there and

R: oh dear

N: She just could not see how high it all could be but she knew

R: oh dear yes she knew

N: and when those birds flew she just could not do so too and she could not sing and cry no matter how much she could try because she was there right in the middle of everything that was around her and how little she could move just a little and a little and the chair was sticking and she was sticking and she could not go down because she would not know where, going down might be anywhere, going up had to be there, dear where was Rose

R: she was there really she was there not stuck there but very nearly really very nearly really stuck there. *(Rose and Narrator walking in opposite directions circle center balloon group.)*

N: And now everything began and if it had not been on a mountain and if it had not been a chair there where she was she would not care

R: but she did not run she never ran, there was no tin can, she was not hungry, oh never that

N: but everything helped to hold her back, but if she stayed she was afraid, run ran a chair can be a man,
(Rose jumps into Narrator's arms, both spin.)

R: oh dear chair oh dear chair be a man so I will not be all scare,

N: that is what Rose said trying not to see her own hair.

R: Dear me hair chair ran man,

N: Rose is beginning to feel as funny as she can.
(Rose and Narrator stop spin.)

R: Anybody try to climb a mountain all alone with only a blue garden chair to hold there and everything on a mountain that is there and then see when it is that ran
(Rose and Narrator play pattycake through following sequence.)

N: Water

R: yes

N: and birds

R: yes

N: and rats

R: yes

N: and snakes

R: yes

N: and lizards

R: yes

N: and cats

R: yes

N: and cows

R: yes

N: and trees

R: yes

N: and scratches

R: yes

N: and sticks

R: yes

N: and flies

R: yes

N: and bees

R: yes but not a Rose with a chair,

N: all a Rose with a chair can dare is just not stare but keep on going up there.

Both: She did.

(Rose and Narrator elephant walk around balloons.)

N: It is hard to go on when you are nearly there but not nearly enough to hurry up to get there.

R: *(Pulling down balloon group.)* That is where Rose was and she well she hardly could go on to get there. *(Rose and Narrator continue elephant walk.)*

N: And where was there. She almost said it she almost whispered it to herself and to the chair. Where o where is there. *(Rose pulls down another balloon group.)* But she went on and the grass was shorter and the slant was steeper and the chair was bluer and heavier and the clouds were nearer and the top was further because she was so near she could not see which way it was and if she went one way and the top was the other way could it be that she would never see what she could see. Oh deary me oh deary me what did she see. *(Rose pulls down balloon group and both resume elephant walk.)*

R: She did see and her eyes were round with fright and her hands and arms did hold her chair tight and suddenly green, became blue and she knew that one would become two and three would become four and never again no never again would there ever be a door for her to go through.

N: But Rose was not like that, stumbling would be the beginning of tumbling and she would not tumble up but tumble down if she began to stumble and so she began to frown and she knew she would have to begin to count. One two one two one two one two. Close your eyes and count one two open your eyes and count one two and then green would not be blue. So Rose began counting.

R: one two one two

N: and she knew that she was counting

R: one two one two

N: and so her eyes were blue although her name was Rose

R: Of course her eyes were blue even though her name was Rose. That is the reason she always did prefer blue because her eyes were blue. *(Rose pulls down balloon group.)* One two one two.

N: And sooner than it could be true there she saw something that was not green nor blue, it was violet and other colors it was high up as high as the sky it was where she could cry it was a rainbow.

R: Oh yes oh no it was a rainbow. *(Rose pulls down center balloon group.)*

N: And Rose just went right through, she went right through the rainbow *(Rose jumps through balloons.)*

R: and she did know that was what she would do. She had it to do

N: *(Jumping through balloons)* and she went right through the rainbow and then there she was right on the top so that there was no other top there just the top with room for the blue chair and Rose put the blue chair there and she sat upon the chair. *(Rose sits on Narrator's shoulders.)*

Both: And Rose was there.

N: She was alone on the top of everything and she was sitting there and she could sing. This is the song she sang, It began

R: Here I am

When I wish a dish
I wish a dish of ham
When I wish a little wish
I wish that I was where I am.

N: She stopped and sat awhile not that she ever got up, she was so pleased with sitting she just sat. She was alone up there. It was getting a little dark and once more Rose began to sing.

R: I am Rose but I am not rosy
All alone and not very cosy
I am Rose and while I am Rose
Well well Rose is Rose.

N: It was darker and darker and the world was rounder rounder and the chair the blue chair was harder and harder Rose was more there than anywhere. Oh dear yes there. And once more Rose began to sing.

R: And I am here
And here is there
Oh where oh where is there
Oh where.
Oh where where where is there. I am here oh yes
   am there oh where oh where is there.

(Rose slides off Narrator's shoulders, both repeat beginning spin.)

Both: Oh where oh where is there oh where oh where is there.

Tell Me a Riddle*

by Tillie Olsen

Adapted by Karen Corley
Directed by Beverly Whitaker Long
University of Texas at Austin

"Tell Me a Riddle," Tillie Olsen's 1961 prize-winning short story (or novella), is a sensitive and intense probe into the lives of two first-generation Americans who struggle both humanly and heroically with each other, their children, old values, the New World, age, poverty, and disease. With a richly original style, Olsen moves the story gracefully from inner to spoken dialogue in a series of lyrical scenes. It was this lyrical quality that first interested us in adapting and staging the story.

Fiction that combines elements of prose and poetry constitutes a rich part of our literary history. Works by Lawrence Durrell, John Hawkes, John Fowles, and Virginia Woolf, are examples of this hybrid form, *lyric fiction*. About Woolf, Leon Edel makes an observation that could just as easily be made of Tillie Olsen:

> Her method was that of the lyric poet. She was interested in the sharpened image, the moment, the condensed experience. She saw

the world around her as if it were a sharp knife, cutting its way into her being.[1]

Sharpened imagery occurs throughout "Tell Me a Riddle"; it begins in the opening paragraph:

> For forty-seven years they had been married. How deep back the stubborn, gnarled roots of the quarrel reached, no one could say—but only now, when tending to the needs of others no longer shackled them together, the roots swelled up visible, split the earth between them, and the tearing shook even to the children, long since grown.

Condensed experiences also occur repeatedly in the story, as in the scenes in which the children learn of their mother's terminal illness and then again when they relate this news to their father.

Lyric fiction also "assumes a unique form which transcends the causal and temporal movement of narrative within the framework of fiction."[2] "Tell Me a Riddle" con-

[1]Leon Edel, *The Modern Psychological Novel,* rev. ed. (New York: Grossett and Dunlap, 1961), p. v.

[2]Ralph Freedman, *The Lyrical Novel* (Princeton, N.J.: Princeton University Press, 1963), p. 1.

169

tains a clear plot line: David, the father, and Eva, the mother quarrel bitterly. David discovers her cancerous condition, they travel and she eventually dies. The chronology of events, however, is not the dominant unifying factor in the story as Olsen discards logically sequential events and ordinary transitions.

Another characteristic of lyric fiction in "Tell Me a Riddle" is the presence of a symbolic hero and heroine, characters whose visions, in effect, make the world of the story. Ralph Freedman explains that

> The symbolic hero in the lyrical novel is analogous to the lyrical "I" in verse poetry. He is the cause of the novel's world, its landscapes and stylized texture of the faces and events. . . . The figures and scenes he confronts signify ideas which, in turn, symbolize his own inner condition.[3]

Certainly Eva and David's inner landscapes, expressed both in outer and inner dialogue and through the reflector-narrator, *cause* this story's world; and with each of the two protagonists, the *inner condition* assumes far more significance than events such as garrulous fights about moving to the Haven or the terrible process of her painful death. A final aspect of lyric fiction, the role of the reader, is succinctly summarized by Suzanne Bennett:

> The reader is asked to participate in the subjective world of lyrical fiction in an imaginative, poetic manner. Just as we experience a dream at the moment of its occurence and accept its distortions of time, space, and logicality of sequence, so we are required to accept the world of lyrical literature. (Subsequent to the reading we may analyze that world just as we frequently re-play and examine dreams the morning after).[4]

"Tell Me a Riddle" invites us time and again to participate, imagine, and accept

[3]*Ibid.*, p. 72.
[4]Suzanne Bennett, "The Aesthetic Conditions of the Lyrical Novel," Unpublished manuscript, University of North Dakota, 1976.

characters and events that are sometimes distorted and almost consistently elliptical.

The language, structure, characterization, and reader role typical of lyric fiction account, in large part, for the rich texture of this profoundly moving story, and for our interest in adapting and staging it.

ORIGINAL PRODUCTION

Production Concept and Staging

In a literal as well as metaphorical sense, "Tell Me a Riddle" is the *trial* of Eva and David. Before their migration to the United States, she had been found guilty and sentenced to penal servitude in Siberia. Now in their old age, they are trials to one another; trials for their children's patience; and finally, they must endure the agonizing trial of her dying. On a symbolic level, the story involves three generations with the last two acting as "jurors" who judge the old man and woman.

The production concept can be clarified by a diagram of the stage floor plan, which embodies this basic metaphor and emphasizes the characteristics of lyric fiction. (See 171.)

This arrangement, with all the members of the family seated on the side stages, while Eva and David in stage center sit in chairs placed on platforms, suggests subtly (1) the alienation of the "family-jurors" and (2) the couple's being in a "witness box." Screen projections are at the back of both side stages. They depict a montage of faces of the group, rather like a distorted family photograph album that emphasizes familial relationships.

Only the narrator moves about freely; he sometimes comes nearer the audience for more direct communication but more often stays near Eva and David when reflecting their thoughts and feelings. With the exception of Jeannie, no family members move from their chairs throughout the production; this indicates a stasis in their under-

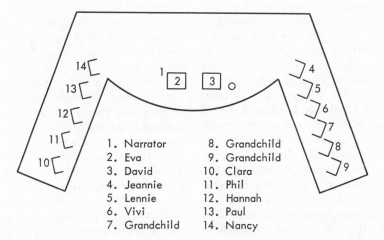

1. Narrator	8. Grandchild
2. Eva	9. Grandchild
3. David	10. Clara
4. Jeannie	11. Phil
5. Lennie	12. Hannah
6. Vivi	13. Paul
7. Grandchild	14. Nancy

standing of the real struggle of the old couple. Jeannie, however, unlike the others, does accept, understand, and love dearly her grandparents. For those final scenes in which she appears, she moves to the stool beside Eva's chair and later to the arm of David's chair.

The rearrangement and minimal movement also suggest the stillness that extends the condensed experiences of lyric fiction and over which the imagery of the language can dominate. The bleakness also provides a neutral background for the abruptly shifting and nonsequentially developed scenes. The starkness, in addition to the multiple focus, also enhances the underlying metaphor for the production and emphasizes the inner conditions of the major characters. The family's chairs, angled toward Eva and David, make it easy for everyone to interact with and attack one another. Yet the couple, when dealing with each other, use offstage focus throughout the show until the end, when they attain at least a partial illumination about their own true needs.

Adaptation

The chief adaptation techniques used were *deletion* and *addition*. The adaptation process also involved the *assignment of lines*.

Because of time limitations, the approximately one hour and forty-five minute story was cut to an hour and fifteen minutes. Our aim was to "cut in" as many parts of the story as possible that deal with family relationships. Once this was done, the necessity for omitting those sections concerning outsiders—Rose, Max, and Mrs. May—became clear. Dialogue tags were not deleted because of their importance in sustaining the rhythm of the lyric prose.

We used the technique of addition several times to underscore the story's thematic elements: the grandchildren's insistent request, "Tell me a riddle" and Eva's desire "never again to be forced to move to the rhythm of others." The addition in the form of repetition was also used when the narrator, who is more understanding of the couple than they are of each other, repeated a line as a *commentary* on its utterance. For example, early in the story, after David's initial plea for a move to the Haven, the narration reads, "but she would not consider it." Eva took the line first, adamantly rejecting the idea. The narrator then repeated the line, delivering the subtext of "I understand why she can't go, but his needs are also clear."

The assignment of lines for the second-

and third-generation family members followed traditional divisions: they spoke their
own dialogue, while the narrator assumed
control by speaking the tags connected to
the lines: By so doing, he signalled the fact
that theirs is *spoken* dialogue. With Eva and
David, however, the assignment was more
challenging and difficult because much of
their dialogue is *unspoken* thought written
in third-person narration. We based our
final decisions about assigning this kind of
narration on the following beliefs: (1) Eva
and David should speak their own dialogue
as well as much of the narration that describes their desires, frustrations, and fears—
if it seemed likely they were conscious of
these feelings, as when Eva speaks of her
early poverty and its attendant humiliations; (2) Eva and David should speak the
narration if the style reflected their own
Yiddish speech rhythms; (3) The narrator
should speak those lines concerning matters
of which Eva and David are ignorant, as
when he describes Paul's action toward
Nancy; (4) The narrator should speak the
passages of heightened poetry, as in the
opening paragraph; and (5) The narrator
should retain control of the story by demonstrating his multiple omniscience, regularly speaking as a *reflector* of each of their
attitudes.

Casting and Rehearsals

"Tell Me a Riddle" requires extremely
strong and sensitive performers for the three
major roles, individuals who can handle
emotional intensity as well as dialect. We
were fortunate in finding three such student
performers.

After casting the supporting roles, we
began rehearsals with a series of sessions
devoted to discussions of Jewish history,
customs, and traditions that so clearly influence the attitudes of the characters. After
those initial meetings and read-through rehearsals, we worked intensively with the
narrator and the two principal characters.
We used many improvisations to help them
each develop a psychological reality and the
characters a sense of a past; the man and
woman who performed Eva and David im-
provised scenes from the old couple's youth
and their young married life to build
"roots" for the characters.

Another objective in these early rehearsals was to help David and Eva become
comfortable with the Yiddish dialect. Leo
Rosten's *The Joys of Yiddish* aided us
greatly in locating the sounds of rhythms
of the speech patterns.

Rehearsals during the ensuing weeks followed the usual pattern with the entire cast
present: sessions began with vocal and physical exercises, and improvisations were followed by work on specific scenes. During the
last week, we added make-up for the old
couple, costumes (mostly blues and golds),
and recorded Russian folk music for the
beginning and ending of the show.

Selected Bibliography

ALTER, ROBERT. *After the Tradition*. New York: E. P. Dutton and Co., Inc., 1969.
BENNETT, SUZANNE. "The Aesthetic Conditions of the Lyrical Novel." Unpublished
    manuscript. University of North Dakota, 1975.
BOUCHER, SANDY. "Tillie Olsen: The Weight of Things Unsaid," *Ms.* (Spring 1975),
    pp. 26–30.

EDEL, LEON. *The Modern Psychological Novel.* New York: Grosset and Dunlap, 1961.

FREEDMAN, RALPH. *The Lyrical Novel.* Princeton, N.J.: Princeton University Press, 1963.

LEBESON, ANITA LIBMAN. *Pilgrim People: A History of the Jews in America from 1492–1974.* New York: Minerva Press, 1975.

O'BRIEN, JILL. "The Interpreter and Ethnic Texts: Jewish-American Literary Experience," *Speech Teacher,* 24 (September 1975), 195–201.

OLSEN, TILLIE. *Tell Me a Riddle.* New York: Dell Publishing Co., Inc., 1960.

———. "Silences: When Writer's Don't Wright," *Harper's* (October, 1965), pp. 153–61.

———. "Women Who are Writers in Our Century: One Out of Twelve," *College English* (October 1972).

ROSTEN, LEO. *The Joys of Yiddish.* New York: Simon and Schuster, 1968.

A side view of the narrator, Eva, and David in the opening scene from *Tell Me a Riddle*. (University of Texas at Austin)

TELL ME A RIDDLE

Cast of Characters

NR: Narrator   **VI:** Vivi
M: Man (David)   **S:** Sammy
W: Woman (Eva)   **L:** Lennie
P: Paul   **J:** Jeannie
H: Hannah   **CH:** Child
PH: Phil   **CL:** Clara
N: Nancy

Part I

(Music for two minutes. Cast enters and takes positions described on page 170.)

NR: For forty-seven years they had been married. How deep back the stubborn, gnarled roots of the quarrel reached, no one could say—but only now, when tending to the needs of others no longer shackled them together, the roots swelled up visible, split the earth between them, and the tearing shook even to the children long since grown.

H: Why now, why now?

NR: Wailed Hannah.

P: As if when we grew up weren't enough.

NR: Said Paul.

VI: Poor Ma. Poor Dad. It hurts so for both of them.

NR: Said Vivi.

175

VI: They never had very much; at least in old age they should be happy.

S: Knock their heads together,

NR: Insisted Sammy,

S: tell 'em: you're too old for this kind of thing; no reason not to get along now.

NR: Lennie wrote to Clara.

L: They've lived over so much together; what could possibly tear them apart?

NR: Something tangible enough. Arthritic hands, and such work as he got, occasional. Poverty all his life, and there was little breath left for the running. He could not, could not turn away from this desire: to have the troubling of responsibility, the fretting with money, over and done with; to be free, to be *care*free where success was not measured by accumulation, and there was use for the vitality still in him. There was a way.

M: There was a way. They could sell the house, and with the money join his lodge's Haven, cooperative for the aged. Happy communal life, and was he not already an official; had he not helped organize it, raise funds, served as a trustee?

NR: But she—would not consider it.

W: But she—would not consider it.

M: What do we need all this for?

NR: he would ask loudly, for her hearing aid was turned down and the vacuum was shrilling.

M: Five rooms. Floors and surfaces to make work. Tell me, why do we need it?

W: Because I'm use't.

M: Because you're use't. This is a reason, Mrs. Word Miser? Used to can get unused!

W: Soon enough we'll need only a little closet, no windows, no furniture, nothing to make work but for worms. Because now I want room . . . Screech and blow like you're doing, you'll need that closet even sooner . . . again!

NR: Over the dishes, coaxingly:

M: For once in your life, to be free, to have everything done for you, like a queen.

W: I never liked queens.

M: You are the one who always used to say: better mankind born without mouths and stomachs than always to worry for money to buy, to shop, to fix, to cook, to wash, to clean.

W: How cleverly you hid that you heard. I said it then because eighteen hours a day I ran. And you never scraped a carrot or knew a dish towel sops. Now—for you and me—who cares? A herring out of a jar is enough. But when *I* want, and nobody to bother.

NR: And she turned off her ear button, so she would not have to hear.

M: Look! In their bulletin. A reading circle. Twice a week it meets.

W: Haumm,

NR: her answer of not listening.

M: A reading circle. Chekhov they read that you like, and Peretz. Cultured people at the Haven that you would enjoy.

W: Enjoy!

NR: She tasted the word.

W: Now, when it pleases you, you find a reading circle for me. And forty years ago when the children were morsels and there was a Circle, did you stay home with them once so I could go? Even once? you trained me well. I do not need others to enjoy. Others! Because you want to be there with others. Already it makes me sick to think of you always around others. Clown, grimacer, floormat, yesman, entertainer, whatever they want of you.

NR: And now it was he who turned on the television loud so he need not hear.

W: Chekhov indeed. She thought without softness of that young wife, who in the deep hours while she nursed the current baby, and perhaps held another in her lap, would try to stay awake for the only time there was to read. She would feel again the weather of the outside of his cheek, when coming late from a meeting, he would find her so, and stimulated and ardent, sniffing her skin, coax: "I'll put the baby to bed, and you—put the book away, don't read, don't read." That had been the most beguiling of all the "don't read, put your book away" her life had been. Chekhov indeed!

NR: Juggling and rejuggling the money to figure:

M: how will I pay for this now?

NR: prying out the storm windows

M: (there they take care of this);

NR: jolting in the streetcar on errands

M: (there I would not have to ride to take care of this or that);

NR: tending the patronizing of relatives just back from Florida

M: (there it matters what one is, not what one can afford),

NR: But as he had no peace, he gave her no peace. Old scar tissue ruptured and the sounds festered anew.

M: In the cottages they buy what you ask, and cook it how you like. *You* are the one who always used to say: better mankind born without mouths and stomachs and always to worry for money to buy, to shop, to fix, to cook, to wash, to clean.

W: Money?

NR: She shrugged him off.

W: Could we get poorer than once we were? And in America, who starves?

NR: But as still he pressed

W: Let me alone about money. Was there ever enough? Seven little ones—for every penny I had to ask—and sometimes, remember, there was nothing. But always *I* had to manage. Now *you* manage. Rub your nose in it good.

NR: But from those years she had had to manage, old humiliations and terrors rose up, lived again, and forced her to relive them.

W: The children's needings; that grocer's face or this merchant's wife she had had to beg credit from when credit was a disgrace, the scenery of the long blocks walked around when she could not pay; school coming, and the desperate going over the old to see what could yet be remade; the soups of meat bones begged "for-the-dog" one winter. . . . Enough. Now they had no children. Let him wrack his head for how they would live. She would not exchange her solitude for anything. *Never again to be forced to move to the rhythms of others.*

NR: Never again to be forced to move to the rhythms of others. For in this solitude she had won a reconciled peace. Tranquility from having the empty house no longer an enemy, for it stayed clean—not as in the days when. . . It was her family, the life

NR: in it, that had seemed the enemy: tracking, smudging, littering, dirtying, engaging her in endless defeating battle—

NR: and on whom her endless defeat had been spewed. The few old books, memorized from rereading; the pictures to ponder (the magnifying glass superimposed on her heavy eye-glasses). Or if she wishes, when he is gone, the phonograph, that if she turns up very loud and strains, she can hear: the ordered sounds, and the struggling. And her one social duty (for she will not go to luncheons or meetings) the boxes of old clothes left with her, as with a life-practiced eye for finding what is still wearable within the worn (again the magnifying glasses superimposed on the heavy glasses) she scans and sorts—this for rag or rummage, that for mending and cleaning, and this for sending abroad.

W: *Being able at last to live within, and not move to the rhythms of others.*

NR: As life had helped her to: denying, removing; isolating; taking the children one by one; then deafening, half-blinding—and at last, presenting her solitude. And in it she had won to a reconciled peace. Now he was violating it with his constant campaigning:

M: Sell the house and move to the Haven. Turn on your ear button—I am talking.

NR: And stubbornly she resisted—so that from wheedling, reasoning, manipulation, it was bitterness he now started with. And it came to where every happening lashed up a quarrel.

M: I will sell the house anyway. I am putting it up for sale. There will be a way to make you sign.

NR: The television blared.

W: She did not know if the tumult was in her or outside.

NR: She turned the sound off.

W: Shadows. Look it is only shadows Did you say that you will sell the house? Look at me, not at that, I am no shadow. You cannot sell without me.

M: Leave on the television. I am watching.

W: Like Paul, like Jenny, a four-year-old. Staring at shadows. *You cannot sell the house.*

M: I will. We are going to the Haven. There you would not have the television when you do not want it. I could sit in the social room and watch. You could lock yourself up to smell your unpleasantness in a room by yourself—for who would want to come near you?

W: No, no selling.

NR: A whisper now.

M: The television is shadows. Mrs. Enlightened! Mrs. Cultured! A world comes into your house—and it is shadows. People you would never meet in a thousand lifetimes. Wonders. When you were four years old, like Paulie, like Jennie, did you know of Indian dances, alligators, how they used bamboo in Malaya? No, you scratched in your dirt with the chickens and thought Olshana was the world. Yes, Mrs. Unpleasant, I will sell the house, for there better can we be rid of each other than here.

NR: She did not know if the tumult was outside, or in it. Always a ravening inside, a pull to the bed, to lie down, to succumb. . . .

P: Have you thought maybe Ma should let a doctor have a look at her?

M: Why not the President too?

P: Seriously, Dad. This is the third Sunday she's lain down like that after dinner. Is she that way at home?

M: A regular love affair with the bed. Every time I start to talk with her.

N: Good protective reaction, observed Nancy to herself. The workings of hos-til-ity.

P: Nancy could take her. I just don't like how she looks. Let's have Nancy arrange an appointment.

M: You think she'll go: All right, we have to have doctor bills, we have to have doctor bills. Something hurts you?

NR: She startled, looked to his lips. He repeated:

M: Mrs. Take It Easy, something hurts?

W: Nothing . . . Only you.

M: A woman of honey. That's why you're lying down?

W: Soon I'll get up to do the dishes, Nancy.

N: Leave them, Mother, I like it better this way.

M: Mrs. Take It Easy, Paul says you should start ballet. You should go see a doctor. and ask: how soon can you start ballet?

W: A doctor? Ballet?

P: We were talking, Ma. You don't seem any too well. It would be a good idea for you to see a doctor for a checkup.

W: I get up now to do the kitchen. Doctors are bills and foolishness, my son. I need no doctors.

M: At the Haven

NR: he could not resist pointing out,

M: a doctor is *not* bills. He lives beside you. You start to sneeze, he is there before you open up a Kleenex. You can be sick there for free, all you want.

W: Diarrhea of the mouth, is there a doctor to make you dumb?

P: Ma. Promise me you'll go. Nancy will arrange it.

N: It's all of a piece when you think of it. The way she attacks my kitchen, scrubbing under every cup hook, doing the inside of the oven so I can't enjoy Sunday dinner, knowing that half-blind or not, she's going to find every speck of dirt. . .

P: Don't Nancy. I've told you—it's the only way she knows to be useful. What did the *doctor* say?

N: A real fatherly lecture. Sixty-nine is young these days. Go out, enjoy life, find interests.

P: So there was nothing physical.

N: Of course there was. How can you live to yourself like she does without there being? Evidence of a kidney disorder, and her blood count is low. He gave her a diet, and she's to come back for follow-up and lab work. . . But he was clear enough: Number One prescription—start living like a human being. When I think of your dad, who could really play the invalid with that arthritis of his, as active as a teenager, and twice as much fun. . .

M: You didn't tell me the doctor says the sickness is in you, how you live.

NR: He pushed his advantage.

M: Life and enjoyments you need better than medicine. And this diet, how can you keep it? To weigh each morsel and scrape away the bits of fat to make this soup, that pudding. There, at the Haven, they have a dietician, they would do it for you.

NR: She is silent.

M: You would feel better there, I know it,

NR: he says gently.

M: There there is life and enjoyments all around.

W: What is the matter, Mr. Important Busy, you have no card game or meeting you can go to?

NR: —turning her face to the pillow. . . .

NR: For a while he cut his meetings and going out, fussed over her diet, tried to wheedle her into leaving the house, brought in visitors:

W: I should come to a fashion tea. I should sit and look at pretty babies in clothes I cannot buy. This is pleasure? . . . No more crushers of people. No more in *my* house. You go to them if you like.

NR: More and more she lay silent in bed, and sometimes did not even get up to make the meals. A bellyfull of bitterness, and every day the same quarrel in a new way and a different old grievance the quarrel forced her to enter and relive. And the new torment.

W: I am not really sick. The doctor said it. Then why do I feel so sick?

NR: One night she asked him:

W: you have a meeting tonight? Do not go. Stay . . . with me.

NR: He had planned to watch "This is Your Life" anyway, but half sick himself from the heavy heat, and sickening therefore the more after the brooks and woods of the Haven, with satisfaction he grated:

M: Hah, Mrs. Live Alone and Like It wants company all of a sudden. It doesn't seem so good the time of solitary when she was a girl exile in Siberia. "Do not go. Stay with me." A new song for Mrs. Free as a Bird. Yes, I am going out, and while I am gone chew this aloneness good, and think how you keep us both from where if you want people you do not need to be alone.

W: Go, go. All your life you have gone without me.

NR: After him she sobbed curses he had not heard in years, old-country curses from their childhood.

W: Grow, oh shall you grow like an onion, with your head in the ground. Like the hide of a drum shall you be, beaten in life, beaten in death. Oh shall you be like a chandelier, to hang, and to burn. . .

NR: She was not in their bed when he came back. She lay on the cot on the sun porch. All week she did not speak or come near him: nor did he try to make peace or care for her. He slept badly, so used to her next to him. It was not the empty bed or the storm that woke him, but a faint singing. *She* was singing. Shaking off the drops of rain, the lightning riving her lifted face, he saw her so; the cot covers on the floor.

M: This is a private concert? Come in, you are wet.

W: I can breathe now. My lungs are rich.

NR: Though indeed the sound was hardly a breath. . . .

NR: He had found a buyer, but before he told her, he called together those children who were close enough to come. Paul, of course, Sammy from New York, Hannah from Connecticut, Vivi from Ohio. What a kindling of energy for her beloved visitors, she arrayed the house, cooked and baked. She was not prepared for the solemn-after-dinner conclave, they too probing in and tearing. Her frightened eyes watched from mouth to mouth as each spoke. His stories were eloquent and funny of her refusal to go back to the doctor, or her stubborn silences of the bile; or her contrariness.

W: (Vinegar he poured on me all his life; I am well marinated; how can I be honey now?)

NR: Deftly he marched in the rightness for moving to the Haven.

M: Their money from social security free for visiting the children, now sucked into daily needs and into the house; the activities in the Haven for him; but mostly the Haven for *her*; her health, her need of care, distraction, amusement, friends who shared her interests.

P: This does offer an outlet for Dad. He's always been an active person. And economic peace of mind isn't to be sneezed at, either. I could use a little of that myself.

H: And you, Ma, how do you feel about it?

W: For him it is good. It is not for me. I can no longer live between people.

VI: You lived all your life *for* people.

W: Not with.

NR: Suffering doubly for the unhappiness on her children's faces.

S: You have to find some compromise. Maybe sell the house and buy a trailer. After forty-seven years there's surely some way you can find to live in peace.

W: There is no help, my children. Different things we need.

M: Then live alone!

NR: He could control himself no longer.

M: I have a buyer for the house. Half the money for you, half for me. Either alone or with me to the Haven. You think we can live any longer as we are doing now?

P: Ma doesn't have to make a decision this minute, however you feel, Dad. And you wouldn't want her to. Let's let it lay a few months, and then talk some more.

H: I think I can work it out to take Mother home with me for a while. You both look terrible, but especially you, Mother. I'm going to ask Phil to have a look at you.

S: Sure

NR: cracked Sammy

S: what's the use of a doctor husband if you can't get free service out of him once in a while for the family? And absence might make the heart . . . you know. . . .

P: There was something after all.

NR: Paul told Nancy in a colorless voice.

P: That was Hannah's Phil calling. Her gall bladder . . . Surgery.

N: Her *gall* bladder. If that isn't classic. Bitter as gall—talk of psychosom—

NR: He stepped forward and said in the same colorless, plodding voice:

P: we have to get Dad. They operated at once. The cancer was everywhere, surrounding the liver, everywhere. They did what they could . . . at best she has a year. Dad . . . we have to tell him.

Part II

NR: Honest in his weakness when they told him, and that she was not to know.

M: I'm not an actor. She'll know right away by how I am. O that poor woman. I am old too, it will break me into pieces. O that poor woman. She will spit on me: "So my sickness was how I live." O Paulie, how she will be, that poor woman. Only she should not suffer. . . I can't stand sickness, Paulie, I can't go with you.

NR: But went. And play-acted.

M: A grand opening and you did not even wait for me. . . A good thing Hannah took you with her.

W: They cut out what tore in me; just in my throat something hurts yet . . . Look! So many flowers, like a funeral. Vivi called, did Hannah tell you? And Lennie from San Francisco, and Clara; and Sammy is coming.

PH: It is impossible to predict in these cases, but once over the immediate effects of the operation, she should have several months of comparative well-being.

M: *The money, where will come the money?*

H: Travel with her, Dad. Don't take her home to the old associations. The other children will want to see her.

M: *The money, where will I wring the money?*

S: Whatever happens, she is not to know. You, you can't ask her to sign papers to sell the house; nothing to upset her. Borrow instead, then after. . .

M: *I had wanted to leave you each a few dollars to make life easier, as other fathers do. There will be nothing left now. (Failure! you and your "business is exploitation." Why didn't you make it when it could be made?—Is that what you're thinking Sammy?)*

H: Sure she's unreasonable, Dad—but you have to stay with her; if there's to be any happiness in what's left of her life, it depends on you.

M: *Prop me up children, think of me, too. Shuffled, chained with her, bitter woman. No Haven, and the little money going. . . How happy she looks, poor creature.*

W: Let's go home.

M: One step from the hospital and she wants to fly. Wait til Doctor Phil says.

W: Let us go home. Let us go home. . . .

NR: Musing; gentleness—but for the incidents of the rabbi in the hospital, and the candles of benediction. Of the rabbi in the hospital.

H: Now tell me what happened, Mother.

W: From the sleep I awoke, and he stands there like a devil in a dream and calls me by name. I cannot hear. I think he prays. Go away please, I tell him, I am not a believer. Still he stands, while my heart knocks with fright.

H: You scared *him*, Mother. He thought you were delirious.

W: Who sent him? Why did he come to me?

H: It is a custom. The men of God come to visit those of their religion they might help. Jew, Protestant, Catholic, the Hospital makes up the list for them, and you are on the Jewish list.

W: Not for rabbis. At once go and make them change. Tell them to write: Born, human; Religion, none.

NR: *And of the candles of benediction*:

M: Look how you have upset yourself, Mrs. Excited Over Nothing. (Pleasant memories you should leave.)

W: Go in, go back to Hannah and the lights.

M: But she asked me. So what was so terrible?

W: Not for pleasure she does it. For emptiness. Because Phil's family does. Because all around her do.

M: That is not a good reason too? But you did not hear her. For heritage, she told you. For the boys, from the past they should have tradition.

W: Superstition! From the savages, afraid of the dark, of themselves: mumbo words and magic lights to scare away ghosts.

M: She told you: how it started does not take away the goodness. For centuries, peace in the house it means.

W: Swindler, does she look back on the dark centuries? Candles brought instead of bread and stuck into a potato for a candlestick. Religion that stifled and said: in Paradise, woman, you will be the footstool of your husband, and in life—poor chosen Jew—ground under, despised, trembling in cellars. And cremated. And cremated.

M: This is religion's fault? You think you are still an orator of the 1905 revolution? Where are the pills for quieting? Which are they?

W: Heritage. How have we come from savages, how no longer to be savages—this to teach. To look back and learn what ennobles man—this to teach. To smash all ghettos that divide man—not to go back, not to go back—this to teach. Learned books in the house, will man live or die, and she gives to her boys—superstition.

M: Hannah that is so good to you. Take your pill, Mrs. Excited For Nothing, swallow.

W: Heritage! But when did I have time to teach? Oh Hannah I asked only hands to help.

NR: Otherwise—musing; gentleness.

W: Not to travel. to go home.

M: The children want to see you. We have to show them you are as thorny a flower as ever.

W: Not to travel.

M: Vivi wants you should see her new baby. She sent the tickets—airplane tickets—a Mrs. Roosevelt she wants to make of you. To Vivi's we have to go.

NR: A new baby. How many warm, seductive babies she had seen. She holds him stiffly, *away* from her, so that he wails.

M: Hush, shush. You should forgive your grandmama, little prince, she has never held a baby before, only seen them in glass cases. Hush, shush.

VI: You're tired, Ma. The travel and the noisy dinner. I'll take you to lie down.

W: *A long travel from, to, what the feel of a baby evokes.* Do not ask me,

NR: she would like to beg.

W: I cannot, cannot. . .

M: *Cannot what?* Unnatural grandmother,

NR: Not able to make herself embrace a baby.

W: It was not that she had not loved her babies, her children. The love—the passion of tending—had risen with the need like a torrent; and like a torrent drowned and immolated all else. But when the need was done—o the power that was lost in the painful damning back and drying up of what still surged, but had nowhere to go. Only the thin pulsing left that could not quiet, suffering over lives one felt, but could not longer hold nor help.

NR: If they would but leave her in the air now stilled of clamor, in the reconciled solitude, to journey to her self. But they put the new baby in her lap. Immediacy to embrace, and the breath of *that* past.

W: Warm flesh like this that had claims and muzzled away all else and with lovely mouths devoured; hot-living like an animal—intensely and now; the turning maze; the long drunkenness; the drowning into needing and being needed.

NR: Severely she looked back—and the shudder seized her again. All that visit she could not touch the baby.

VI: Daddy, is it the . . . sickness she's like that? I was so glad to be having the baby—for her. I told Tim, it'll give her more happiness than anything, being around a baby again. And she hasn't played with him once.

NR: Attentive with the older children; sat through their performance (command performance; we command you to be the audience) helped Ann sort autumn leaves to find the best for a school program; listened gravely to Richard tell about his rock collection; looked for missing socks, books, and bus tickets; watched the children whoop after their grandfather who knew how to tickle, chuck, lift, toss, do tricks, tell secrets, make jokes, match riddle for riddle.

CH: Tell me a riddle, Granny.

W: I know no riddles, child.

CH: Tell me a riddle, Grammy.

W: I know no riddles, child.

NR: After a week she said:

W: Let us go home. Today call about the tickets.

M: You have important business. Mrs. Inahurry? The President waits to consult with you?

NR: He shouted, for the fear of the future raced in him.

M: The clothes are still warm from the suitcase, your children cannot show enough how glad they are to see you, and you want home. There is plenty of time for home. We cannot be with the children at home. Vivi is happy so. The children should have their grandparents a while, she told to me. I should have my momma and daddy. . .

W: Babbler and blind. Do you look at her so tired? How she starts to talk and she cries? I am not strong enough yet to help. Let us go home.

NR: (To reconciled solitude.)

CH: Tell me a riddle, Grandma.

W: (*I know no riddles.*)

CH: Look Grammy. I made it—for you.

NR: From Ann: (Flat paper dolls and aprons that lifted on scalloped skirts that lifted on flowered pants; hair of yarn and great ringed questioning eyes)

CH: Watch me, Grandma.

NR: Richard snaking up the tree, hanging exultant, free, with one hand at the top.

CH: Be my nap bed, Granny.

NR: Morty's abandoned heaviness while his fingers ladder up and down her hearing-aid cord to his drowsy chant:

CH: Eentsiebeensie spider.

NR: *And Vivi's tears and memories,* spilling so fast, half the words not understood. she had started remembering out loud deliberately

VI: so her mother would know the past was cherished, still lived in her.

NR: Nursing the baby:

VI: My friends marvel, and I tell them, oh it's easy to be such a cow. I remember how beautiful my mother seemed nursing my brother, and the milk just flows. . . Was that Davy? It must have been Davy. . .

NR: Lowering a hem:

VI: How did you ever . . . when I think how you made everything we wore. . . Tim, just think, seven kids and Mommy sewed everything . . . do I remember you sang while you sewed: That white dress with the red apples on the skirt you fixed for me. Was it Hannah's or Clare's before it was mine?

M: Strong onion, to still make you cry after so many years

NR: her father said, to turn the tears into laughter. While Richard bent over his homework:

VI: Where is it now, do we still have it, *The Book of the Martyrs?* It always seemed so, well—exalted. You know the book I'm talking about, Daddy, *The Book of the Martyrs,* the first picture was a bust of Socrates? I wish there was something like that for the children, Mommy, to give them what you. . .

NR: (and the tears splashed again)

W: (What I intended and did not? Stop it, daughter, stop it, leave that time. And he, the hypocrite, sitting there with tears in his eyes too—it was nothing to you then, nothing.)

VI: . . . The time you came to school and I almost died of shame because of your accent and because I knew you knew I was ashamed: how could I? . . . Sammy's harmonica and you danced. The time you bundled us up and walked us down to the railroad station to stay the night 'cause it was heated and we didn't have any coal, that winter of the strike, you didn't think I remembered that, did you, Mommy?. . . How you'd call us out to see the sunsets. . .

NR: Day after day, the spilling memories. Worse now, questions, too. Even the grandchildren.

CH: Grandma, in the olden days when. . .

W: (*I know no riddles.*)

NR: Noises that knocked, children screaming.

W: *Who* was screaming? Why was she back in the common room of the prison, the sun motes dancing in the shafts of light, and the informer being brought in, a pirsoner now, like themselves. And Lisa leaping, yes, Lisa, the gentle and tender, biting at the betrayer's jugular. Screaming and screaming. No, it is the children screaming. We have to go home. I grow ill here.

M: It is your own fault, Mrs. Bodybusy, you do not rest, you do too much.

NR: He raged, but the fear was in his eyes.

M: It was a serious operation, they told you to take care. . . All right, we will go to where you can rest. But where? Not home to death, not yet. He had thought of Lennie's, to Clara's; beautiful visits with each of the children. She would have to rest first, be stronger. If they could but go to Florida—it glittered before him, the never-realized promise of Florida. (The money, the money dwindling!) California: of course near Lennie. Los Angeles first for sun and rest, then to Lennie's in San Francisco.

NR: He told her the next day.

M: I called Phil: A prescription, Los Angeles sun and rest.

W: You sold the house, that is why we do not go home. That is why you talk no more of the Haven. Why there is money for travel. After the children you will drag me to the Haven.

M: The Haven! Who thinks of the Haven any more? Tell her, Vivi tell Mrs. Suspicious: a prescription, sun and rest, to make you healthy. . . And how could I sell the house without *you*?

NR: At the place of farewells and greetings, of winds of coming and winds of going, they say their goodbyes.

W: Goodbye my children.

M: Goodbye my children.

Part III

(Jeannie moves to stool.)

NR: It is to the back of the great city he brought her, to that dwelling place of the cast-off old. Bounded by two lines of amusement piers to the north and to the south, and between a long, straight paving rimmed with black benches facing the sand—sands so wide the ocean is only a far fluting. A few newer apartments glint among the low beached squares. It is in one of these Lennie's Jeannie has arranged their rooms.

W: Like a coffin. Rooms and rooms like this.

J: Only a few miles north and south people pay hundreds of dollars a month for just this gorgeous air, Granddaddy, just this ocean closeness.

NR: She had been ill on the plane, lay ill for days in the unfamiliar room. Several times the doctor came by—left medicine she would not take. Several times Jeannie drove in the twenty miles from work, still in her Visiting Nurse uniform the lightness and brightness of her like a healing.

M: Who can believe it is winter? Beautiful it is outside like an ad. Come, Mrs. Invalid, come to taste it. You are well enough to sit in here, you are well enough to sit outside. The doctor said it too.

NR: He took her one Sunday

W: in the evil-smelling bus, past flat miles of blister houses,

NR: to the home of relatives.

W: O what is this? who has done this?

NR: She cried as the light began to smoke and the houses to dim and recede.

M: Smog, everyone knows but you.

NR: Outside he kept his arms about her, but she walked with hands pushing the heavy air as if to open it, whispered:

W: Air.

NR: —her hand claws his.

M: Whenever I enjoy myself. . .

NR: Then he saw the gray sweat on her face.

W: And when will it end? O, the end. That nightmare thought

NR: That nightmare thought, and this time she writhed, crumpled beside him, seized his hand (for a moment again the weight, the soft distant roaring of humanity) and on the strangled-for breath, begged

W: Man. . . Will destroy ourselves?

NR: And looking for an answer—

M: in the helpless pity and fear for her (for *her*) that distorted his face—

W: she understood the last months, and knew that she was dying.

Part IV

W: Let us go home.

M: You are in training for a cross-country trip? That is why you do not even walk across the room? Here, like a prescription Phil said, till you are stronger from the operation. You want to break the doctor's orders?

W: She saw the fiction was necessary for him, was silent, then: At home I will get better. If the doctor here says?

M: And winter? And the visits to Lennie and to Clara? All right,

NR: For he saw the tears in her eyes,

M: I will write Phil, and talk to the doctor.

NR: Days passed. He reported nothing. Jeannie came and took her out for air, to the end of the pier. Back in her bed, while he was gone to the store, she said:

W: Jeannie, this doctor, he is not one I can ask questions. Ask him for me, can I go home?

NR: And closed her eyes.

J: You want to sleep, Granny?

W: Yes, tired from the pleasure of you.

NR: In the kitchenette, helping her grandfather unpack the groceries, Jeannie said in her light voice: *(Jeannie moves to his chair.)*

J: I'm resigning my job, Granddaddy.

M: Something is wrong with the job?

J: With me. I can't be

NR: She searched for the word

J: —professional enough. I let myself feel things. And tomorrow I have to report a family. . . . It's not that, either. I just don't know what I want to do, maybe go back to school, maybe go to art school. I thought if you went to San Francisco I'd come along and talk it over with Mommy and Daddy. But I don't see how you can go. She wants to go home. She asked me to ask the doctor. *(Jeannie returns to the stool.)*

NR: The doctor told her himself.

PH: Next week you may travel, when you are a little stronger.

NR: But next week there was the fever of an infection, and by the time that was over, she could not leave the bed—a rented hospital bed that stood beside the double bed he slept in alone now. Outwardly the days repeated themselves. Every other afternoon and evening he went out to his new-found cronies, to talk and play cards. And the rest of the time, Jeannie was there. Hanna and Phil sent flowers. To deepen her pleasure, he placed one to her hair

M: Like a girl

NR: He said and brought the hand mirror for her to see.

W: She looked at the pulsing red flower, the yellow skull face:

NR: A desolate, excited laugh shuddered from her, and she pushed the mirror away—but let the flower burn. The week Lennie and Helen came, the fever returned. With the excited laugh, and incessant words. She, who in her life had spoken but seldom and then only when necessary (never having learned the easy, social uses of words), now in dying, spoke incessantly.

W: Like Lisa she is, your Jeannie, my son. Have I told you of Lisa, she who taught me to read? Of the highborn she was, but noble in herself. I was sixteen; they beat me, my father beat me so I would not go to her. It was forbidden, she was a Tolstoyan. At night, past dogs that howled, terrible dogs, my son, in the snows of winter to the road, I to ride in her carriage like a lady, to books. To her, life was holy, knowledge was holy, and she taught me to read. They hung her. Everything that happens one must try to understand why. She killed one who betrayed many. Because of betrayal, betrayed all she lived and believed. In one minute she killed, before my eyes in prison with me. (There is so much blood in a human being, my son. All that happens, one must try to understand.) Yes, Jeannie, at your age my mother and grandmother had already buried children . . . yes, Jeannie, it is more than oceans between Olshana and you . . . yes, Jeannie, they danced, and for all the bodies they had they might as well be chicken, and indeed, they scratched and flapped their arms and hopped.

NR: Delirious:

W: Tell them who ask: no rabbis, no ministers, no priests, no speeches, no ceremonies; ah, false—let the living please themselves. Tell Sammy's boy he who flies, tell him to go to Stuttgart and see where Davy has no grave. And what?

NR: A conspirator's laugh.

W: And what? where millions have no graves.

NR: Telling to herself half-memorized phrases from her few books.

W: Pain I answer with tears and cries, baseness with indignation, meanness with repulsion . . . for life may be hated or wearied of, but never despised.

NR: In delirium or not, wanting the radio on; not seeming to listen, the words still jetting, wanting the music on. Once, silencing it abruptly as of old, she began to cry, unconcealed tears this time.

J: You have pain, Granny?

W: The music, still it is there and we do not hear; knocks, and our poor human ears are too weak. What else, what else we do not hear?

NR: Once she knocked his hand aside as he gave her a pill, swept the bottles from her bedside table:

W: No pills, let me feel what I feel.

NR: And laughed as on his hands and knees he groped to pick them up. Nighttimes her hand reached across the bed to hold his. A constant retching began.

D: She will be better off in the hospital now.

NR: He sent the telegrams to the children, was packing her suitcase, when her hoarse voice started. She had roused, was pulling herself to sitting.

W: Where now? Where now do you drag me? Not home yet? Where *is* my home?

NR: Her voice mourned.

M: The doctor, the hospital.

NR: Nighttimes her hand reached across the bed to hold his.

W: Coward,

NR: she hissed,

W: runner.

M: You stand,

NR: he said senselessly. He started to explain, but deftly, like a snake, she had slithered out of bed and stood swaying propped behind the night table.

W: To take me there and run. Afraid of a little vomit.

NR: He reached her as she fell. She struggled against him, half slipped from his arms, pulled herself up again.

W: Weakling,

NR: she taunted,

W: to leave me there and run. Betrayer. All your life you have run.

NR: He sobbed, telling Jeannie.

M: A Marilyn Monroe to run for her virtue. Fifty-nine pounds she weighs, the doctor said, and she beats at me like a Dempsey. Betrayer, she cries, and I running like a dog when she calls; day and night, running to her.

J: She wants you, Granddaddy. Isn't that what they call love? I'll see if she sleeps, and if she does, poor worn-out darling, we'll have a party, you and I; I brought us rum babas.

NR: They did not move her. By her bed now stood the tall hooked pillar that held the solutions—blood and dextrose—to feed her veins. Jeannie moved down the hall to take over the sickroom, her face so radiant, her grandfather asked her once

M: you are in love?

NR: (Shameful with joy, the pure overwhelming joy from being with her grandmother; the peace, the serenity that breathed.)

J: My darling escape

NR: she answered incoherently,

J: My darling Granny

NR: —as if that explained. Now one by one the children came, those that were able. Hannah, Paul, Sammy. Too late to ask: and what did you learn with your living, Mother, and what do we need to know? Clara, the eldest, clenched:

CL: Pay me back, Mother, pay me back for all you took from me. Those others you crowded into your heart. The hands I needed to be for you, the heaviness, the responsibility. Is this she? Noises the dying make, the crablike hands crawling over the covers. The ethereal singing.

NR: She hears that music, that singing from childhood; forgotten sound—not heard since, since . . . And the hardness breaks like a cry:

CL: Where did we lose each other, first mother, singing mother?

NR: Annulled: the quarrels, the gibing, the harshness between; the fall into silence and the withdrawal.

CL: I do not know you, Mother. Mother, I never knew you.

NR: Lennie, suffering not alone for her who was dying, but for that in him which never lived (for that which in him might never live). From him too, unspoken words:

L: Good-by mother who taught me to mother myself. I do not know you, Mother. Mother, I never knew you.

NR: Not Vivi, who must stay with her children; not Davy, but he is already here, having to die again with *her* this time, for the living take their dead with them when they die. Light she grew, like a bird, and, like a bird, sound bubbled in her throat while the body fluttered in agony. Night and day, asleep or awake (though indeed there was no difference now) the songs and the phrases leaping. And he, who had once dreaded the long dying (from fear of himself, from horror of the dwindling money) now desired her quick death profoundly, for *her* sake. He no longer went out, except when Jeannie force him; no longer laughed, except when, in the bright kitchenette, Jeannie coaxed his laughter. The body threshed, her hand clung in his. A melody, ghost-thin, hovered on her lips. Now, heedless of his presence, she floated the melody on and on.

M: How many times you listened to remember it so?

W: An unexamined life   not worth
Strong   with the not yet   in the now
Dogma dead   war dead   one country

M: It helps, Mrs. Philosopher, words from books? It helps?

NR: And it seemed to him that for seventy years she had hidden a tape recorder, infinitely microscopic, within her, that it had coiled infinite mile on mile, trapping every song, every melody, every word read, heard and spoken—

M: that maliciously she was playing back only what said nothing of him, of the children, of their intimate life together. Left us indeed, Mrs. Babbler, you who called others babbler and cunningly saved your words. A lifetime you tended and loved, and now not a word of us, for us. Left us indeed? Left me.

NR: And he took out his solitaire deck, shuffled the cards loudly, slapped them down.

M: Deuce, ten, five.

NR: Dauntlessly she began a song of their youth of belief:

W: *These things shall be, a loftier race*
then e're the world hath known shall rise
with flame of freedom in their souls
and light of knowledge in their eyes

M: King, four, jack. In the twentieth century, hah!

W: *They shall be gentle, brave and strong*
to spill no drop of blood, but dare
all that may plant man's lordship firm
on earth and fire and sea and air

M: To spill no drop of blood, hah! So, cadaver, and you too, cadaver Victor Hugo, in the twentieth century ignorance will be dead, dogma will be dead, war will be dead, and for all mankind one country—of fulfillment. Hah!

W: *And every life*

NR: a long strangled cough.

W: *shall be a song*

NR: The cards fell from his fingers. Without warning, the bereavement and betrayal he

190

had sheltered—compounded through the years—hidden even from himself—revealed itself,

> uncoiled,
> released,
> *sprung*,

and with it the monstrous shapes of what had actually happened in the century. He tried not to listen, as he tried not to look on the face in which only the forehead remained familiar, but trapped with her the long nights in that little room, the sounds worked themselves into his consciousness, with their punctuation of death swallows, simpers, gurglings. *Even in reality life's lack of it.*

M: Lost, how much I lost. Escaped to the grandchildren whose childhoods were childish, who never hungered, who lived unravaged by disease in warm houses of many rooms, had all the school for which they cared, could walk on any street, stood a head taller than their grandparents, towered above—beautiful skins, straight backs, clear straightforward eyes. Yes, you in Olshana,

NR: he said to the town of sixty years ago,

M: they would be *nobility* to you. And was this not the dream then, come true in ways undreamed

NR: he asked.

M: And are there no other children in the world?

NR: As if in her harsh voice he answered,

M: *And the flame of freedom, the light of knowledge? And the drop, the drop of blood?* Dark, ignorant, terrible with hate and disease—how was it that living in it, in the midst of corruption, filth, treachery, degradation, they had not mistrusted man or themselves; had believed so beautifully, so . . . falsely: Aaah, children

NR: He said out loud.

M: How we believed, how we belonged.

NR: And he yearned to package for each of the children, the grandchildren, for everyone

M: That joyous certainty, that sense of mattering, of moving and being moved, of being one and indivisible with the great of the past, with all that freed, ennobled man.

NR: Package it, stand on corners, in front of stadiums and on crowded beaches, knock on doors, give it as a fabled gift.

M: And why not in cereal boxes, in soap packages?

NR: He mocked himself. He left the mute old woman poring over *The Book of the Martyrs*; went past the mother treadling at the sewing machine, singing with the children; past the girl in her wrinkled prison dress, hiding her hair with scarred hands, lifting to him her awkward, shamed, imploring eyes of love; and he took her in his arms, dear, personal, fleshed, in all the heavy passion he had loved to rouse from her.

M: Eva!

NR: Her little claw hand beat the covers.

M: How much, how much can a man stand?

NR: He took up the cards, put them down, circled the beds, walked to the dresser, opened, shut drawers, brushed his hair, moved his hand bit by bit over the mirror to see what of the reflection he could blot out with each move, and felt that any moment he would die of what was unendurable.

M: Went to press the buzzer to wake Jeannie, looked down, saw on Jeannie's sketch pad the hospital bed, with *her*; the double bed alongside, with him; the tall pillar feeding into her veins, and their hands, his and hers, clasped, feeding each other.

NR: And as if he had been instructed he went to his bed, lay down, holding the sketch as if it could shield against the monstrous shapes of loss, of betrayal, of death—and with his free hand took hers back into his. *(He takes her hand and they look at each other briefly.)*

J: So Jeannie found them in the morning.

NR: That last day the agony was perpetual. Time after time it lifted her almost off the bed, so they had to fight to hold her down. He could not endure and left the room; wept as if there never would be tears enough. *(She withdraws her hands, Jeannie puts her arm around him.)*

NR: Jeannie came to comfort him. *(Music begins and continues until several seconds after the ending.)*

J: Granddaddy, Granddaddy, don't cry. She is not there, she promised me. On the last day, she said she would go back to when she first heard music, a little girl on the road of the village where she was born. She promised me. It is a wedding and they dance, while the flutes so joyous and vibrant tremble in the air. Leave her there, Granddaddy, it is all right. She promised me. Come back, come back and help her poor body to die.

NR: *(Stepping forward)*

> For two of that generation
> Seevya and Genya
> Infinite, dauntless, incorruptible.
> Death deepens the wonder.

A Nincompoop*

by Anton Chekhov

Adapted and Directed by Paul H. Gray
University of Texas at Austin

Chekhov began his literary career as a writer of short stories and ended it as a dramatist. Indeed, drama was to prove such an irresistable mode for him that during his last years when he created some of his greatest plays, he wrote only a handful of stories. Yet Chekhov's attraction to drama is manifest in his earliest prose fiction, even in those sketches and stories he tossed off as a medical student, long before he thought of himself as a dramatist or even as a serious writer. Though a number of characteristics contribute to the "dramatic" qualities of Chekhov's stories, three are most prevalent.

First, in a Chekhov story it is frequently dialogue rather than narration which carries the story along. Chekhov's narrators sometimes do little more than set the scene, make clear who is speaking, and summarize at the end. Second, a Chekhov narrator often reveals a character's emotional state by describing not the emotions themselves

but what the character does or how the character looks. Like the dramatist, Chekhov prefers to *show* us the perceivable results of a state of mind than have his narrator describe it directly. Finally, Chekhov anticipates twentieth-century prose writers by dramatizing his narrators. Instead of possessing reliable omniscience, the narrator of a Chekhov story frequently has as limited a perspective on the events he describes as the characters in the story. Indeed, the narrator himself is frequently just another character, and the reader, like the theatergoer, draws conclusions and value judgments based not on an identification with the storyteller's perspective, but on the events of the story.

PRODUCTION CONCEPT

These dramatic qualities of Chekhov's prose served as the organizing principle for a group performance script based on his writings and entitled *Veil of Laughter*. The script included a number of short stories, vignettes, and monologues, but ended with

*The script is adapted from *Anton Chekhov Selected Stories*, translated by Ann Dunnigan. Copyright © 1960 by Ann Dunnigan. Reprinted by arrangement with The New American Library, Inc. New York, N.Y.

one of his first published plays, *The Proposal.* This arrangement underscored Chekhov's gradual evolution from storyteller to dramatist. In this introduction, I want to suggest how one story, "The Nincompoop," lent itself to the production concept behind *Veil of Laughter.*

ORIGINAL PRODUCTION

Adaptation

Written at least a year before Chekhov graduated from medical school, "The Nincompoop" is one of his earliest published stories. Yet this early story possesses all the characteristics I have described as dramatic. Perhaps the dramatic quality most immediately apparent is the prevalence of dialogue and the absence of long narrative passages. The adaptation that follows contains almost all the original story (less than twenty-five words have been cut), yet one laconic sentence from the narrator sets the scene, and another concludes it. The few narrative intrusions into the dialogue are little more than stage directions describing who spoke and how.

Virtually everything we learn about the two characters in this sketch derives from what they do and say. The governess's emotions, for example, are manifested almost exclusively through her acts. Thus while her overbearing master swindles her out of her salary, the narrator tells us not what she felt, but rather, that she "flushed a deep red and picked at the flounce of her dress," her "left eye reddened and filled with moisture. Her chin trembled; she coughed nervously and blew her nose, but—not a word."

In much the same fashion, the "master's" emotional states are equally dramatic. Through the first two thirds of the interview he hides his true feelings from both the girl in the story and the reader. His emotions are not apparent until he tells us late in the scene: "I jumped up and started pacing the room. I was overcome with anger." Thus even when the narrator describes his own emotions he gives us first the action and only then labels the emotion it expresses.

Casting and Rehearsals

Another dramatic element—the considerable difference between the author's perspective and that of his narrator—helped shape our interpretation of characterization. I refer to the disagreement of the implied author with his narrator's amazed conclusion: "how easy it is to crush the weak in this world!" At the start of rehearsals, we assumed Chekhov's agreement with his narrator. As we went through rehearsals, however, we were reminded of the fact that by being a "nincompoop," the governess ends up with her full salary *plus* eleven rubles. Clearly, the script accommodates the interpretation that the meek governess actually gulls her superior, and that the "weak in this world" are not nearly so easily crushed as the master thinks. In fact, the more control over the scene we gave to the governess, the richer her character became, and the more favorably audiences responded to the vignette.

This shift in interpretation affected both line assignments and blocking. One performer played both the narrator and the master since their points of view are nearly identical. After the director and players became convinced that the narrator neither controls his story nor perceives what the governess is doing to him, it seemed appropriate to give all narration describing Julia Vassilyevna's speech and action during the interview to the governess—thereby giving the impression that just as Julia controls the master without his realizing it, she also controls the story.

Stage Composition

Our growing awareness of her control over the story affected the blocking as well. The full script of *Veil of Laughter* involved a number of scene changes and required extreme flexibility of furnishings. These consisted of an oriental rug, Victorian wall hangings, and several turn-of-the-century wooden "ice cream" chairs. For "The Nincompoop," chairs were placed together to form a couch on stage right. Originally, Julia entered upstage right, sitting on the upstage end of the couch with the master-narrator using the down center area. As the scene evolved and the governess took a larger role in its shape, she gradually moved nearer the audience. By the final perform-ance, she was entering downstage right. Acknowledging the audience with a surreptitious curtsey and sitting on the downstage end of the "couch," she played as much to the audience as to the master.

Our conviction of the governess's control over the story evolved over a considerable period of time. We were fortunate enough to have two productions of the sketch spaced some five months apart. The final interpretation was truly an amalgam of our initial impulses and the revelations of both rehearsals and the audiences' response.

Selected Bibliography

Works by Chekhov

CHEKHOV, ANTON. *The Life and Letters of Anton Tcekhov.* Trans. and ed. by S. S. Koteliansky and Philip Tomlinson. New York: B. Blom, 1925.

————. *The Oxford Chekhov.* Trans. and ed. by Ronald Hingley. 8 vols. London: Oxford University Press, 1965–1971.

————. *Selected Stories.* Trans. Ann Dunnigan. New York: American Library, 1960.

Works About Chekhov

HAGAN, JOHN. "The Tragic Sense in Chekhov's Earliest Stories." *Criticism,* 7, 1965, 52–80.

HODGSON, PETER. "Metaliterature: An Excerpt from the Anatomy of a Chekhovian Narrator." *Pacific Coast Philology,* 7 1972, 36–42.

NILSSON, NILS. *Studies in Cechov's Narrative Technique.* Stockholm: Universitetet, Almqvist and Wiksell, 1968.

RAYFIELD, DONALD. *Chekhov: The Evolution of His Art.* London: P. Elek, 1975.

STYAN, J. L. *Chekhov in Performance, A Commentary on the Major Plays.* Cambridge, Eng.: Cambridge University Press, 1971.

CHARLES B. TIMMER. "The Bizarre Element in Cechov's Art." In *Anton Chekhov, 1860–1960: Some Essays.* Ed. T. Eekman. Leiden: E. J. Brill, 1960.

YACHNIN, RISSA. *Chekhov in English: A Selective List of Works by and about Him.* New York: N.Y. Public Library, 1960.

THE NINCOMPOOP

Cast of Characters

M-N: Master-Narrator
J: Julia

The master's study. The Master-Narrator enters to downstage left center, followed by Julia who stops at the downstage right end of the couch.

M-N: A few days ago I asked my children's governess, Julia Vassilyevna, to come to my study. "Sit down, Julia Vassilyevna," I said. "Let's settle our accounts. Although you most likely need some money, you stand on ceremony and won't ask for it yourself. Now then, we agreed on thirty rubles a month . . ."

J: "Forty."

M-N: "No, thirty. I made a note of it. I always pay the governess thirty. Now then, you've been here two months, so . . ."

J: "Two months and five days."

M-N: "Exactly two months. I made a specific note of it. That means you have sixty rubles coming to you. Subtract nine Sundays . . . you know you didn't work with Kolya on Sundays, you only took walks. And three holidays . . ."

J: Julia Vassilyevna flushed a deep red and picked at the flounce of her dress, but—not a word.

M-N: "Three holidays, therefore take off twelve rubles. Four days Kolya was sick and there were no lessons, as you were occupied only with Vanya. Three days you had a toothache and my wife gave you permission not to work after lunch. Twelve and seven—nineteen. Subtract . . . that leaves . . . hmm . . . forty-one rubles. Correct?"

197

J: Julia Vassilyevna's left eye reddened and filled with moisture. Her chin trembled; she coughed nervously and blew her nose, but not a word.

M-N: "Around New Years's you broke a teacup and saucer: take off two rubles. The cup cost more, it was an heirloom, but—let it go. When didn't I take a loss! Then, due to your neglect, Kolya climbed a tree and tore his jacket: take away ten. Also due to your heedlessness the maid stole Vanya's shoes. You ought to watch everything! You get paid for it. So, that means five more rubles off. The tenth of January I gave you ten rubles . . ."

J: "You didn't."

M-N: "But I made a note of it."

J: "Well . . . all right."

M-N: "Take twenty-seven from forty-one—that leaves fourteen."

J: Both eyes filled with tears. Perspiration appeared on the thin, pretty nose. "Only once was I given any money, and that was by your wife. Three rubles, nothing more."

M-N: "Really? You see now, and I didn't make a note of it! Take three from fourteen . . . leaves eleven. Here's your money, my dear. Three, three, three, one and one. Here it is!" I handed her eleven rubles. She took them and with trembling fingers stuffed them into her pocket.

J: "Merci."

M-N: I jumped up and started pacing the room. I was overcome with anger. "For what, this—'merci'?"

J: "For the money."

M-N: "But you know I've cheated you, for God's sake—robbed you! I have actually stolen from you! Why this 'merci'?"

J: "In my other places they didn't give me anything at all."

M-N: "They didn't give you anything? No wonder! I played a little joke on you, a cruel lesson, just to teach you . . . I'm going to give you the entire eighty rubles! Here they are in an envelope all ready for you . . . Is it really possible to be so spineless? Why don't you protest? Why be silent? Is it possible in this world to be without teeth and claws—to be such a nincompoop?" She smiled crookedly and I read in her expression.

J: "It is possible."

M-N: I asked her pardon for the cruel lesson and, to her great surprise, gave her the eighty rubles.

J: *(Exiting)* "Merci, merci, merci."

M-N: I looked after her and thought: "How easy it is to crush the weak in this world."

Twain Sketches[*]

Adapted and Directed by Beverly Whitaker Long
University of Texas at Austin

Twain Sketches, shortened for a one-hour show, originally was a two-and-a-half-hour production that sought to celebrate the American humorist, Samuel Clemens, known the world over as Mark Twain. Acclaimed for a deft wit that transcends time and geography, Twain's work, a perennial favorite of interpreters, is both deceptively simple and perpetually appealing. The source of much of this appeal is expressed in the reported account of Twain's own rejoinder to Matthew Arnold's accusation that he was the worst kind of vulgar funny man: "Twain in his annoyance accepted the charge, claiming to have no interest in the cultivated minority but to be a writer solely for the uncultivated masses."[1]

With this counterattack, Twain announced his most frequent role—a member of the "folk" who wrote in "folksy" style and drew his characters and situations from a "folk community." It is little wonder that Twain's literature has engaged readers for more than ten decades, puzzled literary critics at least since 1910, and intrigued folklorists since the 1930s.

The somewhat nebulous term "folklore" was pivotal both in the compilation and the performance style of *Twain Sketches.*[2] In the compilation, I included several types of folklore: the tall tale and the folk speech in "The Old Ram"; the proverbial sayings in many of the opening epigrams; the exaggerations, or whoppers, in describing his birth and the places he visited, such as Nevada; the traditional customs in the "Cadets" sequence; the "yarn-spinning" in "An Encounter with an Interviewer" in which Twain plays the role of the laconic, poker-faced regional character who tells tall tales to outsiders; and material folk culture expressed in the details of the regional

*All material used in the script are by permission of Harper & Row Publishers. Rights to use in any public performance rest exclusively with Harper & Row.

[1]Henry Nash Smith, "Introduction," *Mark Twain: A Collection of Critical Essays,* ed. Henry Nash Smith (Englewood Cliffs, N.J.: Prentice-Hall, Inc., 1963), p. 3.

[2]See Richard M. Dorson, *American Folklore* (Chicago: University of Chicago Press, 1959). I am indebted for much of this discussion to Elizabeth Fine and Jean Haskell Speer.

199

steamboat construction. Also, in devising the script, it quickly became apparent that as we worked toward a modified chronology of Twain's career, the folkloric elements gradually diminished in importance; in short, his verbal style as well as his attitude and subject matter became increasingly "sophisticated." However, in the closing speech (written when he was seventy years old), he blends the proverbial, folksy elements with a highly cultivated injunction that borders on poetry.

Twain's gradually decreasing—though never totally absent—use of folklore as a rhetorical strategy parallels his development and success as a writer, as well as his increasing impatience with the "damned human race." As his works gained a larger and larger public and his pessissism about the meanness of humans—and even nations—grew, he relied less on traditional folklore, much of which, in his earlier life, he had actually heard and then recorded. Yet, paradoxically, except in the posthumous publications that are sometimes labeled "blasphemous," he retained a sure sense of talking with a real *audience*—whether orally from the public platform or in written narratives, essays, and letters.

This audience, implied or real, is particularly important to the performer of Twain's work, and it greatly influenced the style of the *Twain Sketches* production. We tried to illustrate the especially important elements in folklore as it is performed in the community in which it originates. Richard Bauman, in "Verbal Art as Performance," describes the act of folklore performance as "situated behavior, situated within and rendered meaningful with reference to relevant contexts."[3] Similarly, Roger Abrahams believes that "for folklore to work effectively in a performance there must be . . . a consonance between the situation

which has arisen, the item which is called forth, and the enactment."[4] Thus, in recreating an item of folklore, the performance should match as closely as possible the traditional setting and style.[5]

ORIGINAL STAGING

Much of the concept for this production appears in the program notes, which begin with a quotation from Twain's *The Mysterious Stranger:*

"... For your race, in its poverty, has one really effective weapon—laughter. Power, money, persuasion, supplication, persecution—these can lift at a colossal humbug, push it a little, weaken it a little, century by century, but only laughter can blow it to rags and atoms at a blast. Against the assault of laughter nothing can stand."

Mark Twain earned a position of special esteem in the hearts of most Americans, perhaps because they see in him what they are or think they should be—humorously perceptive and undeceived by sham. Tonight we hope to make theatrically effective a few of Twain's works, drawing from such diverse forms as letters, speeches, short stories, diaries, and newspaper articles. Just as the forms are diverse, so too is the author's tone in describing himself, other men, and events he observed—sometimes with melancholy or affection, but most often with burlesqued indignation or bitter satire.

The style of tonight's show is dictated by the types of literature presented. We have attempted to make nondramatic material vivid and stimulating in the theatre, moving —as the literature seems to move—between conversation, speaking, reading, and dramatization.

My primary aim in devising the script

---

[3]Richard Bauman, "Verbal Art as Performance," *American Anthropologist*, 77 (1975), 20.

[4]Roger Abrahams, "The Complex Relations of Simple Forms," *Genre*, 2 (June 1969), 106.

[5]See Jean Haskell Speer, "Preservation Through Presentation: The Re-Creative Performance of Verbal Art," unpublished manuscript, University of Texas, Austin, 1975.

was to "show off" Twain's versatility as a literary figure, something of his development as a writer, and his mercurial visions of the human race. The cast, it seemed, should be a group of individuals who enjoyed each other as well as the literature and the audience; each performer reflected one of the multiple facets of Twain's work and personality. The wide range of performance styles also nonverbally emphasized this versatility. Furthermore, I tried to bring the *past* and the *present* together by combining elements of more than one epoch: period furniture and authentic late nineteenth-century folk music along with stylized graphics related to the stories on screens behind the furniture, while the performers were in casual, contemporary dress.

In compiling the script, I drew from the volumes of Twain's published work, employing the techniques of *extraction* for the transitions and epigrams, *deletion* for *Letters from the Earth* (to comply with both time limitations and community standards regarding "obscenity"), *addition* from critics' remarks about the movement of his journeys and his progress to fame, and *rearrangement* in "Satan's Letter" and the separately published diaries of Adam and Eve. Also of primary concern in the compilation was a desire to show Twain's skill both as a gentle humorist and a bitter satirist, ending with a blend of his masks, both comic and serious. An outline of the original production follows; asterisks mark the selections omitted in this shortened version:

Introducing—
  Epigrammatist
  Son of Missouri
    "Steamboat a 'Coming"
    *"A Heavenly Place for a Boy"
    *"The Story of the Good and Bad Boys"
  Mississippi Pilot
  Western Traveler
    *"Bemis and the Bull"

Continuing—
  Frontier Newspaperman
  Storyteller
    "The Old Ram"
  Foreign Correspondent
  World Traveler
    *"Letter to the New York *Herald*"
  Lecturer
    "An Encounter with an Interviewer"
  Romancer
  Editor
    *"How I Edited an Agricultural Paper"
Concluding—
  Roving Ambassador
    "Milan: A Poem in Marble"
    *"On the French"
    "Incomparable England"
  Perceiver of Sham
    "Letter to W. D. Howells"
    "Letter from the Earth"
  Spokesman for the First Ones
    "Diaries of Adam and Eve"
  Spokesman for the Septuagenarian
    "Seventieth Birthday Speech"

The staging consisted of six late nineteenth-century chairs arranged in a semicircle. Behind them were paneled screens on which the graphics were attached. In front of the chairs was a long table that also served as a bench. On either side of this central area were two desks, chairs, and stools. All of the areas were used at some point during the show. Music was incorporated both before, during, and after lines at the beginning and the closing of the show.

The performers had slim manuscripts bound in dark stained plywood and used them alternately for "reading" quotes from Twain and for props (as when the interviewer fans herself); the manuscripts were discarded when the performers had to "act out" or assist in acting out a story (as in "The Old Ram" or "An Encounter with an interviewer"). Scripts seemed especially inappropriate for tall tales and yarn-spinning since both items originate in oral composition and gain their credibility from the narrator's appearance of sincerity. Also, when they were not used, the interaction between the performers on stage mirrored the inter- action between folk narrator and audience.

In short, the performers behaved much as we do in convivial social settings: they enjoyed and knew Twain, relished initiating and telling each other of his adventures, experiences, and stories, and all the while, liked helping each other pay tribute to him.

Selected Bibliography

Works by Twain

The Complete Works of Mark Twain. New York Harper and Row, 1907–1935.

Mark Twain's Autobiography. New York: Harper and Row, 1924.

Mark Twain's Letters. Arranged by Albert Bigelow Paine. New York: Harper and Row, 1935.

Mark Twain's Notebook. Prepared by Albert Bigelow Paine. New York: Harper and Row, 1935.

Eve's Diary. New York: Harper and Row, 1906.

Extract's from Adam's Diary. New York: Harper and Row, 1904.

The Love Letters of Mark Twain. Ed. Dixon Wechter. New York: Harper and Row, 1949.

Autobiography of Mark Twain. Ed. Charles Neider. New York: Harper and Row, 1962.

Letters from the Earth. Ed. Bernard DeVoto. New York: Harper and Row, 1940.

Mark Twain in Eruption. Ed. Bernard DeVoto. New York: Harper and Row, 1940.

Mark Twain on the Damned Human Race. Ed. Janet Smith. New York: Farrar, Strauss, and Giroux, 1962.

Mark Twain's Travels with Mr. Brown. Ed. Franklin Walker and G. Ezra Dane. New York: Random House, 1940.

Other Works Consulted

ABRAHAMS, ROGER. "The Complex Relations of Simple Forms." *Genre,* 2 (June 1969), 106.

ANDERSON, FREDERICK, ed., with the assistance of Kenneth Sanderson. *Mark Twain: The Critical Heritage.* New York: Barnes and Noble, 1971.

BALDANZA, FRANK. *Mark Twain: An Introduction and Interpretation.* New York: Barnes and Noble, 1961.

BAUMAN, RICHARD. "Verbal Art as Performance." *American Anthropologist,* 77 (1975), 20.

BROOKS, VAN WYCK. *The Ordeal of Mark Twain.* New York: E. P. Dutton, 1970.

BURRISON, JOHN A. *The Golden Arm: The Folk Tale and Its Literary Uses by Mark Twain and Joel C. Harris.* Atlanta: Georgia State College, 1968.

DEVOTO, BERNARD. *Mark Twain's America.* Boston: Little, Brown, and Company, 1932.

DORSON, RICHARD M. *American Folklore*. Chicago: University of Chicago Press, 1959.

HOWELLS, WILLIAM DEAN. *My Mark Twain: Remembrances and Criticism*. Baton Rouge: Louisiana State University Press, 1967.

MELTZER, MILTON. *Mark Twain Himself: A Pictorial Biography*. New York: Bonanza, 1960.

PAINE, ALBERT BIGELOW. *Mark Twain's Biography*. New York: Harper and Row, 1912.

SMITH, HENRY NASH. *Mark Twain: A Collection of Critical Essays*. Englewood Cliffs, N.J.: Prentice-Hall, Inc., 1963.

SPEER, JEAN HASKELL. "Preservation Through Presentation: The Re-Creative Performance of Verbal Art." Unpublished manuscript, University of Texas, Austin, 1975.

(a) Set for *An Evening with Mark Twain*. Designed by Harold Telford. (Southwest Texas State University)
(b) Performers from *An Evening with Mark Twain* enjoying the opening epigrams. (Southwest Texas State University)

TWAIN SKETCHES

Cast of Characters

M1-4: Four male voices
F1-2: Two female voices

M1: "I was born, the thirtieth of November, 1835, in the almost invisible village of Florida, Monroe County, Missouri. My parents removed to Missouri in the early 30s; I do not remember just when, for I was not born then and cared nothing for such things. It was a long journey in those days and must have been a rough and tiresome one. The village contained a hundred people and I increased the population by one percent. It is more than many of the best men in history could have done for a town. It may not be modest in me to refer to this but it is true. There is no record of a person doing so much, not even Shakespeare." So began the life of Samuel Langhorne Clemens—known to the world as Mark Twain. He was a printer, river pilot, soldier, miner, reporter, editor, lecturer, inventor, investor, businessman, traveler, publisher, and writer. He saw the United States first when the method of transportation was either the stage coach or the steamboat, and later saw five of the earth's continents. His seventy-four years spanned the enormous changes between Andrew Jackson and William Howard Taft. He witnessed a nation divided and a nation reunited; he saw women get the vote and he was present for Queen Victoria's jubilee; he attacked such persons as King Leopold, Jay Gould, and John D. Rockefeller, but he had intense admiration for such diverse characters as Andrew Carnegie, Helen Keller, and General Ulysses Grant . . . but I am getting far ahead of myself. . . Mark Twain is a big territory to roam around in, and there's room here for some help.

F1: It is not surprising that since Mark Twain had an opinion about positively everything and everyone with which he came in contact that he should be the target of a few comments himself. When she was fourteen and he was fifty, Susy Clemens started a biography of her father: "We are a happy family. We consist of Mama, Papa, Jean, Clara, and me. It is Papa I am writing about, and I shall have no trouble in not knowing what to say about him, as he is a very striking character. He is a very good man and a very funny one. He has a temper, but we all have in this family. He is the loveliest man I ever hope to see."

M2: But approval did not always meet Mark Twain. One writer to the *Atlantic Monthly* said, "I lived for ten years with the soul of Robert E. Lee and it really made a little better man of me. Six months of Mark Twain made me worse . . . and I am fifty-six years old." What can he not do to boys and girls of sixteen?

F2: His wife found "Samuel" a name not to her liking; so she named him "Youth" and called him that all her life.

M3: From the late prime minister of Ceylon: "We are not hostile to the United States. How could we be hostile to a country that produced Mark Twain?"

M4: George Bernard Shaw wrote Twain a note, which read; "I am persuaded that future historians of America will find your works as indispensible to them as a French historian finds the political tracts of Voltaire. I tell you because I am the author of a play in which a priest says, 'Telling the truth's the funniest joke in the world,' a piece of wisdom which you helped to teach me." Even George Trevelyan, who had a much greater respect for historical truth than Twain, asserted that "Mark Twain did more than any other man to make plain people in England understand plain people in America."

M1: Finally, from William Dean Howells, Twain's friend of more than thirty years: "Emerson, Longfellow, Lowell, Holmes—I know them all and the rest of our sages, poets, seers, critics, humorists. They were like one another and like all other literary men; but Clemens was sole, incomparable, the Lincoln of our literature." Enough for the editorializing—for the moment, at least. Mark Twain is his own best spokesman:

On Himself: "Compliments always embarrass a man. You do not know anything to say. It does not inspire you with words. There is nothing you can say in answer to a compliment. I have been complimented myself a great many times, and they always embarrass me—I always feel that they have not said enough."

M4: *More On Himself:* "You know, I always am sorry to have my name mentioned as one of the great authors because they have such a sad habit of dying off. Chaucer is dead. Spencer is dead. So is Milton, and so is Shakespeare. And I am not feeling very well myself."

M3: "I can state at this moment that there are two men most remarkable; Kipling is one and I am the other. Between us we cover all knowledge. He knows all that can be known, and I know the rest."

M1: *On the Creatures of the Earth:* "Concerning the difference between man and the jackass; some observers hold there isn't any. But this wrongs the jackass."

F1: "Thanksgiving Day. Let us all give humble, hearty, and sincere thanks now—but the turkeys. In the island of Fiji they do not use turkeys; they use plumbers. It does not become you and me to sneer at the Fiji."

M4: *On Various Professions:* "I always travel with clergymen when I can. It is better for them, it is better for me. And any preacher who goes out with me in stormy weather and without a lightning rod is a good one."

M2: "Now reader, suppose you were an idiot . . . and suppose you were a member of Congress . . . but I repeat myself."

F1: "It could probably be shown by facts and figures that there is no distinctly native criminal class except Congress."

M3: In the first place, God made idiots. This was for practice. Then he made school boards.

F2: *On Men and Women in General:* "I saw men whom thirty years had changed but slightly; but their wives had grown old. These were good women; it is very wearing to be good."

M4: "What I cannot help wishing is, that Adam and Eve had been postponed, and Martin Luther and Joan of Arc put in their places—by neither sugary persuasion nor by hell fire could Satan have beguiled *them* to eat the apple."

F2: "Man is the only creature that blushes or needs to."

M2: "The human race is a race of cowards; and I am not only marching in that procession but carrying a banner."

M1: "Life should begin with old age and its accumulations and vision and close with youth and its capacity to splendidly enjoy such adventures."

M3: The Youth that Twain wished had come last began for him in Hannibal, Missouri . . . a sleepy little town of 200 on the bank of the Mississippi River.

Steamboat A'Comin[1]

When I was a boy there was but one permanent ambition among my comrades in our village on the west bank of the Mississippi River. That was to be a steamboatman. We had transient ambitions of other sorts but they were only transient. When a circus came and went, it left us all burning to become clowns; the first Negro minstrel show that ever came to our section left us all suffering to try that kind of life; now and then we had a hope that, if we lived and were good, God would permit us to be pirates. The ambitions faded out, each in its turn; but the ambition to be a steamboatman always remained.

Once a day a cheap gaudy boat arrived. Before this event, the day was glorious with expectancy; after it, the day was a dead and empty thing. Not only the boys, but the whole village, felt this. After all these years I can picture that old time to myself now, just as it was then; the white town drowsing in the sunshine of a summer's morning; the streets empty, or pretty nearly so; one or two clerks sitting in front of the Water Street stores, with their split-bottomed chairs tilted back against the walls, chins on breasts, hats slouched over their faces—asleep—with shingles-shavings enough around to show what broke them down; a sow and a litter of pigs loafing along the sidewalk, doing a good business in watermelon rind and seeds, and the fragrant town drunkard asleep in the shadow of them; the great Mississippi, the majestic, the magnificent Mississippi, rolling its mile-long tide along, shining in the sun; the dense forest away on the other side; the "point" above the town, and the "point" below, bounding the river-glimpse and turning it into a sort of sea. Presently a Negro drayman, famous for his quick eye and prodigious voice, lifts up the cry, "S-t-e-a-m-b-o-a-t a-comin!" and the scene changes! The town drunkard stirs,

[1]Titles of major sections are included in this script. They were not, however, announced in the performance.

the clerks wake up, a furious clatter of drays follows, every house and store pours out a human contribution, and all in a twinkling the dead town is alive and moving. Drays, carts, men, boys, all go hurrying from many quarters to a common center, the wharf. Assembled there, the people fasten their eyes upon the coming boat as upon a wonder they are seeing for the first time. And the boat is rather a handsome sight, too. She is long and sharp and trim and pretty; she has two tall fanciful chimneys, a fanciful pilot house, all glass and "gingerbread"; the boiler deck, the hurricane deck, and the texas deck are fenced and ornamented with clean white railings, there is a flag gallantly flying from the jack staff; the furnace doors are open and the fires glaring bravely; the upper decks are black with passengers; the captain stands by the big bell, calm imposing, the envy of all; great volumes of the blackest smoke are rolling and tumbling out of the chimneys; the crew are grouped on the forecastle; the broad stage is run far out over the port bow, and an envied deck hand stands picturesquely on the end of it with a coil of rope in his hand, a bell rings, the wheels stop; then they turn back, churning the water to foam, and the steamer is at rest. Then such a scramble as there is to get aboard, and to get ashore, and to take in freight, all at one and the same time; and such a yelling and cursing as the mates facilitate it all with! Ten minutes later the steamer is under way again. After ten more minutes the town is dead again, and the town drunkard asleep by the skids once more.

F2: Hannibal, Missouri, was also the scene of Twain's first encounter with moral injunctions: "Nothing pleases a child so much as to be a member of something or other. Your rightly constituted child don't care shucks what it is either. I joined the Cadets of Temperance once when I was a boy. That was an awful take-in; no smoking or anything allowed—not even any bad language; but they had beautiful red scarves. I never could be truly happy till I wore one of those stunning red scarves and walked in procession when a distinguished citizen died. I stood it four months, but never an infernal distinguished citizen died during the whole time; and when they finally pronounced old Dr. Norton convalescent (a man I had been depending on for seven or eight weeks) I just drew out. I drew out in disgust, and pretty much all the distinguished citizens in the camp died within the next three weeks."

M2: At the age of thirteen, Mark Twain's career as a printer began, first in Hannibal and then in St. Louis, New York, Philadelphia, Washington, and Cincinnati. He left Cincinnati in 1857 for South America—but he got only as far as New Orleans. Because on the steamboat *Paul Jones* . . . Horace Bixby agreed to teach Twain the river, and for the next four glorious years, he realized the ambition of his youth, to be a steamboat pilot on the Mississippi.

"In that brief, sharp schooling I got personally and familiarly acquainted with all the different types of human nature that are to be found. . . . When I find a well-drawn character in fiction or biography, I generally take a warm personal interest in him for the reason that I have known him before—met him on the river."

M4: But the Civil War cut the river career short. Mark Twain enlisted in the Missouri Confederate rangers. "You have heard from a great many people who did something in the war, is it not fair and right that you listen a little moment to one who started out to do something in it, but didn't? Thousands entered the war, got just a taste of it, and then stepped out again permanently. . . . I stayed two weeks. . . . I could have become a soldier myself if I had waited. I had got part of it learned, I knew more about retreating than the man that invented retreating."

The new Lincoln administration appointed Orion Clemens secretary of the Territory of Nevada and Samuel Clemens went along as secretary to the secretary.

M2: The dusty Clemens brothers got off the stage in Carson City, Nevada—population 2,000. Their sister Pamela expressed a desire to come West, so Mark Twain wrote: "Some people are malicious enough to think that if the devil were set at liberty in the Nevada Territory, he would look around awhile, and then get homesick and go back to hell again. Why, I have had my whiskers and moustaches so full of alkali dust that you'd have thought I worked in a starch factory and boarded in a flour barrel."

F1: He roamed this new country, promptly caught the silver mine fever, and went prospecting. With no luck there, he hiked 130 miles to Virginia City, got a job in a newspaper office, and covered local events—such as the legislature. "That was a fine collection of sovereigns, that first Nevada legislature. They levied taxes to the amount of thirty or forty thousand dollars and ordered expenditures to the extent of about a million. Yet they had their little periodical explosions of economy like all other bodies of the kind. A member proposed to save three dollars a day to the nation by dispensing with the Chaplain. And yet that shortsighted man needed the Chaplain more than any other member, perhaps, for he generally set with his feet on his desk, eating raw turnips, during the morning prayer."

M4: Mark Twain's trouble began in May, 1864. Ladies began raising money for the U.S. Sanitary Commission, which provided aid for the wounded Union soldiers. In the midst of the fund-raising, Twain wrote an article for the paper hinting that the funds were being diverted to a "mince genation society" back East. The joke was disastrous, a duel was threatened, and Mark fled west across the mountains. In San Francisco, he worked for three newspapers, covering local news, squabbles, fires, and six theaters. "It was awful slavery for a lazy man." He attacked the corruption of local politicians and the police, and, revolted by the brutal treatment of the Chinese in San Francisco, he damned the mobs that hunted victims in the street. By the end of 1864 San Francisco was too hot for the crusader, so he left for the gold hills and visited Jim Gillis. Jim Gillis knew pocket mining—and he knew story telling. Mark Twain heard a great many stories in that mining shack.

The Old Ram

M3: Every now and then, in those days, the boys used to tell me I ought to get one Jim Blaine to tell me the stirring story of his grandfather's old ram—but they always added that I must not mention the matter unless Jim was drunk at the time—just comfortably and sociably drunk. I got to hunting Blaine; but it was of no use, the boys always found fault with his condition; he was often moderately but never satisfactorily drunk. I never watched a man's condition with such absorbing interest, such anxious solicitude; I never so pined to see a man uncompromisingly drunk before. At last, one evening I hurried to his cabin, for I had learned that this time his situation was such that even the most fastidious could find no fault with it—he was tranquilly, serenely, symmetrically drunk. As I entered, he was sitting upon an empty powder-keg with a clay pipe in one hand the other raised to command silence.

I found a seat at once, and Blaine began:

M1: I don't reckon them times will come again. There never was a more bullier old ram than what he was. Grandfather fetched him from Illinois—got him from a man by the name of Yates—Bill Yates—maybe you might have heard of him; his father was a deacon—Baptist—and he was a rustler too; a man had to get up ruther early to get the start of old Thankful Yates; it was him who put the Greens up to j'ining teams with my grandfather when he moved west. Seth Green was prob'ly the pick of the flock; he married a Wilkerson—Sarah Wilkerson—good cretur, she was—one of the likeliest heifers that was ever raised in Old Stoddard, everybody said that knowed her. She could heft a bar'l of flour as easy as I can flip a flapjack. And spin? Don't mention it! Independent? Hmph! When Sile Hawkins come a browsing around her, she let him know that for all his tin he couldn't trot in harness alongside of her. You see, Sile Hawkins was—no, it warn't Sile Hawkins, after all—it was a galoot by the name of Filking—I disremember his first name; but he was a stump—come into pra'r meeting drunk one night, horraying for Nixon, becuz he thought it was a primary; and Old Deacon Ferguson up and scooted him through the window and he lit on old Miss Jefferson's head, poor old filly. She was a good soul—had a glass eye and used to lend it to old Miss Wagner, that hadn't any, to receive company in; it warn't big enough, and when Miss Wagner warn't noticing, it would get twisted around in the socket, and look up, maybe, or out to one side, and every which way, while t' other one was looking as straight ahead as a spy glass. Grown people didn't mind it, but it 'most always made the children cry, it was so sort of scary. She tried packing it in raw cotton, but it wouldn't work, somehow the cotton would get loose and stick out and look so kind of awful that the children couldn't stand it no way. She was always dropping it out, and turning her old dead light on the company empty, and making them uncomfortable becuz she never could tell when it hopped out, being blind on that side, you see. So somebody would have to punch her and say, "You game eye has fetched loose, Miss Wagner, dear"—and then all of them would have to sit and wait till she jammed it in again—wrong side before, as a general thing, and green as a bird's egg, being a bashful cretur and easy sot back before company. But being wrong side before warn't much difference, anyway becuz her own eye was sky blue and the glass one was yaller on the front side, so witchever way she turned it, it didn't match nohow. Old Miss Wagner was considerable on the borrow, she was. When she had a quilting, or Dorcas S'iety at her house she generally borrowed Miss Higgins' wooden leg to stump around on; it was considerable shorter than her other pin, but much she minded that. She said she couldn't abide crutches when she had company and things had to be done, she wanted to get up and hump herself. She was bald as a jug, and so she used to borrow Mrs. Jacobs' wig—Miss Jacobs was the coffin-peddler's wife—a fatty old buzzard, he was, that used to go roosting around where people was sick, waiting for 'em; and there that old rip would sit all day, in the shade, on a coffin that he judged would fit the can'idate; and if it was a slow customer and kind of uncertain, he fetched his rations and a blanket along and sleep in the coffin nights. He finally moved to Indiany pretty soon—went to Wellsville—Wellsville was the place the Hogadorns was from. Mighty fine family. Old Maryland stock. Old Squire Hogadorn could carry around more mixed licker, and cuss better than 'most any man I ever see. His second wife was the Widder Billings—she that was Becky Martin. Her oldest child, Maria, married a missionary and died in grace—et up by the savages. They et him, too, poor feller—biled him. Don't tell me it was an accident that he was biled. There ain't no such thing as an accident. When my uncle Lem was leaning up against a scaffolding once, sick or drunk or suthin, an Irishman with a hod of bricks fell on him out of the third story and broke the old man's back in two places. People said it was an accident. Much accident there was about that. He didn't know what he was there for, but had been killed. Nobody can ever make me believe anything different from that. Uncle Lem's dog was there. Why didn't the Irishman fall on the dog? Becuz the dog would 'a seen him-a-coming and stood from under. That's the reason the dog warn't app'inted. A dog can't be depended on to carry out a special prov'dence. Mark my words, it was a put-up thing. Accidents don't happen, boys.

M3: Jim Blaine had been growing gradually drowsy and drowsier—his head nodded, once, twice, three times—dropped peacefully upon his breast, and he fell tranquilly asleep. I perceived that I was "sold." I learned then that Jim Blaine's peculiarity was that whenever he reached a certain stage of intoxication, no human power could keep him from setting out, with impressive intention, to tell about a wonderful adventure which he had once with his grandfather's old ram—and the mention of the ram in the first sentence was as far as any man had ever heard him get, concerning it. He always meandered off, interminable, from one thing to another, till his whiskey got to the best of him, and he fell asleep. What the thing was that happened to him and his grandfather's old ram is a dark mystery to this day, for nobody has ever yet found out.

F2: When the heat was off, Twain returned to San Francisco and began writing casual sketches—the real beginning of a long career of fiction publishing. A job with the San Francisco *Union* gave Twain his first assignment as a foreign correspondent . . . in Hawaii. He liked the islanders and their customs, particularly the "demoralizing hula hula, which was forbidden save at night with closed doors." Even though he found "more centipedes, and scorpions and spiders and mosquitoes and missionaries than anywhere else in the world," he was admittedly "taken" by the beauty of the islands. "That peaceful land, that beautiful land, that far-off home of profound repose, and soft indolence, and dreamy solitude, where life is one long slumberous Sabbath, the climate one long delicious summer day, and the good that die experience no change, for they but fall asleep in one heaven and wake up in another."

M2: By the time he got home from Hawaii, Twain was a widely popular reporter. He signed with the Alta *Californian* as a traveling correspondent who would circle the globe and write letters as he went—with New York as the first stop. "There is something about this ceaseless buzz and hurry and bustle that keeps a stranger in a state of unwholesome excitement all the time." During the same spring he was also excited about women's suffrage. "It is time for all good men to tremble for their country. . . . Female suffrage would do harm—it would actually do harm. A large portion of our best and wisest women would still cling to the holy ground of the home circle and refuse to either vote or hold office—but every grand rascal among your sex would work, bribe, and vote with all her might; and behold, mediocrity and dishonesty would be appointed to conduct the affairs of the Government more surely than ever before." But this account, he says, "raised a small female storm, and it occurred to me that it might be uncommon warm for one poor devil against all that crinoline in the camp, so I antied up and passed out."

F2: And he left New York on the steamer *Quaker City* for a voyage that would take him to Spain, France, Russia, Greece, Turkey, Syria, and Egypt. During this first pleasure cruise from America to the old country, Mark Twain wrote over sixty letters to newspapers in the states. Eight months later, when the tourists returned to New York, he wrote a valedictory of the performance of the pilgrims in the foreign lands.

Innocents Abroad

The steamer *Quaker City* has accomplished at last her extraordinary voyage and returned to her old pier at the foot of Wall Street. The expedition was a success in some respects, in some it was not. Originally it was advertised as a "pleasure excursion." Now, anybody's and everybody's notion of a pleasure excursion is that the parties in it will of necessity be young and gay and somewhat boisterous. They will dance a great deal, sing a good deal, make love, but sermonize very little. Three-fourths of the *Quaker City's* passengers were between forty and seventy years of age. There was a picnic crowd for you! It may be supposed that the other fourth was composed of young girls. But it was not. It was chiefly composed of rusty old bachelors and a child of six years. Is any man insane enough to imagine that this picnic of patriarchs sang, danced, made love, dealt in ungodly levity? In my experience they sinned little in these matters.

Wherever we went, in Europe, Asia, or Africa, we made a sensation, and I suppose I may add, created a famine. Many and many a simple community in the Eastern Hemisphere will remember for years the insurgence of that strange horde in the year of our Lord, 1867, that called themselves Americans, and seemed to imagine in some unaccountable way that they had a right to be proud of it.

The people of these foreign countries are very, very ignorant. They looked curiously at the costumes we had brought from the wilds of America. They observed that we talked loudly at table sometimes, and got what we conveniently could out of a franc. In Paris they just simply opened their eyes and stared when we spoke to them in French! We never did succeed in making those idiots understand their own language. One of the passengers said to a shopkeeper, in reference to a proposed return to buy a pair of gloves, "Ze gloves—maybe ve coom Moonday"; and would you believe it, that shopkeeper, a born Frenchman, had to ask what it was that had been said. Sometimes it seems to me, somehow, that there must be a difference between Parisian French and *Quaker City* French.

We didn't much care for Europe. We galloped through all the galleries and through the pictured and frescoed churches of Venice, Naples, and the cathedrals of Spain. Some of us said that certain of the great works of the old masters were glorious creations of genius (we found it out in the guide-book though we got hold of the wrong picture sometimes).

They wouldn't let us land at Malta—quarantine; they would not let us land in Sardinia; nor at Algiers, Africa, not at Malaga, Spain, not Cadiz, nor at the Madeira Islands. So we got offended at all foreigners and turned our backs upon them and came home.

M1: The trip abroad, the lectures, and the books that followed made Mark Twain a sought-after man by audiences and publishers alike. He had struck his bonanza, not in silver or gold, but in selling his alter ego in print and from the platform.

An Encounter with an Interviewer

M2: When I got back to San Francisco I found myself out of a job—so I hired a hall and gave a lecture. I've never had to do a day's work since. I had a new career. I went forth upon the public highway, with all the other bandits, and gave readings from my works. I made the acquaintance of that constant menace to the itinerant lecturer, the local interviewer. It is petrified custom with these people to probe you with personal questions which you try to answer as conscientiously as you can; then they run home and improve you. The result is that you do not recognize yourself in print, unless you happen to be an idiot of long standing, with no prejudices about it.

　　For years I have tried to outwit these people. One of those villains came to me one day. She knocked on my hotel room door and announced that she was connected with the *Daily Thunderstorm*. I was going to break the chair over her, but she sat down on it before I could go into action. I was not at my best that morning. My powers were somewhat under a cloud. So I decided that I had better try to confuse her.

　　She started it off.

F1: You know it is the custom, now, to interview any man who has become notorious.

M2: What do you do it with?

F1: Ah, well, customarily it consists in the interviewer asking questions and the interviewed answering them. It is all the rage now. Will you let me ask you certain questions calculated to bring out the salient points of your public and private life?

M2: I have a very bad memory. . .

F1: Oh, that's all right. Just so you will try to do the best you can.

M2: I will. I will put my whole mind to it.

F1: Thanks. Now. Are you ready to begin?

M2: Ready.

F1: How old are you?

M2: Nineteen.

F1: Well,—I would have taken you to be much older than that.

M2: Thank you very much.

F1: Where were you born?

M2: In Missouri.

F1: When did you first begin to write?

M2: In 1836.

F1: Why, how could that be, if you are only nineteen now?

M2: I don't know. That does strike you as curious, somehow, doesn't it?

F1: Yes. Whom do you consider the most remarkable man you ever met?

M2: Aaron Burr.

F1: Aaron Burr! But you never could have met Aaron Burr if you are only nineteen years—

M2: Now, if you know more about me than I do, what do you ask me for?

F1: Well—it was only a suggestion. How did you happen to meet Burr?

M2: I happened to be at his funeral one day, and he asked me to make less noise. . .

F1: Good heavens! If you were at his funeral, he must have been dead and if he was dead, how could he care whether you made a noise or not?

M2: Oh, he was always a particular kind of a man that way.

F1: Now, let me get this straight; you say he spoke to you, and yet he was *dead*.

M2: I didn't say he was dead.

F1: But . . . wasn't he?

M2: Some said he was, some said he wasn't.

F1: What did you think?

M2: It was none of my business. It wasn't my funeral.

F1: Well, let's drop that. Let me ask about something else. Have you any brothers or sisters?

M2: I—I—I—think so—yes—but I don't remember.

F1: Well, that is the most extraordinary statement I ever heard! I'm sure that you had a brother. Haven't I read that somewhere?

M2: Oh. Yes, now that you mention it; there was a brother William—Bill we called him. Poor old Bill!

F1: Why? Is he dead?

M2: We never could tell. There was a great mystery about that, you see.

F1: That is sad. He disappeared, then?

M2: Well, yes, in a sort of general way. We buried him.

F1: *Buried him*! Without knowing whether he was dead or not?

M2: Oh, no. He was dead enough, anyway, you see, we were twins—defunct and I and we got mixed in the bathtub when we were only two weeks old, and one of us drowned. But we didn't know which. Some think it was Bill. Some think it was me.

F1: What do you think?

M2: I would give worlds to know. This solemn, this awful mystery has cast a gloom over my whole life. But I'll tell you a secret which I've never revealed to anyone before. One of us had a peculiar mark—a large mole on the back of his left hand; that was *me*. That child was the one drowned.
     With that the menace withdrew.

M4: The most important person Twain met on the *Quaker City* voyage was a young man named Charles Langdon. After seeing a photograph of Langdon's sister, he wangled an invitation to spend part of the Christmas vacation in their home. Olivia Langdon and her family received Twain as a caller at ten in the morning on New Year's Day. He left thirteen hours later. The courtship suffered a number of interruptions; Olivia thought there was something "not quite respectable" about being a humorist; but Twain persisted. . . . He wrote his sister; "I love—I worship—Olivia L. Langdon of Elmira—and she loves me. When I am permanently settled—and when I am a Christian and when I have demonstrated that I have a good, steady, reliable character, her parents will withdraw all their objections, and she may marry me—I say she will—I intend she shall—" Two years later, they were finally married and a few weeks later Twain wrote, "If all one's married days are as happy as these new ones have been to me, I have deliberately fooled away thirty years of my life. If it were to do over again I would marry in early infancy instead of wasting time cutting teeth." And later he confides in his family, "Livy gets along better and better with her housekeeping. Now this morning she had a mackerel fricasseed with pork and oysters and I tell you it was a dish to stir the very depths of one's benevolence. We saved every bit of it for the poor. We entirely enjoy these glad days. We sit alone in the loveliest of libraries, in the evening, and I read poetry—and every now and then I come to a passage that brings tears to my eyes, and I look up to her for loving sympathy, and she inquires whether they sell sirloin steaks by the pound or by the yard."

M2: During the next two decades Mark Twain wrote the books that were to bring him wealth, fame, and make his name a household term around the world. With the publication of *Roughing It, Tom Sawyer, Life on the Mississippi,* and *Huckleberry Finn,* the "boy from Mississippi" had most definitely arrived. And he continued to travel, earning for himself the title of "America's informal ambassador to the world."—"Travel is fatal to prejudice, bigotry, and narrow-mindedness, and many of our people need it sorely on these accounts. Broad, wholesome, and charitable views of men and things cannot be acquired by vegetating in one little corner of the earth all one's lifetime."

Well, it seems rather unlikely that he ever vegetated. Twelve years of his life were spent outside the U.S. in Greece, South Africa, Italy, Ceylon, Australia, India—and other places. Sometimes he was humorously perceptive, sometimes indignant, and occasionally almost rhapsodic. . . .

F2: As when he saw the cathedral near Milan

Milan: A Poem in Marble

Toward dusk we drew near Milan, and caught glimpses of the city and the blue mountain peaks beyond. But we were not caring for these things—they did not interest us in the least. We were in a fever of impatience; we were dying to see the renowned cathedral! We watched—in this direction and that—all around—everywhere. We needed no one to point it out—we did not wish any one to point it out—we would recognize it, even in the desert of the great Sahara.

At last, a forest of graceful needles, shimmering in the amber sunlight, rose slowly above the pygmy housetops, as one sometimes sees, in the far horizon, a gilded and pinnacled mass of cloud lift itself above the waste of waves, at sea,—the cathedral! We knew it in a moment.

Half of that night, and all of the next day, this architectural autocrat was the sole object of interest.

What a wonder it is! So grand, so solemn, so vast! And yet so delicate, so airy, so graceful! A very world of solid weight, and yet it seems in the soft moonlight only a fairy delusion of frostwork that might vanish with a breath! How sharply its pinnacled angles and its wilderness of spires were cut against the sky, and how richly their shadows fell upon its snowy roof! It is a vision!—a miracle!—an anthem sung in stone, a poem wrought in marble!

They say that the Cathedral of Milan is second only to St. Peter's at Rome. I cannot understand how it can be second to anything made by human hands.

F1: But of all the countries Mark Twain visited, England was ever the magic land.

Incomparable England

There is only one England. Now that I have sampled the globe, I am not in doubt. There is a beauty of Switzerland, and it is repeated in the glaciers and snowy ranges of many parts of the earth; there is a beauty of the fiord, and it is repeated in New Zealand and Alaska; there is a beauty of Hawaii, and it is repeated in ten thousand islands of the Southern Seas; there is a beauty of the prairie and the plain, and it is repeated here and there in the earth; each of these is worshipful, each is perfect in its way, yet holds no monopoly of its beauty; but that beauty which is England is alone—it has no duplicate. It is made up of very simple details—just grass, and trees, and churches, and castles, and here and there a ruin—and over it all a mellow dream-haze of history. But its beauty is incomparable, and all its own.

Six times Mark Twain visited and revisited England during the thirty-five years between his first and last trips. His last trip was at the invitation of Oxford University to receive an honorary degree. It was a four-week celebration unequaled by any reception ever given by the English to an American up to that time.

M1: "It pleased me beyond measure when Yale made me a Master of Arts, because I didn't know anything about art; I had another convulsion of pleasure when Yale made me a Doctor of Literature, because I was not competent to doctor anyone's literature but my own, and couldn't even keep my own in a healthy condition without my wife's help. I rejoiced again when Missouri University made me a Doctor of Laws because it was all clear profit. I not knowing anything about laws except how to evade them and not get caught. And now at Oxford I am to be made a Doctor of Letters—all clear profit because what I don't know about letters would make me a multimillionaire if I could turn it into cash."

Dressed in academic regalia of scarlet and gray, Mark Twain received the degree from Chancellor Curzon who said "Most amiable and charming sir, you shake the sides of the whole world with your merriment." Twain remarked later that what he liked best about Oxford was the costume he was permitted to wear—a costume he chose to wear again—at his daughter's wedding.

F2: On the continent and in the states, a subject that preoccupied Mark Twain most of his life was "the damned human race." Ironically, as his fame mounted, so did his angry pessimism—a pessimism compounded by tragic deaths in his immediate family, by his financial bankruptcy, and by the wars that continued abroad. From the nineteenth to the twentieth century, he extended a greeting:

M3: "I bring you the stately maiden named Christendom, returning bedraggled, besmirched, and dishonored, from pirate raids in Kiao-Chou, Manchuria, South Africa, and the Philippines, with her soul full of meanness, her pocket full of boodle, and her mouth full of pious hypocrisies. Give her soap and towel, but hide the looking glass."

F2: He continued the same theme in a letter to William Dean Howells, "Dear Howells, You are old enough to be a weary man with paling interests but you do not show it. You do your work in the same old delicate and searching and perfect way. I don't know how you can—but I suspect. I suspect that to you there is still dignity in human life and that man is not a joke—a poor joke—the poorest that was ever contrived. . . . I have been reading the morning paper. I do it every morning—well knowing that I shall find in it the usual depravities and basenesses and hypocrisies and cruelties that make up civilization and cause me to put in the rest of the day pleading for the damnation of the human race. I cannot seem to get my prayers answered. Since I wrote my Bible, man is not to me the respectable worthy person he was before."

M2: "I have no special regard for Satan, but I can at least claim I have no prejudice against him. It may even be I lean a little his way, on account of his not having a fair show . . . we never hear his side." In another assault, not published until after his death, Twain lets us hear Satan's side. He writes a letter to the archangels Gabriel and Michael about his observations of the people on earth.

Letters from the Earth

M4: Earth:

Dear Michael and Gabriel:

Man is a marvelous curiosity. When he is at his very, very best, he is a sort of low-grade, nickel-plated angel; at his worst he is unspeakable, unimaginable. Yet he blandly and in all sincerity calls himself "The noblest work of God." Moreover, if I may put another strain upon you—he thinks he is the creator's pet. He prays to Him and fills his prayer with crude and bald and florid flatteries of Him, and thinks the creator sits and purrs over these extravangancies and enjoys them. I must put one more strain upon you: he has invented a Heaven out of his own head, all by himself. Guess what it is like! In fifteen hundred eternities you couldn't do it. I'll tell you about it.

This heaven he has imagained is like himself: strange, interesting, astonishing, grotesque. I give you my word. It consists, utterly and entirely, of diversions which he cares next to nothing about here in the earth, yet is quite sure he will like in heaven. Isn't it curious? Most men do not sing, most men cannot sing, most men will not stay where others are singing if it be continued more than two hours. Note that. Yet in man's heaven everybody sings! The man who did not sing on earth sings there; the man who could not sing on earth is able to do it there. And this universal singing is not casual, not occasional, not relieved by intervals of quiet; it goes on all day long and every day. And everybody stays! This singing is of hymns alone; nay, only one hymn, and the words are always the same: "Hosannah, Hosannah, Hosannah, Rah! Rah! Siss! Boom! Baah!"

Now then, in the earth, these people cannot stand much church—an hour and a quarter is the limit, and they draw the line at once a week. Of all the men in a church on Sunday, two-thirds are tired when the service is half over, and the rest before it is finished. They quickly weary of this earthly Sabbath, yet they long for that eternal one—a church that lasts forever! They talk about it, they dream of it, they think they are going to enjoy it—with all their simple hearts they think they are going to be happy in it!

Now on earth, all nations look down on all other nations. All nations dislike all other nations.

Yet in their heaven, all the nations of the earth are emptied together in one common jumble. All are on an equality absolute, they have to be "Brothers"; they have to mix together, pray together, harp together, Hosannah together—Whites, Negroes, Jews, Everybody—there's no distinction.

And every pious person adores that heaven and wants to get into it. And when he is in a holy rapture he thinks that if he were only there, he would take all the populace to his heart, and hug, and hug, and hug!

I remain, Your bewildered brother,

Satan.

F2: But confirming his usual contradictory and complex nature, after his wife's death, Twain finished a sketch that contains some support for the human race—at least two members of it—Adam and Eve. He found in Adam "a man who comes down to us without a stain on his name, unless it was a stain to take one apple when most of us would have taken the whole crop." And he found in Eve a rather veiled testimony to the "genuine righteousness" of one person—Olivia. These creatures speak to us in their diaries.

Adam's Diary and Eve's Diary

F1: *Saturday.* I am almost a whole day old, now. I arrived yesterday. That is, as it seems to me. And it must be so, for if there was a day-before-yesterday I was not there when it happened, or I should remember it. It could be, of course, that it did happen and I was not noticing. Very well; I will be watchful now, and if any day-before-yesterdays happen I will make a note of it. It will be best to start right now and not let the record get confused, for some instinct tells me that these details are going to be important to the historian some day.

I followed the other Experiment around, yesterday afternoon, at a distance, to see what it might be for, if I could. But I was not able to make out. I think it is a man. I had never seen a man, but it looked like one, and I feel sure that that is what it is; for it has frowsy hair and blue eyes, and looks like a reptile. It has no hips; it tapers like a carrot; when it stands, it spreads itself apart like a derrick; so I think it is a reptile, although it may be architecture.

I was afraid of it at first, and started to run every time it turned around, for I thought it was going to chase me; but by and by I found it was only trying to get away, so after that I was not timid any more, but tracked it along, several hours, about twenty yards behind, which made it nervous and unhappy. At last it was a good deal worried, and climbed a tree.

M1: *Monday.* This new creature with the long hair is a good deal in the way. It is always hanging around and following me about. I don't like this; I am not used to company. I wish it would stay with the other animals. . . . Cloudy today, wind in the east; think we shall have rain . . . *We?* Where did I get that word? I remember now—the new creature used it.

F1: *Tuesday.* It is in the tree yet. Resting apparently. But that is a subterfuge. I clodded it to make it come down from the tree. One of the clods took it back of the ear, and it used language. It gave me a thrill, for it was the first time I had ever heard speech, except my own. I did not understand the words, but they seemed expressive. When I found I could talk I felt a new interest in it, for I love

218

to talk; I talk, all day, and in my sleep too, and I am very interesting, but if I had another to talk to I could be twice as interesting, and would never stop, if desired.

M1: *Wednesday.* Been examining the great waterfall. . . . It is the finest thing on the estate, I think, the new creature calls it Niagara Falls—why, I am sure I do not know. Says it looks like Niagara Falls. That is not a reason, it is mere waywardness and imbecility. I get no chance to name anything myself. The new creature names everything that comes along, before I can get in a protest. And always the same pretext is offered—it looks like the thing. There is the dodo, for instance. Says the moment one looks at it one sees at a glance that it "looks like a Dodo." It will have to keep that name, no doubt. It wearies me to fret about it, and it does no good, anyway. Dodo! It looks no more like a dodo than I do.

F1: *Next Week Sunday.* All the week I tagged around after him and tried to get acquainted. I had to do the talking, because he was shy, but I didn't mind it. He seemed pleased to have me around and I used the sociable "we" a good deal, because it seemed to flatter him to be included. He does not try to avoid me as much, which is a good sign, and shows that he likes to have me with him. That pleases me, and I study to be useful to him in every way I can, so as to increase his regard. During the last day or two I have taken all the work of naming off his hands, and this has been a great relief, for him, for he has no gift in that line, and is evidently very grateful. I am aware of his defect. Whenever a new creature comes along I name it before he has time to expose himself by an awkward silence. In this way I have saved him many embarrassments. I have no defect like this.

M1: *Wednesday.* Built me a shelter against the rain, but could not have it to myself in peace. The new creature intruded. When I tried to put it out it shed water out of the holes it looks with and wiped it away with the back of its paws and made a noise such as some of the other animals make when they are in distress. I wish it would not talk; it is always talking.
Saturday. The new creature eats too much fruit. We are going to run short, most likely. "We" again—that is *its* word; mine, too, now, from hearing it so much. This morning found the new creature trying to clod apples out of that forbidden tree.

F1: *Next Week Friday.* I tried to get him some of those apples, but I cannot learn to throw straight. I failed, but I think the good intention pleased him. They are forbidden, and he says I will come to harm; but so I come to harm through pleasing him, what shall I care for that harm?

M1: *Saturday.* The new creature says its name is Eve. That is all right, I have no objections. Says it is to call it by, when I want it to come. I said it was superfluous, then. The word evidently raised me in its respect; and indeed it is a large good word and will bear repetition. It says it is not an It, it is a She. This is probably doubtful.

F1: *Sunday.* No, he took no interest in my name. I tried to hide my disappointment, but I suppose I did not succeed. I went away and sat on the mossbank with my feet in the water.
Tuesday. All the morning I was at work improving the estate and I purposely kept away from him in the hope that he would get lonely and come. But he did not. I shall talk with the snake. He is very kindly disposed. . . .

219

M1: *Wednesday.* I have had a variegated time. I escaped last night, and rode a horse all night as fast as he could go, hoping to clear out of the Park and hide in some other country before the trouble should begin; but it was not to be. About an hour after sun-up as I was riding through a flowery plain where thousands of animals were grazing, slumbering, or playing with each other, according to their want, all of a sudden they broke into a tempest of frightful noises, and in one moment the plain was a frantic commotion and every beast was destroying its neighbor. I knew what it meant too. Eve had eaten that fruit, and death was come into the world. I found this place, outside the Park, and was fairly comfortable for a few days, but she found me out. In fact I was not sorry she came, for there are but meager pickings here, and she brought some of those apples. I was obliged to eat them, I was so hungry. It was against my principles, but I find that principles have no real force except when one is well fed. I find that she is a good deal of a companion. I see I should be lonesome, and depressed without her, now that I have lost my property. Another thing, she says it is ordered that we will work for our living hereafter. She will be useful. I will superintend!

F1: *Friday, Six Months Later.* Tuesday—Wednesday—Thursday—and today; all without seeing him. It is a long time to be alone; but he will come back soon.

M1: *Next year.* We have named it Cain. She caught it while I was up country trapping on the North Shore of the Erie; caught it in the timber a couple of miles from our dug-out—or it might have been four, she isn't certain which. It resembles us in some ways, and may be a relation. That is what she thinks, but this is an error, in my judgment. The difference in size warrants the conclusion that it is a different and new kind of animal—a fish, perhaps, though when I put it in the water to see, it sank, and she plunged in and snatched it out before there was opportunity for the experiment to determine the matter. I still think it is a fish, but she is indifferent about what it is, and will not let me have it to try. I do not understand this.

Wednesday. It isn't a fish. I cannot quite make out what it is. It makes curious devilish noises when not satisfied, and says "goo goo' when it is. It is not one of us, for it doesn't walk; it is not a bird, for it doesn't fly; it is not a frog, for it doesn't hop; it is not a snake, for it doesn't crawl. I feel sure it is not a fish, though I cannot get a chance to find out whether it can swim or not.

Three Months Later. The perplexity augments instead of diminishing. I sleep but little. It has ceased from lying around, and goes about on its four legs now. Yet it differs from the other four-legged animals, in that its front legs are unusually short, consequently this causes the main part of the person to stick up uncomfortably high in the air, and this is not attractive.

Three Months Later. The Kangaroo still continues to grow, which is very strange and perplexing. I never knew one to be so long getting its growth. It has fur on his head now; not like kangaroo fur but exactly like our hair except that it is much finer and softer, and instead of being black it's red.

Five Months Later. I have been off hunting and fishing a month. Meantime the bear has learned to paddle around all by itself on its hind legs and says "poppa" and "mamma"! It is certainly a new species. The further study of it will be exceedingly interesting. Meantime I will go off on a far expedition among the forests of the north and make an exhaustive search. There must certainly be another one somewhere, and this one will be less dangerous when it has company of its own species. In my judgment, it is either an enigma or some kind of bug.

Three Months Later. It has been a weary weary hunt, yet I have no success. In the meantime without stirring from the home estate, she has caught another one! I never saw such luck. This new one is as ugly now as the old one was at first; has the same sulphur and raw meat complexion and the same singular head without any fur on it. . . . She calls it Abel.

Ten Years Later. They are *boys*; we found it out long ago. It was their coming in that small immature shape that puzzled us; we were not used to it. There are some girls now. Abel is a good boy, but if Cain had stayed a bear it would have improved him.

F1: *Five Years Later.* When I look back, the Garden is a dream to me. It was beautiful, surpassingly beautiful, enchantingly beautiful, and now it is lost, but I have *him*, and am content. He loves me as well as he can; I love him with all the strength of my passionate nature, and this, I think, is proper. If I ask myself why I love him, I find I do not know, and really do not much care to know; so I suppose that this kind of love is not a product of reasoning and statistics, like one's love for other reptiles and animals. I think that this must be so. I love certain birds because of their song; but I do not love Adam on account of his singing—no, it is not that; the more he sings the more I do not get reconciled to it. Yet I ask him to sing, because I wish to learn to like everything he is interested in. I am sure I can learn, because at first I could not stand it, but now I can. It sours the milk, but it doesn't matter; I can get used to that kind of milk.

It is not on account of his brightness that I love him—no, it is not that. He is not to blame for his brightness, such as it is, for he did not make himself; he is as God made him, and that is sufficient.

It is not on account of his gracious and considerate ways and his delicacy that I love him. No, he has lacked in these regards, but he is well enough just so, and is improving.

It is not on account of his industry that I love him—no, it is not that. I think he has it in him, and I do not know why he conceals it from me.

It is not on account of his chivalry that I love him—no, it is not that. He told on me, but I do not blame him; it is a peculiarity of sex, I think, and he did not make his sex.

Then, why is it that I love him? Merely because he is masculine, I think.

He is strong and handsome and I love him for that, and I admire him and am proud of him, but I could love him without those qualities. If he were plain, I should love him; if he were a wreck, I should love him; and I would work for him, slave over him, and pray for him, and watch by his bedside until I died.

Yes, I think I love him merely because he is *mine* and is *masculine.* There is not any other reason, I suppose. And so I think it is as I first said; that this kind of love is not a product of reasonings and statistics. It just comes—no one knows where—and cannot explain itself and doesn't need to.

It is what I think. But I am only a girl, and the first that has examined the matter, and it may turn out in my ignorance and inexperience I have not got it right.

M1: *Ten Years Later.* After all these years, I see that I was mistaken about Eve in the beginning; it is better to live outside the Garden with her than inside it without her. At first I thought she talked too much; but now I should be sorry to have that voice fall silent and pass out of my life. Blessed be the one that brought us near together and taught me to know the goodness of her heart and the sweetness of her spirit!

F1: *Forty Years Later.* It is my prayer, it is my longing, that we may pass from this life together—a longing which shall never perish from the earth, but shall have place in the heart of every wife that loves, until the end of time; and it shall be called by my name. But if one of us must go first, it is my prayer that it shall be I; for he is strong, I am weak, I am not so necessary to him as he is to me—life without him would not be life; how could I endure it? This prayer is also immortal, and will not cease from being offered up while my race continues. I am the first wife; and in the last I shall be repeated.

M1: *At Eve's Grave.* Wheresoever *she* was, *there* was Eden.

F2: It seems only fair to reject Satan, or Adam, or Eve as the last speaker but instead to turn to Twain speaking for himself as he addressed an imposing group gathered for the celebration of his seventieth birthday.

Seventieth Birthday Speech

M4: This is my seventieth birthday, and I wonder if you all arise to the size of that proposition, realizing all the significance of that phrase, seventieth birthday.

The seventieth birthday! It is the time of life when you arrive at a new and awful dignity; when you may throw aside the decent reserves which have oppressed you for a generation and stand unafraid and unabashed upon your seven-terraced summit and look down and teach—unrebuked. You can tell the world how you got there. It is what They all do. You shall never get tired of telling by what delicate arts and deep moralities you climbed up to that great place. You will explain the process and dwell on the particulars with senile rapture. I have been anxious to explain my own system this long time, and now at last I have the right.

I will now teach, offering my way of life to whomsoever desires to commit suicide by the scheme which has enabled me to beat the doctor and the hangman for seventy years. Some of the details may sound untrue, but they are not. I am not here to deceive; I am here to teach.

We have no permanent habits until we are forty. Then they begin to harden, presently they petrify, then business begins. Since forty I have been regular about going to bed and getting up—and that is one of the main things. I have made it a rule to go to bed when there wasn't anybody left to sit up with; and I have made it a rule to get up when I had to. This has resulted in an unswerving regularity of irregularity. It has saved me sound, but it would injure another person.

I have made it a rule never to smoke more than one cigar at a time. I have no other restriction as regards smoking. I do now know just when I began to smoke, I only know that it was in my father's lifetime, and that I was discreet. He passed from life early in 1847, when I was a shade past eleven; ever since then I have smoked publicly. As an example to others, and not that I care for moderation myself, it has always been my rule never to smoke when asleep, and never to refrain when awake.

I smoke in bed until I have to go to sleep; I wake up in the night, sometimes three times, and I never waste any of these opportunities to smoke. I will grant here that I have stopped smoking now and then, for a few months at a time, but it was not on principle, it was only to show off; it was to pulverize those critics who said I was a slave to my habits and couldn't break my binds.

As for drinking, I have no rule about that. When the others drink I like to help others; otherwise I remain dry, by habit and preference. This dryness does not hurt me, but it could easily hurt you, because you are different. You let it alone.

Since I was seven years old I have seldom taken a dose of medicine, and have still seldomer needed one. But up to seven I lived exclusively on all-opathic medicines. Not that I needed them, for I don't think I did; it was for economy; my father took a drug store for a debt, and it made cod-liver oil cheaper than the other breakfast foods. We had nine barrels of it, and it lasted me seven years.

I have never taken any exercise, except sleeping and resting, and I never intend to take any. Exercise is loathsome. And it cannot be any benefit when you are tired; and I was always tired. But let another person try my way, and see whence he will come out.

Threescore years and ten!

It is the Scriptural statute of limitations. After that, you owe no active duties; for you the strenuous life is over. You are a time-expired man, to use Kipling's military phrase; you have served your term well or less well, and you are mustered out. You are become an honorary member of the republic, you are a man emancipated, compulsions are not for you, nor any bugle call but "lights out." You pay the time-worn duty bills if you choose, or decline if you prefer—and without prejudice—for they are not legally collectable.

The previous-engagement plea, which in forty years has cost you so many twinges, you can lay aside forever; on this side of the grave you will never need it again. If you shrink at the thought of night, and winter, and the late homecoming from the banquet and the lights and the laughter through the deserted streets—a desolation which would not remind you now, as for a generation it did, that your friends are sleeping, and you must creep in a-tiptoe and not disturb them, but would only remind you that you need not things, you need only reply, "Your invitation honors me, and pleases me because you still keep me in your remembrance, but I am seventy; seventy, and would nestle in the chimney corner, and smoke my pipe, and read my book, and take my rest, wishing you well in all affection, and that when you in turn shall arrive at pier No. 70 you may step aboard your waiting ship with a reconciled spirit, and lay your course toward the sinking sun with a contented heart."

Why I Live at the P. O.*

by Eudora Welty

Adapted and Directed by Joanna H. Maclay
University of Illinois at Urbana

"Why I Live at the P. O." is one of Eudora Welty's most frequently anthologized short stories and is consequently familiar to most literature students. Critics usually assume that such widespread interest in this story is due to the vividness of the narrator-protagonist, Sister. Having been variously described as "demented," "paranoid," "schizophrenic," "conniving," and "grimly comic," Sister is nonetheless a most engaging storyteller with a great penchant for detail. But while these various descriptions of Sister may have some general validity, they cannot account for the brilliance of the story. Such brilliance, I believe, lies in Welty's technical mastery and sharp powers of observation. She has not presented us with a simple case study in paranoia. She has rather allowed a young woman with an acute sense of persecution to *show* us how her paranoia manifests itself. We are privileged to see not only how a paranoid person views the world, but how she views *herself* in that world. This two-fold image is a product of Welty's manipulation of the first-person narrator-protagonist.

Stories featuring first-person narrator-protagonists create many interesting and challenging problems for chamber theatre. Certainly no two narrator-protagonists are the same, but their structural similarities make them a readily identifiable group available for some practical generalizations. First of all, the narrator-protagonist is the most subjective of all narrators, telling a story not only as an eyewitness but also as a major participant. Because this narrator is the center of the story he relates and because the action of the story is either precipitated by him or inflicted on him, his view cannot be taken at face value.[1] His is the most prejudiced, biased, and distorted of perspectives. For these reasons, we do not look to his story for a revelation of "fact." We look to the story for an individual's *interpretation* of events. The mirror held up reflects the narrator's own human nature

[1] In order to facilitate ease in reading, the pronoun *he* will be used to refer to narrators in general, where the sex of the narrator is not at issue.

far more than it does the world of his external environment. In such a narrative situation, the distortions of that mirror, not "what really happened," create and sustain our interest; and a successful fiction writer understands and takes advantage of the limitations of this point of view. Granted, the degree of distortion varies considerably among narrator-protagonists. We need, however, to begin with the basic assumptions that (1) it is impossible for a narrator-protagonist to be completely objective, and (2) such a narrator's subjectivity and distortion determine and control our interest as much as, if not more than, the story being told.

In chamber theatre we wish to feature the particular limitations and distortions of a narrator-protagonist's vision, no matter how large or small those restrictions may be. We are not interested in staging such a narrator's story "as it really happened"; we have no way of determining this. We seek, instead, to set on the stage precisely those limitations and interpretations that are imaged forth in the narrator-protagonist's storytelling venture.

One of the first considerations in any chamber theatre adaptation is the relationship between the narrator and the protagonist. We characteristically ask: Is the narrator close to the protagonist? Does the narrator admire the protagonist? Does the narrator even adopt altitudes, even diction, characteristic of the protagonist? Such questions seem foolish when applied to the narrator who is also the central character in his story—they are obviously the same person. Beware, however, of such hasty conclusions. Of course, they have the same name. Furthermore, in some stories, such as Alain Robbe-Grillet's *Jealousy*, the narrator is so involved in reciting his story as it happens that he never mentions himself as the protagonist, because he does not actually see himself in the action. Yet, for the most part, a narrator who tells a story about

himself remembers another self who occupies a different unit of space-time, who may hold attitudes quite different from the narrator's, and whom the narrator tries to view as objectively as possible. The narrator who tells a story about himself is usually older than his "self" in the story, although calendar days are far less important than the changes in temperament and character that occur. In short, the protagonist's image, given us by the narrator in all his finitely subjective wisdom, can differ decidedly from the image we receive of the narrator himself.

What, then, are the implications of such a position for chamber theatre? Should the narrator-protagonist always be bifurcated into two separate performers? Certainly, the answer is not so simple. In most stories where there is a marked age difference between the narrator and his younger self, such a division would appear obvious. Such stories as Peter Taylor's "A Spinster's Tale," George P. Elliott's "Among the Dangs," Katherine Anne Porter's "Holiday," and Frank O'Connor's "My Oedipus Complex" come readily to mind. Yet even in "My Oedipus Complex," where the division between the adult narrator and the child protagonist seems patently clear, the narrator's sophisticated diction belies his childlike emotional responses to his mother. The small boy in the story does not have an Oedipus complex; the narrator does. Perhaps in this story, the comic tone created by the narrator's voicing the child's emotions in adult terminology could be reinforced by using the same performer for narrator and protagonist. In a story such as J. D. Salinger's *The Catcher in the Rye*, on the other hand, where the narrator sees himself in a variety of roles (e.g., the "phoney" Holden Caulfield and the "nice" one), a chamber theatre adaptation could clarify those multiple divisions within the narrator-protagonist. In short, there is no fixed rule for translating the narrator-protagonist relationship onto the stage. Careful attention to the dimensions of the relationship between the narrator and the protagonist self should provide guidelines for decisions about character assignments.

In addition to translating the narrator-protagonist relationship into theatrical terms, chamber theatre also creates on the stage the world of the story as the narrator perceives it. If the narrator's perception is distorted, as is the case to varying degrees with narrator-protagonists, then our purpose is to realize those distortions. In the case of "Why I Live at the P. O.," the distortions are quite striking.

PRODUCTION CONCEPT

"Why I Live at the P. O." is a story about two sisters—the narrator-Sister who tells the story and is presently occupying the P. O. and the protagonist-Sister who participated in the events at home that led to her move to the P. O. The bifurcation of self is central to the story's structure. Because Sister is a vivid and highly circumstantial story-teller who *shows* most of her story through scene and dialogue, a fairly clear picture of her home life in China Grove emerges as she *tells* her story. In relating the crucial incidents at Mama's house, Sister dramatizes herself as a Cinderella figure—a pitiable, mistreated, misjudged, and misunderstood girl who tries desperately to be a dutiful member of her family. Such filial efforts, as she perceives them for her listener, are continuously thwarted by the prejudices of her own kin. Lest her auditor fail to understand the full impact of the Cinderella image she creates through the scenes of her home life, Sister frequently interrupts the flow of the story's action with asides to her listener, in order to point out how such scenes should be interpreted (e.g., "I stood up for Uncle Rondo, please remember").

This production attempted to demonstrate the essential bifurcation of Sister's

self and to show how carefully Welty orchestrates Sister's technique of blending distorted scenes and overt commentary. Such a presentation could give an audience a two-fold image of the tensive relationship between selves within Sister: an image of the paranoid Sister narrating her story and an image of the persecution-filled world in which protagonist-Sister is the sole victim.

PRODUCTION PLAN

Devising the Script. The major decisions involved assigning lines to the individual characters. No parts of the story were rearranged and nothing was added; most of the story remained intact. All of the dialogue tags were retained, not because they were necessary to identify who was speaking, but because they play an important role in the rhythm of the narration and because they provide constant reminders of the narrator's presence and control over the story she is telling. Two small sections of Sister's narration were deleted because I felt that while her comments about "the niggers" were integral to her narrative style, they could be misconstrued easily by a contemporary audience. Cutting these sections of narration does not seriously affect the audience's perception of Sister, whereas retaining them could elicit a response extraneous to the story.

Selection of Characters. My interpretation of the story suggested that there are two Sisters vividly present in "Why I Live at the P. O.," and that the other characters in Sister's story are highly dramatized. Sister No. 1, the narrator, received those narrative lines occurring within a scene in which other characters are present for the most part. In those scenes where Sister the narrator is alone with her listener, the narration was shared by the two Sister characters in this way: Sister No. 1 was assigned all lines that indicated a paranoic judgment;

and Sister No. 2 was assigned lines of narration that suggested her immersion in the past scene.

ORIGINAL PRODUCTION

Rehearsals

Rehearsals were held daily for four weeks before the performance. The first week of rehearsals was devoted to the two Sisters only, in order to solidify their relationship. Sister No. 2 needed to understand her role as a Cinderella figure who would be subservient to the family and to Sister No. 1. Sister No. 1 needed to develop her sense of power and control over her story and her audience. As the family members moved into rehearsals, I emphasized ensemble playing and Sister No. 1's control over the movement of action within the story.

Stage Composition

Setting and Properties. Sister's scenic details are vivid but sparse in projecting the setting of Mama's China Grove home. Although she speaks of home as if it were an actual place, complete with furnished rooms and simmering food, her story clearly takes place in her own imagination. In such a location, ukeleles, pickling pots, charm bracelets, and entire rooms appear and disappear at will. It therefore seemed appropriate to use relatively flexible set pieces (in our case, four bentwood chairs downstage and one four-foot platform upstage) that could become furniture in several rooms. All properties were mimed in order to underscore their illusory nature. Because of the apparent spontaneity and oral style of Sister's storytelling, no scripts were used.

Costumes. Costumes vivified the distorted images of the characters created by Sister. Sister No. 2 wore dirty, torn clothing, an apron, and no shoes. Mama was padded to look obese and wore a dress to emphasize her fatness. Uncle Rondo wore plain trousers and a loud Hawaiian shirt; and Papa Daddy's costume of overalls and shirt was virtually hidden by his floor-length beard. Shirley T. was dressed in a Shirley Temple costume, complete with curly blond wig. And Stella Rondo was dressed and made up to look like a "hussy," with a tight dress, gaudy jewelry, too much make-up, clock stockings, and ankle-strap shoes. One important costume piece was the flesh-colored kimono, which was a close duplicate of the one described by Sister. Sister No. 1 was dressed simply in a cotton dress and sandals.

Blocking. Although Sister says at the end of the story, referring to the P. O., "It's ideal, as I've been saying," we hardly believe her. This is her first mention of her epic situation. The large, vivid scenes all take place at Mama's house, and the P. O. seems rather pale and small by comparison. Consequently, a small area downstage right was given over to the P. O., and had its own special spotlight. The remainder of the stage space was for the scenes at home. Because we wished to emphasize that the story's realism is psychological rather than social, we did not attempt to divide the stage space into separate rooms in Mama's house. The same area became the kitchen, dining room, hall, or whatever downstairs room was needed. The platform situated upstage center identified the upstairs playing area where Sister has her major confrontations with Stella Rondo. Characters came and went, either by physically entering and exiting or by being blacked out, as they were directed by Sister No. 1.

All the scenes at home were played with onstage focus and explicitly mimed action. Sister No. 2 always speaks her lines either to a character in a scene or to Sister No. 1. Sister No. 1, however, is not actually at home and she is not reporting factually; she is creating the story anew for her audience and herself. Consequently, she appears at times to direct a scene or call it into existence. In her capacity as director of the scene, (e.g.,

"Just then, something perfectly horrible occurred to me") she often addresses her observation to Sister No. 2. At other times her sympathy for Sister No. 2 is demonstrated by sharing with her a comment about the family (e.g., "She went right upstairs and hugged the baby"). Finally, the narrator addresses those lines to the audience that are designed to elicit sympathetic responses (e.g., "Do you remember who it was really said that?"). The shifting focus of Sister No. 1's line delivery is intended to reinforce the tension in her narrative technique.

Selected Bibliography

APPEL, ALFRED. *A Season of Dreams: The Fiction of Eudora Welty.* Baton Rouge: Louisiana State University Press, 1965.

BREEN, ROBERT S. "Chamber Theatre." Unpublished manuscript, Evanston, Illinois, 1964. Mimeographed.

BRYANT, JOSEPH ALLEN. *Eudora Welty.* Minneapolis: University of Minnesota Press, 1968.

ROMBERG, BERTIL. *Studies in the Narrative Technique of the First-Person Novel.* Transl. Michael Taylor and Harold W. Borland. Stockholm: Almquist & Wiksell, 1962.

RUBIN, LOUIS D., JR. *Writers of the Modern South: The Faraway Country.* Seattle: University of Washington Press, 1966.

———— and ROBERT JACOBS. *Southern Renascence.* Baltimore: The Johns Hopkins Press, 1953.

VANDE KIEFT, RUTHE M. *Eudora Welty.* New York: Twayne Publishers, 1962.

WELTY, EUDORA. *One Time, One Place: Mississippi in the Depression, a Snapshot Album.* New York: Random House, Inc., 1971.

————. *Selected Stories.* New York: Modern Library, 1943.

————. *Three Papers on Fiction.* Northampton, Mass: Smith College Press, 1962.

WHY I LIVE AT THE P.O.*

Cast of Characters

SIS 1: Sister 1
SIS 2: Sister 2
MAMA: Mama
STEL: Stella-Rondo
UNCLE: Uncle Rondo
PAPA: Papa-Daddy

SIS 1: *(Sister No. 1 alone in spot, downstage right. Sister No. 1 speaks lines to the audience, unless otherwise noted.)*
I was getting along fine with Mama, Papa-Daddy, and Uncle Rondo until my sister Stella-Rondo just separated from her husband and came back home again. Mr. Whitaker! Of course, I went with Mr. Whitaker first, when he first appeared here in China Grove, taking 'Pose Yourself' photos, and Stella-Rondo broke us up. Told him I was one-sided. Bigger on one side than the other, which is a deliberate, calculated falsehood: I'm the same. Stella-Rondo is exactly twelve months to the day younger than I am and for that reason she's spoiled.

She's always had anything in the world she wanted and then she'd throw it away. Papa-Daddy gave her this gorgeous Add-a-Pearl necklace when she was eight years old and she threw it away playing baseball when she was nine, with only two pearls.

So as soon as she got married and moved away from home the first thing she did was separate! From Mr. Whitaker! This photographer with the

*Reprinted by permission of Russell & Volkening, Inc. as agents for the author. Copyright ©
1941, renewed 1969.

popeyes she said she trusted. Came home from one of those towns in Illinois and to our complete surprise brought this child of two. Mama said she like to made her drop dead for a second.

MAMA: *(Lights up on family, center stage.)* Here you had this marvelous blond child and never so much wrote your mother a word about it,

SIS 1: says Mama.

MAMA: I'm thoroughly ashamed of you.

SIS 1: But of course she wasn't. Stella-Rondo just calmly takes off this *hat.* I wish you could see it. She says,

STEL: Why Mama, Shirley-T's adopted, I can prove it.

MAMA: How?

SIS 1: says Mama, but all I says was

SIS 1 & 2: *(to each other)* H'm!

SIS 1: There I was over the hot stove, trying to stretch two chickens over five people and a completely unexpected child into the bargain, without one moment's notice.

STEL: What do you mean, "H'm"?

SIS 1: says Stella-Rondo, and Mama says,

MAMA: I heard that, Sister.

SIS 2: I said that oh, I didn't mean a thing, only that whoever Shirley-T was, she was the spit-image of Papa-Daddy if he'd cut off his beard, *(to Sister 1)* which of course he'd never do in the world.

SIS 1: Papa-Daddy is Mama's Papa and sulks. Stella-Rondo got furious. She said,

STEL: Sister, I don't need to tell you you got a lot of nerve and always did have and I'll thank you to make no further reference to my adopted child whatsoever.

SIS 2: Very well, I said. Very well, very well. *(to Sister 1)* Of course I noticed at once she looks like Mr. Whitaker's side too.

SIS 1: *(to Sister 2)* That frown.

SIS 2: She looks like a cross between Mr. Whitaker and Papa-Daddy.

STEL: Well, all I can say is she isn't.

MAMA: She looks exactly like Shirley Temple to me,

SIS 1: says Mama, but Shirley-T just ran away from her. So, the first thing Stella-Rondo did at the table was turn Papa-Daddy against me.

STEL: *(Family members arrange chairs for dinner, DL)* Papa-Daddy,

SIS 1: she says.

SIS 2: *(to Sister 1)* He was trying to cut up his meat.

STEL: Papa-Daddy!

SIS 2: *(to Sister 1)* I was taken completely by surprise.

SIS 1: Papa-Daddy is about a million years old and's got this long beard.

STEL: Papa-Daddy, Sister says she fails to understand why you don't cut off your beard.

SIS 2: *(to Sister 1)* So Papa-Daddy l-a-y-s down his knife and fork!

SIS 1: He's real rich. Mama says he is, he says he isn't. So he says,

PAPA: Have I heard correctly? You don't understand why I don't cut off my beard?

SIS 2: Why,

SIS 1: I says,

SIS 2: Papa-Daddy, of course I understand, I did not say any such of a thing, the idea.

SIS 1: He says,

PAPA: Hussy!

SIS 2: I says, Papa-Daddy, you know I wouldn't any more want you to cut off your beard than the man in the moon. It was the farthest thing from my mind. Stella-Rondo sat there and made that up while she was eating breast of chicken.

SIS 1: But he says,

PAPA: So the postmistress fails to understand why I don't cut off my beard. Which job I got you through my influence with the government. Bird's nest—is that what you call it?

SIS 1: Not that it isn't the next to the smallest P. O. in the entire state of Mississippi. I says,

SIS 2: Oh, Papa-Daddy,

SIS 1: I says,

SIS 2: I didn't say any such of a thing, I never dreamed it was a bird's nest. I have always been grateful, though this is the next to the smallest P. O. in the state of Mississippi, and I do not enjoy being referred to as a hussy by my own grandfather.

SIS 1: But Stella-Rondo says,

STEL: Yes, you did say it too. Anybody in the world could of heard you, that had ears.

MAMA: Stop right there,

SIS 1: says Mama, looking at *me*. So I pulled my napkin straight back through the napkin ring and left the table. *(Sister 2 crosses C)* As soon as I was out of the room, Mama says,

MAMA: Call her back, or she'll starve to death.

SIS 1: But Papa-Daddy says,

PAPA: This is the beard I started growing on the Coast when I was fifteen years old and *(Papa-Daddy continues to mumble under Sister's speech until Shirley-T loses the Milky Way)*

SIS 1: He would of gone on till nightfall if Shirley-T hadn't lost the Milky Way she ate in Cairo. So Papa-Daddy says,

PAPA: *(Rising)* I am going out and lie in the hammock, and you can all sit here and remember my words: I'll never cut off my beard, as long as I live, not one inch, and I don't appreciate it in you at all. *(Papa-Daddy crosses R and exits.)*

SIS 2: Passed right by me in the hall and went straight out and got in the hammock. *(Lights down on family. They exit in dark.)*

SIS 1: *(Crosses C to Sister 2)* It would be a holiday. *(Uncle Rondo appears UC and crosses down to Sister 2)* It wasn't five minutes before Uncle Rondo suddenly appeared in the hall, in one of Stella-Rondo's flesh-colored kimonos, all cut on the bias, like something Mr. Whitaker probably thought was gorgeous.

SIS 2: Uncle Rondo, I didn't know who that was! Where are you going?

UNCLE: Sister, get out of my way, I'm poisoned.

SIS 2: If you're poisoned, stay away from Papa-Daddy. Keep out of the hammock. Papa-Daddy will certainly beat you on the head if you come within forty miles of him. He thinks I deliberately said he ought to cut off his beard after he got me the P.O., and I've told him and told him, and he acts like he doesn't hear me. Papa-Daddy must of gone stone deaf.

UNCLE: He picked a fine day to do it, then,

SIS 2: *(to Sister 1)* and before you could say "Jack Robinson" flew out in the yard. *(Uncle Rondo exits DR.)*

SIS 1: What he'd really done, he'd drunk another bottle of that prescription.

SIS 2: *(to Sister 1)* He does it every Fourth of July as sure as shooting.

SIS 1: *(to Sister 2)* And it's horribly expensive.

SIS 2: *(to Sister 1)* Then he falls over in the hammock

SIS 1: *(to Sister 2)* and snores. *(to audience)* So he insisted on zigzagging right out to the hammock, looking like a half-wit.

SIS 2: Papa-Daddy woke up with this horrible yell and right there without moving an inch he tried to turn Uncle Rondo against me.

SIS 1: *(to Sister 2, moving her DR to listen to Papa-Daddy)* I heard every word he said.

SIS 2: Oh he told Uncle Rondo I didn't learn to read till I was eight years old and he didn't see how in the world I ever got the mail put up at the P. O. much less read it all! And he said if Uncle Rondo could only fathom the lengths he had gone to to get me that job! And he said on the other hand he thought Stella-Rondo had a brilliant mind and deserved credit for getting out of town. All the time he was just lying there swinging as pretty as you please and looping out his beard, and poor Uncle Rondo was *pleading* with him to slow down the hammock, it was making him dizzy as a witch to watch it.

SIS 1: *(to Sister 2)* But that's what Papa-Daddy likes about a hammock. *(to audience)* Uncle Rondo was too dizzy to get turned against me for the time being. He's Mama's only brother and is a good case of a one-track mind.

SIS 2: *(to Sister 1)* Ask anybody. A certified pharmacist.

SIS 1: *(to Sister 2)* Just then I heard Stella-Rondo raising the upstairs window. *(to audience)* While she was married she got this peculiar idea that it's cooler with the windows shut and locked. So she has to raise the window before she can make a soul hear her outdoors. *(Lights up on Stella-Rondo on platform UC.)* So she raises the window and says,

STEL: OH!

SIS 1: You would have thought she was mortally wounded. Uncle Rondo and Papa-Daddy didn't even look up, but kept right on with what they were doing. *(to Sister 2)* I had to laugh. *(Sister 2 laughs.)* I flew up the stairs and threw the door open! *(Sister 2 crosses onto platform; Sister 1 follows to left edge of platform.)*

SIS 2: What in the wide world's the matter, Stella-Rondo? You mortally wounded?

STEL: No, I am not mortally wounded but I wish you would do me the favor of looking out that window there and telling me what you see.

SIS 1: *(to Sister 2)* So I shade my eyes and look out the window.

SIS 2: I see the yard, I says.

STEL: Don't you see any human beings?

SIS 2: I see Uncle Rondo trying to chase Papa-Daddy out of the hammock, I says. Nothin more. Naturally, it's so suffocating hot in the house, with all the windows shut and locked, everybody who cares to stay in their right mind will have to go out and get in the hammock before the Fourth of July is over.

STEL: Don't you notice anything different about Uncle Rondo?

SIS 2: Why, no, except he's got on some terrible-looking flesh-colored contraption I wouldn't be found dead in, is all I see, I says.

STEL: Never mind, you won't be found dead in it, because it happens to be part of my trousseau, and Mr. Whitaker took several dozen photographs of me in it. What on earth could Uncle Rondo mean by wearing part of my trousseau out in the broad open daylight without saying so much as "Kiss my foot," knowing I only got home this morning after my separation and hung my negligee up on the bathroom door, just as nervous as I could be?

SIS 2: I'm sure I don't know, and what do you expect me to do about it? I says. Jump out the window?

STEL: No, I expect nothing of the kind. I simply declare that Uncle Rondo looks like a fool in it, that's all. It makes me sick to my stomach.

SIS 2: Well, he looks as good as he can, I says. As good as anybody in reason could.

SIS 1: *(to audience)* I stood up for Uncle Rondo, please remember. *(to Sister 2)* And I said to Stella-Rondo,

SIS 2: I think I would do well not to criticize so freely if I were you and come home with a two-year old child I had never said a word about, and no explanation whatever about my separation.

STEL: I asked you the instant I entered this house not to refer one more time to my adopted child, and you gave me your word of honor you would not,

SIS 1: was all Stella-Rondo would say, and started pulling out every one of her eyebrows with some cheap Kress tweezers. *(Sister 1 crosses to right edge of platform and holds open imaginary door for Sister 2.)* So I merely slammed the door behind me and went down and made some green-tomato pickle. *(Sisters 1 and 2 move to LC as lights come up there and go down on UC platform.)*

SIS 2: *(to Sister 1)* Somebody had to do it.

SIS 1: So Mama trots in. Lifts up the lid and says,

MAMA: H'm! Not very good for your Uncle Rondo in his precarious condition, I must say. Or poor little adopted Shirley-T. Shame on you!

SIS 1: *(to Sister 2)* That made me tired. I says,

SIS 2: Well Stella-Rondo had better thank her lucky stars it was her instead of me came trotting in with that very peculiar-looking child of two. Now if it had been me that trotted in from Illinois and brought a peculiar-looking child of two, I shudder to think of the reception I'd of got, much less controlled the diet of an entire family.

MAMA: *(shaking a spoon at Sister 2)* But you must remember, Sister, that you were never married to Mr. Whitaker in the first place and didn't go up to Illinois to live,

SIS 1: says Mama shaking a spoon in my face.

MAMA: If you had I would of been just as overjoyed to see you and your little adopted girl as I was to see Stella-Rondo, when you wound up with your separation and came on back home.

SIS 2: You would not, I says.

MAMA: Don't contradict me, I would.

SIS 2: But I said she couldn't convince me though she talked till she was blue in the face. Then I said, Besides you know as well as I do that that child is not adopted.

MAMA: She most certainly is adopted,

SIS 1: says Mama, stiff as a poker.

SIS 2: I says, Why, Mama, Stella-Rondo had her just as sure as anything in this world, and just too stuck up to admit it.

MAMA: Why, Sister, here I thought we were going to have a pleasant Fourth of July, and you start right out not believing a word your own baby sister tells you!

SIS 2: Just like Cousin Annie Flo. Went to her grave denying the facts of life,

SIS 1: I remind Mama.

MAMA: I told you if you ever mentioned Annie Flo's name I'd slap your face,

SIS 1: says Mama and slaps my face.

SIS 2: All right, you wait and see, I says. I, says Mama,

MAMA: I prefer to take my children's word for anything when it's humanly possible.

SIS 1: You ought to see Mama, she weighs two hundred pounds and has real tiny feet. Just then something perfectly horrible occurred to me. *(Sister 1 moves closer to Sister 2 and whispers in her ear.)*

SIS 2: Mama, I says, can that child talk?

SIS 1: I simply had to whisper!

SIS 2: Mama, I wonder if that child can be—you know—in any way? Do you realize that she hasn't spoken one single solitary word to a human being up to this minute? This is the way she looks, I says,

SIS 1: and I looked like this. *(Sister 1 makes the face for audience and Sister 2. Sister 2 mimics it for Sister 1's approval, then shows it to Mama.)* Well, Mama and I just stood there and stared at each other. It was horrible!

MAMA: I remember well that Joe Whitaker frequently drank like a fish, I believe to my soul he drank chemicals. *(As Mama moves to left edge of UC platform, lights come up to reveal Stella-Rondo and Shirley-T.)*

SIS 1: And without another word she marches to the foot of the stairs and calls Stella-Rondo.

MAMA: Stella-Rondo? o-o-o-o-o! Stella-Rondo!

STEL: What?

SIS 1: says Stella-Rondo from upstairs.

SIS 2: *(to Sister 1)* Not even the grace to get up off the bed.

MAMA: Can that child of yours talk?

STEL: Can she what?

MAMA: Talk! Talk! Burdyburdyburdyburdy!

SIS 1: So Stella-Rondo yells back,

STEL: Who says she can't talk?

MAMA: Sister says so,

SIS 1: says Mama.

STEL: You didn't have to tell me, I know whose word of honor don't mean a thing in this house.

SIS 1: And in a minute the loudest Yankee voice I ever heard in my life yells out.

STEL: *(Stella-Rondo stands behind Shirley-T, like a puppeteer; Shirley-T mimes the singing.)* OE'm Pop-OE the Sailor-r-r-r Ma-a-an! *(Stella-Rondo tap dances while Shirley-T jumps up and down.)*

SIS 2: and then somebody jumps up and down in the upstairs hall. In another second the house would of fallen down.

STEL: Not only talks, she can tap dance. Which is more than some people I won't name can do.

MAMA: Why the precious darling thing!

SIS 1: Mama says, so surprised.

MAMA: Just as smart as she can be!

SIS 2: *(to Sister 1)* Starts talking baby talk right there.

SIS 1: *(to Sister 2)* Then she turns on me. *(Lights fade on platform.)*

MAMA: Sister, you ought to be thoroughly ashamed! Run upstairs this instant and apologize to Stella-Rondo and Shirley-T.

SIS 2: Apologize for what? I says, I merely wondered if the child was normal, that's all. Now that she's proved she is, why, I have nothing further to say.

SIS 1: *(Mama crosses UR onto darkened platform.)* But Mama just turned on her heel and flew out, furious. She ran right upstairs and hugged the baby. *(to Sister 2)* She believed it was adopted. Stella-Rondo hadn't done a thing but turn her against me from upstairs while I stood there helpless over the hot stove. *(to audience)* So that made Mama, Papa-Daddy, and the baby all on Stella-Rondo's side.

(Sisters 1 and 2 begin cross to P. O. area, DR. Lights fade C stage as P. O. spot comes up.)

Next, Uncle Rondo.

I must say that Uncle Rondo had been marvelous to me at various times in the past and I was completely unprepared to be made to jump out of my skin, the way it turned out. Once Stella-Rondo did something perfectly horrible to him—broke a chain letter from Flanders Field—and he took the radio back he had given her and gave it to me. Stella-Rondo was furious! For six months we all had to call her Stella instead of Stella-Rondo, or she wouldn't answer. I always thought Uncle Rondo had all the brains of the entire family. Another time he sent me to Mammoth Cave, with all expenses paid.

SIS 2: *(to Sister 1)* But this would be the day he was drinking that prescription, the Fourth of July. *(Sisters 1 and 2 move to C stage where lights come up to reveal family seated for supper. Sister 2 sits)* So at supper Stella-Rondo speaks up and says she thinks. . .

STEL: Uncle Rondo ought to try to eat a little something.

SIS 2: So finally Uncle Rondo said he would try a little cold biscuits with ketchup,

UNCLE: But that was all.

SIS 1: So *she* brought it to him. *(Stella-Rondo fetches ketchup for Uncle Rondo.)*

SIS 2: Do you think it wise to disport with ketchup in Stella-Rondo's flesh-colored kimono? I says. *(to Sister 1)* Trying to be considerate!

SIS 1: *(to Sister 2)* If Stella-Rondo couldn't watch out for her trousseau, somebody had to.

UNCLE: Any objections?

SIS 1: asks Uncle Rondo,

SIS 2: *(to Sister 1)* just about to pour out all the ketchup.

STEL: Don't mind what she says, Uncle Rondo. Sister has been devoting this solid afternoon to sneering out my bedroom window at the way you look.

UNCLE: What's that?

SIS 1: Uncle Rondo has got the most terrible temper in the world. Anything is liable to make him tear the house down if it comes at the wrong time. So Stella-Rondo says,

STEL: Sister says, Uncle Rondo certainly does look like a fool in that pink kimono!

SIS 1: Do you remember who it was really said that?

SIS 2: *(to Sister 1)* Uncle Rondo spills out all the ketchup and jumps out of his chair and tears off the kimono and throws it down on the dirty floor and puts his foot on it.

SIS 1: It had to be sent all the way to Jackson to the cleaners and re-pleated.

UNCLE: So that's your opinion of your Uncle Rondo is it? I look like a fool, do I? Well, that's the last straw. A whole day in this house with nothing to do, and then to hear you come out with a remark like that behind my back!

SIS 2: I didn't say any such of a thing, Uncle Rondo, I says, and I'm not saying who did either. Why, I think you look all right. Just try to take care of yourself and not talk and eat at the same time, I says. I think you better go lie down.

UNCLE: Lie down my foot.

SIS 2: *(to Sister 1)* I ought to of known by that he was fixing to do something perfectly horrible.

SIS 1: *(Sister 1 moves DR as lights fade on family scene DC and come up on P. O. area.)* So he didn't do anything that night in the precarious state he was in—just played Casino with Mama and Stella-Rondo and Shirley-T and gave Shirley-T a nickel with a head on both sides. It tickled her nearly to death and she called him "Papa." But at 6:30 A.M. the next morning, he threw a whole five-cent package of some unsold one-inch firecrackers from the store as hard as he could into my bedroom and they everyone went off.

SIS 2: *(Sister 2 joins Sister 1 in P. O. spot)* Not one bad one in the string.

SIS 1: *(to Sister 2)* Anybody else, there'd be one that wouldn't go off. *(to audience)* Well, I'm just terribly susceptible to noise of any kind, the doctor has always told me I was the most sensitive person he had ever seen in his whole life, and I was simply prostrated. I couldn't eat! People tell me they heard it as far away as the cemetery, and old Aunt Jep Patterson, that had been holding her own so good, thought it was Judgment Day and she was going to meet the whole family. It's usually so quiet here. And I'll tell you it didn't take me any longer than a minute to make up my mind what to do. There I was with the whole entire house on Stella-Rondo's side and turned against me.

SIS 2: *(to Sister 1)* If I have anything at all I have pride.

SIS 1: So I just decided I'd go straight down to the P. O.

SIS 2: *(to Sister 1)* There's plenty of room there in the back, I says to myself.

SIS 1: *(to Sister 2)* Well! I made no bones about letting the family catch on to what I was up to. I didn't try to conceal it. *(Lights come up for entire stage, revealing family as described. As action unfolds, Sister 2 follows the directions of Sister 1 who helps her gather her belongings.)* The first thing they knew, I marched in where they were all playing Old Maid and pulled the electric oscillating fan out by the plug, and everything got real hot. Next I snatched the pillow I'd done the needlepoint on right off the davenport from behind Papa-Daddy. *(to audience)* He went,

PAPA: Ugh!

SIS 1: *(to Sister 2)* I beat Stella-Rondo up the stairs *(Sister 2 moves onto platform UC)* and finally found my charm bracelet in her bureau drawer

SIS 2: under a picture of Nelson Eddy.

UNCLE: So that's the way the land lies,

SIS 1: says Uncle Rondo. There he was, piecing on the ham. *(Sister 2 moves UL to Uncle Rondo)*

UNCLE: Well, Sister, I'll be glad to donate my army cot if you got any place to set it up, providing you'll leave right this minute and let me get some peace.

SIS 1: Uncle Rondo was in France.

SIS 2: Thank you kindly for the cot and "peace" is hardly the word I would select if I had to resort to firecrackers at 6:30 A.M. in a young girl's bedroom, I says back to him. And as to where I intend to go, you seem to forget my position as postmistress of China Grove, Mississippi, I says. I've always got the P. O.

SIS 1: Well, that made them all sit up and take notice. *(to Sister 2, moving her DC)* I went out front and started digging up some four-o'clocks to plant around the P. O.

MAMA: *(crosses DC and raises imaginary window)* Ah-ah-ah!

SIS 1: says Mama, raising the window.

MAMA: Those happen to be my four-o'clocks. Everything planted in that yard is mine. I've never known you to make anything grow in your life.

SIS 2: Very well, I says. But I take the fern. Even you, Mama, can't stand there and deny that I'm the one *watered* that fern. And I happen to know where I can send in a box top and get a packet of one thousand mixed seeds, no two the same, free.

MAMA: Oh, where? . . .

SIS 1: Mama wants to know. *(to Sister 2)* But I says,

SIS 2: Too late. You 'tend to your house, and I'll 'tend to mine. You hear things like that all the time if you know how to listen to the radio. Perfectly marvelous offers. Get anything you want free.

SIS 1: *(to Sister 2, as she moves her into house area)* So I hope to tell you I marched in and got that radio, *(to audience)* and they could of all bit a nail in two, especially Stella-Rondo, that it used to belong to, and she knew she couldn't get it back, I'd sue for it like a shot. *(to Sister 2, moving her around the "room" to collect items)* And I very politely took the sewing machine motor I helped pay the most on to give Mama for Christmas back in 1929, and a good big calendar, with the first aid remedies on it. The thermometer and the Hawaiian ukulele certainly were rightfully mine, and I stood on the stepladder and got all my watermelon-rind preserves and every fruit and vegetable I'd put up, every jar. Then I began to pull the tacks out of the bluebird wall vases on the archway to the dining room. *(Sister 2 moves DRC)*

MAMA: *(Mama, fanning, crosses DRC to Sister 2)* Who told you you could have those, Miss Priss?

SIS 1: says Mama, fanning as hard as she could.

SIS 2: I bought 'em and I'll keep track of 'em, I says. I'll tack 'em up one on each side of the post office window, and you can see 'em when you come to ask me for your mail, if you're so dead to see 'em.

MAMA: Not I! I'll never darken the door to that post office again if I live to be a hundred. Ungrateful child! After all the money we spent on you at the Normal.

STEL: *(crosses DC)* Me either. You can just let my mail lie there and *rot*, for all I care. I'll never come and relieve you of a single, solitary piece.

SIS 2: I should worry,

SIS 1: I says.

SIS 2: And who you think's going to sit down and write you all those big fat letters and postcards, by the way? Mr. Whitaker? Just because he was the only man ever dropped down in China Grove and you got him—unfairly—is he going to sit down and write you a lengthy correspondence after you come home giving no rhyme nor reason whatsoever for your separation and no explanation for the presence of that child? I may not have your brilliant mind, but I fail to see it. *(Sister 2 moves UL, followed by Mama.)*

MAMA: Sister, I've told you a thousand times that Stella-Rondo simply got homesick, and this child is far too big to be hers. Now why don't you all just sit down and play Casino? *(Shirley-T crosses to Stella-Rondo and sticks out her tongue at Sister 2.)*

SIS 2: *(to Sister 1)* Then Shirley-T sticks out her tongue at me in this perfectly horrible way.

SIS 1: *(to Sister 2)* She has no more manners than the man in the moon.

SIS 2: *(to Shirley-T)* I told her she was going to cross her eyes like that some day and they'd stick.
It's too late to stop me now, I says. You should have tried that yesterday. I'm going to the P. O. and the only way you can possibly see me is to visit me there.

SIS 1: So Papa-Daddy says,

PAPA: *(rising from "sofa")* You'll never catch me setting foot in that post office, even if I should take a notion into my head to write a letter some place. I won't have you reaching out of that little old window with a pair of shears and cutting off any beard of mine. I'm too smart for you!

STEL: We all are, *(sits C)*

SIS 1: says Stella-Rondo.

SIS 2: *(crosses to Stella-Rondo)* But I said, If you're so smart, where's Mr. Whitaker?

SIS 1: So then Uncle Rondo says,

UNCLE: I'll thank you from now on to stop reading all the orders I get on postcards and telling everybody in China Grove what you think is the matter with them.

SIS 2: *(crosses UR to Uncle Rondo)* But I says, I draw my own conclusions and will continue in the future to draw them. I says, If people want to write their inmost

MAMA: *(crosses DC to sit with Stella-Rondo)* And if you think we'll ever *write* another postcard you're sadly mistaken.

SIS 2: *(crosses C, above Mama and Stella-Rondo)* Cutting off your nose to spite your face then, I says. But if you're all determined to have no more to do with the U.S. mail, think of this: what will Stella-Rondo do now, if she wants to tell Mr. Whitaker to come after her?

STEL: WAH!

SIS 1: I knew she'd cry. She had a conniption fit right there in the kitchen.

SIS 2: It will be interesting to see how long she holds out, I says. And now—I am leaving.

UNCLE: Good-bye.

MAMA: Oh, I declare, to think that a family of mine should quarrel on the Fourth of July, or the day after, over Stella-Rondo leaving old Mr. Whitaker and having the sweetest little adopted girl! It looks like we'd all be glad!

STEL: Wah!

SIS 1: Stella-Rondo has a fresh conniption fit.

SIS 2: *He* left *her*—you mark my words, I says. That's Mr. Whitaker. I know Mr. Whitaker. After all, I knew him first. I said from the beginning he'd up and leave her. I foretold every single thing that's happened.

MAMA: Where did he go?

SIS 2: Probably to the North Pole, if he knows what's good for him. But Stella-Rondo just bawled and wouldn't say another word. *(Stella-Rondo runs to UC platform)* She flew to her room and slammed the door.

MAMA: Now look what you've gone and done, Sister. You go apologize.

SIS 2: I haven't got time, I'm leaving, I says.

UNCLE: Well, what are you waiting around for?

SIS 1: *(to Sister 2 as they cross R together)* So I just picked up the kitchen clock and marched off, without saying "Kiss my foot" or anything and never did tell Stella-Rondo good-bye. *(Sister 1 moves to DR spot as lights go out on remainder of stage. Sister 2 stays in blacked out area)* And that's the last I've laid eyes on any of my family or my family laid eyes on me for five solid days and nights. Stella-Rondo may be telling the most horrible tales in the world about Mr. Whitaker, but I haven't heard them. As I tell everybody—I draw my own conclusions.

SIS 2: But oh, I like it here. It's ideal, as I've been saying. You see, I've got everything cater-cornered, the way I like it. Hear the radio? All the war news. Radio, sewing machine, book ends, ironing board, and that great big piano lamp—peace, that's what I like. Butterbean vines planted all along the front where the strings are.

Of course, there's not much mail. My family are naturally the main people in China Grove, and if they prefer to vanish from the face of the earth, for all the mail they get or the mail they write, why, I'm not going to open my mouth. Some of the folks here in town are taking up for me and some turned against me. I know which is which. There are always people who will quit buying stamps just to get on the right side of Papa-Daddy.

But here I am, and here I'll stay. I want the world to know I'm happy. And if Stella-Rondo should come to me this minute, on bended knees, and *attempt* to explain the incidents of her life with Mr. Whitaker, I'd simply put my fingers in both my ears and refuse to listen.

(Lights fade.)

III

SCRIPTS FOR GROUP PERFORMANCE

Alice in Wonderland

by Lewis Carroll

Adapted and Directed by Jean Haskell Speer
Virginia Polytechnique Institute & State University

PRODUCTION CONCEPT

A group performance of *Alice in Wonderland* was chosen as a production vehicle that could simultaneously entertain children and adults. Bearing in mind the dual nature of our audience and the nature of the literature, two objectives for the production emerged: (1) For adults, the script and staging would emphasize the verbal intricacies of *Alice in Wonderland*—the puns, the parodies, the latent sense in the nonsense, and (2) for the children, we emphasized telling a story that was filled with memorable characters and the visual and physical illusions of a fantasy world.

Selected Bibliography

AYRES, HARRY MORGAN. *Carroll's Alice.* New York: Columbia University Press, 1936.

BLAKE, KATHLEEN. *Play, Games, and Sport: The Literary Works of Lewis Carroll.* Ithaca: Cornell University Press, 1974.

CAMMAERTS, EMILE. *The Poetry of Nonsense.* London: George Routledge, 1925.

CARROLL, LEWIS. *Alice's Adventures in Wonderland.* London: Collier-Macmillan Ltd., 1962.

————. *The Annotated Alice.* Introduction and Notes by Martin Gardner. New York: Bramhall House, 1960.

————. *The Nursery "Alice."* New York: McGraw-Hill, 1966.

DE LA MARE, WALTER. *Lewis Carroll.* London: Faber & Faber, 1932.

PHILLIPS, ROBERT, ed. *Aspects of Alice: Lewis Carroll's Dreamchild as seen through the Critics' Looking-Glasses, 1865–1971.* London: Victor Gollanez, 1972.

RACKIN, DONALD. "The Critical Interpretations of *Alice in Wonderland:* A Survey and Suggested Reading." Unpublished doctoral dissertation, University of Illinois, 1968.

WOOD, JAMES. *The Snark was a Boojum: A Life of Lewis Carroll.* New York, Pantheon, 1966.

(a) The narrator introduces Alice to the Audience.

(b) "I'm late! I'm late! For a very important date!"

Scenes from *Alice In Wonderland.* (Virginia Polytechnic Institute and State University)

(c) Alice tries to keep peace between the Queen of Hearts
and the Duchess.

(d) The Mock Turtle and the
Gryphon entertain Alice with
a song.

(e) Alice is a guest at a Mad
Tea-Party!

ALICE IN WONDERLAND

Cast of Characters

A: Alice   **H:** Hatter
C: Caterpillar   **K:** King
CC: Cheshire Cat   **KN:** Knave
CD2: Card #2   **M:** Mouse
CD5: Card #5   **MH:** March Hare
CD7: Card #7   **N:** Narrator
D: Dormouse   **Q:** Queen
DH: Duchess   **R:** Rabbit
AL: All   **T:** Turtle
G: Gryphon

PROLOGUE

The Narrator, Alice, the Mouse, the Caterpillar, and the Cheshire Cat enter down left in a black-out. The Narrator stands beside his chair, down left, as the light comes up on him.

N: Alice! A childish story take,
    And, with a gentle hand,
    Lay it where Childhood's dreams are twined
    In Memory's mystic band,
    Like pilgrim's wither'd wreath of flowers
    Plucked in a far-off land.[1]

[1]This is the last stanza of Carroll's own prefatory verses to *Alice's Adventures in Wonderland*. For the full poem, see *The Annotated Alice,* ed. Martin Gardner (New York: Bramhall House, 1960), p. 21.

N: Alice was beginning to get very tired of sitting by her sister on the bank and of having nothing to do; once or twice she had peeped into the book her sister was reading, but it had no pictures or conversations in it.

A: What is the use of a book without pictures or conversations?

N: So she was considering getting up and making a daisy chain, when suddenly a white rabbit with pink eyes ran close by her. There was nothing so very remarkable in that; nor did Alice think it so very much out of the way to hear the Rabbit say to itself:

R: Oh, dear! Oh, dear! I shall be too late!

N: But, when the Rabbit actually took a watch out of its pocket, and looked at it, and then hurried on, Alice started to her feet, for it flashed across her mind that she had never before seen a rabbit with either a pocket or a watch to take out of it. Burning with curiosity, she ran after it and was just in time to see it pop down a large rabbit-hole. In another moment down went Alice after it, never once considering how in the world she was to get out again.

Episode I

N: The rabbit hole went straight down like a tunnel. Either it was very deep or Alice fell very slowly, for she had plenty of time as she fell to look about her, and to wonder what was going to happen next.

A: I wonder if I shall fall right through the earth! How funny it'll seem to come out near the center of the earth. Let me see: that would be four thousand miles down, I think—
I wonder if I shall fall right through the earth! How funny it'll seem to come out among the people that walk with their heads downwards!

N: Suddenly, thump! thump! down she came upon a heap of sticks and the fall was over. Alice saw before her the White Rabbit, still hurrying along.

R: Oh my ears and whiskers, how late it's getting!

N: Alice was close behind it, when suddenly the Rabbit was no longer to be seen. Poor Alice! She sat down and began to cry, shedding gallons of tears, until there was a large pool all around her.

A: Stop it this moment, I tell you!

N: As she said these words, her foot slipped, and in another moment, splash! she was up to her chin in salt water.

Episode II

N: Just then Alice heard something splashing about in the pool a little way off. She soon made out that it was only a mouse, that had slipped in like herself.

A: O Mouse, do you know the way out of this pool? I am very tired of swimming about here, O Mouse!

N: Alice thought this must be the right way of speaking to a mouse; she had never done such a thing before, but she remembered seeing in her brother's Latin Grammar—

A: A mouse—of a mouse—to a mouse—a mouse—O mouse! Perhaps it doesn't understand English. I daresay it's a French mouse, come over with William the

Conquerer. *Ou est ma chatte?* Oh, I beg your pardon! I quite forgot you didn't like cats.

M: Not like cats! Would you like cats, if you were me?

A: Well, perhaps not. And yet I wish I could show you our cat, Dinah. She's such a capital one for catching mice—oh, I beg your pardon! We won't talk about her any more if you'd rather not.

M: Don't let me hear the name again!

A: Oh, dear! I'm afraid I've offended it!

N: For the Mouse was swimming away from her as hard as it could go. Then Alice managed to swim to shore.

Episode III

N: There was a large mushroom growing near her, and when she had looked under it, on both sides of it, and behind it, she stretched herself up on tiptoe and peeped over the edge. Her eyes immediately met those of a large blue caterpillar, sitting on top, with its arms folded, quietly smoking a long hookah. The Caterpillar and Alice looked at each other for some time in silence; at last the Caterpillar took the hookah out of its mouth, and addressed her in a languid, sleepy voice.

C: Who are you?

A: I—I hardly know, Sir, just at present—at least I know who I *was* when I got up this morning, but I think I must have changed since then.

C: What do you mean by that? Explain yourself.

A: I can't explain *myself*, I'm afraid, Sir, because I'm not myself you see.

C: I don't see.

A: I'm afraid I can't put it more clearly, for I can't understand it myself—

C: You! Who are you?

A: I think you ought to tell me who you are first.

C: Why?

N: This was another puzzling question; and Alice could not think of any good reason, and the Caterpillar seemed to be in a very unpleasant state of mind, so she turned away.

C: Come back. I've something important to say!

N: This sounded promising, certainly. Alice turned and came back again.

C: Keep your temper.

A: Is that all?

C: No.

N: Alice thought she might as well wait, as she had nothing else to do. For some minutes it puffed away without speaking; but at last, it unfolded its arms, took the hookah out of its mouth again and said—

C: So you think you're changed, do you?

A: I'm afraid I am, Sir. I can't remember things as I used to—

C: Can't remember *what* things?

A: Well, I've tried to say "How doth the little busy bee" but it all came out different!

C: Repeat "You are old Father William."

A: You are old, Father William, the young man said
    and your hair has become very white:
And yet you incessantly stand on your head—
    Do you think at your age, it is right?

In my youth, Father William replied to his son,
    I feared it might injure the brain;
But, now that I'm perfectly sure I have none,
    Why, I do it again and again.[2]

C: That is not said right.

A: Not *quite* right, I'm afraid, some of the words have got altered.

C: It is wrong from beginning to end.

N: This time Alice waited patiently for the Caterpillar to speak again. In a minute or two the Caterpillar took the hookah out of its mouth, yawned once or twice, and shook itself. Then it got down off the mushroom and crawled away into the grass.

Episode IV

N: Alice began talking to herself as usual.

A: How puzzling all these changes are. I'm never sure where I'm going to be, from one minute to another!

N: Alice came suddenly upon an open place, where she was a little startled by seeing a Cheshire Cat sitting on a bough of a tree a few yards off. The cat only grinned when it saw Alice. It looked good-natured, she thought: still it had *very* long claws, and a great many teeth, so she felt it ought to be treated with respect.

A: Cheshire-Puss. (Come, it's pleased so far.) Could you tell me please, which way I ought to go from here?

CC: That depends a good deal on where you want to get to.

A: I don't much care where.

CC: Then it doesn't matter which way you go.

A: So long as I get somewhere.

CC: Oh, you're sure to do that, if you only walk long enough.

A: What sort of people live about here?

CC: In that direction lives a Hatter; and in that direction lives a March Hare. Visit either you like; they're both mad.

A: But I don't want to go among mad people.

CC: Oh, you can't help that, we're all mad here. I'm mad, you're mad.

A: And how do you know you're mad?

CC: To begin with, a dog's not mad. You grant that?

A: I suppose so.

CC: Well, then, you see a dog growls when it's angry, and wags its tail when its

[2]This poem is a parody of Robert Southey's didactic poem, *The Old Man's Comforts and How He Gained Them*. For the complete poem, and Carroll's entire parody, see *The Annotated Alice*, p. 69.

pleased. Now I growl when I'm pleased and wag my tail when I'm angry. Therefore, I'm mad.

A: I call it purring, not growling.

CC: Call it what you like. Do you play croquet with the Queen today?

A: I should like it very much, but I haven't been invited yet.

CC: You'll see me there.

N: And the Cat vanished quite slowly, beginning with the end of the tail, and ending with the grin, which remained some time after the rest of it had gone.

A: Well! I've often seen a cat without a grin, but a grin without a cat! It's the most curious thing I ever saw in all my life!

N: Alice waited a little, half expecting to see it again, but it did not appear, and after a minute or two she walked on in the direction in which the March Hare was said to live.

Episode V

A: I've seen hatters before; the March Hare will be much the most interesting, and perhaps, as this is May, it won't be raving mad—at least not so mad as it was in March.

N: She had not gone much farther before she came in sight of the house of the March Hare.

A: Suppose it should be raving mad after all! I almost wish I'd gone to see the Hatter instead!

N: There was a table set out under a tree in front of the house, and the March Hare and the Hatter were having tea at it. A Dormouse was sitting between them, and the other two were using it as a cushion. The table was a large one, but the three were all crowded together at one corner of it.

AL: No room! No room!

A: There's *plenty* of room!

MH: Have some wine.

A: I don't see any wine.

MH: There isn't any.

A: It wasn't very civil of you to offer it.

MH: It wasn't very civil of you to sit down without being invited.

H: Your hair wants cutting.

A: You should learn not to make personal remarks. It's very rude.

H: Why is a raven like a writing desk?

A: Come, we shall have some fun now! I'm glad they've begun asking riddles—I believe I can guess that.

MH: Do you mean that you think you can find the answer to it?

A: Exactly so.

MH: Then you should say what you mean.

A: I do, at least—at least I mean what I say—that's the same thing, you know.

H: Not the same thing a bit! Why you might just as well say that "I see what I eat" is the same thing as "I eat what I see."

253

MH: You might just as well say that "I like what I get" is the same thing as "I get what I like"!

D: *(waking momentarily)* You might just as well say that "I breathe when I sleep" is the same thing as "I sleep when I breathe"! *(Dormouse falls asleep.)*

H: It is the same thing with you. Have you guessed the riddle yet?

A: No, I give it up. What's the answer?

H: I haven't the slightest idea.

MH: Nor I.

A: I think you might do something better with the time than wasting it in asking riddles that have no answers.

H: If you knew Time as well as I do, you wouldn't talk about wasting *it*. It's *him*.

A: I don't know what you mean.

H: Of course you don't! I dare say you never even spoke to Time.

A: Perhaps not, but I know I have to beat time when I learn music.

H: Ah! That accounts for it. He won't stand beating. Now, if you only kept on good terms with him, he'd do almost anything you liked with the clock.

MH: Suppose we change the subject, I'm getting tired of this. I vote the young lady tell us a story.

A: I'm afraid I don't know one.

H &
MH: Then the Dormouse shall! Wake up, Dormouse!

D: I wasn't asleep, I heard every word you fellows were saying.

MH: Tell us a story!

A: Yes, please do!

H: And be quick about it or you'll be asleep again before it's done.

D: Once upon a time there were three little sisters, and their names were Elsie, Lacie, and Tillie, and they lived at the bottom of a well—

A: What did they live on?

D: They lived on molasses.

A: But why did they live at the bottom of the well?

D: It was a molasses-well.

A: There's no such thing!

H &
MH: Sh! Sh!

D: If you can't be civil, you'd better finish the story for yourself.

A: No, please go on! I won't interrupt you again. I dare say there may be *one*.

D: One, indeed! And so these three little sisters—they were learning to draw, you know—

A: What did they draw?

D: Molasses.

A: But I don't understand. Where did they draw the molasses from?

H: You can draw water out of a water-well, so I should think you could draw molasses out of a molasses-well, eh, stupid?

D: They were learning to draw and they drew all manner of things—everything that begins with an M—

254

A: Why with an M?

MH: Why not?

D: —that begins with an M, such as mouse-traps, and the moon, and memory, and muchness—you know you say things are "much of a muchness"—did you ever see such a thing as a drawing of a muchness?

A: Really, now you ask me, I don't think—

H: Then you shouldn't talk.

N: This piece of rudeness was more than Alice could bear; she got up in great disgust, and walked off; the Dormouse fell asleep instantly, and neither of the others took the least notice of her going, though she looked back once or twice, half hoping that they would call after her; the last time she saw them, they were trying to put the Dormouse into the teapot.

A: At any rate I'll never go there again! It's the stupidest teaparty I ever was at in all my life!

N: Just as she said this, she found herself in a beautiful garden, among bright flower-beds and cool fountains.

Episode VI

N: A large rose-tree stood growing near the entrance of the garden; the roses growing on it were white, but there were three gardeners at it, busily painting them red. Alice thought this a very curious thing, and she went nearer to watch them.

CD2: Look out now, Five! Don't go splashing paint over me like that!

CD5: I couldn't help it. Seven jogged my elbow.

CD7: That's right, Five! Always lay the blame on others!

CD5: *You'd* better not talk! I heard the Queen say only yesterday you deserved to be beheaded—just like the Duchess.

CD2: What for?

CD7: That's none of *your* business!

CD5: Yes, it *is* his business! And I'll tell him—it was for bringing the cook tulip-roots instead of onions.

CD7: Well, of all the unjust things—

N: His eye chanced to fall upon Alice, as she stood watching them. The others looked around also, and all of them bowed low.

A: Would you please tell me why you are painting those roses?

CD2: Why, the fact is, you see, Miss, this here ought to have been a *red* rose-tree, and we put in a white one by mistake; and if the Queen was to find it out, we should all have our heads cut off, you know. So you see, Miss, we're doing our best, before she comes, to—

CD5: The Queen! The Queen!

N: The three gardners instantly threw themselves flat upon their faces. There was a sound of footsteps and Alice looked round, eager to see the Queen. First came the White Rabbit; then came the Queen of Hearts.

Q: Who is this? What's your name, child?

A: My name is Alice, so please your Majesty. *(aside)* Why, they're only a pack of cards, after all. I needn't be afraid of them!

Q: Can you play croquet?

A: Yes.

Q: Come on then!

N: Alice followed the Queen, wondering very much what would happen next.

R: It's—it's a very fine day!

A: Very. Who's the Duchess? The painters said she was to be beheaded!

R: Hush! Hush!

N: He looked anxiously over his shoulder as he spoke, and then raised himself up on tiptoe, put his mouth·close to her ear, and whispered—

R: She's under sentence of execution.

A: What for?

R: Did you say "What a pity"?

A: No, I didn't. I don't think it's at all a pity. I said, "What for?"

R: She boxed the Queen's ears—*(Alice screams with laughter.)* Oh, hush! The Queen will hear you! You see, the Duchess came rather late, and the Queen said—

Q: Off with her head!

A: It belongs to the Duchess; you'd better ask *her* about it.

Q: She's in prison; fetch the Duchess!

DH: You can't think how glad I am to see you, you dear *old* thing! You're thinking about something, my dear, and that makes you forget to talk. I can't tell you just now what the moral of that is, but I shall remember it in a bit.

A: Perhaps it hasn't one.

DH: Tut, tut, child! Everything's got a moral, if only you can find it. And the moral of that is—Oh, tis love, tis love, that makes the world go round!

A: Somebody said that it's done by everybody minding their own business!

DH: Ah well! It means much the same thing, and the moral of *that* is—take care of the sense, and the sounds will take care of themselves.

A: *(aside)* How fond she is of finding morals in things!

DH: I dare say you're wondering why I don't put my arm round your waist; the moral of that is—Birds of a feather flock together. And the moral of that is—Be what you would seem to be—or, if you'd like it put more simply—Never imagine yourself not to be otherwise than what it might appear to others that what you were or might have been was not otherwise than what you had been would have appeared to them to be otherwise.

A: I think I should understand that better, if I had it written down; but I can't quite follow it as you say it.

DH: That's nothing to what I could say if I chose.

A: Pray don't trouble yourself to say it any longer than that.

DH: Oh, don't talk about trouble! I make you a present of everything I've said as yet.

N: The Duchess began to tremble. Alice looked up, and there stood the Queen in front of them, with her arms folded, frowning like a thunderstorm.

DH: A fine day, your Majesty!

Q: Now, I give you fair warning; either you or your head must be off, and that in about half no time! Take your choice!

N: The Duchess took her choice, and was gone in a moment!

Q: Have you seen the Gryphon and the Mock Turtle yet?

A: No, I don't even know what a Mock Turtle is.

Q: It's the thing Mock Turtle soup is made from.

A: I never saw one, or heard one.

Q: Go, then, and he shall tell you his history. I must go back and see after some executions I have ordered.

Episode VII

N: Alice had not gone far before she saw the Gryphon and the Mock Turtle in the distance. As she came nearer, Alice could hear the Mock Turtle sighing as if his heart would break. She pitied him deeply.

A: What is his sorrow?

G: It's all his fancy that; he hasn't got no sorrow, you know.

N: The Mock Turtle looked at them with large eyes full of tears, but said nothing.

G: This here young lady, she wants for to know your history, she do.

T: I'll tell it to her. Sit down, both of you, and don't speak a word till I've finished.

A: I don't know how he can *ever* finish, if he doesn't begin.

T: Once, I was a real turtle. When we were little, we went to school in the sea. The master was an old Turtle—we used to call him Tortoise—

A: Why did you call him Tortoise, if he wasn't one?

T: We called him Tortoise because he taught us. Really you are very dull!

G: You ought to be ashamed of yourself for asking such a simple question. Drive on, old fellow!

T: Yes, we went to school in the sea, though you mayn't believe it—

A: I never said I didn't.

T: You did.

G: *(to Alice)* hold your tongue!

T: We had the best of educations. I only took the regular courses.

A: What was that?

T: Reeling and Writhing, of course, to begin with, and then the different branches of Arithmetic—Ambition, Distraction, Uglification, and Derision.

A: I never heard of "uglification." What is it?

G: Never heard of uglifying! You know what to beautify is, I suppose?

A: Yes, it means—to—make—anything—prettier.

G: Well, then, if you don't know what to uglify is, you *are* a simpleton.

A: What else had you to learn?

T: Well, there was Mystery—Mystery, ancient and modern, with Seaography; then Drawling—the Drawling-master was an old conger-eel, that used to come once a week; he taught us Drawling, Stretching and Fainting in Coils.

A: What was *that* like?

T: Well, I can't show you myself. I'm too stiff. And the Gryphon never learnt it.

G: Hadn't time. I went to the Classical master, though. He was an old crab, *he* was.

T: I never went to him. He taught Laughing and Grief, they used to say.

G: So he did, so he did.

G: That's enough about lessons. Would you like the Mock Turtle to sing you a song?

A: Oh, a song, please, if the Mock Turtle would be so kind.

G: Sing her "Turtle Soup," will you old fellow?

T: *(sighing deeply, sobbing)*
Beautiful Soup, so rich and green,
Waiting in a hot tureen!
Who for such dainties would not stoop?
Soup of the evening, beautiful Soup!

Soup of the evening, beautiful Soup!
   Beau—ootiful Soo—oop!
   Beau—ootiful Soo—oop!
Soo—oop of the e—e—evening,
Beautiful, beautiful Soup!

Beautiful Soup! Who cares for fish,
   Game, or any other dish?
Who would not give all else for two
pennyworth only of Beautiful Soup?
Pennyworth only of Beautiful Soup?
   Beau—ootiful Soo—oop!
   Beau—ootiful Soo—oop!
Soo—oop of the e—e—vening.
Beautiful, beauti—FUL, SOUP![3]

G: Chorus again!

N: The Mock Turtle had just begun to repeat the chorus when a cry of "The trial's beginning!" was heard in the distance.

G: Come on!

N: The Gryphon hurried off, without waiting for the end of the song.

Episode VIII

N: The King and Queen of Hearts were seated on their throne when Alice arrived, with a great crowd assembled about them; the Knave was standing before them in chains, and near the King was the White Rabbit, with a trumpet in one hand and a scroll in the other. In the middle of the court was a table, with a large dish of tarts upon it. Alice had never been in a court of justice before, but she had read about them in books, and she was quite pleased to find that she knew the name of nearly everything there.

A: That's the judge, because of his great wig.

[3]The song is a parody of a nineteenth-century popular song, "Star of the Evening," with words and music by James M. Sayles. For original song, see *The Annotated Alice*, p. 141. In our production, we used the tune to "Beautiful Dreamer," which called for some "murdering of the time"; however, we felt the tune would be much more recognizable and therefore funnier for a modern audience.

N: The judge, by the way, was the King; and, as he wore his crown over the wig, he did not look at all comfortable, and it was certainly not becoming.

A: And that's the jury-box, and those creatures (*Duchess, Gryphon, and Card enter*) I suppose they are the Jurors.

N: The jurors were all writing very busily on slates.

A: What are they doing? They can't have anything to put down yet, before the trial begins.

R: They're putting down their names, for fear they should forget them before the end of the trial.

A: Stupid things!

N: Alice could see that all the jurors were writing down "stupid things!" on their slates, and she could make out that one of them didn't know how to spell "stupid" and he had to ask his neighbor to tell him.

A: A nice muddle their slates'll be in, before the trial's over!

R: Silence in the court!

K: *(to Rabbit)* Herald, read the accusation!

R: The Queen of Hearts, she made some tarts,
    All on a summer's day:
The Knave of Hearts, he stole those tarts,
    And took them quite away!

K: Consider your verdict.

R: Not yet, not yet! There's a great deal to come before that!

K: Call the first witness.

R: First witness!

N: The first witness was the Hatter. He came in with a teacup in one hand and a piece of bread and butter in the other.

H: I beg pardon, your Majesty, for bringing these in; but I hadn't quite finished my tea when I was sent for.

K: You ought to have finished. When did you begin?

N: The Hatter looked at the March Hare, who had followed him into court, arm-in-arm with the Dormouse.

H: Fourteenth of March, I *think* it was.

MH: Fifteenth.

D: Sixteenth.

K: *(to Jury)* Write that down.

N: The jury eagerly wrote down all three dates on their slates, and then added them up, and reduced the answer to nickels and dimes.

K: Take off your hat.

H: It isn't mine.

K: *(to Jury) Stolen!*

N: The jury instantly made a memorandum of the fact.

K: Give your evidence.

H: I keep them to sell, I've none of my own. I'm a hatter.

N: Here the Queen put on her spectacles and began to stare hard at the Hatter, who turned pale and fidgeted.

K: Give your evidence, and don't be nervous, or I'll have you executed on the spot. Give your evidence, or I'll have you executed, whether you are nervous or not.

H: I'm a poor man, your Majesty, and I hadn't begun my tea—not above a week or so—and what with the bread-and-butter getting so thin—and the twinkling of the tea—

K: The twinkling of what?

H: It *began* with the tea.

K: Of course twinkling begins with a T! Do you take me for a dunce? Go on!

H: I'm a poor man, and most things twinkled after that—only the March Hare said—

MH: I didn't!

H: You did!

MH: I deny it!

K: *(to Jury)* He denies it, leave that part out.

H: Well, at any rate, the Dormouse said. . . . After that, I cut some bread-and-butter—

R: But what did the Dormouse say?

H: That I can't remember.

K: You *must* remember, or I'll have you executed.

H: I'm a poor man, your Majesty.

K: You're a *very* poor *speaker*. If that's all you know about it, you may stand down.

H: I can't go no lower. I'm on the floor as it is.

K: Then you may *sit* down. *(to Jury)* Consider your verdict.

R: There's more evidence to come yet, please your Majesty; this paper has just been picked up. It seems to be a letter, written by the prisoner to—to somebody.

Q: Who is it directed to?

R: It isn't directed at all; in fact, there's nothing written on the *outside*. It isn't a letter after all, it's a set of verses.

K: Are they in the prisoner's handwriting?

R: No, they're not, and that's the queerest thing about it.

K: He must have imitated somebody else's hand.

KN: Please, your Majesty, I didn't write it, and they can't prove that I did; there's no name signed at the end.

K: If you didn't sign it, that only makes it worse. You must have meant some mischief, or else you'd have signed your name like an honest man.

Q: That *proves* his guilt, of course, so off with—

A: It doesn't prove anything of the sort! Why, you don't even know what they're about!

K: Read them.

R: Where shall I begin, please your Majesty?

K: Begin at the beginning and go on till you come to the end; then stop.

R: They told me you had been to her,
    And mentioned me to him;
  She gave me a good character,
    But said I could not swim.

> He sent them word I had not gone
>   (We know it to be true);
> If she would push the matter on,
>   What would become of you?
>
> I gave her one, they gave him two,
>   You gave us three or more;
> They all returned from him to you
>   Though they were mine before.
>
> My notion was that you had been
>   (Before she had this fit)
> An obstacle that came between
>   Him, ourselves, and it.

K: That's the most important piece of evidence we've heard yet, so now let the jury—

A: If any one of them can explain it *(gestures to jury)*, I'll give him sixpense. *I* don't believe there's an atom of meaning in it.

K: If there's no meaning in it, that saves a world of trouble, you know, as we needn't try to find any. And yet, I don't know, I seem to see some meaning in them after all.—"said I could not swim"—you can't swim, can you?

KN: Do I look like it?

N: Which he certainly did *not*, being made entirely of cardboard.

K: All right, so far. "We know it to be true"—that's the jury of course—"If she should push the matter on"—that must be the Queen—"What would become of you?"—What, indeed!—"I gave her one, they gave him two"—why, that must be what he did with the tarts, you know—

A: But it goes on "they all returned from him to you."

K: Why, there they are! Nothing can be clearer than *that*. Then again—"before she had this fit"—you never had *fits*, my dear, I think?

Q: Never!

K: Then the words don't *fit* you. It's a pun! Let the jury consider their verdict.

Q: No, no! Sentence first—verdict afterwards.

A: Stuff and nonsense! The idea of having the sentence first!

Q: Hold your tongue!

A: I won't!

Q: Off with her head!

A: Who cares for you? You're nothing but a pack of cards!

N: At this the whole pack of cards rose up into the air, and came flying down upon her; she gave a little scream, half of fright and half of anger, and tried to beat them off.

Epilogue

N: And she found herself lying on the bank, with her head in the lap of her sister, who was gently brushing away some dead leaves that had fluttered down from the trees upon her face.

Educating the Young King Arthur
Episodes from "The Sword In the Stone"*

by T. H. White

Adapted and Directed by Margaret Davidson
University of Northern Iowa

PRODUCTION CONCEPT

Two interrelated concerns were central to the production concept: (1) the antiwar theme that so dominated White's revised conception of the book and, (2) the biographically influenced representation of author T. H. White as the narrator of the production. The first concern greatly affected my cutting of the script, and the second gave a strong, dominating narrative presence to the performance.

*Script reprinted from T. H. White, *The Once and Future King*, by permission of David Higham Associates, Ltd., London.

Selected Bibliography

GARNETT, DAVID, ed. *The White Garnett Letters.* New York: The Viking Press, 1968. 1968.

WARNER, SYLVIA TOWNSEND. *T. H. White: A Biography.* New York: The Viking Press, 1967.

WHITE, T. H. *The Sword in the Stone.* New York: G. P. Putnam's Sons, 1939.

———. *The Once and Future King.* London: Collins, 1958.

(a) When he first meets Merlyn, the Wart (or the young Arthur) struggles to make a "W" by looking only in a mirror.

(b) As T. H. White, the narrator, looks on, Archimedes, Merlyn's owl, startles the Wart.

(c) Badger relates the story of Man to the Wart as T. H. White listens.

Scenes from *Educating the Young King Arthur*. (Northwestern University)

"EDUCATING THE YOUNG KING ARTHUR" *FROM* THE SWORD IN THE STONE

Cast of Characters

N: Narrator (T. H. White) **A:** Archimedes
W: Wart **B:** Badger
M: Merlyn

Exposition

Music for 3 minutes, house lights down. The cast enters down left and take their positions: Wart on stool center stage, Merlyn and Archimedes, platform 1 upstage right, Badger platform 2 upstage left, the Narrator standing center stage by Wart. [The stage is divided into 3 general areas; extreme upstage with platforms for performers not in scene; center stage for the nonmagical sequences (R); and downstage for the magical sequences (F).] General lights up on R.

N: *(as if rereading a manuscript from his book)* More than anything else the Wart . . .

W: *(taking over for N)* wanted to be a knight and go on a quest.

N: *(to the audience)* The Wart was called the Wart because it more or less rhymed with Art, which was short for his real name, Arthur. He lived with his uncle, Sir Ector. Sir Ector's castle stood in an enormous clearing in a still more enormous forest. It had a courtyard and a moat. The castle was surrounded by the Forest Sauvage. *(Wart rises and moves downstage right still in R.)* It was there that the Wart found himself one day, after chasing a lost hawk, Cully, into the woods. The Wart would not have been frightened of an English forest nowadays, but the great jungle of Old England was a different matter.

W: *(to N)* It was not only that there were wild boars in it, nor that one of the surviving wolves might be slinking behind a tree.

N: There were magicians in the forest in those legendary days, as well as strange animals not known to modern works of natural history. The forest was trackless and nobody in the castle knew what was on the other side. *(N moves between stool and Wart.)*

Episode I

W: *(W crosses to left, Merlyn moves to R, blocked from W's sight by N)* The Wart walked further and further into the forest in search of Cully.

N: Suddenly there was a clearing in the forest, *(N moves from between Merlyn and Wart)* and in this clearing

W: there was a snug cottage built of stone. There was a well in front of the cottage.

N: A very old man was drawing water from the well.

M: "Drat the whole thing!"

N: *(moves to join Merlyn)* said the old gentleman.

M: *(to N)* "You would think that after all these years of study you could do better for yourself than a by-our-lady well with a by-our-lady bucket, whatever the by-our-lady cost. By this and by that, why can't they get us the electric light and company's water?"

W: *(crossing to Merlyn)* "Excuse me, sir, but can you tell me the way to Sir Ector's castle, if you don't mind?"

M: "Your name would be the Wart."

W: "Yes, sir, please, sir."

M: "My name is Merlyn."

W: "How do you do?"

M: "How do. Do you like peaches?"

W: "Very much indeed."

M: "They're scarcely in season,"

N: said the old man reprovingly and *(Merlyn moves toward stools)* walked off in the direction of the cottage. The Wart followed after,

W: *(following Merlyn)* since it seemed the simplest thing to do, and offered to carry the bucket

N: which seemed to please Merlyn, who gave it to him,

W: and waited while he counted the keys—while he muttered and mislaid them and dropped them in the grass.

N: Finally, when they had got their way into the black and white home with as much trouble as if they were burgling it, he found himself in the main room.

W: It was the most marvellous room that he had ever been in

N: *(locus of most objects in the room is offstage)* There was a real corkindrill hanging from the rafters, very lifelike and horrible with glass eyes and scaly tail stretched out behind it. When its master came into the room it winked one eye in salutation, although it was stuffed. There were thousands of brown books in leather bindings, some chained to the bookshelves and others propped against each other as if they had had too much to drink and did not really trust themselves. These gave out a smell of must and solid brownness which was most secure.

M: There were stuffed birds, popinjays, maggot-pies, and kingfishers and peacocks with all their feathers but two,

N: *(cutting in)* a guncase with all sorts of weapons which would not be invented for half a thousand years, a rod box ditto, a chest of drawers full of salmon flies

M: *(cutting in)* which had been tied by Merlyn himself,

N: a bunch of turkey feathers and goose-quills for making pens and an astrolabe, twelve pairs of boots, twelve corkscrews, some ants' nests between two glass plates, darning-needles, a gold medal,

M: *(cutting in)* for being the best scholar at Winchester,

N: two skulls, the fourteenth edition of the *Encyclopaedia Britannica*

M: *(cutting in)* (marred as it was by the sensationalism of the popular plates)

N: three globes of the known geographical world, a few fossils, some glass retorts with cauldrons, bunsen burners, etc.,

M: *(Archimedes moves to R beside Wart)* and a complete set of cigarette cards depicting wild fowl by Peter Scott.

N: At that moment an owl appeared from a corner of the room.

W: "Oh, what a lovely owl."

N: But when he went up to it, the owl grew half as tall again, stood stiff as a poker, closed its eyes and said in a doubtful voice,

A: "There is no owl."

M: "It is only a boy."

A: "There is no boy,"

N: said the owl hopefully. The Wart was so startled by finding that the owl could talk that he forgot his manners and came closer. The bird became so nervous that it flew off *(crosses right in R)* to a perch on the other side of the room.

M: "We see so little company," explained Merlyn, "that Archimedes is a little shy of strangers. Come Archimedes, I want you to meet a friend of mine called Wart. Say how d'you do properly."

A: "I will not."

W: "Oh, he is lovely! I wish he would talk to me!"

M: "Let him alone. Perhaps he does not want to be friends with you until he knows what you are like. With owls, it is never easy-come and easy-go."

W: The Wart was so impressed by the kindness of the old man and particularly by the lovely things which he possessed, that he hardly liked to ask him personal questions.

N: At last his curiosity got the better of him,

W: and he asked something which had been puzzling him for some time. "Would you mind if I asked you a question?"

M: "It is what I am for."

W: "How did you know my name?"

N: The old man leaned back in his chair and lighted an enormous meerschaum pipe

W: *(to N)* good gracious, he breathes fire, thought Wart

N: who had never heard of tobacco.

M: "Have you ever tried to draw in a looking glass?"

W: "I don't think I have."

M: "Looking-glass." *(snaps fingers)*

N: Immediately there was a tiny lady's vanity-glass in his hand.

M: "Not that kind you fool. I want one big enough to shave in."

N: The vanity-glass vanished, and in its place there was a shaving mirror about six inches square. He then demanded

M: pencil and paper, *(snapping fingers)*

N: got an unsharpened pencil and the *Morning Post:*

M: sent it back, and flew into a passion in which he said by-our-lady several times and ended up with

N: a carbon pencil and some cigarette papers

M: *(to N)* which he said would have to do.

N: He put one of the papers in front of the glass and made five dots.

M: "Now I want you to join those five dots to make a W, looking only in the glass."

W: The Wart took the pencil and tried to do as he was bid.

M: "Well, it's not bad and in a way it does look a bit like an M."

W: "About my name?"

M: "Ah, yes. That was why I showed you the looking-glass. Now ordinary people are born forwards in Time, if you understand what I mean, and nearly everything in the world goes forward too. This makes it quite easy for the ordinary people to live, just as it would be easy to join those five dots into a W if you were allowed to look at them forwards, instead of backwards and inside out. But I unfortunately was born at the wrong end of time, and I have to live backwards from in front, while surrounded by a lot of people living forwards from behind. Some people call it having second sight. Have I told you this before?"

W: "No, we only met about ten minutes ago."

M: "So little time to pass? Am I going to tell it to you again?"

W: "I don't know unless you have not finished telling me yet."

M: "You see, one gets confused with Time, when it is like that. If I know what is going to happen to people, and not what has happened to them, it makes it difficult to prevent it happening, if you don't want it to have happened, if you see what I mean? Like drawing in the mirror."

N: The Wart did not quite see, *(Archimedes crosses in back to beside Wart)* but was just going to say that he was sorry for Merlyn if these things made him unhappy when

M: "Don't jump!"

N: Archimedes had eased himself over to the Wart's ear.

A: "How d'you do?"

W: "Oh, owl!"

N: cried the Wart, forgetting about Merlyn's troubles instantly.

W: "Look, he has decided to talk to me! I shall call him Archie!"

M: "I trust you will do nothing of the sort," exclaimed Merlyn.

A: and the owl moved away.

W: "Is it wrong?"

A: "You might as well call me Wol, or Olly and have done with it. Or Bubbles."

M: "You are young and do not understand these things. But you will learn that owls are the most courteous, single-hearted, and faithful creatures living. You must never be familiar, rude, or vulgar with them, or make them look ridiculous. Their mother is Athene, the goddess of wisdom, and although they are often buffoons to amuse you, such conduct is the prerogative of the truly wise. No owl can possibly be called Archie."

W: "I'm sorry, owl."

A: "And I'm sorry, boy. I can see that you spoke in ignorance and I bitterly regret that I should have been so petty as to take offense when none was intended."

M: "Well, now that we have that settled, I think it is high time that we should all three find our way back to Sir Ector."

W: "Are you really coming all the way home with me?" asked Wart who could hardly believe the good news.

M: "Why not? How else can I be your tutor?"

W: "My! I must have been on a quest!"

(Freeze for count of 3. Wart moves away from Merlyn and turns his back. N moves toward audience.)

Episode II

N: And that's how Merlyn became the Wart's tutor.

M: *(joins N)* But he was not just an ordinary tutor.

N: Instead of giving the Wart lessons in arithmetic and astrology, he used his magical powers to turn the Wart into different animals so he could learn from them. *(Merlyn to one of the stools)* One cold, wet evening the Wart *(Wart turns to audience and then moves to Merlyn and paces in front of him)* couldn't think of anything to do. Finally he dragged off to the tower room, where Merlyn was busy knitting himself a woolen nightcap for the winter.

W: "Oh, Merlyn, please give me something to do, because I feel so miserable. Nobody wants me for anything today, and I just don't know how to be sensible."

M: "You could learn to knit."

W: "Could I go out and be something, a fish or anything like that?"

M: "You've been a fish. Nobody with any go needs to do their education twice."

W: "What do you suggest for me just now?"

M: "Let me see. We have had short six years of this and in that time I think I am right in saying that you have been many kinds of animal, vegetable, mineral, etc.—many things in earth, air, fire, and water?"

W: "I don't think I know much about the animals and earth."

M: "Then I think you had better meet my friend the badger."

W: "I have never met a badger."

M: "Good. Except for Archimedes, he is the most learned creature, I know. You will like him. By the way there is one thing I ought to tell you. This is the last time I shall be able to turn you into anything. All the magic for that sort of thing has been used up, and this will be the end of your education. When your cousin Kay has been knighted, my labours will be over. You will have to go away then, to be his squire in the wide world, and I shall go elsewhere. Do you think you have learned anything?"

W: "I have learned and been happy."

M: "That's right then. Try to remember what you learned."

N: He proceeded with the spell, pointed his wand of *lignum vitae* at the Little Bear and called out cheerfully.

M: "Have a good time for the last visit, and give my love to Badger." *(MS1)*

B: "So Merlyn sent you to me to finish your education, well. I can only teach you two things—to dig, and to love your home. These are the true ends of philosophy.

W: "What enormous arms you have. So have I for that matter."

N: And he looked down at his own bandy-legged muscles. He was mainly a tight chest holding together a pair of forearms, mighty as thighs.

B: "It is to dig with. Mole and I, I suppose you would have to dig pretty quick to match us. Well, now what could have possessed Merlyn to send you to me?"

W: "He was talking about learning."

B: "Ah, well, if it is learning you are after, you have come to the right shop. But, don't you find it rather dull?"

W: "Sometimes I do, and sometimes I don't. On the whole, I can bear a good deal of learning if it is about natural history."

B: "I am writing a treatise just now which is to point out why Man has become the master of animals. Perhaps you would like to hear it? It's for my doctor's degree, you know,"

N: he added hastily, before the Wart could protest. He got few chances of reading his treatise to anybody, so he could not bear to let the opportunity slip by.

W: "Thank you very much."

B: "It will be good for you, dear boy. It is just the thing to top off an education. Study birds and fish and animals: then finish off with Man. How fortunate that you came! Now where the devil did I put that manuscript? *(Wart and Badger move to edge of stage and sit)* Hem."

N: He immediately became paralyzed with shyness, and sat blushing at his papers, unable to begin.

W: "Go on."

B: "It is not very good. It is just a rough draft, you know. I shall alter it a lot before I send it in."

W: "Oh, I am sure it must be interesting."

B: "Oh, no, it is not a bit interesting. But still this is how it begins. Hem. People often ask, as an idle question, whether the process of evolution began with the chicken or the egg. Was there an egg out of which the first chicken came, or did the chicken lay the first egg? I am in a position to say that the first thing created was the egg. When God manufactured all the eggs out of which the fishes and the serpents and the birds and the mammals and even the duck-billed platypus would eventually emerge, he called the embryos before Him, and saw that they were good, and He addressed them: 'Now, you embryos, here you are, all looking exactly the same and We are going to give you the choice of what you want to be. You may alter any parts of yourselves into anything which you think would be useful to you in later life. For instance, at the moment you cannot dig. Anybody who would like to turn his hands into a pair of spades or garden forks is allowed to do so. Or, put it another way, at present you can only use your mouths for eating. Anybody who would like to use his mouth as an offensive weapon, can change it by asking. Now then, step up and choose your tools, but remember that what you choose you will grow into and will have to stick to.' All the embryos thought the matter over politely, and then, one by one they stepped up before the eternal throne. Some chose to use their arms as flying machines and their mouths as weapons, or crackers, or drillers, or spoons, while others selected to use their bodies as boats and their hands as oars. We badgers thought very hard and decided to ask three boons. We wanted our skins changed to shields, our mouths to weapons, and our arms to garden forks. These boons were granted. Everybody specialized in one way or another. The asking and granting took up two long days—they were the fifth and sixth, so far as I remember—and at the very end of the sixth day, just before it was time to knock off for Sunday, they had got through all the little embryos except one. This embryo was Man *(N moves to become embryo Man.)* 'Well, Our little man. You have waited till the last, and slept on your decision, and We are sure you have been thinking hard all the time. What can We do for you?'

N: 'Please, God, I think that You made me in the shape in which I am for reasons best known to Yourselves, and that it would be rude to change. If I am to have my choice I will stay as I am. I will not alter any of the part which You gave me for other and doubtless inferior tools, and I will stay a defenseless embryo all my life. Probably I have been very silly in refusing to take advantage of Your kind offer, but I have done my best to think it out carefully, and now hope that the feeble decision of this small innocent will find favor with Yourselves.'

B: 'Well, done. Here all you embryos, come here with your beaks and whatnots to look upon Our first Man. He is the only one who has guessed Our riddle, out of all of you, and We have great pleasure in conferring upon him the Order of Dominion over the Fowls of the Air, and the Beasts of the Earth, and the Fishes of the Sea. Now let the rest of you go along, and love and multiply, for it is time to knock off for the week-end. As for you, Man, you will look like an embryo till they bury you, but all others will be embryos before your might. Eternally undeveloped you will always remain potential in Our image, able to see some of Our sorrows and to feel some of Our joys. Run along then, and do your best. And listen, Man, before you go . . .'"

N: "Well."

B: "'We are only going to say, well, We are just going to say, God bless you.'"

W: "It's a good story and it is interesting."

B: "No, no, dear boy. You exaggerate. A minor parable at most. Besides I fear it a trifle optimistic."

W: "How?"

B: "Well, it is true that man has the Order of Dominion and is the mightiest of the animals—if you mean the most terrible one—but I have sometimes doubted lately whether he is the most blessed."

W: "I don't think Sir Ector is terrible."

B: "All the same, if even Sir Ector was to go for a walk beside a river, not only would the birds fly from him and the beasts run away from him, but the very fish would dart to the other side. They don't do this for each other."

W: "Man is king of animals."

B: "Perhaps. Or ought one to say the tyrant? And then again we do have to admit that he has a quantity of vices."

W: "King Pellinore has not got many."

B: "He would go to war, if King Uther declared one. Do you know that *Homo sapiens* is almost the only animal which wages war?"

W: "Ants do."

B: "Don't say 'Ants do' in that sweeping way, dear boy. There are more than four thousand different sorts of them and from all those kinds I can only think of five which are belligerent. There are the five ants, one termite, and Man."

W: "But the pack of wolves from the Forest Sauvage attack our flocks of sheep every winter."

B: "Wolves and sheep belong to different species, my friend. True warfare is what happens between bands of the same species. True warfare is rarer in Nature than cannibalism. Don't you think that is a little unfortunate?"

W: "Personally, I should have liked the banners and the trumpets of war, the flashing armor and the glorious charges. And oh, I should have liked to do great deeds, and be brave, and conquer my own fears. Don't you have courage in warfare, Badger, and endurance and comrades whom you love?"

B: "Which did *you* like better, the belligerent ants or the peaceful wild geese?"

(Freeze count of 5. Lights fade out slowly. Opening music begins.)

From the Bible: The Plight of Man

Adapted and Directed by David A. Williams
University of Arizona

PRODUCTION CONCEPT

We hoped ultimately (1) to present a dramatic historical condensation of the rise and fall of the Israelite community and (2) to show the history of Israel as a symbol of Everyman's exodus and his struggles with a meaning in life. As such, we hoped further to appeal to a widely diverse audience— those who knew the story, those who did not, and those who might arbitrarily reject it in the light of twentieth-century existential thought.

Selected Bibliography

ACKERMAN, JAMES S., ALAN WILKIN JENKS, EDWARD B. JENKINSON, and JAN BLOUGH. *Teaching the Old Testament in English Classes.* Bloomington: Indiana University Press, 1973.

AKIN, JOHNNYE, SETH A. FESSENDEN, P. MERVILLE LARSON, and ALBERT N. WILLIAMS. *How to Read the Bible Aloud.* New York: Association Press, 1965.

ANDERSON, BERNHARD W. *Understanding the Old Testament.* Englewood Cliffs, N.J. Prentice-Hall, Inc., 1966.

ARMSTRONG, CHLOE. *Oral Interpretation of Biblical Literature.* Minneapolis: Burgess, 1968.

BREWER, JULIUS A. *The Literature of the Old Testament.* New York: Columbia University Press, 1962.

BURROWS, MILLAR. *What Mean These Stones?* New York: Meridian Books, 1957.

CHILDS, BREVARD S. *Myth and Reality in the Old Testament.* London: SCM Press, 1968.

DINSMORE, CHARLES ALLEN. *The English Bible as Literature*. Boston: Houghton Mifflin, 1931.

HARRELSON, WALTER. *Interpreting the Old Testament*. New York: Holt, Rinehart and Winston, 1964.

HENN, T. R. *The Bible as Literature*. New York: Oxford University Press, 1970.

HILLERS, DELBERT. *Lamentations: The Anchor Bible*. New York: Doubleday, 1972.

KELLNER, ESTHER. *The Background of the Old Testament*. New York: Doubleday, 1963.

LEE, CHARLOTTE I. *Oral Reading of the Scriptures*. Boston: Houghton Mifflin, 1974.

McKENZIE, S. J. *The World of the Judges*. Englewood Cliffs, N.J.: Prentice-Hall, Inc., 1966.

RECE, E. H., and WILLIAM A. BEARDSLEE. *Reading the Bible: A Guide*. Englewood Cliffs, N.J.: Prentice-Hall, Inc., 1964.

FROM THE BIBLE: THE PLIGHT OF MAN

Cast of Characters

M: Male voice
F: Female voice
All: Chorus
AM: All males

AF: All females
M1-8: Eight males
F1-2-3: females
N: Narrator

Prologue

N: I will tell you a story with a meaning,
I will expound the riddle of things past,
things that we have heard and know,
and our fathers have repeated to us,
so that it might be known to a future generation,
to children yet unborn.
Listen! For I will speak clearly,
you will have plain speech from me;
for I will speak nothing but the truth.

F1: Man born of woman is short-lived and full of disquiet.
He blossoms like a flower and then he withers;
he slips away like a shadow and does not stay;
he is like a wine-skin that perishes
or a garment that moths have eaten.

F2: My days die like an echo;
my heart-strings are snapped.

Day is turned into night,
and morning light is darkened before me.

M3: Has not man hard service on earth,
and are not his days like those of a hired laborer,
like those of a slave longing for the shade
or a servant kept waiting for his wages?
So months of futility are my lot.

M4: Why should the sufferer be born to see the light?
Why is life given to men who find it so bitter?
They wait for death but it does not come,
They seek it more eagerly than hidden treasure.
They are glad when they reach the tomb.

N: I would rather be choked outright;
I would prefer death to all my sufferings.
I am in despair, I would not go on living;
leave me alone, for my life is but a vapor.

F2: Consider: God is so great that we cannot know him;
the number of his years is beyond reckoning.

M3: He draws up drops of water from the sea
and distils rain from the mist he has made;
the rain-clouds pour down in torrents,
they descend in showers on mankind;

F1,2: thus he sustains the nations
and gives them food in plenty.

M3: Proud men rage against him
and do not cry to him for help when caught in his toils;
so they die in their prime,
like male prostitutes, worn out.

N: The Lord created me the beginning of his words,
before all else that he made, long ago.
Alone, I was fashioned in terms long past,
at the beginning, long before earth itself.
When there was yet no ocean I was born, you were born,

All: We were born.

N: Before the mountains were settled in their place,
long before the hills I was born,
when as yet he had made neither land nor lake
nor the first clod of earth.
When he set the heavens in their place I was there,
you were there

All: We were there

N: when he girdled the ocean with the horizon,
when he fixed the canopy of clouds overhead
and set the springs of ocean firm in their place,
when he prescribed its limits for the sea
and knit together earth's foundations.
I applied my mind to understand wisdom and knowledge
I undertook great works
I amassed silver and gold

Then I turned and reviewed my handiwork
Everything was emptiness and chasing the wind

F1: God has made everything to suit its time

AF: A time to be born

AM: A time to die

AF: A time to pull down

AM: A time to build up

AF: A time to love

AM: A time to hate

AF: A time for war

AM: A time for peace

N: And I know that there is nothing good for a man except to be
happy and live the best life he can while he is alive

F2: Men have no advantage over beasts
For man is a creature of chance and the beasts are creatures of chance
All came from dust and to the dust all return
Everything is emptiness

N: Everything is empty
Everything that is to come will be emptiness.

Genesis

F1: In the beginning, God created the heaven and the earth

M3,4: Emptiness

F2: And the earth was without form and void.

M3,4: All is emptiness

F1: And God said, "Let there be light," and there was light

M3,4: All is emptiness

F1: And God said

M3,4: All things are wearisome

F1: "Let us make a man."

M3,4: Generations come and generations go.
What has happened will happen again

F2: And the Lord God planted a garden eastward in Eden

M3,4: What has been done will be done again

F2: And there he put the man whom he had formed

M3,4: The wind blows south, the wind blows north

F2: And the Lord God said, "It is not good that man should be alone"

M3,4: All things are wearisome

F2: and he took one of Adam's ribs and made he a woman

M3,4: And there is nothing new under the sun

F1: And when the woman saw that the tree was good for food, she took some of it
and ate it.

M3,4: The sun rises and the sun goes down

F1: She also gave her husband some and he ate it

M3,4: All things are wearisome

F1: So the Lord God drove them out of the Garden of Eden

M3,4: It is a sorry business that God has given men to busy themselves with

F2: And Adam knew Eve his wife and she bore him a son Cain and also his brother Abel

M3,4: And all his deeds under the sun are emptiness

F1: When the Lord God saw that man had done much evil on earth and that his inclinations were always evil, he was grieved at heart.

F2: But Noah was a righteous man and had won the Lord's favor. "Make yourself an ark with ribs of cypress, and you shall bring creatures of every kind into the ark to keep them alive." Exactly as God had commanded him, so Noah did. It rained upon the earth forty days and forty nights but God remembered Noah. Back to the place from which the streams ran, they return—to run again. And God made a wind to pass over the earth.

F1,2: Round and round it goes and the waters subsided. And returns full circle.

F1: And God said,

M3: "I do set my bow in the cloud, and it shall be a token of a convenant which I establish between myself and you and every living creature, to endless generations. Never again shall the waters become a flood to destroy all living creatures."

M4: And in that day all the world spoke a single language and used the same words. "Come," they said, "Let us build ourselves a tower with its top in the heavens, and make a name for ourselves." So the Lord scattered them from there all over the earth.

F1: That is why it is called Babel, because the Lord there made a babble of the languages of all the world.

M3,4: All the deeds that were done under the sun are emptiness and chasing the wind.

M3: Now the Lord had said unto Abram, "Get thee out of thy country unto a land that I will show thee and I will make thee a great nation."

F2: So Abram departed and Lot went with him. Lot chose for himself all the plain of Jordan and pitched his tent toward Sodom. And there came two angels to Sodom and to Lot saying,

M3: "The outcry over Sodom and Gomorrah is very great because their sin is grievous. Get any who belong to you out of this place because the Lord has sent us to destroy it. Flee for your lives. Do not look back or you will be swept away!"

F1: But Lot's wife, behind him, looked back and she turned into a pillar of salt.

M3,4: The Lord God will be obeyed.

F2: And when Abram was ninety and nine years old, the Lord appeared to him and said,

M3: "I am the Almighty God. Walk before me and be perfect and thou shall be a father of many nations. Neither shall thy name anymore be called Abram, but thy name shall be Abraham and kings shall spring from you. For your part, you must keep my covenant, you and your descendants after you, generation by generation."

F2: And Abraham was a hundred years old when his son Isaac was born unto him.

And it came to pass that God put Abraham to the test and said unto him,

M3: "Abraham, take your son Isaac, your only son, and offer him as a sacrifice in a place which I will show you."

F2: So Abraham took the wood for the sacrifice and laid it on his son Isaac's shoulder; he himself carried the fire and the knife. Abraham built an altar and bound his son Isaac and laid him on it. Then he stretched out his hand and took the knife to kill his son, but the angel of the Lord called to him, "Abraham, Abraham, do not raise your hand against the boy. You have not withheld from me your son, your only son. Now I know you are a God-fearing man."

F2: And Abraham gave all that he had to Isaac.

F1: After the death of Abraham, God blessed Isaac and gave him twin sons: Jacob and Esau.

F2: Now Jacob was a smooth man

M2: but Esau was a hairy man.

F1: When Isaac grew old, his eyes became so dim that he could not see. And Jacob dressed in Esau's best clothes and put goatskins on his hands and the smooth nap of his neck and went in unto his father Isaac and said,

M4: "I am Esau, your elder son. Give me your blessing."

F1: Isaac then said to Jacob,

M3: "Come close and let me feel you my son to see whether you are really my son Esau."

F1: Jacob came near and Issac felt his hands and smelt of his clothes and he blessed him.

F2: Now Esau bore a grudge against Jacob because of the blessing and the birthright and threatened to kill him. And Jacob went to Padan-aram to Laban, the brother of Rebecca, his mother. At a certain place on his journey, he dreamt that he saw a ladder which rested on the ground with its top reaching to heaven and the Lord was standing on it and said,

M3: "This land on which you are lying I will give to you and your descendants. I will be with you and I will protect you wherever you go and I will bring you back to this land."

F1: Jacob continued his journey and came upon a well where Rachel came with her father's sheep and Jacob loved her. He served her father Laban seven years for her. And it came to pass after the wedding feast that Laban took his daughter Leah and brought her to Jacob and Jacob slept with her.

F1: But when morning came, Jacob saw that he was deceived and said,

M4: "What have you done to me? Did I not work for Rachel?" Laban answered,

M3: "It is not right that the younger should marry before the elder. Take Leah and Rachel shall be given you for a further seven years work."

F2: Jacob did so and Rachel and Leah and their handmaidens bore him twelve sons. After twenty years, Jacob returned to his father's country. One night a man wrestled with him until daybreak and when the man saw that he could not throw Jacob, he said,

M3: "Your name shall no longer be Jacob but Israel because you strove with God. The land which I gave to Abraham and Isaac I give to you."

F2: So Jacob lived in Canaan, the country which his father had settled.

F1: Now Israel loved Joseph, Jacob's son, more than all his children because he was a child of his old age and made him a coat of many colors. When his brothers saw how their father loved Joseph they hated him. And it came to pass that when Joseph came unto his brothers in the field that they stripped off his coat of many colors and said,

M4: "We will sell him to the Ishmaelites for twenty pieces of silver."

F1: And Joseph was brought down to Egypt. The Lord was with Joseph and he prospered in all that he undertook. The Pharaoh dreamed a dream and called unto Joseph,

M3: "I have had a dream and there is none that can interpret it."

M4: "Not I, but God, shall give Pharaoh an answer. There are to be seven years of great plenty throughout the land. After them will come seven years of famine and the famine will ruin the country."

M3: "Since a God has made this known to you, you shall be in charge of my household, and all my people will depend on your every word."

F1: When the seven years of plenty in Egypt came to an end, seven years of famine began, as Joseph had foretold. The whole world came to Egypt to buy corn from Joseph. Jacob sent Joseph's brothers, ten of them, down to buy corn from Egypt. Although Joseph recognized his brothers, they did not recognize him and Joseph turned away from them and wept. He commanded them to fill their sacks with corn and they returned to Jacob. When they had used up the corn, the famine was still sore in the land, so Jacob said

M4: "Go again. Buy us a little food."

F1: The brothers returned to Egypt with Benjamin the youngest because Joseph had commanded it. When Joseph saw his brother Benjamin with them, he commanded,

M4: "Fill the sacks with food and put my cup in the youngest's sack."

F1: When they were gone to return to Israel, Joseph sent his steward after them to search for the cup and it was found in Benjamin's sack. They returned to the city to Joseph's presence and he revealed himself to them.

M4: "I am your brother Joseph whom you sold into Egypt. It was not you who sent me here but God to preserve you all."

F1: He kissed all his brothers and wept over them. Pharaoh said to Joseph,

M3: "Say to your brethren, fetch your father and your household goods and I will give you the best that there is in Egypt." So Israel set out with all that he had and dwelt in the land of Goshen.

Exodus

F: Joseph remained in Egypt and took an oath of the Children of Israel,

M: "God will not fail to come to your aid and take you to the land of milk and honey which he promised to Abraham, Isaac, and Jacob.

F: So Joseph died at the age of a hundred and ten and was laid in a coffin in Egypt. Then a new king ascended the throne of Egypt, one who knew nothing of Joseph. He said to his people,

M: "These Israelites have become too many and too strong for us. Throw every newborn Hebrew boy into the Nile, but let the girls live."

F: A descendent of Levi married a Levite woman who conceived and bore a son. When she saw what a fine child he was, she hid him for three months, but she could conceal him no longer. So she got a rush basket and laid him in it and put it among the reeds by the bank of the Nile. Pharaoh's daughter found him and called him Moses. Years passed and the king of Egypt died but the Israelites still groaned in slavery. They cried out, and their appeal for rescue from slavery rose up to God. He heard their groaning, and remembered his covenant with Abraham, Isaac, and Jacob.

M: Moses was minding the flock of his father-in-law Jethro near the mountain of God. There the Lord appeared to him in the flame of a burning bush. "Why does not the bush burn away?"

F: And the Lord called to Moses, and told him to take off his sandals, for the place where he was standing was Holy. He told Moses that he was the God of Jacob. He told Moses that he had seen the misery of His people in Egypt, and He told Moses that he had come down to rescue them from the power of Egypt, and to bring them up out of the country into a fine broad land, a land flowing with milk and honey.

M: "Let my people go."

All: No!

AF: And the waters were turned to blood.

M: "Let my people go!"

All: No!

AM: And frogs covered the land of Egypt.

M: "Let my people go!"

All: No!

AM: Flies!

M: "Let my people go!"

All: No!

AF: Cattle plague!	**All:** No!	
AM: Boils and blains!	**All:** No!	
AF: Pestilence!	**All:** No!	
AM: Hail!	**All:** No!	
AF: Locusts!	**All:** No!	
AM: Darkness!	**All:** No!	

M: "LET MY PEOPLE GO!"

All: No!

F: And the Lord smote all the first born in Egypt, from the first born of Pharaoh unto the firstborn of the captive in the dungeon. There was a great cry in Egypt; for there was not a house where there was not one dead. But the firstborn of the children of Israel were passed over. And Pharaoh rose up in the night and said,

M: "Go! Get you forth from among my people."

F: At the end of four hundred and thirty years, all the tribes of the Lord came out of Egypt. When the king of Egypt was told that the Israelites had slipped away, he was again made obstinate by the Lord and said,

M: "What have we done? We have let our Israelite slaves go free."

F: Then Pharaoh, king of Egypt, pursued the Israelites as they marched defiantly away. The Egyptians, all Pharaoh's chariots and horses, cavalry, and infantry, were almost upon them when the Israelites looked up and saw the Egyptians close behind. In their terror they clamored to the Lord, "Were there no graves in Egypt, that you should have brought us here to die in the wilderness?"

M: Then Moses stretched out his hand over the sea, and the Lord drove the sea away all night with a strong east wind and turned the sea bed into dry land. The waters were torn apart and the Israelites went through on dry ground. The Egyptians went in pursuit of them far into the sea and the waters returned to their accustomed place. Not one man among the Egyptians was left alive.

F: Moses led Israel from the Red Sea out into the wilderness. They set out from Rephidim and entered the wilderness of Sinai, where they encamped, pitching their tents opposite the mountain. Moses went up the mountain of God. And God told him,

M: "Thou hast seen with your own eyes what I did to Egypt, and how I have carried you on eagles' wings and brought you here to me. If only you will now listen to me and keep my covenant, then out of all peoples you shall become my special possession; for the whole earth is mine. You shall be my kingdom of priests, my holy nation. These are the words you shall speak to the Israelites. Be attentive to every word of mine.

All: Thou shalt have no other gods before me.

AM: Thou shall not	**AF:** Make any graven image
AM: Thou shall not	**AF:** take the name of the Lord thy God in vain
AM: Remember the Sabbath day	**AF:** to keep it holy
AM: Honor thy father	**AF:** and thy mother
AM: Thou shall not	**AF:** kill
AM: Thou shall not	**AF:** commit adultery
AM: Thou shall not	**AF:** steal
AM: Thou shall not	**AF:** bear false witness against thy neighbor
AM: Thou shall not	**AF:** covet thy neighbor's house

F: Moses was a hundred and twenty years old when he died; his sight was not dimmed nor had his vigor failed. There has never yet risen in Israel a prophet like Moses, whom the Lord knew face to face.

Joshua

M1: After the death of Moses the Lord said to Joshua,

M2: "My servant Moses is dead; now it is for you to cross the Jordan, you and this whole people of Israel to the land of milk and honey which I am giving them. You must not turn to the right or the left. This book of the law must be ever on your lips, day and night. This is my command. Be strong. Be resolute. For the Lord your God is with you."

M1: That day the Lord made Joshua stand very high in the eyes of all Israel, and the people revered him as they had revered Moses all his life. When Joshua came near Jericho he looked up and saw that Jericho was bolted and barred. No one went in, no one came out. The Lord said to Joshua,

M2: "Look I have delivered Jericho and her king into your hands. On the seventh day you shall march round the city seven times and the priests shall blow their trumpets and all of the people shall shout a great shout and the walls of the city shall fall down."

M1: So Joshua summoned the people and gave them their orders. They marched around the city, the trumpets sounding as they marched.

M2: But Joshua ordered the people not to shout till the day came when he would tell them to shout. This they did for six days. But on the seventh day they rose at dawn and marched seven times round the city. The priests blew the trumpets and Joshua commanded the people,

M1: "Shout! The Lord has given you the city. Everything in the city belongs to the Lord, all the silver and gold, all the vessels of copper and iron shall be holy; you must take none of it for yourselves."

M2: So they blew the trumpets and when the people heard the trumpet sound, they raised a great shout, and down fell the walls.

M1: The people advanced on the city, every man straight ahead, and took it. They destroyed everything in the city, they put every one to the sword, men and women, young and old. But the Lord said to Joshua,

M2: "Israel has sinned: they have broken the covenant which I laid on them by taking forbidden things for themselves. The man who has them shall be burnt, he and all his people because he has committed outrage in Israel."

M1: Early in the morning Joshua rose and brought Israel forward tribe by tribe, and man by man, and Achan was chosen. Then Joshua said to Achan, "My son, confess before the Lord God of Israel, tell me what you have done, hide nothing from me." Achan answer Joshua,

M2: "I confess, I have sinned against the Lord. I kept for myself a fine mantle, two hundred weights of silver, and a bar of gold."

M1: Then Joshua took Achan with the silver, the mantle, and the bar of gold, together with his sons and daughters, his oxen, his asses, and his sheep, his tent, and everything he had. Joshua said, "What trouble you have brought on us! Now the Lord will bring trouble on you." Then all the Israelites stoned him to death; and they raised a great pile of stones over him.

M2: Thus the Lord was with Joshua and his fame spread throughout the country. So Joshua massacred the population of the whole region and all their kings. He left no survivor, destroying everything that drew breath, for the Lord God of Israel fought for Israel. By this time Joshua had become very old. He summoned all Israel, their elders and heads of families, their judges and officers, and said to them,

M1: "You have seen for yourself all that the Lord our God has done for your sake; it was the Lord God himself who fought for you. Observe and perform everything written in the book of the law of Moses, without swerving to right or to left. If you forsake the Lord and worship foreign gods, we will turn and bring adversity upon you and will make an end of you."

Judges

M2: After these things Joshua died. Israel served the Lord during the life time of Joshua. After the death of Joshua the Israelites made an assault on Jerusalem and captured it, put its people to the sword, and set fire to the city. Of that whole generation, all were gathered to their forefathers, and another generation followed it who did not acknowledge the Lord and did not know what he had done for Israel. Then the Israelites did what was wrong in the eyes of the Lord and worshipped Baalim. And the Lord set judges over them. Yet they did not listen even to those judges, but turned wantonly to worship other gods and bowed down before them. The Lord said, "I brought you up out of Egypt and into a country which I vowed I would give to your forefathers. But look what you have done. You did not obey me, so I say I will not drive out the inhabitants of the land before you, they will destroy you, and their gods will shut you fast in the trap." Once again the Israelites did what was wrong in the eyes of the Lord. At that time Deborah, a prophetess, was judge in Israel.

All: Hear ye oh kings
Ye princes give ear

F1: I, even I, Deborah
will sing unto the Lord

F2: I will sing praise
to the Lord God of Israel.

F3: O Lord
At the setting forth
from Seir
when then comest marching
out of the plains of Edom

F1: earth trembled

F2: heaven quaked

F3: the clouds streamed down
in torrents.

F1: Mountains shook in fear
before the Lord

F2: the Lord of Sinaï,

F:1 before the Lord
the God of Israel.

F3: The inhabitants of the villages ceased,

F1: until that I Deborah arose,

F2: that I arose a mother of Israel.

All: They chose new gods,

F1: then there was war in the gates.

F2: Then down marched the column
and its chieftains.

F3: The people of the Lord
marched down like warriors.

All: Kings come,

F1: they fought.

F2: Then fought
the kings of Canaan.

F3: They fought from heaven
the stars in their courses
fought against Sisera.

All: Blest above women
be Jael.

F1: She put her hand to the nail,

F2: and her right hand to the workmen's hammer

F3: and with her right hand she smote Sisera,

All: she smote off his head,

F1: when she had pierced and stricken though his temples.

F2: At her feet he bowed

F3: he fell

F1: he lay down:

F2: at her feet he bowed

F3: he fell:

F1: where he bowed
there he fell down dead.

M2: Once more the Israelites did what was wrong in the eyes of the Lord, worshipping the Baalim and the Ashtaroh. And the Lord delivered them into the hands of the Philistines for forty years.

I Samuel

M1: In those days there was no king in Israel and every man did what was right in his own eyes. And the Lord raised Samuel as judge over the people and Samuel's words had great authority throughout Israel.

M2: And it came to pass, when Samuel was old, that he made his sons judges over Israel, but his sons were corrupt and took bribes and perverted judgment. Then all the elders of Israel gathered themselves together and came to Samuel and said,

M1: "Behold, you are old, and your sons walk not in your ways. Make us a king to judge us like the other nations."

M2: Their request displeased Samuel and he prayed to the Lord who answered,

M1: "Hear what the people have to say. They have not rejected you, it is I whom they have rejected. They are doing to you just what they have done to me since I brought them up from Egypt. But give them a solemn warning and tell them what sort of king will govern them."

M2: And Samuel said, "This will be the manner of the king who will reign over you. He will take your sons and make them serve in his chariots and with his cavalry. He will take your daughters for perfumers and cooks, and will seize the best of your cornfields, vineyards, and olive trees and give them to his lackeys. He will take a tenth of all that you have and you yourselves will become his slaves and you will cry out in that day, because of your king and the Lord will not hear you."

M1: But the people refused to listen to the voice of Samuel and said, "We will have a king over us that we may be like the other nations with a king to judge us and go out before us and fight our battles."

M2: There was a man from the district of Benjamin whose name was Saul, a choice young man, there was no better among all the children of Israel.

M1: He was head and shoulders taller than any of his people. And the Lord disclosed his intention to Samuel to anoint Saul king over Israel. Samuel took a flask of oil and poured it over Saul's head, and he kissed him and said,

M2: "The Lord makes you prince over his people Israel. Look at the man whom the

Lord has chosen; there is none like him among all the people."

A: "Long live the king!"

M1: But there were scoundrels who said, "How can this fellow deliver us?" They thought nothing of him and brought him no gifts.

M1: Saul reigned over Israel for twenty-two years and there was bitter warfare with the Philistines throughout Saul's lifetime; any strong man and any brave man that he found, he took into his own service. Samuel came to Saul and said,

M2: "This is the very word of the Lord of Hosts. I am resolved to punish the Amalekites because they attacked Israel on the way up from Egypt. Go now, fall upon the Amalekites. Spare no one; put them all to death, men and women, children and babes in arms, herds and flocks, camels and asses."

M1: Then Saul cut the Amalekites to pieces, he destroyed all the people, putting them to the sword. But Saul and his army spared Agag the king of the Amalekites and the best of the sheep and cattle and everything worth keeping.

M2: Then the word of the Lord came to Samuel, "I repent of having made Saul king, for he has turned his back on me and has not obeyed my commands. Fill your horn with oil and take it with you. I have chosen myself a king." The Lord sent him unto David the youngest son of Jesse of Bethlehem. Now he was handsome, with ruddy cheeks and bright eyes. The Lord said, "Arise and anoint him: this is the man." Then the spirit of the Lord came upon David and was with him from that day onwards. But the spirit of the Lord departed from Saul, and an evil spirit troubled him.

M1: And Saul said to his servants, "Find me a man who is a cunning player on the harp and bring him to me." And David came to Saul, and stood before him; and he loved him greatly. And it came to pass, when the evil spirit from God was upon Saul that David took his harp and played with his hand so that Saul was refreshed and the evil spirit departed from him.

M2: The Philistines collected their forces for war, and a champion came out from the camp, a man named Goliath; he was over nine feet tall. He stood and shouted to the ranks of Israel, "Why do you not come out to do battle, you slaves of Saul?" Then David picked up his shepherd's stick, chose five smooth stones from the brook and put them in a shepherd's bag which served as his pouch. He walked out to meet the Philistine. "You have come against me with sword and spear, but I have come against you in the name of the Lord of Hosts." David took a stone, slung it, and it sank deep into the Philistine's forehead and he fell on his face on the ground.

AF: "Saul has slain his thousands and David his tens of thousands."

M2: The saying displeased Saul and he said, "They have given David tens of thousands and me only thousands, what more can he have but the kingdom?" From that day forward Saul looked upon David with a jealous eye and determined to kill him;

M2: but Jonathan, Saul's son, loved David greatly and told him of Saul's intentions. And David left Saul's company and hid himself in the land of Nob.

M1: Saul's anger was kindled against Jonathan, "You have brought confusion upon yourself and upon your mother's nakedness, for as long as David lives, your right to the kingdom will never be established." And Saul went out with a party of three thousand men and searched for David day after day, but the Lord did not put him into his hands.

M2: David hid himself in a cave.

M1: During the search, Saul and his men came to the mouth of the cave and Saul went in to cover his feet. "God forbid that I should harm my Master, the Lord's anointed."

M2: Then David arose and cut off the skirt of Saul's robe stealthily.

M1: Saul rose up out of the cave, and went on his way,

M2: whereupon David came out of the cave and called after Saul, "My Lord the King," and David stooped with his face to the earth and said to Saul, "Why do you listen when they say that David is out to do you harm. Today the Lord put you in my power in the cave and I spared your life because I cannot lift a finger against my master, for he is the Lord's annointed. Look, my dear Lord, look at this piece of your robe in my hand. I cut it off, but I did not kill you." And it came to pass that when David had finished speaking Saul said,

M1: "Is this your voice, my son David?" And Saul lifted up his voice and wept. "You are more righteous than I. And now I know that you will surely become king and that the kingdom of Israel will become a great nation under your rule. Swear to me before the Lord that you will not cut off my descendants and blot out my name from my father's house."

M2: David swore an oath to Saul and Saul went back to his home. The Philistines fought a great battle against Israel, and the men of Israel were routed, leaving their dead on Mount Gilboa. When the children of Israel came back to minister to their dead they found Saul and his three sons lying dead on Mount Gilboa.

N: Leaders, kings, and judges: what has happened once will happen again.

F1: David caught his clothes and rent them, and so did all the men with him. They beat their breasts and wept, because Saul and Jonathan his son and the people of the Lord, the house of Israel, had fallen in battle.

II Samuel

F2: One morning David got up from his couch, and as he walked about on the roof of the palace, he saw from there a woman bathing, and she was very beautiful. When he sent to inquire who she was, the answer came, "It must be Bathsheba, daughter of Elram and wife of Uriah the Hittite."

F3: The following morning David wrote a letter to Joab in the field of battle and sent Uriah with it. "Put Uriah opposite the enemy where the fighting is fiercest and then fall back, and leave him to meet his death."

F1: When Uriah's wife heard that her husband was dead, she mourned for him; after the period of mourning was over, David sent for her and brought her into his house. She became his wife and bore him a son. But what David had done was wrong in the eyes of the Lord.

F2: The Lord struck the boy and he became very ill. On the seventh day the boy died.

F3: David's other son, Absolom, invited all the king's sons to his sheep-shearing. A rumor reached David that Absolom had murdered all the royal princes.

F2: News reached David that the men of Israel had transfered their allegiance to Absolom. He said to those who were with him in Jerusalem, "We must get away at once; or there will be no escape from Absolom for any of us."

F3: Some of David's men caught sight of Absolom. He was riding a mule, and as it passed a great oak, his head was caught in its boughs; he found himself in mid-air and the mule went on from under him. Then ten young men who were Joab's armor-bearers closed in on Absolom, struck at him, and killed him. The king was deeply moved and went up to the roof chamber over the gate and wept.

M2: "O, my son! Absolom my son, my son Absolom! If only I had died instead of you! O Absolom, my son, my son."

F1: So David came back to the Jordan. The men of Judah met him and escorted him across the river.

F2: He who rules men in justice,
who rules in the fear of God,
is like the light of morning at sunrise,
a morning that is cloudless after rain
and makes the grass sparkle from the earth.

F3: But the ungodly put forth no shoots,
they are like briars tossed aside;
none dare put out his hand to pick them up,
none touch them but with tool of iron or of wood;
they are fit only for burning in the fire.

Kings

F1: When David rested with his forefathers, Solomon succeeded his father as king and was firmly established on the throne.

F2: God gave Solomon depth of wisdom and insight and understanding as wide as the sand of the seashore.

F3: Men of all races came to listen to the wisdom of Solomon, and from all the kings of the earth who had heard of his wisdom he received gifts.

F1: Thus, King Solomon outdid all the kings of the earth in wealth and wisdom, and all the world courted him to hear him, to hear the wisdom which God had put in his heart.

F2: King Solomon was a lover of women, and besides Pharaoh's daughter he married many foreign women from the nations with whom the Lord had forbidden the Israelites to intermarry.

F3: When he grew old, his wives turned his heart from the truth to follow other gods, and he did not remain wholly loyal to the Lord. He followed Ashtoreth, goddess of the Sidonians, and Milcom, the loathsome god of the Ammonites. The Lord was angry with Solomon and said to him,

F1: "Because you have done this and have not kept my covenant as I commanded you, I will tear the kingdom from you and will bring great strife in Israel generation after generation."

F2: And it was as the Lord had said it would be, there was strife in Israel year after year, generation after generation until Nebuchadnezzar, king of Babylon, advanced with all his army against Jerusalem and the city of David and brought ruin to Solomon's temple.

F3: Nebuchadnezzar carried the people of Jerusalem into captivity in Babylon, all the best and the strongest; only the weakest of the people were left.

All: By the rivers of Babylon, there we sat down, yea, we wept, when we remembered Zion.

F1: We hanged our harps upon the willows in the midst thereof,

F2: for there they that carried us away captive required of us a song;

F3: and they that wasted us required of us mirth, saying, "Sing us one of the songs of Zion."

All: How shall we sing the Lord's song in a strange land?

F1: If I forget thee, O Jerusalem, let my right hand forget her cunning.

F2: If I do not remember thee, O, Jerusalem, let my tongue cleave to the roof of my mouth;

AF: Remember, O Lord, the children of Babylon in the day of Jerusalem,

F3: who said, "Down with it, Down with it."

F2: How solitary lies the city, once so full of people!

F3: Once great among nations, now become a widow;

F1: once queen among provinces, now put to forced labor!

F2: Bitterly she weeps in the night, tears run down her cheeks;

F3: she has no one to bring her comfort among all that love her;

F1: all her friends turned traitor and became her enemies.

N: There is nothing new under the sun, what has happened once will happen again.

Epilogue

M1: Israel is like a rank vine ripening its fruit; his fruit grows more and more and more and more his altars; they are crazy now, they are mad. God himself hacks down their altars. The Lord will be like a panther to Israel. King after king falls from power, but not one of them calls upon the Lord. Return, O Israel, to the Lord your God; for you have stumbled in your evil courses.

F1: There is no peace for the wicked. You women that live at ease, stand up and hear what I have to say. Strip yourselves bare; put a cloth round your waists and beat your breasts. Because you have walked with necks outstretched and wanton glances, instead of perfume you shall have the stench of decay, and branding instead of beauty. Your men shall fall by the sword, and your warriors in battle.

M2: The Lord is leaving his dwelling-place for the crime of Jacob and the sin of Israel. Her wound cannot be healed; for the stroke has bitten deep into Judah, it has fallen on the gate of my people, upon Jerusalem itself. Zion becomes a ploughed field, Jerusalem a heap of ruins.

N: If only I could go back to the old days, to the time when God was watching over me.

M3: The Lord is a sure refuge for those who look to him in time of distress; he cares for all who seek his protection and brings them safely through the sweeping flood; he makes a final end of all who oppose him and pursues his enemies into darkness.

N: Whoever heard of me spoke in my favor and those bore witness to my merit. I was eyes to the blind and feet to the lame. But now, I am laughed to scorn by men whose fathers I would have disdained to butt with the dogs who keep my flocks. Now I have become the target of their taunts. I am the man who has known affliction.

M4: Proclaim this amongst the nations: Declare a holy war. Beat your mattocks into swords and your pruning-hooks into spears. Let all the nations hear the call to arms and come to the Valley of the Lord's judgment.

F2: The Lord has done what he planned to do, all that he ordained from days of old.

M5: I have seen all deeds that are done under the sun. Devastation and violence confront me; strife breaks out, discord raises its head, and so law grows effete.

F3: Make a joyful noise unto the Lord, all ye lands. Serve the Lord with gladness; come before his presence with thanksgiving.

M6: This is what is wrong with all that is done here under the sun; that one and same fate befalls every man. Where is the God of justice?

F4: Sing unto the Lord a new song.

M7: Make a loud noise and rejoice and sing praise.

M8: The more words one uses the greater is the emptiness of it all; and where is the advantage to a man?

M1: I will take up my position on the watchtower.

M2: I will watch to learn who can tell me what is to happen next here under the sun.

AF: *(Begin the Twenty-third Psalm and continue it until "a curse on the day I was born.")*

M3: All is vanity.

M4: The Lord is in his holy temple, let all the earth keep silence before him.

M5: The Lord will be obeyed.

M6: All is emptiness and chasing the wind.

M7: Rescue me, O Lord, from evil man.

M8: O praise God in his holy place.

M1: The son of righteousness shall rise with healing in his wings.

M2: All prophetic wisdom has become for you like a sealed book.

M3: How long, O Lord, how long.

M4: Unto us a child is born, unto us a song is given.

M5: I reveal the end from the beginning.

N: A curse on the day that I was born.

F1: Comfort, comfort my people. His name shall be called wonderful, counselor, the mighty God, the everlasting father, the prince of Peace

N: I will tell you a story with a meaning,
I will expound the riddle of things past,
things that we have heard and know.
And our fathers have repeated to us,
so that it might be known to a future generation,
to children yet unborn.
Men, it is to you I call,

N: I appeal to every man:

N: understand you simple fools, what it is to be shrewd;
you stupid people, understand what sense means.
Listen! For I will speak clearly,
you will have plain speech from me;
for I will speak nothing but the truth.

Indians Speak: Words, Music, and Art by and about Them

Compiled and Directed by Ruth Arrington and Louis Baker

Northeastern Oklahoma State University

PRODUCTION CONCEPT

Two themes found in American Indian writings are the love of nature shown in literature of the past and present; and the attempt to reconcile the old way of living with the new. Other art forms produced by the Native American reflect these themes. In order to communicate an impression of the creative American Indian the adapters of "Indians Speak" selected literature, music, and other art forms on colored slides and combined them into a multi-media performance.

Selected Bibliography

ALLEN, T. D., (pseud. Terry D. Allen and Don B. Allen) ed. *Arrows Four: Prose and Poetry by Young American Indians.* New York: Washington Square Press, 1974.

———. *The Whispering Wind.* New York: Doubleday, 1972.

ARMSTRONG, VIRGINIA IRVING, ed. *I Have Spoken.* Chicago: The Swallow Press, 1971.

BABCOCK, C. MERTON, ed. *Walk Quietly the Beautiful Trail.* Kansas City, Mo.: Hallmark Cards, Inc., 1973.

BASS, ALTHEA. *The Arapaho Way.* New York: Clarkson N. Potter, Inc., 1967.

BILLARD, JULES B., ed. *The World of the American Indian.* Washington, D.C.: National Geographic Society, 1974.

CRONYN, GEORGE W., ed. *American Indian Poetry.* New York: Ballantine Books, 1972.

DODGE, ROBERT K., and McCULLOUGH, JOSEPH B., eds. *Voices from Wah'Kon-Tah: Contemporary Poetry of Native Americans.* New York: International Publishers, 1974.

GRINNELL, GEORGE BIRD, *Pawnee Hero Stories and Folk-Tales.* Lincoln: University of Nebraska Press, 1961.

HASLAM, GERALD W., *Forgotten Pages of American Literature.* Boston: Houghton Mifflin Co., 1970.

MATHEWS, JOHN JOSEPH. *Wah'Kon-Tah.* Norman: University of Oklahoma Press, 1968.

McGINNIS, DUANE. *After the Death of an Elder Klallam.* Phoenix, Ariz.: Baleen Press, 1970.

ROSEN, KENNETH, ed. *The Man to Send Rain Clouds.* New York: The Viking Press, 1974.

———. *Voices of the Rainbow.* New York: The Viking Press, 1975.

SANDERS, THOMAS, and PECK, WALTER, eds. *Literature of the American Indian.* New York: The Glencoe Press, 1973.

TURNER, FREDERICK W. III, ed. *The Portable North American Indian Reader.* New York: The Viking Press, 1974.

WITT, SHIRLEY HILL, and STEINER, STAN, eds. *The Way.* New York: Random House, 1972.

INDIANS SPEAK

Cast of Characters

N: Narrator
V1-5: Voices

As audience enters, a campus scene is displayed on a colored slide. Five minutes before production begins, a tape of Pow-Wow music is played, while slides of Pow-Wow dancers are displayed. As narrator enters, music fades and screen is empty. Slide changes and descriptions are indicated in script by "S."

N: Welcome to this multimedia presentation, *Indians Speak: Words, Music, and Art, by and about Them*. We have endeavored to present a variety of art works of the American Indians for your interpretation, for we believe that the culture of a people is reflected in their art forms. Let me introduce our readers: (Insert names of performers and narrator).

Music: Up and under (*Indian flute tape*).

N: Our program is divided into two parts—the first contains material to recreate a view of the past and in the second we use selections written in the twentieth century—from 1900 to now. Listen to *Indians Speak*.

V1: (S—"Dog Soldier Dance," Richard West)
These words come from a speech of the chief of the Stockbridge tribe to the Massachusetts Congress, in the year 1775.

V2: You remember, when you first came over the great waters, I was great and you were little, very small. I then took you in for a friend; and kept you under my arms, so that no one might injure you. Since that time we have ever been true friends, there has never been any quarrel between us. (S—"End of the Trail")

293

But now our conditions are changed. You are become great and tall. You reach to the clouds. You are seen all round the world.

(S—"Warfare") Brothers! I am sorry to hear of this great quarrel between you and Old England. It appears that blood must soon be shed to end this quarrel. We never till this day understood the foundation of this quarrel between you and the country you came from. (S—"Wild Horses," G. Catlin) Brothers! Whenever I see your blood running, you will soon find me about you to revenge my brothers' blood. Although I am low and very small, I will grip hold of your enemy's heel, that he cannot run too fast, and so light, as if he had nothing at his heels. (S—"Buffalo's Child," G. Catlin)

Brothers! One thing I ask of you, if you send me to fight, that you will let me fight in my own Indian way. I am not used to fight English fashion; therefore you must not expect I can train like your men. Only point out to me where your enemies keep, and that is all I shall want to know.

V5: (S—"Trail of Tears," J. Tiger)

Town's Fourth Reader, published in 1847, contained the following description of the Trail of Tears. Though the author is not identified, remember, it was written and read at the time of, and shortly after, the removal of the Five Tribes from their homes in the southeastern states to the eastern half of what is now the state of Oklahoma.

V1: (S—"Our Warriors Return," C. M. Russell)

We hear the rustling of their footsteps like that of the withered leaves of autumn, and they are gone forever. They pass mournfully by us, and they return no more. Two centuries ago, the smoke of their wigwams and the fires of their councils rose in every valley, from Hudson's Bay to the farthest Florida, from the ocean to the Mississippi, and the lakes.

V5: (S—The Trail of Tears poster)

The winds of the Atlantic fan not a single region which they may now call their own. Already, the last feeble remnants of the race are preparing for their journey beyond the Mississippi. I see them leave their miserable homes, the aged, the helpless, the women, and the warriors, "few and faint, yet fearless still."

V4: (S—part of "Trail of Tears," J. Tiger)

The ashes are cold on their native hearths. The smoke no longer curls round their lowly cabins. They move on with a slow, unsteady step. The white man is upon their heels for terror or despatch; but they heed him not. (S—another part of "Trail of Tears," J. Tiger) They turn to take a last glance upon the graves of their fathers. They shed no tears; they utter no cries; they heave no groans.

V1: (S—"Her Heart Is on the Ground," C. Russell)

There is something in their hearts which passes speech. There is something in their looks, not of vengeance or submission, but of hard necessity, which stifles both; which chokes all utterance; which has no aim or method. (S—"Cune Shote") It is courage absorbed in despair. They linger but for a moment. Their look is onward. They have passed the fatal stream. It shall never be repassed by them; no never. Yet there lies not between us and them an impassable gulf. (S—"Black Hawk and his Son") They know and feel that there is for them still one removed farther not distant, nor unseen. It is to the general burial ground of the races.

V3: (S—"Sioux Council," G. Catlin)

At a later time the Sioux leader, Sitting Bull, was asked why he did not surrender and allow his starving followers to live on a reservation. Sitting Bull replied:

V5: (S—picture of Sitting Bull)

"Because I am a red man. If the Great Spirit had desired me to be a white man he would have made me so in the first place. He put in your heart certain wishes and plans, in my heart he put other and different desires. Each man is good in his sight. Now we are poor but we are free. No white man controls our footsteps. If we must die we die defending our rights."

V1: (S—picture of Chief Joseph)

The surrender speech of Chief Joseph of the Nez Perce terminated a tragic yet admirable attempt to take his people to Canada.

V2: (S—close-up of Chief Joseph)

"I am tired of fighting. Our chiefs are killed. Looking Glass is dead. The old men are all dead. It is cold and we have no blankets. The children are freezing to death. My people, some of them, have run away to the hills and have no blankets, no food; no one knows where they are—perhaps freezing to death. I want to have time to look for my children and see how many of them I can find. Maybe I shall find them among the dead. Hear me, my chiefs. I am tired; my heart is sick and sad. From where the sun now stands I will fight no more forever."

Music: Up and under (*Indian flute*)

V4: (S—"Cornstalk Shooter," W. Stone)

Beginning in the twentieth century, Alex Posey, editor of the *Eufaula Indian Journal* in the Creek Nation, was a voice of some of the citizens of Indian Territory. In addition to his newspaper work he was a poet, an Indian poet, who wrote of nature, the world he loved and respected!

V2: (S—cloud scene)
Like a truant boy, unmindful
Of the herd he keeps, thou, idle
Breeze, hast left the white clouds scattered
All about the sky, (S—landscape) and wandered
Down to play at leapfrog with the
Grass, and rest in the branches; (S—another cloud scene)
While, one by one, the white clouds stray
Apart, and disappear forever.

V1: (S—scene at twilight)
O Twilight, fold me, let me rest within
    Thy dusky wings;
For I am weary, weary. Lull me with
    Thy whisperings,
So tender; (S—river and hills scene) let my sleep be fraught with dreams
    Of beauteous things.

V5: Cherokee writer Maggie Culver Fry wrote of the tragic drowning of Alex Posey at the age of thirty-five.

V3: S—picture of Posey)
The river welled high, as the skittering, leafy-like rowboat
Pitched here and there by the dark, tawny crest of the water,
Flipped the frail wisp, as it lifted and spilled out its cargo

Of men in the muddy brown maelstrom, the river.
(S—another picture of Posey)
Out in the path of the rapids, a figure was clinging . . .
Hour by hour, still swaying, bobbing; enduring . . .
A line then . . . at last . . . a long and merciful towline.
Reeling to shoreward a catch . . . a fellow . . . a human . . .
Then suddenly, slackness . . . such terrible, sickening slackness . . .
A rope without weight, as limp as warm puddle-water.
Meanwhile the form of a man sank down, deep down in the rushing;
The churning and roaring closed over the head of the poet.

V4: (S—picture of Will Rogers)
Another man of Indian heritage won national recognition and, like Posey,
suffered an untimely death. This man was Will Rogers. Fellow Cherokee
Maggie Culver Fry wrote a tribute to him, too.

V5: I have no flower here, for your lapel;
Somehow I failed to find
The one for you.
Although your great compassion for mankind
I understand, in part . . .
And yet, somehow, to plunge into your heart
And hold to view this vital, golden thing
That made you servant while you were a king
Is next to sacrilege . . .
And could I heap up praises high, they are
Unable to add luster to your star.
The homey thing you prized no fame could kill—
Was just the privilege to be yourself—
Plain Will.

V1: (S—another picture of Will Rogers)
When Will was offered an honorary degree he responded:

V2: "Degrees have lost prestige enough as it is without handing 'em around to
second-hand comedians, and it's this handing 'em out too promiscuously that
has helped to cheapen 'em. Let a guy get in there and battle four years if he
wants one, and don't give him one just because he happens to hold a good job
in Washington, or manufactures more monkey-wrenches than anybody else or
because he might be fool enough to make people laugh. Keep 'em for those
kids that have worked hard for 'em."

V4: (S—"Stomp Dance," Mike Pasha-Topah)
Some Indians today continue the traditions of the past as described by Bob
Chesbro, Northeastern student, in "Stomp Dance."

V3:   The fire was low and only its red coals glowed when the cold wind blew. It
was peaceful.
    A loud scream pierced the air, and the singing started. (S—"Shell Shaker,"
Willard Stone) The dancers followed and repeated what he said. Their
movements quickened. The fire blazed! Everybody danced!
    The song went on and on but was finally over. All dancers slowed down from
an almost frantic frenzy. (S—"Shell Shaker and Corn Stalk Shooter," W. Stone)
Another song began. The cycle repeated itself.
    Late. Late. The fire burned low on a tall pile of grey ashes.

V4: (S—Bisbee Turquoise)
Some react to present treatment as in "Turquoise Tears."

V1: you read a book about my past
and how the west was won.
and while your nose was in a book
the stealing still goes on. (S—Old Navajo jewelry)
you look into a jewelry store
admiring turquoise rings
not knowing that they were pawned out
for flour and cheaper things.

V3: (S—"Long Hair," Paul Pasha-Topah)
look away from books and turquoise—
look onto our eyes instead!
see the fire slowly dying
from the tears that did no good
often failing, always trying . . .
but you never understood.
we asked you once in pain,
we ask you now in rage,
—consider our humanity! (S—Eagle dancer ring)
(turquoised finger turns a page)

V2: (S—"Beadworker," O. C. Seltzer)
Other Indians have been successful in expressing themselves in music, on
canvas, in dance, in writing. These Indians speak:

V1: (S—"Cochiti Gourd Dance")
Moscelyn Larkin, Shawnee-Peoria, is a ballet dancer.

V4: "The dancer's path through discipline and the mastery of technique has given
me inspiration and tools for greater self-expression and has led me to a deeper
understanding as well, for I have now come to the realization that the American
Indian has what man has been seeking all along—harmony with the universe."

V1: (S—Seminary Hall mural)
John Joseph Mathews, Osage, is a writer.

V3: "I got my feet on my own bit of earth . . . to express, by physical action, my
harmony with the natural flow of life. . . ."

V1: (S—"Dreams," Paul Pasha-Topah)
Alex Posey, Creek Indian poet, journalist, and statesman said of the American
Indian:

V5: "All of my people are poets."

Music: Up and under (*Indian flute*)

V4: (S—"Peyote Scene," Terry Saul)
May the Great Spirit send his choicest gifts to you;
May the Sun Father and the Moon Mother shed their softest beams on you;
May the Four Winds of Heaven blow gently upon you and
Upon those with whom you share your heart and home.

Music: Up as audience leaves. (S—"Madonna," W. Stone)

Lily Daw and the Three Ladies*

by Eudora Welty

Adapted and Directed by Judy Baker Goss
The University of Arkansas at Little Rock

PRODUCTION CONCEPT

My objective in adapting and producing "Lily Daw and the Three Ladies" was to demonstrate the story's form, style, and humor. My interpretation of the story dictated decisions that are central to the production concept: (1) a realistic style, both in performance and technical design; (2) the literalization of selected movement, set pieces, stage properties, and costumes; (3) an onstage focus to dramatize all scenes; and (4) the mobility of the narrator.

In addition, this production concept offered the performers practice in several specific aspects of performance: (1) developing broad characterization that borders on caricature; (2) establishing rhythm and pace through style of language; (3) achieving ensemble interaction to advance scenes; and (4) using movement, set pieces, stage properties, and costumes with clarity and economy.

Selected Bibliography

APPEL, ALFRED, JR. *A Season of Dreams: The Fiction of Eudora Welty*. Baton Rouge: Louisiana State University Press, 1965.

BUCKLEY, WILLIAM F. "The Southern Imagination: An Interview with Eudora Welty and Walker Percy" *Mississippi Quarterly*, 26, 4 (Fall 1973), 493–516.

DRAKE, ROBERT Y., JR. "Comments on Two Eudora Welty Stories." *Mississippi Quarterly*, 13, 3 (Fall 1960), 123–31.

HOWELL, ELMO. "Eudora Welty's Comedy of Manners." *South Atlantic Quarterly*, 69, 3 (Autumn 1970), 469–79.

KUEHL, LINDA. "The Art of Fiction XLVII: Eudora Welty." *Paris Review*, 55 (Fall 1972), 72–97.

LANDESS, THOMAS H. "The Function of Taste in the Fiction of Eudora Welty." *Mississippi Quarterly*, 26 (Fall 1973), 543–58.

OATES, JOYCE CAROL. "The Art of Eudora Welty." *Shenandoah*, 20 (1969), 54–57.

PICKETT, NELL. "Colloquialism as a Style in the First-Person-Narrator Fiction of Eudora Welty." *Mississippi Quarterly*, 26, *4* (Fall 1973), 559–76.

RUBIN, LOUIS D., JR. *The Faraway Country: Writers of the Modern South*. Seattle: University of Washington Press, 1963.

VANDE KIEFT, RUTH M. "The Vision of Eudora Welty." *Mississippi Quarterly*, 26, *4* (Fall 1973), 517–42.

————. *Eudora Welty*. New York: Twayne Publishers, 1962.

WELTY, EUDORA. *One Time, One Place: Mississippi in the Depression, A Snapshot Album*. New York: Random House, 1971.

————. "Place in Fiction." *South Atlantic Quarterly*, 55, *1* (January 1956), 57–72.

————. *Selected Stories of Eudora Welty: "A Curtain of Green and Other Stories" and "The Wide Net and Other Stories."* New York: The Modern Library, 1943.

————. "Some Notes on Time in Fiction." *Mississippi Quarterly*, 26, *4* (Fall 1973), 483–92.

LILY DAW AND THE THREE LADIES

AS: Aimee Slocum
C: Mrs. Carson
EN: Ed Newton
EM: Estelle Mabers
L: Lily Daw
LA: Loralee Adkins

L1: Lady No. 1
L2: Lady No. 2
L3: Lady No. 3
M: Musician (Xylophone player)
N: Narrator
W: Mrs. Watts

N: Mrs. Watts and Mrs. Carson were both in the post office in Victory when the letter came from the Ellisville Institute for the Feeble-Minded of Mississippi. Aimee Slocum, with her hand still full of mail, ran out in front and handed it straight to Mrs. Watts, and they all three read it together. Mrs. Watts held it taut between her pink hands, and Mrs. Carson underscored each line slowly with her thimbled finger. Everybody else in the post office wondered what was up now.

C: What will Lily say,

N: beamed Mrs. Carson at last,

C: when we tell her we're sending her to Ellisville!

W: She'll be tickled to death,

N: said Mrs. Watts, and added in a guttural voice to a deaf lady,

W: Lily Daw's getting in at Ellisville!

AS: Don't you all dare go off and tell Lily without me!

N: called Aimee Slocum, trotting back to finish putting up the mail.

C: Do you suppose they'll look after her down there?

N: Mrs. Carson began to carry on a conversation with a group of Baptist ladies

301

waiting in the post office. She was the Baptist preacher's wife.

L1: I've always heard it was lovely down there, but crowded.

L2: Lily lets people walk over her so.

L3: Last night at the tent show—

C: Don't mind me, I know there are such things in the world,

N: said Mrs. Carson, looking down and fingering the tape measure which hung over her bosom.

L3: Oh, Mrs. Carson. Well, anyway, last night at the tent show, why, the man was just before making Lily buy a ticket to get in.

C: A ticket!

L3: Till my husband went up and explained she wasn't bright, and so did everybody else.

N: The ladies all clucked their tongues.

L3: Oh, it was a very nice show,

N: said the lady who had gone.

L3: And Lily acted so nice. She was a perfect lady—just set in her seat and stared.

C: Oh, she can be a lady—she can be,

N: said Mrs. Carson, shaking her head and turning her eyes up.

C: That's just what breaks your heart.

L3: Yes'm, she kept her eyes on—what's that thing makes all the commotion?—the xylophone. Didn't turn her head to the right or to the left the whole time. Set in front of me.

W: The point is, what did she do after the show?

N: said Mrs. Watts practically.

W: Lily has gotten so she is very mature for her age.

C: Oh, Etta!

N: protested Mrs. Carson, looking at her wildly for a moment.

W: And that's how come we are sending her to Ellisville,

N: finished Mrs. Watts.

AS: I'm ready, you all,

N: said Aimee Slocum, running out with white powder all over her face.

AS: Mail's up. I don't know how good it's up.

L2: Well, of course, I do hope it's for the best.

N: said several of the other ladies. They did not go at once to take their mail out of their boxes; they felt a little left out. The three women stood at the foot of the water tank.

AS: To find Lily is a different thing.

W: Where in the wide world do you suppose she'd be?

N: It was Mrs. Watts who was carrying the letter.

C: I don't see a sign of her either on this side of the street or on the other side,

N: Mrs. Carson declared as they walked along. Ed Newton was stringing Redbird school tablets on the wire across the store.

EN: If you're after Lily, she came in here while ago and tole me she was fixin' to git married,

N: he said,

302

W, C, AS: Ed Newton!

N: cried the ladies all together clutching one another. Mrs. Watts began to fan herself at once with the letter from Ellisville. She wore widow's black, and the least thing made her hot.

C: Why she is not. She's going to Ellisville, Ed.

N: said Mrs. Carson gently.

C: Mrs. Watts and I and Aimee Slocum are paying her way out of our own pockets. Besides, the boys of Victory are on their honor. Lily's not going to get married, that's just an idea she's got in her head.

EN: More power to you, ladies,

N: said Ed Newton spanking himself with a tablet. When they came to the bridge over the railroad tracks, there was Estelle Mabers, sitting on a rail. She was slowly drinking an orange Ne-Hi.

W, C, AS: Have you seen Lily?

EM: I'm supposed to be out here watching for her now,

N: said the Mabers girl, as though she weren't there yet.

EM: But for Jewel—Jewel says Lily came in the store while ago and picked out a two-ninety-eight hat and wore it off. Jewel wants to swap her something else for it.

AS: Oh, Estelle, Lily says she's going to get married!

EM: Well, I declare,

N: said Estelle; she never understood anything. Loralee Adkins came riding by in her Willys-Knight, tooting the horn, to find out what they were talking about. Aimee threw up her hands and ran out into the street.

AS: Loralee, Loralee, you got to ride us up to Lily Daw's. She's up yonder fixing to get married!

LA: Hop in, my land!

W: Well, that just goes to show you right now,

N: said Mrs. Watts, groaning as she was helped into the back seat.

W: What we've got to do is persuade Lily it will be nicer to go to Ellisville!

C: Just to think!

N: While they rode around the corner, Mrs. Carson was going on in her sad voice, sad as the soft noises in the hen house at twilight.

C: We buried Lily's poor defenseless mother. We gave Lily all her food and kindling and every stitch she had on. Sent her to Sunday school to learn the Lord's teachings, had her baptized a Baptist. And when her old father commenced beating her and tried to cut her head off with the butcher knife, why, we went and took her away from him and gave her a place to stay.

N: The paintless frame house with all the weather vanes was three stories high in places and had yellow and violet stained-glass windows in front and gingerbread around the porch. It leaned steeply to one side, toward the railroad, and the front steps were gone. The car full of ladies drew up under the cedar tree.

C: Now Lily's almost grown up,

N: Mrs. Carson continued.

C: In fact, she's grown,

N: she concluded getting out.

W: Talking about getting married.

N: said Mrs. Watts disgustedly.

W: Thanks, Loralee, you run on home.

N: They climbed over the dusty zinnias onto the porch and walked through the open door without knocking.

AS: There certainly is always a funny smell in this house. I say it every time I come.

N: Lily was there, in the dark of the hall, kneeling on the floor by a small open trunk. When she saw them she put a zinnia in her mouth, and held still.

C: Hello, Lily.

N: said Mrs. Carson reproachfully.

L: Hello.

N: said Lily. In a minute she gave a suck on the zinnia stem that sounded exactly like a jay bird. There she sat, wearing a petticoat for a dress, one of the things Mrs. Carson kept after her about. Her milky-yellow hair streamed freely down from under a new hat. You could see the weavy scar on her throat if you knew it was there. Mrs. Carson and Mrs. Watts, the two fattest, sat in the double rocker. Aimee Slocum sat on the wire chair donated from the drugstore that burned.

W: Well, what are you doing, Lily?

N: asked Mrs. Watts, who led the rocking. Lily smiled. The trunk was old and lined with yellow and brown paper, with an asterisk pattern showing in darker circles and rings. Mutely the ladies indicated to each other that they did not know where in the world it had come from. It was empty except for two bars of soap and a green washcloth, which Lily was now trying to arrange in the bottom.

AS: Go on and tell us what you're doing, Lily.

L: Packing, silly.

AS: Where are you going?

L: Going to get married, and I bet you wish you was me now,

N: said Lily. But shyness overcame her suddenly, and she popped the zinnia back into her mouth.

C: Talk to me, dear. Tell old Mrs. Carson why you want to get married.

L: No,

N: said Lily, after a moment's hestitation.

C: Well, we've thought of something that will be so much nicer. Why don't you go to Ellisville!

W: Won't that be lovely? Goodness, yes.

AS: It's a lovely place,

N: said Aimee Slocum uncertainly.

L: You've got bumps on your face,

N: said Lily.

C: Aimee, dear, you stay out of this, if you don't mind.

N: said Mrs. Carson anxiously.

C: I don't know what it is comes over Lily when you come around her.

N: Lily stared at Aimee Slocum meditatively.

C: There! Wouldn't you like to go to Ellisville now?

L: No'm.

W, C, AS: Why not?

N: All the ladies leaned down toward her in impressive astonishment.

L: 'Cause I'm goin' to get married.

W: Well, and who are you going to marry, dear?

N: asked Mrs. Watts. She knew how to pin people down and make them deny what they'd already said. Lily bit her lip and began to smile. She reached into the trunk and held up both cakes of soap and wagged them.

W: Tell us,

N: challenged Mrs. Watts.

W: Who you're going to marry, now.

L: A man last night.

N: There was a gasp from each lady. The possible reality of a lover descended suddenly like a summer hail over their heads. Mrs. Watts stood up and balanced herself.

W: One of those show fellows! A musician!

N: she cried. Lily looked up in admiration.

W: Did he—did he do anything to you?

N: In the long run, it was still only Mrs. Watts who could take charge.

L: Oh, yes'm.

N: said Lily. She patted the cakes of soap fastidiously with the tips of her small fingers and tucked them in with the washcloth.

AS: What?

N: demanded Aimee Slocum rising up and tottering before her scream.

AS: What?

C: Don't ask her what. Tell me, Lily—just yes or no—are you the same as you were?

L: He had a red coat,

N: said Lily graciously.

L: He took little sticks and went *ping pong! ding-dong!*

AS: Oh, I think I'm going to faint,

N: said Aimee Slocum, but they said,

W,C: No, you're not.

W: The xylophone! The xylophone player! Why, the coward, he ought to be run out of town on a rail!

AS: Out of town? He is out of town, by now,

N: cried Aimee.

AS: Can't you read?—the sign in the cafe—Victory on the ninth, Como on the tenth? He's in Como. Como!

W: All right! We'll bring him back! He can't get away from me!

C: Hush. I don't think it's any use following that line of reasoning at all. It's better in the long run for him to be gone out of our lives for good and all. That kind of a man. He was after Lily's body alone and he wouldn't ever in this world make the poor little thing happy, even if we went out and forced him to marry her like he ought—at the point of a gun.

AS: Still—

N: began Aimee, her eyes widening.

W: Shut up. Mrs. Carson, you're right, I expect.

L: This is my hope chest—see?

N: said Lily politely in the pause that followed.

L: You haven't even looked at it. I've already got soap and a washrag. And I have my hat—on. What are you all going to give me?

W: Lily,

N: said Mrs. Watts, starting over.

W: We'll give you lots of gorgeous things if you'll only go to Ellisville instead of getting married.

L: What will you give me?

C: I'll give you a pair of hemstitched pillowcases.

W: I'll give you a big caramel cake.

AS: I'll give you a souvenir from Jackson—a little toy bank. Now will you go?

L: No.

C: I'll give you a pretty little Bible with your name on it in real gold.

W: What if I was to give you a pink crepe de Chine brassiere with adjustable shoulder straps?

N: asked Mrs. Watts grimly.

C: Oh, Etta.

W: Well, she needs it. What would they think if she ran all over Ellisville in a petticoat looking like a Fiji?

AS: I wish *I* could go to Ellisville,

N: said Aimee Slocum luringly.

L: What will they have for me down there?

N: asked Lily softly.

C: Oh! lots of things. You'll have baskets to weave, I expect . . .

N: Mrs. Carson looked vaguely at the others.

W: Oh, yes indeed, they will let you make all sorts of baskets,

N: said Mrs. Watts; then her voice too trailed off.

L: No'm, I'd rather get married.

W: Lily Daw! Now that's just plain stubbornness! You almost said you'd go and then you took it back!

C: We've all asked God, Lily,

N: said Mrs. Carson, finally,

C: and God seemed to tell us—Mr. Carson, too—that the place where you ought to be, so as to be happy, was Ellisville.

AS: We've really just got to get her there—now!

N: screamed Aimee Slocum all at once.

AS: Suppose—! She can't stay here!

C: Oh, no, no, no,

N: said Mrs. Carson hurriedly.

C: We mustn't think that.

N: They sat sunken in despair.

L: Could I take my hope chest—to go to Ellisville?

N: asked Lily shyly, looking at them sidewise.

C: Why, yes,

N: said Mrs. Carson blankly. Silently they rose once more to their feet.

L: Of, if I could just take my hope chest!

AS: All the time it was just her hope chest,

N: Aimee whispered. Mrs. Watts struck her palms together.

W: It's settled!

C: Praise the fathers,

N: murmured Mrs. Carson. Lily looked up at them, and her eyes gleamed. She cocked her head and spoke out in a proud imitation of someone—someone utterly unknown.

L: O.K.—Toots!

N: The ladies had been nodding and smiling and backing away toward the door.

C: I think I'd better stay,

N: said Mrs. Carson, stopping in her tracks.

C: Where—where could she have learned that terrible expression?

W: Pack up. Lily Daw is leaving for Ellisville on Number One.

N: In the station the train was puffing. Nearly everyone in Victory was hanging around waiting for it to leave. The Victory Civic Band had assembled without any orders and was scattered through the crowd. Ed Newton gave false signals to start on his bass horn. A crate full of baby chickens got loose on the platform. Everybody wanted to see Lily all dressed up, but Mrs. Carson and Mrs. Watts had sneaked her onto the train from the other side of the tracks. The two ladies were going to travel as far as Jackson to help Lily change trains and be sure she went in the right direction. Lily sat between them on the plush seat with her hair combed and pinned up into a knot under a small blue hat which was Jewel's exchange for the pretty one. She wore a traveling dress made out of part of Mrs. Watt's last summer's mourning. Pink straps glowed through. She had a purse and a Bible and a warm cake in a box, all in her lap. Aimee Slocum had been getting the outgoing mail stamped and bundled. She stood in the aisle of the coach now, tears shaking from her eyes.

AS: Good-bye, Lily,

N: she said. She was the one who felt things.

L: Good-bye, silly.

AS: Oh, dear, I hope they get our telegram to meet her in Ellisville,

N: Aimee cried sorrowfully, as she thought how far away it was.

AS: And it was so hard to get it all in ten words, too.

W: Get off, Aimee, before the train starts and you break your neck,

N: said Mrs. Watts, all settled and waving her dressy fan gaily.

W: I declare, it's so hot, as soon as we get a few miles out of town I'm going to slip my corset down.

AS: Oh, Lily, don't cry down there. Just be good, and do what they tell you—it's all because they love you.

N: Aimee drew her mouth down. She was backing away, down the aisle. Lily laughed. She pointed across Mrs. Carson's bosom out the window toward a man. He had stepped off the train and just stood there, by himself. He was a stranger and wore a cap.

L: Look,

N: she said, laughing softly through her fingers.

C: Don't—look,

N: said Mrs. Carson very distinctly, as if, out of all she had ever spoken, she would impress these two solemn words upon Lily's soft little brain. She added,

C: Don't look at anything till you get to Ellisville.

N: Outside, Aimee Slocum was crying so hard she almost ran into the stranger. He wore a cap and was short and seemed to have on perfume if such a thing could be.

M: Could you tell me, madam, where a little lady lives in this burg name of Miss Lily Daw?

N: He lifted his cap—and he had red hair.

AS: What do you want to know for?

N: Aimee asked before she knew it.

M: Talk louder.

N: said the stranger. He almost whispered, himself.

AS: She's gone away—she's gone to Ellisville!

M: Gone?

AS: Gone to Ellisville!

M: Well, I like that!

N: The man stuck out his bottom lip and puffed till his hair jumped.

AS: What business did you have with Lily?

N: cried Aimee suddenly.

M: We was only going to get married, that's all.

N: Aimee Slocum started to scream in front of all those people. She almost pointed to the long black box she saw lying on the ground at the man's feet. Then she jumped back in fright.

AS: The xylophone! The xylophone!

N: she cried, looking back and forth from the man to the hissing train. Which was more terrible? The bell began to ring hollowly, and the man was talking.

M: Did you say Ellisville? That in the state of Mississippi?

N: Like lightning he had pulled out a red notebook entitled, "Permanent Facts & Data." He wrote down something.

M: I don't hear well.

N: Aimee nodded her head up and down, and circled around him. Under "Ellis-ville Miss" he was drawing a line; now he was flicking it with two little marks.

M: Maybe she didn't say she would. Maybe she said she wouldn't.

N: He suddenly laughed very loudly, after the way he had whispered. Aimee jumped back.

M: Women!—Well, if we play anywheres near Ellisville, Miss., in the future I may look her up and I may not,

N: he said. The brass horn sounded the true signal for the band to begin. White steam rushed out of the engine. Usually the train stopped for only a minute in Victory, but the engineer knew Lily from waving at her, and he knew this was her big day.

AS: Wait!

N: Aimee Slocum did scream.

AS: Wait, mister! I can get her for you. Wait, Mister Engineer! Don't go!

N: Then there she was back on the train, screaming in Mrs. Carson's and Mrs. Watt's faces.

AS: The xylophone player! The xylophone player to marry her! Yonder he is!

W: Nonsense,

N: murmured Mrs. Watts, peering over the others to look where Aimee pointed.

W: If he's there I don't see him. Where is he? You're looking at One-Eye Beasley.

AS: The little man with the cap—no, with the red hair! Hurry!

C: Is that really him?

N: Mrs. Carson asked Mrs. Watts in wonder.

C: Mercy! He's small, isn't he?

W: Never saw him before in my life!

N: cried Mrs. Watts. But suddenly she shut up her fan.

AS: Come on! This is a train we're on!

N: cried Aimee Slocum. Her nerves were all unstrung.

W: All right, don't have a conniption fit, girl. Come on,

N: she said thickly to Mrs. Carson.

L: Where are we going now?

N: asked Lily as they struggled down the aisle.

W: We're taking you to get married. Mrs. Carson, you'd better phone up your husband right there in the station.

L: But I don't want to git married,

N: said Lily, beginning to whimper.

L: I'm going to Ellisville.

C: Hush, and we'll all have some ice-cream cones later,

N: whispered Mrs. Carson. Just as they climbed down the steps at the back end of the train, the band went into "Independence March." The xylophone player was still there, patting his foot. He came up and said,

M: Hello, Toots. What's up—tricks?

N: and kissed Lily with a smack, after which she hung her head.

W: So you're the young man we've heard so much about,

N: said Mrs. Watts. Her smile was brilliant.

W: Here's your little Lily.

M: What say?

C: My husband happens to be the Baptist preacher of Victory,

N: said Mrs. Carson in a loud, clear voice.

C: Isn't that lucky? I can get him here in five minutes: I know exactly where he is. They were in a circle around the xylophone player, all going into the white waiting room.

AS: Oh, I feel just like crying, at a time like this,

N: said Aimee Slocum. She looked back and saw the train moving slowly away, going under the bridge at Main Street. Then it disappeared around the curve.

AS: Oh, the hope chest!

N: Aimee cried in a stricken voice.

W: And whom have we the pleasure of addressing?

N: Mrs. Watts was shouting, while Mrs. Carson was ringing up the telephone. Some of the people thought Lily was on the train, and some swore she wasn't. Everybody cheered, though, and a straw hat was thrown into the telephone wires.

Miss Kindergarten America*

by Carol Schacter

Adapted and Directed by Ron Pelias and Mary Vance
University of Illinois at Urbana

PRODUCTION CONCEPT

We hoped to achieve three aims with the production: (1) demonstrate the two con-

*Script reprinted by permission of Martin Levin and Saturday Review, Inc. for "Miss Kindergarten America," by Carol Schacter from *"Phoenix Nest,"* *Saturday Review*, Feb. 8, 1964. © 1964 by Saturday Review, Inc.

flicting aspects of Miss Kindergarten—her absurdist "adult" sphere, and her typical childhood world; (2) illustrate the narrator's control of, and basically sarcastic attitude toward, the situation; and (3) illustrate the humor of the piece to an audience and suggest that they are also the target of the satire.

MISS KINDERGARTEN AMERICA

Cast of Characters

N: Narrator
MK: Miss Kindergarten

N: Miss Kindergarten America of 1984 hitched up her garters and teetered back to her hotel room overlooking the boardwalk. She was a very small beauty queen and it had been a tiring day.

MK: The most exciting day of her whole life. She had done it! She had won the title and next year

N: Mommy promised

MK: she could enter the preliminaries for the Miss Pre-Sub Teen America pageant. Oh, Mommy was so happy!

N: Oh, Mommy was so happy!
As soon as she closed her door, she stepped out of her high heels and ripped off her girdle.

MK: Gee, that felt good! Standing all afternoon at the Coketail press party had been awful.

N: She undressed and stood at the mirror, looking at her figure. When she had reached the semifinals, she had stopped eating cookies and icecream and started smoking. Then she had really lost a lot of weight.

MK: Daddy called it "baby fat" and said leave it alone, but Mommy said after all, the child *is* five and it's about time she thought about her shape.

N: (She didn't really like the taste of cigarettes too much, but ever since the sixth graders got their own smoking lounge at school, all the younger kids sneaked a few drags at recess, hiding under the slide. And then it got to be a habit.) She carefully removed her makeup with Big Idea Moisturizing Cleanser, slapped on some Big Idea Skin Freshener and Big Idea Hormone Night Cream. She considered not setting her hair but knew it was hopeless.

MK: Her perm was going out and this morning Kenneth had teased her hair so much

N: (to make it look natural)

MK: she knew it would collapse overnight. Maybe she'd run in for a comb-out after breakfast.

N: A half hour later all the rollers were in place and she rubbed her aching arms. She laid out her dress for the next day's festivities—a stunning little nothing from Saks, all shape and line.

MK: She'd be able to wear it to the PTA first-grade dancing classes next year, so $89.95 wasn't really expensive.

N: Even Mommy had said it was a thoughtful investment. She set her clock-TV for 6:30 and tucked in her doll family for the night. Santa Claus had brought her the whole set last Christmas. It came in a big box with three double beds and a new educational toy, "The Mating Game."

MK: There was Grandma Barbie and Grandpa Ken and Daughter Sally and Son-in-Law Rob and their daughter Lolly and her boyfriend Tom. Sally came equipped with snap-on bosoms and snap-on tummies and a yummy wardrobe of maternity clothes so you could pretend she was in all different "months."

N: She got under the covers and lay on her side, her arms and legs curled up under her chin.

MK: The rollers hurt like anything. She thought how nice it would be to go home and see Daddy. She really hadn't spent much time with him since Tabitha Carleton's fifth-birthday coming-out party. Ever since that night, she'd been busy working for the title. The party had been lots of fun but, gee, what a mess after those third-grade boys crashed it and spiked all the Cokes.

N: All those broken windows and doll furniture thrown all over the beach. . . . But, still, it was the publicity that had started her on the road to the crown. Mommy took her straight to the modeling agency in New York, and she hadn't been so busy since she was three and a cheerleader for the Little Punks Tiny Football League.

MK: Now here she was, at last, Miss Kindergarten America.

N: She tried and tried to find a comfortable position, but something didn't feel quite right. Something was missing. Then she remembered.

MK: Oh good!

N: With her mangy teddy bear, cuddled fiercely in her arms, she fell sound asleep.

The Nineteenth Great American Laugh

Compiled and Directed by Josephine Moran
University of Houston

PRODUCTION CONCEPT

An anthology of nineteenth-century American humor seemed an appropriate way to celebrate the Bicentennial of the Republic. Yet because the past is in constant need of understanding, this script does not depend upon anniversaries. The two-fold purpose is: (1) to underscore laughter as a salutary vehicle in interpreting and meeting the problems of human behavior; and (2) to heighten the consciousness of our past as a prologue to the present in which challenges and afflictions contain the seeds of laughter.

Selected Bibliography

ASWELL, JAMES R., ed. *Native American Humor.* New York: Harper & Brothers, 1947.

AULT, PHILIP H., ed. *The Home Book of Western Humor.* New York: Dodd, Mead & Co., 1967.

BLAIR, WALTER. *Native American Humor.* San Francisco: Chandler Publishing Co., 1960.

BOATRIGHT, MODY C. *Folk Laughter on the American Frontier.* New York: Macmillan, 1949.

BROWNE, CHARLES FARRAR. *Complete Works of Artemus Ward.* New York: G. W. Dillingham Company, 1898.

BRUERE, MARTHA BENSLEY, and BEARD, MARY RITTER, eds. *Laughing Their Way.* New York: Macmillan, 1934.

COHEN, HENNING and DILLINGHAM, WILLIAM B., eds. *Humor of the Old Southwest.* New York: Houghton Mifflin Company, 1964.

CONROY, JACK, ed. *Midland Humor*. New York: Harper & Brothers, 1947.

DUNNE, FINLEY PETER. *Mr. Dooley at His Best*. New York: Charles Scribner's Sons, 1938.

FRENCH, JOSEPH LEWIS, ed. *Sixty Years of American Humor*. Boston: Little, Brown and Company, 1928.

HUDSON, ARTHUR PALMER. *Humor of the Old Deep South*. New York: Macmillan, 1930.

LARSON, T. A., ed. *Bill Nye's Western Humor*. Lincoln: University of Nebraska Press, 1968.

SHAW, HENRY W. *Complete Works of Josh Billings*. New York: M. S. Donahue & Co., 1919.

WEBER, BROM, ed. *An Anthology of American Humor*. New York: Thomas Y. Crowell, 1962.

WILT, NAPIER. *Some American Humorists*. New York: Johnson Reprint Corp., 1970.

THE NINETEENTH GREAT AMERICAN LAUGH

Cast of Characters

N:	Narrator	**MF:**	Mrs. Flint
R1-5:	Five readers	**WT:**	Widow Tompkins
Y:	Yorker	**WS:**	Widow Stokes
J:	Jonathan	**BN:**	Bill Ney
S:	Sam Slick	**SA:**	Samantha Allen
D:	Deacon	**JB:**	Josh Billings

(Six readers enter single file dressed in basic costume from off stage. The Narrator moves downstage center to face the audience as the other five readers stand in front of their stools, which have been placed in a wide semi-circle. The properties have been placed previously on shelves under the stools.)

N: Of all the sorts of writing which have flourished in these United States our native humor has been the one enjoyed by most kinds of people. In the early days you could probably say that folks paid as much attention to the salty sayings in their almanacs as they paid to the Bible. For instance, "If you'd lose a troublesome visitor, lend him money."

R1-5: *(Each reader takes one line in sequence around the circle and sits after the line.)*
"Three may keep a secret, if two of them are dead."
"Mary's mouth costs her nothing, for she never opens it but at others expense."
"If your head is wax, don't walk in the sun."
"Better slip with the foot than the tongue."
"Keep your eyes wide open before marriage and half shut afterwards."

N: What is native American humor? The simplest equation is "horse-sense" plus the "horse-laugh." In our general way of thinking, of course, horse-sense is the same as common sense or gumption. It means you don't have to look in a book to find the answers. Naturally Americans didn't invent common sense; but when you add to it the racy sort of humor that comes from people constantly on the move in new frontiers, you get a horse-sense laugh.

I

The authors we're bringing you reveal some home-grown laughter in different regions, in changing times, and show us—to quote a nineteenth-century writer—"our blessed American faith in the sufficiency of born gumption." We're going to skip over the well-known names such as Davy Crocket and Mark Twain and dip into short stories and yarns of writers immensely popular in their own day but not so well known to us now. The first two stories come from New England, and are examples of "Down-East Humor."

Episode 1   "Green Mountain Boy"

Narrator takes a position downstage right. Yorker ambles to position right of center and pantomimes throwing stones directly front.

N: On the banks of the Hudson River a bunch of village loafers were standing seeing who could throw stones the farthest into the stream. *(Jonathan shuffles to position left of center.)* A tall, rawboned, slabsided Yankee, and no mistake, came up and looked on. For awhile he said nothing til a Yorker in a tight jacket began to try his wit on Jonathan. He hurled a stone away out into the river.

Y: You can't beat that.

J: Mebbe not. But up in Vermont in the Green Mountains we have a pretty big river, considerin', and t'other day I hove a man clear across it and he come down fair and squar on t'other side.

N: The onlookers yelled in derision. *(The other three readers, as onlookers, shout and laugh.)*

J: Well now, you may laugh but I kin do it again.

Y: Do what?

J: I kin take an' heave you acrost that river yonder jest open and shut.

Y: Bet you ten dollars on it!

J: Done!

N: So Jonathan drew forth a ten note which covered the Yorker's shinplaster.

J: Can you swim, feller?

Y: Like a duck.

N: Without further parley, the Vermonter seized the Yorker by the nape of the neck and the basement of his pants, and dashed him heels over head into the Hudson! *(Onlookers shout with laughter.)* A shout ran through the crowd as he floundered in the cold water. *(Jonathan pantomimes throwing the Yorker as the Yorker pantomimes being thrown forward and falling on his knees.)* He put back to shore and scrambled up the bank. *(Yorker pantomimes pulling himself up to his feet again.)*

Y: I'll take that ten spot if you please. You took us for greenhorns, eh? We'll show you how to do things down here in York.

J: Well, I reckon you won't take no ten spot jest yet, cap'n.

Y: Why? You lost the bet.

J: Not 'xactly. I didn't wager to do it the first time. Jest said I could do it and I tell you I can.

N: Jonathan seized the loafer by the scuff and seat and pitched him farther into the river than upon the first trial. Again the Yorker floundered back through the icy water. *(Repeat the previous pantomime.)*

J: *Third* time never fails. I can do it I tell you—*(Pantomimes preparing to grab the Yorker again.)*

Y: *(Shaking with cold.)* Ho-old on!

J: And I will do it—if I try till tomorrow mornin' *(Crowd laughter.)*

Y: I-I-I give up! T-take the m-m-money!

J: Oh, well—if that's the way it's done in York State.

N: And Jonathan pocketed the money and coolly turned away. *(Readers return to their stools.)*

Episode 2 *"Soft Sawder and Human Natur"*

Narrator takes position downstage right, with Sam Slick standing on his left.

N: "How is it," said I to Sam Slick, "that you manage to sell such an immense number of clocks, which certainly can't be called necessary articles, among people with whom there seems to be so great a scarcity of money?"

S: Well I don't care if I do tell you, for the market is glutted and I shall quit this circuit. It's done by a knowledge of soft sawder an' human natur'. *(Pointing and moving to center.)* Here's Deacon Flint. I've got but one clock left and I guess I'll sell it to him.

N: At the gate of a most comfortable looking farmhouse stood Deacon Flint, *(Deacon moves haltingly to position left of center)* a respectable old man who had understood the value of time better than most of his neighbors to judge by the appearance of the place. After the usual salutation *(both men nod)* an invitation to alight was accepted by Sam. We had hardly entered the house when Sam said—

S: *(Pointing out window)* If I was to tell them down in Connecticut that there was such a farm as this away down east here they wouldn't believe me. Why there ain't such a location in all New England. The water privilege alone must be worth three thousand dollars—twice as much as Governor Case paid fifteen hundred dollars for. I wonder, Deacon, you don't put up a cardin' mill on it and a turnin' lathe, a shingle machine, a circular saw—

D: Too old—too old for all these speculations.

S: Old? Not you! Why you're worth half dozen of the young men we see nowadays. You're young enough to—*(moves closer and cups his hand over his mouth to whisper to Deacon).*

N: Here he said something in a lower tone of voice which I did not distinctly hear, but whatever it was the Deacon was pleased. *(Both men snicker.)*

D: *(Guffawing)* Well I do not think of such things now. But your horses, your horses must be put in and have a feed. *(Turns back to audience.)*

N: As the old gentleman closed the door after him, Sam drew near to me and said in an undertone—*(Sam moves back to Narrator.)*

S: That's what I call soft sawder.

N: He was cut short by the entrance of Mrs. Flint. *(Mrs. Flint moves to position right of the Deacon.)*

S: *(Moves to center, on right of Mrs. Flint.)* Just come to say goodbye, Mrs. Flint.

MF: What? Have you sold all your clocks?

S: Yes and very low too. Money is scarce and I wished to close the concern. But I'm wrong in saying all, for I have just one left. Neighbor Steel's wife asked to have the refusal of it but I guess I won't sell it. I had but two of 'em, this one and the feller of it, that I sold to Governor Lincoln . . . give me fifty dollars for it. It has composition wheels and patent axles. A beautiful article, a real first chop and no mistake, genuine superfine. But I guess I'll take it back.

MF: Dear me, I should like to see it. Where is it?

N: Sam Slick, willing to oblige, produced the clock—a gaudy, highly varnished trumpery affair. He placed it on the chimney piece *(Sam pantomimes placing the clock)* where its beauties were pointed out and duly appreciated by Mrs. Flint, who was about to make a proposal when Deacon Flint returned. *(Deacon turns to face audience again.)* He too, praised the clock.

D: It is indeed a handsome one. But I have a watch. I am sorry, but I can see no occasion for a clock.

S: I guess you're in the wrong furrow this time Deacon. It ain't for sale. And if it was I reckon Neighbor Steel's wife would have the refusal of it for she gives me no peace about it.

MF: Mr. Steel has enough to do, poor man, to pay his interest without buying clocks for his wife!

S: It's no concern of mine what he has to do as long as he pays me. But I guess I don't want to sell it. And besides it comes too high. That clock couldn't be made at Rhode Island under forty dollars. *(Looking at pocket watch.)* Why as I'm alive it's four o'clock and how on earth shall I reach River Philip tonight! I tell you what, Mrs. Flint. I'll leave the clock in your care until I return. I'll set it a-goin' and put it to the right time.

N: As soon as this operation was performed he delivered the key to the Deacon, telling him to wind it up every Saturday night. *(Sam pantomimes business with the key. Deacon and Mrs. Flint turn backs to audience. Sam moves to left of Narrator.)* When we were mounted and on our way Sam said—

S: That's what I call human natur'. Now that clock is sold for forty dollars. It cost me jest six dollars and fifty cents. Mrs. Flint will never let Mrs. Steel have the refusal nor will the Deacon learn until I call for the clock how hard it is to give it up. . . . We can do without any article of luxury we never had but once we've had it, it's not in human natur' to surrender it voluntarily. Of fifteen thousand sold by myself and my partners in this state, twelve thousand were left in this manner. And only ten clocks were ever returned when we came back around. You see we trust to soft sawder to get the clocks *in* the house and to human natur' that they never come *out* of it. *(Readers return to stools.)*

II

N: Another flourishing area of native humor was known as the Old Southwest, which then included the state of Georgia on the Atlantic seaboard and all the states over to Louisiana and Arkansas. The ways of living differed greatly among the inhabitants, for there were various stages of settled communities separated by long stretches of frontier. People were eternally swapping stories—in stage coaches and riverboats, in taverns and courthouses. So the tradition of oral storytelling thus had a great influence on the literature that found its way into print.

Episode 3 "Taking the Census"

N: *(Moving to downstage right.)* The Census Law of 1840 called for the collection of statistical information concerning the resources and industry of the country over and above the counting of noses. But the popular impression of this investigation caused the censustaker to be viewed in the light of a tax collector. I rode up one day to the house of a widow rather past the prime of life—just the period at which nature supplies most abundantly the oil which lubricates the female tongue—*(Widow Tompkins stands and moves a few paces downstage toward center)*—and hitching my horse to the fence, walked to the house. . . . Good morning, mam. *(Narrator towards Widow Tompkins, staying right of center.)*

WT: Mornin'.

N: I'm the man, madam, that takes the census, and—

WT: The mischief you are! Yes I've hearn of you! Parson Williams told me you was comin' and I told him jist what I'll tell you—that I'd set the dogs on ye! Here, Bull! Here, Pomp!

N: Two wolfish curs responded by smelling at my feet with a slight growl, and then laid down on the steps.

WT: Now them's the severest dogs in this county. If I was to sic 'em on your old hoss yonder, they'd eat him up afore you could say Jack Roberson. And it's jist what I shall do if ye try to pry into my consarns. They're none of your business nor Van Buren's neither! Sendin' men to take down that little stuff people's got jist to tax it when its taxed enuff already!

N: When she paused I remarked that if she was determined not to answer the questions about the produce of the farm, we would just set down the age, sex, and complexion of each member of her family.

WT: You'll do no sich thing! I've got five in my family and they're all between five and a hundred years. They are all a plaguey sight whiter than you!

N: I told her I would report her to the U.S. Marhsall and she would be fined, but it only augmented her wrath.

WT: Yes you do that! Send your marshall, or your president, Mr. Van Buren down here! I'd cut his head off!

N: That might kill him.

WT: I don't care if it did. A pretty feller like that to be eatin' his vittles out of gold spoons, and raisin' an army to git hisself made king of Ameriky! That outdacious, nasty, stinking old scamp! Now lessen here, mister, don't you be sendin' no lies 'bout me to Washington City. Just put down Judy Tompkins, *ageable woman and four children! (Whirls around and returns to her stool.)*

N: And, perforce, that is how the entry had to be made in the census of 1840. . . . My next encounter was with an old lady who lived nearby and seemed more than anxious to help us in our undertaking. *(Widow Stokes pulls her stool down into center area.)* Striding into the cabin and taking out my papers, I said, "Taking the Census Mam."

WS: Ah, well! Bless your soul, honey, take a seat. Now do! *(Narrator pulls stool toward the right of Widow Stokes.)* Are you the gentleman that Mr. Van Buren has sent out? Well, good Lord look down, how *was* Mr. Van Buren and family when you seen him last?

N: I explained that I had never seen the president and that I had been *written to* to take the census.

WS: Well, now, *that* agin! Lord love your soul. I suppose thar's mighty little here to take down. Times is hard, God's will be done, and it looks like people can't git their jist rights in this country. The law is all for the rich and none for the poor. *(She is not accusing him, just gossiping.)*

N: Here I interposed that I wished to take down the members of her family and produce raised last year and be off. "How many yards of cotton cloth did you weave in 1840, mam?"

WS: Well, now! The Lord have mercy, less see! You know Sally Higgins that used to live in the Smith Settlement? Poor thing, her daddy druv her off, on account of her havin' a little baby. Poor gal, she couldn't help it, I dare say. Well, Sally, she came to stay with me, and she was a powerful good hand to weave, and I *did* think she'd help me a power. Well, after she'd been here awhile her baby it tuck sick, and old Miss Stringer, she undertuck to help it. She is a powerful good hand, Ole Miss Stringer, on yerbs and sich like. Well, the Lord look down from above! She made a sort of tea and give it to Sally's baby, but it got wuss—the poor creature—and she *give* it tea and she *give* it tea and looked like the more tea she *give* it, the more—

N: My dear madam, I am in a hurry. Please tell me how many yards of cotton cloth you wove in 1840?

WS: *(Retains cheerful attitude.)* Well, the Lord-a-mercy! Who'd a-thought you'd a been so snappish. Well, as I was a-sayin' the baby got wurse, and old Miss Stringer, who kept a-givin' it the yerb tea, till at last the child it looked like to *would* die anyhow. And bout the time the child was at its wurst old Daddy Sykes he came along. And he said if we'd git some nightshed berries and stew 'em with a little cream and hog's lard—now old Daddy Sykes is a mighty fine man and when my boys had that case in court, he give 'em a heap of mighty good counsel—

N: In God's name, tell about your cloth, and let the sick child and Miss Stringer and Daddy Sykes go to the—

WS: *(Surprised but still consoling.)* Gracious bless your dear soul! Now, don't get aggravated. I was jist a-tellin' you how it come I didn't weave no cloth last year.

N: Oh—well. You didn't weave *any* cloth last year. We'll go on to the next article.

WS: Yes. You see, the child, it begun to swell and turn yaller, and it kept a wallin' its eyes and a moanin' and I *knowed*—

N: Never mind about the child. Just tell me the value of the poultry you raised last year.

WS: Oh—yes—the chickens, you mean. Why, the Lord love your poor soul, the *owls* destroyed in and about the best half that I did raise. Every blessed night the Lord sent they'd come and set on the comb of the house and hoo-hoo-o-hoo-o-o-o! And one night pertiklar, I remember, I had jist got up to git the nightshed salve to rub Sally Higgenses' ailin' little gal with—

N: *(Exhausted.)* Madam, I am very tired and would beg you to answer directly and without any circumlocution.

WS: The Lord love your dear heart, honey, I'm a-tellin' you as fast as I can. The owls they got wuss *and* wuss, so Bryant—that's one of my boys—he 'lowed he'd shoot the pestersome critters. And so one night after that, we hearn one holler, and Bryant he tuck the old musket and went out and sure enough, there was *owley*, as *he* thought, a-settin' on the comb of the house. *(Pantomines shooting the rifle.)* So he blazes away and down come—what on earth *did* come down, do you reckon, when Bryant fired?

N: The owl, I suppose.

WS: No sich a thing, no sich! The owl *warn't there*! 'Twas my old house cat come a-tumblin' down, a-spittin', sputterin', and a-scratchin' and the fur a-flyin' every time she jumped! Like you'd a-busted a feather bed open. Bryant said the way he come to shoot the cat instead of the owl *(pantomimes rifle again)*, he seed somethin' white and—

N: *(Stands).* For heaven's sake, Mrs. Stokes, give me the value of your poultry or say you will not. Do one thing or the other!

WS: Oh, well, dear Lord love your soul, I reckon I had last year nigh about the same as I've got this. I'll let you see for yourself. *(She stands and pantomimes the following action.)*

N: And she took an ear of corn out of a crack between the logs of the cabin and began shelling off a handfull, scattering the grain on the floor, all the while screaming—

WS: Here chick-a-chick-chick-chick-chickee—here chick-chick-a-chick . . .

N: Here they came, roosters and hens, pullets and chicks, and the old lady seemed delighted thus to exhibit her feathered stock—

WS: A nice passel, ain't they? A mighty nice passel! *(She turns her back to the audience as she continues pantomime of feeding chickens until Narrator concludes.)*

N: But she never would say what they were wroth. And so our papers at Washington contain no estimate of the value of Mrs. Stokes poultry—though as she said herself, she had a "mighty nice passel." *(Returns to his stool.)*

III

N: The Literary Comedians were a group of writers who appeared just prior to the Civil War and continued until the end of the century. They were men of wide experience and had in common an association with newspapers—whether as editors, reporters, or journeyman printers. Most of them wrote in the guise of comic characters; and after achieving popularity in print many of them took to the lecture circuit, presenting their characters from the platform.

Episode 4   "A Resignation"

BN: *(Moves front and center.)* Post office Divan, Laramie City, Wyoming Territory, October 1883. To the President of the United States. Sir: I beg leave at this time to officially tender my resignation as postmaster at this place and in due form to deliver the great seal and the key to the front door. The safe combination is set on the numbers 33, 66, and 99 though I do not remember which comes first, or how many times you revolve the knob to make it operate. You will find the postal cards that have not been used under the distributing table, and the coal down in the cellar. If the stove draws too much, close the damper in the pipe and shut the General Delivery Window. Mr. President, I cannot close this letter without thanking yourself and the heads of departments at Washington for your active, cheery, and prompt cooperation. But now we must separate. Here the roads seem to fork and you and I and the cabinet must leave each other. You had better turn the cat out at night. If she does not go readily, you can make it clearer by throwing the cancelling stamp at her. Once more I become a private citizen, clothed only with the right to read such postal cards as may be addressed to me personally. And to curse the inefficiency of the post office department. Sincerely yours, Bill Nye. *(Returns to his stool)*

Episode 5   "My Opinions and Betsey Bobbet's"

SA: *(Moves front and center.)* In the first days of our married life, I strained nearly every nerve to help my husband Josiah along and take care of his children by his former consort. But as we prospered and the mortgage was cleared, a voice kept a-sayin' inside me, "Josiah Allen's wife, write your views on the great subject of Wimmin's Rites." Now, take Betsey Bobbet, a neighborin' female of ourn. Betsey hain't married and she is awful opposed to wimmin's rites. She thinks it is wimmin's only sphere to marry—which makes it hard and wearin' on the single men around here. Well, one day I had a fortnite's washin' to do, the house to clean up, churnin' to do, and bakin', and then I had a batch of maple sugar to do off, for the trees had begun to run—and well doth the poet say 'that a woman never gets her work done up' for she don't. An' Betsey Bobbet come to spend the day. Says she, "I have always felt that it was woman's only mission to cling, to smile, to coo, to soothe lacerations, to be a sort of poultice to the noble, manly breast when it is torn with the cares of life." This was too much in the agitated frame of mind I then was. "Am I a poultice, Betsey Bobbet? What has my sex done that they have got to be lacerator soothers, when they got everythin' else under the sun to do!" Here I stirred down the preserves that was a-runnin' over with one hand and removed a cake from the oven with the other. "An' if men have got to be soothed," says I, "they might jest as well be soothin' each other, as to be hangin' round grocery stores, or settin' by the fire whittlin'." Now some weeks later, the Methodist minister went home with us to supper. He was a widower, an' awful opposed to wimmin havin' any rights—only the right to marry. So that day I put it fair and square to him. Says I, "Elder, how can a woman marry without a man is forthcomin'? An' if a man is obstinate and hangs back, what's she to do?" He began to look a little sheepish and kinder tried to turn off the subject onto religion. But I fixed my eyes on him with seemin'ly an arrow in each one, and says, "which had you rather do, Elder, let Betsy Bobbet vote or cling to you? She is fairly achin' to make a runnin' vine of herself, and" says I, "are you willin' to be a tree?" *(Returns to her stool.)*

Episode 6 "Josh Billings"

JB: *(Comes down to center front.)* I kum to the conclusion lately that life was so unsartin that the only way for me to stand a fair change with other folks was to git my life insured. So I called on the Agent of the Garden Angel Life Insurance Co. and answered the following questions: 1. Are you male or female? If so, please state how long you have been so. 2. Are you subject to fits, and if so do you have more than one at a time. 3. Did you ever have any ancestors, and if so how much. 4. Do you believe in a future state? If you do, state it. 5. Have you ever committed suicide, and if so how did it seem to affect you. After answering the above questions, the agent said I was insured for life and probably would remain so for a term of years. I thanked him and smiled one of my most pensive smiles.

    So many folks write in wantin' my meditations, I thot I'd give you a few of 'em right now. First, on Politics . . . *(returns to his stool)*

R6: A man runnin' fer orfice puts me in mind of a dog that's lost—he smells of everybody he meets and wags hisself all over.

R1: To be a successful politician, a man shud be buttered on both sides then keep away from the fire.

R2: I argy this way—if a man is right he can't be too radikul. If he is rong, he kant be too conservatiff.

JB: On Women . . .

R1: Adam invented "luv at first sight," which is one of the greatest labor-savin' mersheens the world ever saw.

R2: Why is it so many wimmin who are so thin in the face stick out so everywhar else?

R3: As a gineral thing when a woman wares the britches she has a good rite to 'em.

R4: They tell me females are so skarse in the Far West that a great many marrid wimmin are already engaged to ther secund and third husbands.

R6: If you got a real good wife, keep perfeckly still and thank God every twenty minits.

JB: On Fools . . .

R4: It's dredful easy to be a fool—a man can be one and not know it.

R3: God save the fools and don't let em run out. Fer if it wasn't for 'em wise men couldn't git a livin.

JB: Good advice . . .

R6: "Bee yee as wise as a sarpint and as harmelss as a dove." Then if a feller cums a foolin' round your dove, you kin set yer sarpint at 'em.

R3: I have heard a great deal said about broken harts, and ther may be a few. But its my experience that next to the gizzard the hart is the toughest piece o'meat in the hole critter.

JB: On Americans . . . *(During the following sequence each reader exits after his line, in an increasingly rapid tempo.)*

R1: I guess the English have more wit, and the Americans have more humor.

R6: We haven't had time yit to bile down our humor and git the wit out of it.

R5: An American loves to laugh, but he doen't make a business of it—

R2: He works, eats, and haw-haws on a gallop.

R4: If you tickle or convince an American—

R3: You have to do it quick!

The Wind in the Willows[*]

by Kenneth Grahame

Adapted and Directed by Beth Greenway
Parkview High School, Little Rock, Arkansas

PRODUCTION CONCEPT

My objective in presenting a chamber theatre production of *The Wind in the Willows* was to reenact the experiences in the book for a child audience. A chamber theatre production of this novel by Kenneth Grahame was a natural extension of the novel's origin and style. Like other popular fantasies such as *Alice in Wonderland* and *The Hobbit, The Wind in the Willows* was first told as a story to a child. Grahame's tale began in the nursery with his son, "Mouse," who interrupted occasionally to argue a point or laugh at his father's imaginings. When Grahame later wrote the story, he retained the orality of the earlier spoken version, a dimension sought to retain by utilizing the technique of chamber theatre.

A staged production would hopefully (1) preserve the natural oral composition of the novel for children to enjoy; (2) clarify the relationship of the narrator to the characters in the story and to the child audience; and (3) vivify, through action, the life experiences in the novel for the child.

I used both slides and a fast-motion film in the production. The film sequence portraying Toad's escape from Toad Hall substituted for lengthy deleted narrative sections. The film was not only a convenient capsule of the incident, but was humorous and particularly captivating for a child audience.

*The script is an adaptation of Kenneth Grahame's *The Wind in the Willows* and is reprinted by permission of Charles Scribner's Sons.

Selected Bibliography

About Kenneth Grahame

BRAYBROOKE, NEVILLE. "Kenneth Grahame 1859–1932." *Elementary English*, 36 (January 1959), 11–15.

CHALMERS, PATRICK R. *Kenneth Grahame: Life, Letters and Unpublished Work.* London: Methuen and Co. Ltd., 1933.

GREEN, PETER. *Kenneth Grahame: A Biography.* New York: The World Publishing Co., 1959.

KARL, JEAN. *From Childhood to Childhood: Children's Books and Their Creators.* New York: John Day Co., 1970.

About the Wind
in the Willows

ARBUTHNOT, MAY HILL. *Children and Books.* 3rd. ed. rev. Glenview, Ill.: Scott, Foresman & Co., 1964.

GRAHAME, ELSPETH. *First Whisper of "The Wind in the Willows."* London: Methuen & Co. Ltd., 1946.

HEDGES, NED S. "The Fable and the Fabulous: The Use of Traditional Forms in Children's Literature." Unpublished Doctor's dissertation, University of Nebraska, 1968.

"Kindly Beasts," *Time* (December 28, 1953), p. 58.

TAYLOR, S. KEITH. "Universal Themes in Kenneth Grahame's *The Wind in the Willows.*" Unpublished Doctor's dissertation, Temple University, 1968.

Scenes from *The Wind in the Willows.*
(University of Texas at Austin)

(a) Mole is "intoxicated with the sparkle, the ripple, the scents and the sounds" of the water as Rat takes him for his first ride on the river.

(b) Poor Toad thinks it's "a hard world" when Rat, Mole, and Badger refuse him one little song of praise for his glorious deeds.

(c) The hour has come for the four friends to rout the lawless Stoats and Weasels from Toad Hall.

(d) The narrator and the traveling trio catch their first "Moment's glimpse of the magnificent motor car."

THE WIND IN THE WILLOWS

Cast of Characters

B:	Badger	**MN:**	Man
C:	Clerk	**N:**	Narrator
CM:	Chief Magistrate	**O:**	Otter
E:	Engineer	**R:**	Rat
G:	Girl	**T:**	Toad
L:	Lady	**V:**	Voices
M:	Mole	**W:**	Washerwoman

Scene I

N: The Mole had been working very hard all the morning, spring-cleaning his little home. First with brooms; then with dusters; then on ladders and steps and chairs, with a brush and a pail of whitewash; till he had dust in his throat and eyes, and splashes of whitewash all over his black fur, and an aching back and weary arms. Spring was moving in the air above and was penetrating even his dark and lowly little house. It was small wonder, then, that he suddenly flung down his brush on the floor, and said,

M: Bother!

N: and

M: O blow!

N: and also

M: Hang spring-cleaning!

N: and bolted out the house without even waiting to put on his coat. Something up

331

above was calling him imperiously, and so he scraped and scratched and scrabbled and scrooged, and then he scrooged again and scrabbled and scraped and scratched, working busily with his little paws and muttering to himself,

M: Up we go! Up we go!

N: til at last, pop! His snout came out into the sunlight, and he found himself rolling in the warm grass of a great meadow.

M: This is fine! This is better than whitewashing.

N: Jumping off all his four legs at once, in the joy of living and the delight of spring without its cleaning, he pursued his way across the meadow till he reached the hedge on the further side. It all seemed too good to be true. Hither and thither through the meadows he rambled busily.

He thought his happiness was complete when suddenly he stood by the edge of a full-fed river. Never in his life had he seen a river before. It was all a-shake and a-shiver, rustle and swirl, chatter and bubble. The Mole was bewitched, entranced, fascinated.

As he sat on the grass and looked across the river, a dark hole in the bank opposite, just above the water's edge, caught his eye, and dreamily he fell to considering what a nice snug dwelling place it would make for an animal. As he gazed, something bright and small seemed to twinkle down in the heart of it, vanished then twinkled once more like a tiny star. But it could hardly be a star in such an unlikely situation. Then, as he looked, it winked at him, and so declared itself to be an eye; and a small face began gradually to grow up round it, like a frame round a picture. A brown little face, with whiskers. Small neat ears and thick silky hair. It was the Water Rat!

R: Hullo, Mole!

M: Hullo, Rat!

R: Would you like to come over?

M: Oh, it's all very well to *talk*.

N: The Rat said nothing, but stooped and unfastened a rope and hauled on it; then lightly stepped into a little boat which the Mole had not observed. It was painted blue outside and white within, and was just the size for two animals; and the Mole's whole heart went out to it at once.

R: Come Mole, hop in. Lean on that! Now then, step lively.

M: This has been a wonderful day! Do you know, I've never been in a boat before in all my life.

R: What? Never been in a—you never—well, I—what have you been doing, then?

M: Is it so nice as all that?

R: Nice? It's the only thing. Believe me, my young friend, there is *nothing*—absolutely nothing—half so much worth doing as simply messing about in boats. Simply messing, messing—about—in—boats; messing—

M: Look ahead, Rat!

N: It was too late. The boat struck the bank full tilt. The dreamer, the joyous oarsman, lay on his back at the bottom of the boat, his heels in the air.

R: —about in boats—or *with* boats. In or out of 'em, it doesn't matter. Look here! If you've really nothing else on hand this morning, suppose we drop down the river together, and have a long day of it?

M: *What* a day I'm having! Let us start at once!

R: Hold hard a minute, then! Shove that under your feet.

M: What's inside it?

R: There's cold chicken inside it, coldtonguecoldhamcoldbeefpickledgherkins saladfrenchrollscressandwidgespottedmeatgingerbeerlemonadesodawater—

M: O stop, stop. This is too much!

R: Do you really think so? It's only what I always take on these little excursions and the other animals are always telling me that I'm a mean beast and cut it *very* fine!

N: The Mole never heard a word he was saying. Absorbed in the new life he was entering upon, intoxicated with the sparkle, the ripple, the scents, and the sounds, and the sunlight, he trailed a paw in the water and dreamed long, waking dreams.

M: I beg your pardon. You must think me very rude; but all this is so new to me. So—this—is—a—River!

R: *The* river!

M: And you really live by the river? What a jolly life!

R: By it and with it and on it and in it. It's brother and sister to me, and aunts, and company, and food and drink, and (naturally) washing. What it hasn't got is not worth having, and what it doesn't know is not worth knowing. Lord! the times we've had together! Whether in winter or summer, spring or autumn, it's always full of fun and excitement.

M: What lies over *there*?

R: That? O, that's just the Wild Wood. We don't go there very much, we river-bankers.

M: Aren't they—aren't they very *nice* people in there?

R: W-e-ll, let me see. The squirrels are all right. *And* the rabbits—some of 'em, but rabbits are a mixed lot. And then there's Badger, of course. He lives right in the heart of it; wouldn't live anywhere else, either. Dear old Badger! Nobody interferes with *him*. And . . . well, of course—there—are others, Weasels—and stoats—and foxes—and so on. They're all right in a way, but you really can't trust them, and that's the fact.

N: The Mole knew well that it is quite against animal-etiquette to dwell on possible trouble ahead, or even to allude to it; so he dropped the subject.

M: And beyond the Wild Wood?

R: Beyond the Wild Wood comes the Wide World. And that's something that doesn't matter, either to you or me. I've never been there, and I'm never going, nor you either, if you've got any sense at all. Now then! Here's our backwater at last, where we're going to lunch.

N: The Rat brought the boat alongside the bank, made her fast, helped the still awkward Mole safely ashore and swung out the luncheon-basket. The Mole begged as a favor to be allowed to unpack it all by himself; and the Rat was pleased to indulge him, and to sprawl at full length on the grass and rest, while his excited friend shook out the tablecloth and spread it, took out all the mysterious packets one by one, gasping,

M: O my! O my!

R: Now, pitch in, old fellow! What are you looking at?

N: A broad glistening muzzle showed itself above the edge of the bank, and the Otter hauled himself out and shook the water from his coat.

O: Greedy beggars! Why didn't you invite me, Ratty?

R: This was an impromptu affair. By the way—my friend Mr. Mole.

O: Proud, I'm sure.

N: And the two animals were friends forthwith.

O: Such a rumpus everywhere! All the world seems out on the river to-day.

N: There was a rustle behind them, proceeding from a hedge, and a stripy head, with high shoulders behind it, peered forth on them.

R: Come on, old Badger!

B: H'm! Company!

R: That's just the sort of fellow he is! Simply hates Society! Now we shan't see any more of him today. Well, tell us *who's* out on the river?

O: Toad's out for one. In his brand new wager-boat; new togs, new everything! Such a good fellow, too. But no stability—especially in a boat.

N: From where they sat they could get a glimpse of the main stream across the island that separated them; and just then a wager-boat flashed into view, the rower—a short, stout figure—splashing badly, but working his hardest. The Rat stood up and hailed him, but Toad—for it was he—shook his head and settled sternly to his work.

R: He'll be out of the boat in a minute if he rows like that.

O: Of course he will. Did I ever tell you that good story about Toad and the lock-keeper. It happened this way. Toad . . .

N: An errant May-fly swerved unsteadily across the current. A swirl of water and a "cloop!" and the May-fly was visible no more. Neither was the Otter. The Mole looked down. The voice was still in his ears, but the turf whereon he had sprawled was clearly vacant. Not any Otter to be seen, as far as the distant horizon.

The Rat hummed a tune, and the Mole recollected that animal-etiquette forbade any sort of comment on the sudden disappearance of one's friends at any moment, for any reason or no reason whatever.

R: Well, well. I suppose we ought to be moving. I wonder which of us had better pack the luncheon-basket?

N: He did not speak as if he was frightfully eager for the treat.

M: O, please let me!

N: So, of course, the Rat let him. The afternoon sun was getting low as the Rat sculled gently homewards in a dreamy mood, murmuring poetry-things over to himself, and not paying attention to Mole. But the Mole was very full of lunch, and self-satisfaction, and pride, and already quite at home in a boat.

This day was only the first of many similar ones for the emancipated Mole, each of them longer and fuller of interest as the ripening summer moved onward. He learnt to swim and to row, and entered into the joy of running water; and with his ear to the reed-stems he caught at intervals, something of what the wind was whispering so constantly among them.

Scene II

M: Ratty,

N: said the Mole suddenly, one bright summer morning,

M: if you please, I want to ask you a favor. Won't you take me to call on Mr. Toad? I've heard so much about him, and I do so want to make his acquaintance.

R: Why, certainly. Get the boat out, and we'll paddle up there at once. It's never the wrong time to call on Toad. Early or late he's always the same fellow. Always good-tempered, always glad to see you, always sorry when you go!

M: He must be a very nice animal.

R: He is indeed the best of animals. So simple, so good-natured, and so affectionate. Perhaps he's not very clever—we can't all be geniuses; and it may be that he is both boastful and conceited. But he has got some great qualities, has Toady.

N: Rounding a bend in the river, they came in sight of a handsome, dignified old house, with well-kept lawns reaching down to the water's edge.

R: There's Toad Hall, and that creek on the left, where the notice board says, "Private. No landing allowed," leads to his boathouse, where we'll leave the boat. The stables are over there to the right. That's the banqueting-hall you're looking at now—very old, that is. Toad is rather rich, you know, and this is really one of the nicest houses in these parts, though we never admit as much to Toad.

N: They glided up the creek and the Mole shipped his sculls as they saw many handsome boats, slung from the crossbeams or hauled up on a slip, but none in the water; and the place had an unused and a deserted air.

R: Oh, I understand. Boating is played out. He's tired of it, and done with it. I wonder what new fad he has taken up now? Come along and let's look him up. We shall hear all about it quite soon enough.

N: They strolled across the gay flower-decked lawns in search of Toad, whom they presently happened upon resting in a wicker garden-chair, with a preoccupied expression of face, and a large map spread out on his knees.

T: Hooray! this is splendid! How *kind* of you! I was just going to send a boat down the river for Ratty, with strict orders that you were to be fetched up here at once, whatever you were doing. I want you badly—both of you. Now what will you take? Come inside and have something! You don't know how lucky it is, your turning up just now.

R: Let's sit quiet a bit, Toady!

M: Delightful residence!

T: Finest house on the whole river. Or anywhere else, for that matter.

N: Here the Rat nudged the Mole. Unfortunately the Toad saw him do it, and turned very red. There was a moment's painful silence. Then Toad burst out laughing,

T: All right, Ratty, it's only my way, you know. Now, look here. Let's be sensible. You are the very animals I wanted. You've got to help me. It's most important!

R: It's about your rowing, I suppose. You're getting on fairly . . .

T: O, pooh! boating! Silly boyish amusement. I've given that up long ago. Sheer waste of time, that's what it is. No, I've discovered the real thing, the only genuine occupation for a lifetime. I propose to devote the remainder of mine to it, and can only regret the wasted years, that lie behind me, squandered in trivialities. Come with me, dear Ratty, and your amiable friend also, if he will be so very good, just as far as the stableyard, and you shall see what you shall see!

N: He led the way to the stableyard accordingly, the Rat followed with a most mistrustful expression; and there, drawn out of the coach house into the open, they saw a gypsy caravan, shining with newness, painted a canary-yellow picked out with green, and red wheels.

T: There you are! There's real life for you, embodied in that little cart. The open road, the dusty highway, the heath, the rolling downs! The whole world before you! And mind, this is the very finest cart of its sort that was ever built, without any exception. And inside, all complete with biscuits, potted lobster, sardines—everything you can possibly want. You'll find that nothing whatever has been forgotten, when we make our start this afternoon.

R: I beg your pardon, but did I overhear you say something about "*we*," and "*start*," and "*this afternoon*"?

T: Now you dear good old Ratty, don't begin talking in that stiff and sniffy sort of way, because you know you've got to come. You surely don't mean to stick to your dull fusty old river all your life, and just live in a hole in a bank, and *boat*? I want to show you the world! I'm going to make an *animal* of you, my boy.

R: I don't care. I'm not coming, and that's flat. And I am going to stick to my old river, *and* live in a hole, *and* boat, as I've always done. And what's more, Mole's going to stick to me and do as I do, aren't you, Mole?

M: Of course I am. I'll always stick to you, Rat, and what you say is to be—has got to be. All the same, it sounds as if it might have been—well, rather fun, you know!

N: Poor Mole! The Life Adventurous was so new a thing to him, and so thrilling; and this fresh aspect of it was so tempting; and he had fallen in love at first sight with the canary-colored cart.

The Rat saw what was passing in his mind, and wavered. He hated disappointing people, and he was fond of the Mole, and would do almost anything to oblige him. Somehow, it soon seemed taken for granted by all three of them that the trip was a settled thing.

It was a golden afternoon when they set off, all talking at once. Out of thick orchards on either side of the road, birds called and whistled to them cheerily; good-natured wayfarers, passing them, gave them "Good day," or stopped to say nice things about their beautiful cart; and rabbits, sitting at their front doors, help up their forepaws, and said, "O, my! O my!"

At last, late in the evening, tired and happy and miles from home, they drew up on a remote common far from habitations, turned into their little bunks; and Toad, kicking out his legs, sleepily said,

T: Well, good night, you fellows! This is the real life for a gentleman! Talk about your old river!

R: I *don't* talk about my river. You *know* I don't, Toad. But I think about it—I think about it—all the time!

N: The Mole reached out from under his blanket, felt for the Rat's paw in the darkness, and gave it a squeeze,

M: I'll do whatever you like, Ratty. Shall we run away tomorrow morning, quite early—*very* early—and go back to our dear old hole on the river?

R: No, no, we'll see it out. Thanks awfully, but I ought to stick by Toad till this trip is ended. It wouldn't be safe for him to be left to himself. It won't take very long. His fads never do. Good night!

N: The end was indeed nearer than even the Rat suspected. Their way lay, as before, across country by narrow lanes, and it was not till the afternoon that they came out on the high road; and there disaster, fleet and unforeseen, sprang out on them—disaster momentous indeed to their expedition, but simply overwhelming in its effect on the after-career of Toad.

They were strolling along the high road easily, the Mole by the horse's head, talking to him, since the horse had complained that nobody considered him in the least; the Toad and the Water Rat were walking behind the cart talking together, when far behind them they heard a faint warning hum, like the drone of a distant bee. Glancing back, they saw a small cloud of dust, with a dark center of energy advancing on them at incredible speed; in an instant the peaceful scene was changed, and with a blast of wind and a whirl of sound that made them jump for the nearest ditch, it was on them. From out of the dust a "poop-poop!" rang with a brazen shout in their ears. They had a moment's glimpse of the magnificent motor-car, and then it dwindled to a speck in the far distance, and changed back into a droning bee once more.

R: You villains! you—you—roadhogs—I'll have the law of you! I'll report you! I'll take you through all the courts!

M: Hi! Toad! Come and bear a hand, can't you!

N: The Toad never answered a word, or budged from his seat in the road; so they went to see what was the matter with him. They found him in sort of a trance, a happy smile on his face, his eyes still fixed on the dusty wake of their destroyer. At intervals he was still heard to murmur,

T: Poop-poop!

R: Are you coming to help us, Toad?

T: Glorious, stirring sight! The poetry of motion! The *real* way to travel! O bliss! O poop-poop! O my! O my!

M: What are we to do with him?

R: Nothing at all. You see, I know him from old. He is now possessed. He has got a new craze, and it always takes him that way. He'll continue like that for days now. Never mind him. Let's go. It's five or six miles to the nearest town, and we shall have to walk it.

N: The following evening the Mole, who had risen late and taken things very easy all day, was sitting on the bank fishing, when the Rat, who had been looking up his friends and gossiping, came strolling along to find him,

R: Heard the news? There's nothing else being talked about, all along the river bank. Toad went up to Town by an early train this morning. And he has ordered a large and very expensive motor-car.

Scene III

N: In the winter time the Rat slept a great deal, retiring early and rising late. So the Mole, who had a good deal of spare time on his hands, formed the resolution to go out by himself and explore the Wild Wood, and perhaps strike up an acquaintance with Mr. Badger.

It was a cold, still afternoon with a hard, steely sky overhead when he slipped out of the warm parlor into the open air. The country lay bare and entirely leafless around him, but the Mole with a cheerful spirit, pushed towards the Wild Wood, which lay before him low and threatening, like a black reef in some still, southern sea. He penetrated to where the light was less, and holes made ugly mouths at him on either side. Everything was very still now. The dusk advanced on him steadily, rapidly, gathering in behind and before; and the light seemed to be draining away like flood water. At last he took refuge in the deep dark hollow of an old beech tree, which offered shelter. As he lay there panting and trembling, and listening to the whistlings and the patterings outside, he knew it at last, that dread thing which other little dwellers in field and hedgerow had encountered here, and known as their darkest moment—that thing which the Rat had tried to shield him from—the Terror of the Wild Wood!

R: Moly, Moly! Where are you? It's me—it's old Rat!

N: The Rat had patiently hunted through the wood for an hour or more, when at last to his joy he heard a little answering cry.

M: Ratty! Is that really you? Oh Rat! I've been so frightened, you can't think!

R: O, I quite understand. You shouldn't really have gone and done it, Mole. I did my best to keep you from it. We river-bankers, we hardly ever come here by ourselves. Of course if you were Badger or Otter, it would be quite another matter.

M: Surely the brave Mr. Toad wouldn't mind coming here by himself, would he?

R: Old Toad? He wouldn't show his face here alone, not for a whole hatfull of golden guineas, Toad wouldn't.

N: The Mole was greatly cheered by the sound of Rat's careless laughter, and he stopped shivering and began to feel bolder and more himself again.

R: Now then, we really must pull ourselves together and make a start for home while there's still a little light left. It will never do to spend the night here, you understand. Too cold, for one thing.

   Uh, oh! here—is—a—go!

M: What's up, Ratty?

R: Snow is up, or rather, *down*. It's snowing hard. Well, well, it can't be helped. We must make a start, and take our chance, I suppose. The worst of it is, I don't exactly know where we are. And now this snow makes everything look so very different.

N: It did indeed. The Mole would not have known that it was the same wood. However, they set out bravely, and took the line that seemed most promising, holding on to each other and pretending with invincible cheerfulness that they recognized an old friend in every fresh tree that grimly and silently greeted them, or saw openings, gaps, or paths with familiar turns in them, in the monotony of white space and black tree-trunks that refused to vary. An hour or two later—they had lost all count of time—there seemed to be no end to this wood, and no beginning, and, worst of all, no way out. They pulled up, dispirited, weary, and hopelessly at sea, and sat down on a fallen tree-trunk to recover their breath and consider what was to be done.

R: We can't sit here very long. We shall have to make another push for it. The cold is too awful for anything, and the snow will soon be too deep for us to wade through.

N: So once more they got on their feet, and struggled on, when suddenly:

M: O my leg! O my poor shin!

R: Poor old Mole; you've cut your shin, sure enough. It's a very clear cut. Looks as if it was made by a sharp edge of something in metal. Funny!

M: Well, never mind what done it.

N: The Mole had quite forgotten his grammar in his pain.

M: It hurts just the same, whatever done it.

R: Hooray! Hooray—oo—ray—oo—ray—oo—ray!

M: What have you found, Ratty?

R: Come and see!

N: In the side of what had seemed to be a snow-bank stood a solid looking little door, painted a dark green. On a small brass plate, neatly engraved in square capital letters, they could read by the aid of moonlight:

MR. BADGER

They waited patiently for what seemed a very long time, stamping in the snow to keep their feet warm. At last they heard the sound of slow shuffling footsteps approaching the door from the inside. It seemed, as the Mole remarked to the Rat, like someone walking in carpet slippers that were too large for him, which was intelligent of Mole, because that was exactly what it was.

There was the noise of a bolt shot back, and the door opened a few inches, enough to show a long snout and a pair of sleepy blinking eyes.

B: Now, the *very* next time this happens, I shall be exceedingly angry. Who is it *this* time, disturbing people on such a night? Speak up!

R: O, Badger, let us in, please. It's me, Rat, and my friend Mole, and we've lost our way in the snow.

B: What, Ratty, my dear little man! Come along in, both of you, at once.

N: The two animals tumbled over each other in their eagerness to get inside. The kindly Badger thrust them down on a settee to toast themselves at the fire, and bade them remove their wet coats and boots. When at last they were thoroughly toasted, the Badger summoned them to the table. Conversation was impossible for a long time; and when it was slowly resumed, it was that regrettable sort of conversation that results from talking with your mouth full. The Badger did not mind that sort of thing at all, nor did he take any notice of elbows on the table, or everybody speaking at once. As he did not go into Society himself, he had got an idea that these things belonged to the things that didn't really matter. (We know of course that he was wrong, and took too narrow a view; because they do matter very much, though it would take too long to explain why.)

B: Now then! tell us the news from your part of the world. How's old Toad going on?

R: O, from bad to worse. Another motor-car smash-up only last week, and a bad one.

B: How many has he had?

R: Smashes, or motor-cars? O, well, after all, it's the same thing—with Toad. This is the seventh. As for the others—you know that coach-house of his? Well, it's piled up—literally piled up to the roof—with fragments of motor-cars none of them bigger than your hat! That accounts for the other six—so far as they can be accounted for.

M: He's been in the hospital three times, and as for the fines he's had to pay, it's simply awful to think of.

R: Yes, and that's part of the trouble. Toad's rich, as we all know; but he's not a millionaire. And he's a hopelessly bad driver, and quite regardless of law and order. Killed or ruined—it's got to be one of the two things, sooner or later. Badger! we're his friends—oughtn't we to do something?

B: Now look here! Of course you know I can't do anything *now*?

N: His two friends assented, quite understanding his point. No animal, according to the rules of animal-etiquette, is ever expected to do anything strenuous, or heroic, or even moderately active during the off-season of winter. All are sleepy—some actually asleep.

B: Well, *then*, we—that is, you and me and our friend the Mole here—we'll—you're asleep, Rat!

R: Not me!

M: He's been asleep two or three times since supper.

B: Well, it's time we were all in bed. Come along, you two, and I'll show you your quarters. And take your time tomorrow morning—breakfast at any hour you please!

N: In accordance with the kindly Badger's injunctions, the two tired animals came down to breakfast very late the next morning. The Mole took the opportunity to tell Badger how comfortable and homelike it all felt to him.

M: Once well underground you know exactly where you are. Nothing can happen to you, and nothing can get at you. You're entirely your own master, and you don't have to consult anybody or mind what they say.

B: That's exactly what I say. There's no security, or peace and tranquillity, except underground.

When breakfast is over, I'll take you all round this little place of mine. I can see you'll appreciate it. You understand what domestic architecture ought to be, you do.

N: But after breakfast, the Rat was anxious to be off and attend to his river, so the Badger, taking up his lantern again, led the way along a damp and airless tunnel. At last daylight began to show itself confusedly through tangled growth overhanging the mouth of the passage; and the Badger bade them a hasty good-bye. They found themselves standing on the very edge of the Wild Wood. Rocks and brambles and tree-roots behind them, in front, a great space of quiet fields, and, far ahead, a glint of the familiar old river, while the wintry sun hung red and low on the horizon.

(Film sequence depicting, in slow motion, Mole, Rat, and Badger locking Toad in his room and Toad's escape in his motor car.)

Scene IV

CM: To my mind,

N: observed the Chairman of the Bench of Magistrates cheerfully,

CM: the *only* difficulty that presents itself in this otherwise very clear case is, how we can possibly make it sufficiently hot for the incorrigible rogue and hardened ruffian whom we see cowering in the dock before us. Let me see: he has been found guilty, on the clearest evidence, first, of stealing a valuable motor-car; secondly, of driving to the public danger; and, thirdly, of gross impertinence to the rural police. Mr. Clerk, will you tell us, please, what is the very stiffest penalty we can impose for each of these offenses? Without, of course, giving the prisoner the benefit on any doubt, because there isn't any.

C: Some people would consider that stealing the motor-car was the worst offense; and so it is. But cheeking the police undoubtedly carries the severest penalty; and so it ought. Supposing you were to say twelve months for the theft, which is mild; and three years for the furious driving, which is lenient; and fifteen years for the cheek, which was pretty bad sort of cheek, judging by what we've heard from the witness-box, even if you only believe one-tenth part of what you heard, and I never believe more myself—those figures, if added together correctly, total up to nineteen years—

CM: First-rate!

C: —So you had better make it a round twenty years and be on the safe side.

CM: An excellent suggestion! Prisoner! Pull yourself together and try and stand up straight. It's going to be twenty years for you this time. And mind, if you appear before us again, upon any charge whatever, we shall deal with you very seriously!

N: Then the brutal minions of the law fell upon the hapless Toad; loaded him with chains, and dragged him from the Court House to the door of the grimmest dungeon that lay in the heart of the innermost keep. The rusty key creaked in the lock, the great door clanged behind him; and Toad was a helpless prisoner in the remotest dungeon on the best-guarded keep of the stoutest castle in all the length and breadth of Merry England.

T: This is the end of everything, at least it is the end of the career of Toad, which is the same thing. The popular and handsome Toad, the rich and hospitable Toad, the Toad so free and careless and debonair! How can I hope to be ever set at large again. Stupid animal that I was, now I must languish in this dungeon, till people who were proud to say they knew me, have forgotten the very name of Toad! O wise old Badger! O clever, intelligent Rat and sensible Mole! What sound judgments, what a knowledge of men and matters you possess! O unhappy and forsaken Toad!

N: Now the goaler of this great dungeon had a daughter, a pleasant wench and good-hearted, who assisted her father in the lighter duties of his post, pitied the misery of Toad. So one day she went on her errand of mercy, and knocked at the door of Toad's cell.

G: Toad? Cheer up, Toad? Listen to what I have to say. I have an aunt who is a washerwoman.

T: There, there, never mind; think no more about it. I have several aunts who *ought* to be washerwomen.

G: Do be quiet a minute, Toad. As I said, I have an aunt who is a washerwoman; she does the washing for all the prisoners in this castle—we try to keep any paying business of that sort in the family, you understand. She takes out the washing on Monday morning, and brings it in on Friday evening. This is a Thursday. Now, this is what occurs to me: you're very rich—at least you're always telling me so—and she's very poor. A few pounds wouldn't make any difference to you, and it would mean a lot to her. Now, I think if she were properly approached—squared, I believe is the word you animals use—you could come to some arrangement by which she would let you have her dress and bonnet and so on, and you could escape from the castle as the official washerwoman. You're very alike in many respects—particularly about the figure.

T: We're *not* I have a very elegant figure—for what I am.

G: So has my aunt, for what *she* is. But have it your own way. You horrid, proud, ungrateful animal, when I'm sorry for you and trying to help you!

T: Yes, yes, that's all right; thank you very much indeed. But look here! you wouldn't surely have Mr. Toad, of Toad Hall, going about the country disguised as a washerwoman!

G: Then you can stop here as a Toad. I suppose you want to go off in a coach-and-four!

N: Honest Toad was always ready to admit himself in the wrong,

T: You are a good, kind, clever girl, and I am indeed a proud and a stupid toad. Introduce me to your worthy aunt, if you will be so kind, and I have no doubt that the excellent lady and I will be able to arrange terms satisfactory to both parties.

N: The next evening the girl ushered her aunt into Toad's cell, bearing his week's washing pinned up in a towel. The old lady had been prepared beforehand for the interview, and the sight of certain golden coins that Toad had thoughtfully placed on the table practically completed the matter. In return for his cash, Toad received a cotton print gown, an apron, a shawl, and a rusty black bonnet.

N: With a quaking heart, Toad set forth cautiously. As he walked along his attention was caught by some red and green lights a little way off, and the sound of the puffing and snorting of engines fell on his ear.

T: Aha! This is a piece of luck! A railway-station is the thing I want most in the whole world at this moment.

N: He made his way to the station accordingly, consulted a timetable and found that a train, bound more or less in the direction of his home, was due to start in half an hour.

T: More luck!

N: But as he started off to the booking-office to buy his ticket, he suddenly recollected that he had left both coat and waistcoat behind him in his cell, and with them his pocket-book, money, keys, watch, matches, pencilcase—all that makes life worth living. Full of despair he wandered blindly down the platform where the train was standing, and tears trickled down each side of his nose.

E: Hullo, mother! What's the trouble? You don't look particularly cheerful.

T: O, sir! I am a poor unhappy washerwoman, and I've lost all my money, and can't pay for a ticket, and I *must* get home tonight somehow, and whatever I am to do I don't know. O dear, O dear!

E: That's a bad business, indeed. Lost your money—and can't get home—and got some kids, too, waiting for you, I dare say?

T: Any amount of 'em. And they'll be hungry—and playing with matches—and upsetting lamps, the little innocents!—and quarrelling, and going on generally. O dear! O dear!

E: Well, I'll tell you what I'll do. You're a washerwoman to your trade, says you. If you'll wash a few shirts for me when you get home, and send 'em along, I'll give you a ride on my engine.

N: The Toad's misery turned into rapture as he eagerly scrambled up into the cab of the engine. Of course, he had never washed a shirt in his life, and couldn't if he tried and, anyhow, he wasn't going to begin; but he thought,

T: When I get safely home to Toad Hall, and have money again, and pockets to put it in, I will send the engine-driver enough to pay for quite a quantity of washing, and that will be the same thing, or better.

N: They had covered many and many a mile, and Toad was already considering what he would have for supper as soon as he got home, when he noticed that the engine-driver, with a puzzled expression on his face, was leaning over the side of the engine and listening hard.

E: It's very strange; we're the last train running in this direction, yet I could be sworn that I heard another following us!

I can see it clearly now! It is an engine, on our rails, coming along at a great pace! It looks as if we are being pursued!

N: The miserable Toad, crouching in the coal-dust, tried hard to think of something to do, with dismal want of success.

E: They are gaining on us fast! And the engine is crowded with the queerest lot of people! Men like . . . policemen; all waving, and all shouting the same thing—"Stop, stop, stop!"

T: Save me, only save me, dear kind Mr. Engine-driver, and I will confess everything! I am not the simple washerwoman I seem to be! I have no children waiting for me. I am a toad—the well-known and popular Mr. Toad, a landed proprietor; and I have just escaped, by my great daring and cleverness, from a loathsome dungeon into which my enemies had flung me; and if those fellows on that engine recapture me, it will be chains and bread-and-water and straw and misery once more for poor, unhappy, innocent Toad!

E: Now tell the truth. What were you put in prison for?

T: It was nothing very much. I only borrowed a motor-car while the owners were at lunch; they had no need of it at the time. I didn't mean to steal it, really!

E: I fear you have been indeed a wicked toad, and by rights I ought to give you up to offended justice. But you are evidently in sore trouble and distress, so I will not desert you. I'll do my best, and we may beat them yet!

N: They piled on more coals, shoveling furiously; the engine leapt and swung, but still their pursuers slowly gained.

E: I'm afraid it's no good. Toad. There's just one thing left for us to do, and it's your only chance, so attend very carefully to what I tell you. A short way ahead of us is a long tunnel, and on the other side of that the line passes through a thick wood. Now, I will put on all the speed I can while we are running through the tunnel. When we are through, I will put on brakes as hard as I can, and the moment it's safe to do so you must jump and hide in the wood, before they get through the tunnel and see you.

N: The train shot into the tunnel, and the engine rushed and roared and rattled, till at last they shot out at the other end. The driver put on brakes, and as the train slowed down to almost a walking pace the Toad heard the driver call out,

E: Now, jump!

N: Toad jumped, picked himself up unhurt, scrambled into the wood, and hid. Then out of the tunnel burst the pursuing engine with her motley crew shouting, "Stop, stop, stop!"

As he tramped along gaily, he thought of his adventures and escapes and how when things seemed at their worst he had always managed to find a way out; and his pride and conceit began to swell within him.

T: Ho, ho! what a clever Toad I am! There is surely no animal equal to me for cleverness in the whole world! This is real life again. Oh, ho! I will hail them, my brothers of the wheel.

N: He stepped confidently out into the road to hail the motor-car; when suddenly he became very pale, his knees shook and yielded under him. And well he might, the unhappy animal; for the approaching car was the very one he had stolen out of the yard of the Red Lion Hotel on that fatal day when all his troubles began!

T: It's all up! It's all over now! Chains and policemen again! Prison again! Dry bread and water again! O, what a fool I have been!

N: The terrible motor-car drew slowly nearer and nearer, till at last he heard it stop just short of him. A lady and a gentleman got out and walked round the trembling heap of crumpled misery lying in the road.

L: O dear! this is very sad! Here is a poor old thing—a washerwoman apparently—who had fainted in the road! Let us take her to the nearest village, where doubtless she has friends.

MN: Look! she is better already. The fresh air is doing her good. How do you feel now, ma'am?

T: Thank you kindly sir. I'm feeling a great deal better!

T: Please, sir, I wish you would kindly let me try and drive the car for a little. I've been watching you carefully, and it looks so easy and so interesting, and I should like to be able to tell my friends that once I had driven a motor-car!

L: Bravo, ma'am! I like your spirit. Let her have a try, and look after her. She won't do any harm.

MN: How well she does it!

L: Fancy a washerwoman driving a car as well as that, the first time!

N: Then Toad went a little faster; then faster still, and faster.

MN: Be careful, washerwoman!

T: Washerwoman, indeed! Ho! ho! I am the Toad, the motor-car snatcher, the prison-breaker, the Toad who always escapes! Sit still, and you shall know what driving really is, for you are in the hands of the famous, the skillful, the entirely fearless Toad!

MN: Seize the Toad, the wicked animal. Down with the desperate and dangerous Toad!

N: Alas! they should have remembered to stop the motor-car somehow before playing any pranks of that sort. With a half-turn of the wheel the Toad sent the car crashing through the low hedge that ran along the roadside. One mighty bound, a violent shock, and the wheels of the car were churning up the thick mud on the side of the road. Splash! Toad found himself head over ears in deep water, rapid water, and he knew that he had fallen into the river!

T: O, my! if I ever steal a motor-car again! If I ever sing another conceited song—

N: Then suddenly he saw a big dark hole in the bank, just above his head—

Scene V

T: O, Ratty! I've been through such times since I saw you last, you can't think! Such trials, such sufferings, and all so nobly borne! Then such escapes, such subterfuges, and all so cleverly planned and carried out! Been in prison—got out of it, of course! Humbugged everybody—made 'em all do exactly what I wanted! Oh, I *am* a clever Toad, and no mistake! What do you think my last exploit was? Just hold on till I tell you—

R: Toad, you go off upstairs at once, and take off that old cotten rag that looks as if it might have belonged to some washerwoman, and clean yourself thoroughly, and try and come down looking like a gentleman if you *can*; I'll have something to say to you later!

N: By the time he came down, luncheon was on the table, and very glad Toad was to see it. While they ate Toad told the Rat all his adventures, dwelling chiefly on his own cleverness, and so on. But the more he talked and boasted, the more grave and silent the Rat became.

T: There, there! don't take on so, old chap; I won't talk any more about it now. We'll have our coffee, *and* a smoke, and a quiet chat, and then I'm going to stroll gently down to Toad Hall . . .

R: Stroll gently down to Toad Hall? What are you talking about? Do you mean to say you haven't *heard*?

T: Heard what? Go on, Ratty! Quick! Don't spare me! What haven't I heard?

R: Do you mean to tell me that you've heard nothing about the Stoats and Weasels? And how they've been and taken Toad Hall?

T: What, the Wild Wooders? No, not a word!

R: It's a long story, Toad, and I am convinced that we can do nothing until we have seen the Mole and the Badger, and heard their latest news, and taken their advice in this difficult matter.

T: O, ah, yes, of course, the Mole and the Badger. What's become of them, the dear fellows? I had forgotten all about them.

R: Well may you ask! While you were riding about the country in expensive motor-cars, these two poor devoted animals have been camping out in the open, in every sort of weather; watching over your house, patrolling your boundaries, keeping a constant eye on the stoats and weasels, scheming and planning and contriving how to get your property back for you. You don't deserve to have such true and loyal friends, Toad, you don't, really. Some day, when it's too late, you'll be sorry you didn't value them more while you had them!

T: I'm an ungrateful beast, I know. Let me go out and find them, out into the cold, dark night, and share their hardships, and try and prove by—Hold on a bit!

B: Welcome home, Toad! Alas! what am I saying? Home, indeed! This is a poor homecoming. Unhappy Toad!

M: Hooray! Here's old Toad! Fancy having you back again! We never dreamt you would turn up so soon! Why, you must have managed to escape, you clever, ingenious, intelligent Toad!

T: Clever? O, no! I'm not really clever, according to my friends. I've only broken out of the strongest prison in England, that's all! And captured a railway train and escaped on it, that's all! And disguised myself and gone about the country humbugging everybody, that's all! O, no! I'm a stupid ass, I am! I'll tell you one or two of my little adventures, Mole, and you shall judge for yourself!

R: Toad, do be quiet, please! And Mole, tell us as soon as possible what the position is, and what's best to be done, now that Toad is back at last.

M: The position's about as bad as it can be, and as for what's to be done, why, blest if I know! Sentries posted everywhere, guns poked out at us, stones thrown at us; always an animal on the look-out.

T: Then it's all over. I shall go and enlist for a soldier, and never see my dear Toad Hall anymore!

B: Come, cheer up, Toady! I'm going to tell you a great secret.

N: Toad sat up slowly and dried his eyes. Secrets had an immense attraction for him, because he never could keep one. (We know of course that secrets should be kept.)

B: There—is—an—underground—passage, that leads from the river bank, quite near here right up into the middle of Toad Hall.

T: How's this passage of yours going to help us?

B: I've found out a thing or two lately. There's going to be a big banquet tomorrow night. It's somebody's birthday—the Chief Weasel's, I believe—and all the weasels will be gathered together in the dining-hall, eating and drinking and laughing and carrying on, suspecting nothing. The weasels will trust entirely to their excellent sentinels. And that is where the passage comes in. That very useful tunnel leads right up under the butler's pantry, next to the dining-hall!

T: Aha! that squeaky board in the butler's pantry. Now I understand it!

M: We shall creep out quietly into the butler's pantry—

R: —with our pistols and swords and sticks—

B: —and rush in upon them—

T: —and whack 'em and whack 'em, and whack 'em!

N: When all was quite ready, the Badger took a dark lantern in one paw, grasped his great stick with the other,

B: Now then, follow me! Mole first, cos I'm very pleased with him; Rat next; Toad last. And look here, Toady! Don't you chatter so much as usual, or you'll be sent back, as sure as fate!

N: At last they were in the secret passage, and the expedition had really begun! The procession moved on. They hurried along the passage till it came to a full stop, and they found themselves standing under the trap-door that led up into the butler's pantry.

B: Now, boys, all together!

T: Only just let me get at him!

B: Hold hard a minute! Get ready, all of you! The hour is come! Follow me!

N: The affair was soon over. In five minutes the four friends had cleared the room. The following morning, Toad, who had overslept as usual, came down to breakfast disgracefully late. Through the French windows of the breakfast-room he could see the Mole and the Water Rat sitting in wicker chairs out on the lawn, evidently telling each other stories. The Badger was in an armchair and deep in the morning paper.

B: I'm sorry, Toad, but I'm afraid there's a heavy morning's work in front of you. You see, we really ought to have a banquet at once, to celebrate this affair. So you must write the invitations.

T: O, all right, anything to oblige.

N: He quitted the room. He *would* write the invitations; and he would take care to mention the leading part he had taken in the fight, and how he had laid the Chief Weasel flat; and he would hint at his adventures, and what a career of triumph he had to tell about; and on the flyleaf he would give a sort of programme of entertainment for the evening—something like this, as he sketched it out in his head:—

T: Speech

N: by Toad.

T: There will be other speeches during the evening

N: by Toad.

T: Address

N: by Toad.

T: Synopsis—Our Prison System—Property, its rights and duties—Back to the Land—A typical English Squire. Song

N: by Toad.

R: Now, look here, Toad. It's about this Banquet, and very sorry I am to have to speak to you like this. But we want you to understand that there are going to be no speeches and no songs. Try and grasp the fact that on this occasion we're not arguing with you; we're just telling you.

N: Toad saw that he was trapped. His pleasant dream was shattered.

T: Mayn't I sing them just one *little* song?

R: No, not *one* song. It's no good, Toady; you know well that your songs are all conceit and boasting and vanity; and your speeches are all self-praise and—and—well, and gross exaggeration and—and—

B: And gas!

R: It's for your own good, Toady. You know you *must* turn over a new leaf sooner or later, and now seems a splendid time to begin; a sort of turning-point in your career.

T: You are right, I know, and I am wrong. Henceforth I will be a very different Toad. My friends, you shall never have occasion to blush for me again. But, O dear, O dear, this is a hard world!

N: At last the hour for the banquet began to draw near, and Toad who on leaving the others had retired to his bedroom, was still sitting there, melancholy and thoughtful. His brow resting on his paw, he pondered long and deeply. Gradually his countenance cleared, and he began to smile long, slow smiles. Then he took to giggling in a shy, self-conscious manner. At last he got up, locked the door, collecting all the chairs in the room and arranged them in a semicircle, and took up his position in front of them, swelling visibly. Then he bowed, coughed twice, and letting himself go, with uplifted voice he sang, to the enraptured audience that his imagination so clearly saw, TOAD'S LAST LITTLE SONG!

T: The Toad—came—home!
There was panic in the parlor
   and howling in the hall,
There was crying in the cow-shed
   and shrieking in the stall,
When the Toad—came—home!

When the Toad—came—home!
There was smashing in of window
   and crashing in of door,
There was chivying of weasels
   that fainted on the floor,
When the Toad—came—home!

Bang! go the drums!
The trumpeters are tooting and

the soldiers are saluting,
And the cannon they are shooting
   and the motor-cars are hooting,
As the Hero—comes!

Shout—Hooray!
And let each one of the crowd try
   and shout it very loud,   .
In honor of an animal of whom
   you're justly proud,
For it's Toad's—great—day!

N: Quietly Toad went down the stairs to greet his guests, who he knew must be assembling in the drawing-room.
   All the animals cheered when he entered.

V: Toad! Speech! Speech from Toad! Song! Mr. Toad's Song!

N: But Toad only shook his head gently, raised one paw in mild protest.
   He was indeed an altered Toad!

Scene VI

N: After this climax, the four animals continued to lead their lives in great joy and contentment, undisturbed by further risings or invasions. Sometimes, in the course of long summer evenings, the friends would take a stroll together in the Wild Wood, now successfully tamed so far as they were concerned; and it was pleasing to see how respectfully they were greeted by the inhabitants, and how the mother-weasels would bring their young ones to the mouths of their holes, and say, pointing, "Look, baby! There goes the great Mr. Toad! And that's the gallant Water Rat, a terrible fighter, walking along o' him! And yonder comes the famous Mr. Mole, of whom you so often have heard your father tell!" But when their infants were quite beyond control, they would quiet them by telling how, if they didn't hush, the terrible Badger would up and get them. This was a base libel on Badger, who, though he cared little about Society, was rather fond of children; but it never failed to have its full effect.
   Thus they continued their joyous life, catching at intervals something of what the wind was whispering so constantly in the willows.

Index